Feminist Interpretations and Political Theory

*To Kate and Anthony Chromey
and the memory of
Harry Pateman*

Feminist Interpretations and Political Theory

*Edited by Mary Lyndon Shanley
and Carole Pateman*

The Pennsylvania State
University Press

Copyright individual essays: 1 © 1977 Princeton University Press;
2 © 1985 Praeger Publishers; 3 © 1989 Carole Pateman;
4 © 1978 American Political Science Association; 5 © 1981 *Social Theory and Practice*; 6 © 1991 Moira Gatens; 7 © 1991 Seyla Benhabib;
8 © 1991 Christine Di Stefano; 9 © 1981 Sage Publications, Inc.;
10 © 1989 Basic Books, Inc.; 11 © 1988 Elizabeth V. Spelman;
12 © 1986 Hypatia, Inc.; 13 © 1991 Mary G. Dietz; 14 © 1989 The
Regents of the University of Minnesota.
This collection and the introduction © 1991 Mary Lyndon Shanley
and Carole Pateman

First published 1991 in the United States by
The Pennsylvania State University Press,
Suite C, 820 North University Drive, University Park, PA 16802

ISBN 0–271–00736–2 (cloth)
ISBN 0–271–00742–7 (paper)

Library of Congress Cataloging-in-Publication Data
Feminist interpretations and political theory / edited by Carole
    Pateman and Mary Lyndon Shanley.
        p. cm.
    ISBN 0–271–00742–7 (pbk)
    ISBN 0–271–00736–2 (alk. paper)
    1. Feminist theory.   2. Political science.   I. Pateman, Carole.
II. Shanley, Mary Lyndon, 1944–
HQ1190.F46   1991   90–43290
305.42′01—dc20

Typeset in 10 on 12pt Baskerville
by Hope Services (Abingdon) Ltd.
Printed in Great Britain

Contents

Contents

Contributors

Seyla Benhabib is associate professor of philosophy and women's studies at the State University of New York at Stony Brook. She is the author of *Critique, Norm and Utopia* (Columbia University Press, 1986) and co-editor with D. Cornell of *Feminism as Critique: On the Politics of Gender* (University of Minnesota Press and Polity Press, 1987). She is currently working on a reinterpretation of Hannah Arendt's political philosophy from a feminist perspective.

Melissa Butler is associate professor of political science at Wabash College. She is currently completing a book on Jean-Jacques Rousseau and the idea of self-love.

Mary G. Dietz is associate professor of political science at the University of Minnesota. She is author of *Between the Human and the Divine: The Political Thought of Simone Weil* (Rowman and Littlefield, 1988), and editor of *Thomas Hobbes and Political Theory* (University of Kansas Press, 1990) as well as articles on the history of ideas and feminist political theory.

Christine Di Stefano teaches political theory at the University of Washington in Seattle. She is currently at work on a study of "Autonomy: The Fate of an Ideal." Her forthcoming book, *Configurations of Masculinity: A Feminist Rereading in Modern Political Theory*, offers gender-inflected readings of Hobbes, Marx and J. S. Mill.

Nancy Fraser teaches philosophy at Northwestern University. She is the author of *Unruly Practices: Power, Discourse, and Gender in Contemporary Social Theory* (University of Minnesota Press and Polity Press, 1989). She is currently at work on a new book, *Keywords of the Welfare State*, which she will co-author with Linda Gordon.

Moira Gatens lectures in philosophy at the Australian National University. She is author of *Feminism and Philosophy* (Polity Press, 1990). Her current research concerns philosophies of the body (Spinoza, Nietzsche, and Freud) and their relations to theories of ethics.

Lynda Lange teaches feminist philosophy at the University of Toronto, Scarborough campus. She has published articles on Rousseau and feminist theory, and is co-editor (with L. Clark) of *The Sexism of Social and Political Theory: Women and Reproduction from Plato to Nietzsche* (University of Toronto Press, 1979). Her current research is mainly on the development of democratic feminist thought.

Susan M. Okin is professor of political science at Stanford University. She is the author of *Women in Western Political Thought* (Princeton University Press, 1979) and *Justice, Gender, and the Family* (Basic Books, 1989).

Carole Pateman is professor of political science at the University of California, Los Angeles. Her most recent books are *The Sexual Contract* and *The Disorder of Women: Democracy, Feminism and Political Theory* (both Polity Press and Stanford University Press, 1988 and 1990). She is currently continuing her research on women and democratic citizenship.

Jana Sawicki is associate professor of philosophy at the University of Maine. She has published many articles on Foucault and feminism which address issues in the philosophy of desire, motherhood, and technology. A collection of her essays on sexuality and reproduction will be published by Routledge Press in 1991.

Arlene Saxonhouse is professor of political science at the University of Michigan. She is author of *Women in the History of Political Thought: Ancient Greece to Machiavelli* (Praeger, 1985). She has published widely in the area of ancient political theory, and is currently working on a book, *The Fear of Diversity in Greek Thought*.

Mary Lyndon Shanley is professor of political science at Vassar College. She is the author of *Feminism, Marriage and the Law in Victorian England, 1850–1895* (Princeton University Press, 1989) and many articles on the history of political theory. She is currently working on a book on liberal theory, feminism, and contemporary family law.

Elizabeth V. Spelman teaches in the philosophy department at Smith College, and is the author of *Inessential Woman: Problems of Exclusion in Feminist Thought* (Beacon, 1988). Her writings have focused on the mutual construction of gender, race and class and the implications of their interconnections for feminist theory and politics. Her next long-term project is an examination of the treatment of suffering in Western philosophy.

Acknowledgments

The editors and publishers are grateful for permission to reproduce the following:

Susan Moller Okin, "Philosopher Queens and Private Wives: Plato on Women and the Family," first published in *Philosophy and Public Affairs*, 6(4), Summer 1977, pp. 345–69. Reprinted with permission of Princeton University Press. The essay has also appeared in Jean Elshtain (ed.), *The Family in Political Thought* (Amherst: University of Massachusetts Press, 1982), pp. 31–50.

Arlene Saxonhouse, "Aristotle: Defective Males, Hierarchy and the Limits of Politics," abridged from the original published in Arlene Saxonhouse, *Women in the History of Political Thought: Ancient Greece to Machiavelli* (New York: Praeger, 1985). Abridged and reprinted with permission of the author and Praeger Publishers, a division of Greenwood Press, Inc.

Melissa Butler, "Early Liberal Roots of Feminism: John Locke and the Attack on Patriarchy," first published in the *American Political Science Review*, 72, 1978, pp. 135–50. Reprinted by permission of the American Political Science Association. It appears here in a shortened version.

Lynda Lange, "Rousseau and Modern Feminism," which originally appeared, in a longer version, in *Social Theory and Practice*, 7, 1981, pp. 245–77; by permission of the editorial board of *Social Theory and Practice*, Florida State University.

Mary Lyndon Shanley, "Marital Slavery and Friendship: John Stuart Mill's *The Subjection of Women*," first published in *Political Theory*, 9(2), May 1981, pp. 229–47. Reprinted by permission of Sage Publications, Inc.

Susan Moller Okin, "John Rawls: Justice as Fairness – For Whom?" which is drawn from "Justice and Gender," *Philosophy and Public Affairs*, 16(1), Winter 1987, pp. 42–72, copyright © 1987 by Princeton University Press, excerpt adapted with permission of Princeton University Press; and "Reason and Feeling in Thinking about Justice," *Ethics*, 99(2), January 1989, pp. 229–49, by permission of University of Chicago Press. This version is adapted from that in Susan Moller Okin, *Justice, Gender, and the Family* (New York: Basic Books, 1989) and is reprinted by permission of Basic Books, Inc., Publishers, New York.

Elizabeth V. Spelman, "Simone de Beauvoir and Women: Just Who Does She Think 'We' Is?" abridged from the original published in Elizabeth V. Spelman, *Inessential Woman* (Boston: Beacon Press, 1988). Copyright © 1988 by Elizabeth V. Spelman. Reprinted by permission of Beacon Press.

Jana Sawicki, "Foucault and Feminism: Toward a Politics of Difference," which originally appeared in *Hypatia: A Journal of Feminist Philosophy*, 1 (2), Fall 1986, pp. 23–36.

Nancy Fraser, "What's Critical about Critical Theory: The Case of Habermas and Gender": a longer version of this essay was published in *New German Critique*, 35, Spring/Summer 1985, pp. 97–131, and in Nancy Fraser, *Unruly Practices: Power, Discourse and Gender in Contemporary Social Theory* (Minneapolis: University of Minnesota Press; Cambridge: Polity, 1989). Reprinted by permission of the University of Minnesota Press.

Introduction

Carole Pateman and
Mary Lyndon Shanley

Since the early 1970s, feminist theorists have been examining the familiar, and some not so familiar, texts of political theory. Their rereadings and reinterpretations have revolutionary implications for an understanding not only of the books themselves, but also of such central political categories as citizenship, equality, freedom, justice, the public, the private, and democracy. Despite the importance of the new feminist scholarship, it has developed for the most part alongside rather than as part of "mainstream" political theory. Remarkably little attention has been paid to the implications of feminist arguments in the ever-increasing volume of commentary on the famous texts, or in discussions of contemporary political problems.

This volume illustrates the range and depth of feminist studies of the texts and, by collecting the essays together, we hope that their significance for political theory and practice will be more readily acknowledged. Some contributions have been published before, the earliest in 1977 and the most recent in 1989; others have been specially commissioned for this collection. The interpretations presented here could be challenged by other feminist readings of each of the texts, but we are not aiming to collect together a set of definitive accounts. Rather, our aim is to make a reasonably wide selection of feminist scholarship more easily accessible to political theorists and to the general reader.

Each of the chapters raises the question of how useful the texts of political theory are or can be to feminist theorists. The standard commentaries on the texts invariably either ignore or merely mention in passing the arguments of the great writers about sexual difference. These essays show, on the contrary, that arguments about the characters and attributes of men and women are fundamental to political theory. As

Susan Okin commented in *Women in Western Political Thought*, "it is by no means a simple matter to integrate the female half of the human race into [the Western] tradition of political theory."[1]

When feminists first turned to the classic texts they were mainly concerned with exposing the misogyny of many famous theorists and the way in which virtually every writer assumed that women's stunted rationality and moral and political capacities made them unfit for citizenship and political life. Indeed, one initial reaction was to reject the whole tradition of political theory and to call for feminists to begin again on completely new terrain. Thus, Lorenne Clark and Lynda Lange announced that "traditional political theory is utterly bankrupt in the light of present [feminist] perspectives . . . [It] is up to us to remedy this by providing new theories which reflect a deeper understanding of our historical position."[2] Most of the authors in this volume (including Lange) now suggest that the theorists whom they discuss do have something valuable to offer to feminist political theory. For example, Butler sees Locke as an embryonic "equal rights" feminist; Lange presents Rousseau as providing insights into the problems for women if social life is based on generalized competition between individuals; Okin argues that Rawls's theory has subversive potential for reconceptualizing familial as well as political justice; Dietz suggests that Arendt's notion of the *vita activa* should be incorporated into any feminist vision of the good life; and Sawicki claims that Foucault offers feminists a critical method and a "set of recommendations" about how to assess feminist theories.

The order of the chapters follows the conventional manner of discussing political thinkers and there is a rough thematic pairing throughout; Plato and Aristotle come first and we conclude with Mill and Rawls, de Beauvoir and Foucault, and Arendt and Habermas. The volume is not entirely conventional, however; two theorists included here, Mary Wollstonecraft and Simone de Beauvoir, do not usually make an appearance in the canon of texts that make up the standard curriculum of "political theory." Feminist scholarship has raised some awkward questions about the construction of this canon. Why, for example, are Mary Wollstonecraft and Simone de Beauvoir so rarely studied in courses on political theory? William Godwin (Wollstonecraft's husband) and Jean-Paul Sartre (de Beauvoir's companion) are much more likely to be read, and many more obscure, minor male authors of both the eighteenth and twentieth centuries are discussed.

Both Wollstonecraft and de Beauvoir were the friends of the leading radicals of their time, led unconventional lives and wrote novels as well as books of political theory and philosophy. Their major feminist works, *A Vindication of the Rights of Woman* and *The Second Sex*, are important works in the history of political thought, raising questions that other advocates of the "rights of men and citizens," and existentialist and individualist philosophers, repressed and ignored. The neglect of both writers appears to be because they were feminists writing about the relation between the sexes, a matter treated by contemporary political theorists as outside their subject matter. John Stuart Mill wrote on the same issue from a feminist perspective, and, until very recently, his feminist writings have also been largely ignored by political theorists, despite the very extensive discussion of his other work.

The authors of these chapters write from a variety of perspectives from within political theory and feminism; there is no single "feminist view" of the texts, nor is there a feminist conclusion about the theoretical way forward. Rather, this volume reflects the great diversity of both feminist argument in general and feminist approaches to the history of political thought. Nonetheless, despite the varied approaches of the contributors, the chapters are related because these scholars have approached the texts with specifically feminist questions in mind. The questions concern the political significance of sexual difference and men's power over women; the patriarchal construction of central categories of political thought; the relation between nature, the sexes, reason and politics; the relation between the private (in the sense of the domestic, the familial, the intimate) and the public (in the sense of the economy and the state); and the political importance of differences among women.

Notwithstanding all the differences between theorists from Plato to Habermas, the tradition of Western political thought rests on a conception of the "political" that is constructed through the exclusion of women and all that is represented by femininity and women's bodies. Sexual difference and sexuality are usually treated as marginal to or outside of the subject matter of political theory, but the different attributes, capacities and characteristics ascribed to men and women by political theorists are central to the way in which each has defined the "political." Manhood and politics go hand in hand, and everything that stands in contrast to and opposed to political life and the political virtues has been represented by women, their capacities and the tasks seen as natural to their sex, especially motherhood. Many political theorists have seen women as having a vital part to play in social life – but not as citizens and political actors. Rather, women have been designated as the upholders of the private foundation of the political world of men; or, as Saxonhouse argues of Aristotle, femininity symbolizes the private ties, restraint and stability that support the *polis*.

The question of sexual difference, that is to say, is inseparable from the question of the relationship between the "private" and the "public," which also runs through this volume. Mainstream political theory takes for granted, but generally ignores, a major distinguishing feature of modern

Western societies: the fact that they are divided into two spheres, only one of which, the public sphere, is seen to be of political relevance. Long before the separation of the world of women and the household from the masculine realm of politics and citizenship took its peculiarly modern form, political theorists had set the "political" in opposition to "private" concerns. On the face of it, this may seem untrue of Plato, who, in Book V of the *Republic*, had included women among his guardian class. Okin argues that although Plato's view that the most able upper-class women could share in political rule was "more revolutionary than [that] of any other major political philosopher," whether or not women ruled depended on Plato's willingness to abolish the private family and with it women's subordination as wives and their consequent exclusion from political activity. In the *Laws*, Plato demonstrated his unwillingness to undermine the patriarchal household, and so inaugurated a tradition in which the political and women were seen as incompatible.

For Aristotle there was no question about women's exclusion from the reasoned discourse and activities of the *polis*. Aristotle insisted that the natural order prescribed that the superior must govern the inferior. Saxonhouse stresses that, although Aristotle did not believe that all males were naturally superior to all females, even those women who might be fit for political life were precluded from it; in nourishing the young with their bodies and preserving the household, women lacked the necessary leisure to engage in politics. Nonetheless, Saxonhouse argues, women performed a vital political role in sustaining the life of the *polis*. The view that women must remain outside the public world of politics, even though they have a fundamentally important political task to perform, recurs in many of the classic texts.

In the modern period, however, the idea that women, by virtue of their natural capacities, had a distinctive political part to play gave rise to a problem that still remains unresolved. Before the proclamation of the revolutionary modern doctrine that all men were by nature, or by birthright, free and equal to each other, the exclusion of women from political life was unremarkable; many other categories of the population (such as the poor, the propertyless, or slaves) were deemed unfit by nature for citizenship. But once the "rights of man" became the currency of modern political argument, women posed a special problem – precisely because they are not the same as men. Standard accounts of the history of political theory assume that the statement that "all men" are born free and equal should be read as "all humankind"; that is, the doctrine of individual freedom and equality is assumed to be universal, to apply to everyone. On this reading, the incorporation of women into citizenship poses exactly the same problem in principle as the inclusion of, say, propertyless men or men of racial minorities. The only difficulty is putting theory into practice.

Such a view is shared by contemporary feminists who press for equal rights for women and men and for all differences between the sexes as citizens to be swept away through the enactment of gender-neutral laws and policies.

At this point textual interpretation becomes important. The standard commentaries pay virtually no attention to the fact that almost all the famous modern political theorists agree that "human nature" is sexually differentiated; womanhood and manhood do not have the same political meaning. But now the crucial question arises: what exactly is the significance of sexual difference? Do the different natures and capacities of women and men mean that women cannot be citizens? Or does it mean that, if women are citizens, their citizenship will differ in some ways from that of men? Feminists have recently been conducting a vigorous debate about equality, difference and citizenship, and some contemporary feminists argue that women can make a distinctive and valuable contribution to political life. Sexual difference (women's specific attributes, capacities and tasks), they claim, should be acknowledged in law and public policy.

The readings of the modern texts in these chapters reflect the wide difference of opinion over sexual difference and equality, and also illustrate the complexity of the relationship between masculinity and femininity, and the political and the private, equality, freedom and citizenship. The modern construction of separate public and private spheres was developed in the seventeenth century, and two contrasting interpretations are offered here of texts from that period. Hobbes stands alone in the tradition of political thought, although his singularity receives little attention from mainstream theorists. Hobbes is the only writer received into the "tradition" who assumed that the same human nature is common to women and men. Hobbes's theory begins from the premise that women, like men, are born free and are men's equals. Why, then, did he endorse the dominion of men over women in civil society, and how does he make the theoretical move from sexual equality in the state of nature to patriarchal rule in civil society? Pateman's reading of Hobbes is that all the women in the state of nature are conquered by men and so incorporated as servants into "families." Having lost their status as free and equal "individuals," women lack the standing to participate in the original contract. Men thus make a contract that creates modern patriarchal marriage and the private sphere and that legitimates men's jurisdiction over women in civil society.

Locke did not share Hobbes's view that the state of nature was a condition of sexual equality. Butler's reading of Locke, however, is that his theory has the potential to be expanded to allow the incorporation of women into political life on the same basis as men. The crucial factor is that Locke argued that women, like men, could be educated; thus women's political fate was not determined by their nature. Women, Butler states, are capable "of satisfying Locke's requirements for political life." Moreover, Locke stands at the beginning of liberal individualism, a doctrine with universal implications. Locke's legacy, Butler argues, meant that "liberals would be forced to bring their views on women into line with their theory of human nature."

The feminist John Stuart Mill was one liberal who saw the subjection of women as a glaring anomaly in the modern world. Mill tried (albeit without success) to bring the relation between the sexes into line with his wider liberal principles, which meant that he had to attempt to bridge the divide between public and private. The tenets of liberalism, Mill argued, applied to marriage as well as political life. Shanley interprets Mill as arguing for friendship, not domination, in marriage and she sees Mill's demand for equal opportunity for women as a means to marital friendship rather than an end in itself. But Mill's attempt to universalize liberal principles remains an exception in political theory. Other writers, including twentieth-century theorists who figure prominently in the canon of modern political theory, construct their arguments around the separation between public and private.

For example, Hannah Arendt's examination of labor, work and action assumes a strict division between the worlds of productive (male) and reproductive (female) work and labor. As Dietz points out, "the fundamental activities Arendt designates have actually been lived out as either male or female *identities. Animal laborans*, 'the reproducer,' has been structured and experienced as if it were natural to the female, and *homo faber*, 'the fabricator,' has been constructed as if it were appropriate to the male," rather than taken as irreducible dimensions of humanness itself. As Fraser shows, Habermas's extremely elaborate and sophisticated analysis, with his distinctions between material and symbolic reproduction and between socially integrated and system integrated action contexts, similarly maintains the patriarchal division between private and public. Habermas's theory has an implicit "gender subtext," and, because he fails to investigate how the public – the (masculine) worker and the workplace – are linked to the private – the family – his theory defends "an institutional arrangement which is widely held to be one, if not the, linchpin of modern women's subordination."

The example of Habermas illustrates how even radical theorists are oblivious to the problem of sexual difference and sexual subordination. Thus they rarely ask any questions about Rousseau's credentials as the father of radical democracy. Yet Rousseau could not be more explicit in his exclusion of women, whom he sees as natural political subversives, from citizenship. Many feminists have seen Rousseau as merely inconsistent in his argument about the sexes, but Lange argues against this reading.

Within the structure of Rousseau's theory, political order requires that the public world reflect the sexual order of nature. The education of men and women must be different and women must maintain the family, the foundation of the state. If both men and women acted as competitors, making decisions on the basis of private advantage and subjective interest – that is to say, if both sexes acted in the manner seen as properly masculine – then, Rousseau believed, women would always lose because men already have an advantage in the competition. The lesson to be learnt from Rousseau, Lange argues, is that women should be cautious about equality with men; "meaningful equality of right, or privilege, or social consideration, may have to be based on an accommodation of sexual differences."

Like Rousseau, Hegel made his views on men's and women's political place clear enough; indeed, Hegel not only confined women to the private family but even excluded them from history. Yet Hegel, as Benhabib emphasizes, was an Enlightenment thinker who upheld the transformation begun in the French Revolution – at least, where the freedom of the male subject of the modern state is concerned. He drew back when faced with the emancipated women of his day; his "views on love and sexuality . . . reveal him to be a counter-Enlightenment thinker." Benhabib states that Hegel is "women's grave digger"; he confines women to a doomed phase of the dialectic. Hegel called women "an everlasting irony" in the life of the community, and Benhabib urges the restoration of irony and the "otherness of the other" – that is, the difference of women – that Hegel sought to expunge from political theory.

The pervasive and protracted unwillingness of political theorists to examine and question the arguments of theorists such as Rousseau and Hegel about sexual difference and the public and private is exacerbated by the exclusion of feminist works from the canon of texts. Mary Wollstonecraft, for instance, insisted that public and private, and, hence, the characters of men and women, could only be understood in relation to each other. Wollstonecraft is especially interesting, too, because two different arguments can be found in her writings, an argument for women's political equality with men and an argument that motherhood, women's special capacity or what she called their "peculiar destination," meant that women's citizenship must differ from that of men. Wollstonecraft was by no means alone in this mixture of arguments. In the late nineteenth and early twentieth centuries, the suffragists also argued, on the one hand, that (political) virtue had no sex, and that justice demanded that women should have the same political rights and be enfranchised on the same basis as men; on the other hand, they argued that women had a unique contribution to make (and so had a different claim to the vote than men) because of their special responsibilities as mothers.

In many of her comments on motherhood, Wollstonecraft sounds like the precursor of contemporary feminist thinkers who advocate bringing the traditionally female practices and values associated with motherhood into the public realm. In this volume, such arguments are represented by Di Stefano's discussion of Marx. Di Stefano makes the sweeping charge against Marx that – regardless of or despite what he said explicitly about women – the very structure and style of his thought is masculinist and denies the importance, and even the existence, of mothers, mothering activity and maternal labor. "Marx has essentially denied and then reappropriated the labor of the mother in his historical and labor-based account of self-created man." The denial of the mother, in Di Stefano's view, maintains the domination of women and nature, and "the case of the missing (m)other in western political theory," not unique to Marx, supports a deep misogyny in the tradition of political thought.

Wollstonecraft provides a necessary counter to this aspect of the tradition, but one problem in her arguments, Gatens states, is that she treats women's tasks as mothers as necessarily following from women's embodiment and biology; a political division of labor between women and men is then justified as natural. Wollstonecraft agreed with Rousseau that the family was the foundation of the state, but sharply disagreed that women could be good mothers in conditions of marital despotism or without public standing as citizens. Yet their duties as citizens coincided with their duties as mothers. At the same time, Gatens stresses, Wollstonecraft also insisted that reason had no sex. Women's apparent incapacity was due to lack of education, and their natures were corrupted by passion – the passion of men. Thus Wollstonecraft argues simultaneously that the bodily difference between the sexes is crucial for their citizenship, and appeals to a disembodied reason, or what Gatens calls "the essential sexual neutrality of the rational agent," in her defence of the rights of woman.

A defence of the rational agent is presented by Dietz and Okin in their analyses of Arendt and Rawls. They argue that to pay attention to sexual difference in policy and public law is not only detrimental to women but wrongly conceptualizes the nature and purpose of political life. Dietz recoils from the strand of contemporary feminist theory that shares "an emancipatory vision that defends the moral (or subversive) possibilities of women's role as reproducer, nurturer, and preserver of vulnerable human life." Okin takes Rawls to task for failing to see the need to apply liberal principles of justice to the private sphere, and thus for not considering how his acceptance of the conventional sexual division of labor excludes women from public life and relieves men of domestic burdens. While both Dietz and Okin argue that in the past the concept of the "universal citizen," or neutral rational agent, has not been universal or neutral but masculine, they think that one should be able to discern, and articulate and act according to, universal, gender-neutral standards of justice.

In contrast, Spelman and Sawicki reject a unitary model of citizenship. In their discussions of the works of de Beauvoir and Foucault they defend difference and also go further by emphasizing that, if women differ from men, so women also differ from each other. Spelman and Sawicki acknowledge the danger that to sweep away universally applicable rules and precepts may put women back into a position where they have different, but also lesser and secondary, obligations and rights from men. However, they see the possibility of second-class citizenship as less of a problem than the failure to recognize that "equality" (at least as presently conceived) rests on binary oppositions – such as private/public, feminine/masculine, citizen/woman – and denies the myriad and crosscutting differentiations between individuals and groups.

De Beauvoir's famous observation that "one is not born, but rather becomes, a woman" may undermine notions that biology determines women's destiny, but it also suggests to Spelman that there is no single, prototypical "woman" whose interests can shape a single feminist agenda. The lesson we must learn from the fact that, as Spelman argues, de Beauvoir implicitly wrote from the perspective of a middle-class white woman, is not simply that political theory has ignored or not adequately accounted for women's political position, but that there is no "woman's place" unmediated by class, race, ethnicity, religion, sexual orientation and other factors. Similarly, Sawicki argues that Foucault's theory helps feminists to see that it is not necessary for all differences between women to be obliterated if women are to be able to resist male domination. She argues that difference theory puts the "sexuality debate" that has polarized American feminists into a new perspective. It becomes possible to see that the two sides share common conceptions of power, freedom and sexuality that obscure and deny the historical character and diversity of women's sexual experiences. Unless the multiplicity of women's voices and interests are taken into account, women in dominant groups are likely to neglect or silence other women just as they have been neglected or silenced by most political theorists.

Political theory is often taught as if reading (selected) classic texts – the "history of political thought" – can be kept separate from pressing, current political problems. Feminist interpretations of the texts show that this is far from the case. This volume illustrates that one of the major tasks facing feminist theorists is to develop democratic theory into a theory of political and civil equality that encompasses the differences between the sexes and among women so that full citizenship for varied women can be secured. Despite the disagreements among the authors, they agree that among the greatest wrongs done to women has been their exclusion from taking part as full members and citizens of the polity in political debate, deliberation and contest. The classic theorists, and the construction of the academic canon of political theory, have been instrumental in achieving and maintaining this exclusion. We hope that the very diversity of feminist perspectives that follow will encourage many others to join in reinterpretating the texts, and so in the reconstruction of the discipline of political theory itself. To join in the theoretical dialogue is to participate in the vital argument over the purposes and goals of our common life which lies at the heart of politics.

Notes

1 Susan Okin, *Women in Western Political Thought* (Princeton, NJ: Princeton University Press, 1979), p. 286.
2 Lorenne M. G. Clark and Lynda Lange, *The Sexism of Social and Political Theory* (Toronto: University of Toronto Press, 1979), p. xvii.

1

Philosopher Queens and Private Wives: Plato on Women and the Family

Susan Moller Okin

Plato's ideas about women have attracted considerable attention in recent years.[1] This is not surprising, since his proposals for the education and role of the female guardians in Book V of the *Republic* are more revolutionary than those of any other major political philosopher, not excluding John Stuart Mill. However, Plato on the subject of women appears at first to present his reader with an unresolvable enigma, especially when his other dialogues are taken into account. One might well ask how the same, generally consistent philosopher can assert, on the one hand, that the female sex was created from the souls of the most wicked and irrational men and can argue, on the other hand, that if young girls and boys were trained identically, their abilities as adults would be practically the same. How can the claim that women are "by nature" twice as bad as men be reconciled with the radical idea that they should be included among the exalted philosophic rulers of the ideal state?

While I cannot here discuss all the relevant dialogues, the following paper attempts, through analysis of Plato's arguments about private property and the family in relation to the *polis*, to explain why he appears so inconsistent about the nature and the proper role of women. I contend that when one compares the arguments and proposals of the *Republic* with those of the *Laws*, it becomes clear that the absence or presence of the private family determines whether Plato advocates putting into practice his increasingly radical beliefs about the potential of women. Only by examining the proposals of *Republic* V in the context of the overall aims and structure of the ideal society, and by doing likewise with the contrasting proposals regarding women in the *Laws*, will we find the differences intelligible.

The aim of the true art of ruling, as Plato conceives of it, is not the welfare of any single class or section, but the greatest possible happiness of the entire community.[2] "Happiness," however, can be a misleading word, for if it leads us to thoughts of freedom, individual rights, or equality of opportunity, we are far from Plato's idea of happiness (*eudaimonia*). Neither equality nor liberty nor justice in the sense of fairness were values for Plato. The three values on which both his ideal and his second-best cities are based are, rather, harmony, efficiency, and moral goodness; the last is the key to his entire political philosophy. Because of his belief in the intrinsic value of the soul and the consequent importance of its health, Plato does not think that happiness results from the freedom to behave just as one wants; it is in no way attainable independently of virtue. Statesmen, therefore, should "not only preserve the lives of their subjects but reform their characters too, so far as human nature permits of this."[3] Though the ultimate aim of the true ruler is the happiness of all his subjects, the only way he can attain this is by raising them all, by means of education and law, to the highest possible level of wisdom and virtue.

The gravest of all human faults, however, one considered by Plato to be inborn in most people is that "excessive love of self" which is "the cause of all sins in every case."[4] Worse still, whereas the soul and next the body should take priority, man's all too prevalent tendency is to give his property – in truth the least valuable of his possessions – his greatest attention. Thus, in the *Laws* the currency and system of production, while allowing for private property, are so designed as to ensure that "a man by his money-making [will not] neglect the objects for which money exists: . . . the soul and the body . . . Wherefore we have asserted (and that not once only) that the pursuit of money is to be honoured last of all."[5] Clearly Plato's citizens were never to forget that material possessions were but means to far more important ends.

The ruler's task in promoting his subjects' virtue is therefore two-fold. He must aim to overcome their extremes of self-love and their fatal preference for material possessions over the welfare of their souls. A man who is to be virtuous and great must be able to transcend his own interests and, above all, to detach himself from the passion to acquire. As Glenn Morrow has noted, there is abundant evidence in both the *Republic* and the *Laws* that Plato regarded the maintenance of a temperate attitude towards property as essential for the security and well-being of the state.[6] It was acquisitiveness, after all, that had led the first city Socrates depicted – the simple, "true" and "healthy" city – into war with its neighbors and all the complications that this entailed. Again, corruption that results from increasing possessiveness is the recurrent theme of *Republic* VIII, which analyzes the process of political degeneration.[7]

The *Republic* is an extremely radical dialogue. In his formulation of the ideal state, Plato questions and challenges the most sacred contemporary conventions. The solution he proposes for the problem of selfishness and divisive interests is that private property and hence private interests be abolished to the greatest possible extent. For in this city, not just harmony but unity of interests is the objective. "Have we any greater evil for a city," asks Socrates, "than what splits it and makes it many instead of one? Or a greater good than what binds it together and makes it one?" He concludes that the best governed city is that "which is most like a single human being."[8] Nothing can dissolve the unity of a city more readily than for some of its citizens to be glad and others to grieve over the same thing, so that all do not work or even wish in concert. The highest possible degree of unity is achieved if all citizens feel pleasure and pain on the same occasions, and this "community of pleasure and pain" will occur only if all goods are possessed in common. The best governed city will be that "in which most say 'my own' and 'not my own' about the same thing, and in the same way."[9]

If he had thought it possible, Plato would certainly have extended the communal ownership of property to all the classes of his ideal city. The first of the "noble lies," according to which all citizens are told that they are one big family, can be read as the complete expression of an ideal which can be realized only in part. Because he believes in the tendency of most human beings to selfishness, Plato considers the renunciation of private property to be something that can be attained only by the best of persons. This is made clear in the *Laws*, where he rejects the possibility of eliminating ownership for the citizens of his projected "second-best" city, since tilling the soil in common is "beyond the capacity of people with the birth, rearing and training we assume."[10] What is impossible for the citizens of the second-best city, with all their carefully planned education, must regretfully be regarded as beyond the capacity of the inferior classes in the ideal city. Thus it is the guardian class alone which is to live up to the ideal of community of property and unity of interests.[11]

The overcoming of selfish interests is regarded as most necessary for those who are to have charge of the welfare and governance of all the other citizens – quite apart from their greater capacity for it. Since a person will always take care of what he loves, the guardians, especially, must love the whole community, and have no interests other than its welfare. Above all, then, the permitted property arrangements for them must be "such as not to prevent them from being the best possible guardians and not to rouse them up to do harm to the other citizens."[12] Plato argues that the possession by the rulers of private lands and wealth would inevitably lead to their formation into a faction, whereupon they would consitute "masters and enemies instead of allies of the other citizens."[13] The combination of wealth and private interests with political power can lead only to the destruction of the city.

Plato's ideal for the guardians is expressed by the proverb, "friends have all things in common."[14] But if communal ownership of inanimate property is a great aid to the unity of the city, it appears to him to follow that communal ownership of women and children will conduce to even greater unity. It is clear from the way Plato argues that he thinks the communalization of property leads directly to the abolition of the family. He does not regard them as distinct innovations requiring separate justifications. In fact, he slides over the first mention of the abolition of the family, almost as a parenthesis,[15] and in both the *Republic* and the brief summary of this aspect of it presented in the *Laws*, the two proposals are justified by the same arguments and often at the same time. In the *Laws* especially, when Plato looks back to the institutions of the ideal city, the classification of women and children with other possessions occurs frequently. Thus he talks of "community of wives, children, and all chattels," and later, by contrast, of that less desirable state of affairs in which "women and children and houses remain private, and all these things are established as the private property of individuals."[16]

Women are classified by Plato, as they were by the culture in which he lived, as an important subsection of property.[17] The very expression "community (or common having) of women and children," which he uses to denote his proposed system of temporary matings, is a further indication of this, since it could just as accurately be described as "the community of men," were it not for its inventor's customary way of thinking about such matters.[18]

Just as other forms of private property were seen as destructive of society's unity, so "private wives" are viewed by Plato as diverse and subversive in the same way. Thus, in contrast to the unified city he is proposing, he points to those institutional arrangements that foster the ascendance of particularism and factionalism, with "one man dragging off to his own house whatever he can get his hands on apart from the others, another being separate in his own house with separate women and children, introducing private pleasures and griefs of things that are private."[19] Again, in the *Laws*, he strikes simultaneously against contemporary Athenian practices with regard both to private property and to women: "we huddle all our goods together, as the saying goes, within four walls, and then hand over the dispensing of them to the women . . ."[20] It is clear that conventional marriage and woman in her traditional role as guardian of the private household were seen by Plato as intimately bound up with that system of private possessions which was the greatest impediment to the unity and well-being of the city.

In *Republic* VIII, however, as Plato reviews the successively degenerate forms of the political order, we can see his association of private women with corruption at its most graphic. Just as women were communalized at the same time as other property, so are they now, without separate explanation, made private at the same time as other property, as the course of the city's degeneration is described. Once private, moreover, women are depicted as hastening the course of the decline, due to their exclusive concern with the particular interests of their families. First, when the rulers begin to want to own land, houses, and money, and to set up domestic treasuries and private love-nests, they will begin to fail as guardians of the people, and the city will start to degenerate.[21] Thereafter, private possession of women is depicted as a major cause of further corruption. The mother's complaints that her husband's lack of concern for wealth and public prestige disadvantages her among the other women make the timocratic youth begin to despise his worthy father and to feel challenged into showing that he is more of a man. The wife with her selfish concerns, who "chants all the other refrains such as women are likely to do in cases of this sort," is, like Pandora, the real originator of the evils that follow.[22]

The fact that Plato identifies the abolition of the family so closely with the communalization of property, and does not appear to regard the former as a more severe emotional deprivation than the latter, must be understood in the context of the functions and status of women and the family in contemporary upper-class Athenian life. In view of the chattel status of Athenian women and the "peculiarly close relation thought to hold between a family and its landed property," Plato's blending of two issues, which to us appear to be much more distinct, is far from inexplicable.[23] There is abundant evidence in classical Greek literature that the women who were eligible to become the wives of Plato's contemporaries were valued for silence, hard work, domestic frugality, and, above all, marital fidelity. Confined to the functions of household management and the bearing of heirs, they were neither educated nor permitted to experience the culture and intellectual stimulation of life outside their secluded quarters in the house. Accordingly, it was almost impossible for husbands and wives to be either day-to-day companions or emotional and intellectual intimates.[24] Consequently, as recent scholars of Greek life agree, "the family does not bulk large in most Greek writing, its affective and psychological sides hardly at all," and "family life, as we understand it, hardly existed" in late fifth-century Athens.[25] The prevailing bisexuality meant that "two complementary institutions coexisted, the family taking care of what we may call the material side, pederasty (and the courtesan) the affective, and to a degree the intellectual, side of a man's intimate life."[26]

On the other hand, while the family was certainly no center of the upper-class Greek's emotional life, it did function in ways that the modern family does not – ways which rendered it potentially far more socially divisive. The single-family household had emerged from the clan in comparatively recent times, and only gradually did the *polis* gain the loyalty that had once belonged to the autonomous clan. Antigone represents the paradigm example of this conflict of loyalties; there were, in fact, various areas of life where it had not yet become clear whether family or civic obligations should prevail. The extent to which the victim's kin, rather than the rulers, were responsible for ensuring that crime was properly avenged is well documented in the *Laws*.[27] Again, the predominance of duties to parents over any notion of legal justice is clearly indicated in the *Euthyphro*, where Socrates is incredulous that a man could even think of prosecuting his own father for the murder of anyone who was not a relative.[28] Despite its minimal functioning as an emotional base, then, the Athenian family of the early fourth century, as a firm economic entity and the focus of important duties, constituted an obviously divisive force and potential threat to civic loyalty.

Those Plato scholars who have expressed profound horror at the idea that the family be abolished and replaced by those mating arrangements designed to produce the best offspring seem to have treated the issue anachronistically, by neglecting the function of the family in Athenian life. When G. M. A. Grube, for example, objects to the system of temporary matings advocated for the guardians as "undesirable because it does violence to the deepest human emotions" and "entirely ignores the love element between the 'married' pair,"[29] he seems to be forgetting that at the time, the family was simply not the locus for the expression of the deepest human emotions. Even a cursory knowledge of the *Symposium*, with its deprecating comparison of those who turn their love towards women and raise families with those whose superior, spiritual love is turned towards boys and philosophy, reveals that Plato and his audience would not have regarded the abolition of the family as a severe limitation of their intimate lives. Stranger still is the attitude taken by Leo Strauss, who not only assumes that the family is "natural" and any move to abolish it "convention," but makes the issue of whether the abolition of the family is possible or not into an acid test for determining the feasibility of the entire ideal state.[30] Those passages of the *Republic* to which he refers in order to demonstrate the supposed "fact that men seem to desire naturally to have children of their own" are remarkably inadequate to prove his point. Moreover, his objection that Plato's controls on heterosexual behaviour mean that "the claims of *eros* are simply silenced" implies a complete denial of the prevailing homosexual *eros* of the time. It is very probable that Plato's listeners would have regarded the ideal state's restrictions on their homosexual behavior as more repressive of their sexual feelings than the abolition of the family and the controls placed on heterosexual intercourse.

The same scholars – Grube, Taylor, and Strauss – who reject the abolition of the family as impossible, are those most intolerant of the proposed alternative, in which partners are chosen for each other, supposedly by lot but, in fact, for eugenic purposes. Those who reject such proposals as quite impracticable, given human nature, because of their "intolerable severity"[31] would do well to consider the position of respectable Greek women. For they were just as controlled and deprived in their sexual lives as both sexes of guardians were to be in the ideal city, and without having available to them the compensations of any participation in life outside the domestic sphere. The Greek woman was not permitted to choose her sexual partner, any more than Plato's guardians were. Moreover, in her case the partner had not only the absolute right to copulate with and reproduce via her for the rest of her life, but also all the powers which her father had previously wielded over her. Once married, a woman had no condoned alternative sexual outlets, but was entirely dependent on a husband, who might have any number of approved hetero- or homosexual alternatives, for any satisfaction that he might choose to give her. The extent of the double standard is brought clearly into relief by the fact that the Greek word for adultery *meant* nothing but sexual intercourse between a married woman and a man who was not her husband. Needless to say, the punishments were very severe. Even if her husband died, a woman had no control over her life or her body, since she was returned to the custody of her father or guardian, who could remarry her at his pleasure. Alternatively, a citizen could give his sister or daughter into concubinage, from which she could be sent to a brothel without any reproach to her owner.[32]

If Athenian women of the highest class, living in one of the most highly cultured societies the world has known, could be controlled and deprived to this extent, it is hardly arguable that the exigencies of human nature render the Platonic mating system, with its requirement of supposedly "unnatural continence,"[33] impossible to enact. Women's sexual lives have been restricted throughout the greater part of world history, just as rigidly as Plato proposes to control the intimate lives of his guardians. "The claims of *eros*" have been "simply silenced" in women with considerable success. It is apparent from much of the history of the female sex that, with suitable indoctrination and strong sanctions, human beings can be conditioned to accept virtually any extent of control on their sexual and emotional lives. The point is, of course, that the scholars concerned have

used the terms "human emotions" and "human nature" to refer only to
men. What seems really horrific to Grube, Taylor, and Strauss is that
whereas the Greeks, like many other peoples, merely reserved women for
the production of legitimate issue and controlled their lives accordingly,
Plato has dared to suggest that the sexual lives of both male and female
guardians should be controlled for the purpose of producing the best
possible offspring for the community.

The significance of Plato's abolition of the family is profound; the
proposal has been echoed by a number of subsequent theorists or rulers of
utopian societies that depend to a very high degree on cohesion and unity.
As Stanley Diamond has asserted, in an illuminating essay which analyzes
the significance of Plato's treatment of the family, "The obvious aim is to
disengage [the guardians] from all connections and motives which might
diminish their dedication to the state . . . Plato clearly sensed the antagonism
between state and family, and in order to guarantee total loyalty to the
former, he simply abolished the latter."[34] It is important to notice that
Plato's revolutionary solution to the conflict was not to obliterate the
primary ties of kinship, but to extend them throughout the entire ruling
class. The guardians were in fact "to imagine that they were all one
family,"[35] and it is stressed in many ways that the formation of the rulers
into one family is to be no mere formality. They are required not only to
address but to behave towards each other as brother, parent, and so on.
"It would be ridiculous," Glaucon agrees, "if they only mouthed, without
deeds, the names of kinship."[36] Thus, the fear and shame associated with
violence towards a parent will operate as an unusually strong sanction
against attack on anyone at all of the older generation. Likewise, lawsuits
and factional disputes will be no more common than they would be within
a family, and the city's success in war will be in large part due to the fact
that soldiers will be no more likely to desert their comrades than to
abandon members of their own families.[37] Indeed, as Gregory Vlastos has
concisely stated, "The ideal society of the *Republic* is a political community
held together by bonds of fraternal love."[38]

The most radical implication of Plato's transforming the guardian class
into a single family concerns the role of women. Rousseau, in the course of
a bitter attack on Plato both for doing away with the family and for giving
equal opportunities to women, nevertheless reveals a perceptive understanding of the connection between the two innovations. "I am well aware
that in the *Republic* Plato prescribes the same exercises for women as for
men," he says. "Having dispensed with the individual family in his system
of government, and not knowing any longer what to do with women, he
finds himself forced to turn them into men."[39] It appears that he is correct,
except that in place of "men" we should substitute "people," since for
Rousseau in many important respects only men were people. Scholars

who have considered the connection between the first two "waves of paradox" of Book V – the granting of equal opportunities to women and the abolition of the family – do not, however, agree. Some have stressed the independence of the two proposals, some have maintained that there is probably a causal link between them but have not committed themselves on its direction, and at least one has asserted, without giving any reasons, that it is the emancipation of women which renders necessary the abolition of the family.[40] For a number of reasons, however, it seems that any causal connection that exists between the two paradoxes goes the other way, as Rousseau claims.

In the ideal city, since there is no private wealth or marriage for those in the guardian class and since their living arrangements are to be communal, there is no domestic role such as that of the traditional housewife. Since planned breeding and communal childrearing minimize the unpredictability of pregnancy and the time demanded of mothers, maternity is no longer anything approaching a full-time occupation. Thus, women can no longer be defined by their traditional roles. However, every person in the ideal city is defined by his or her function; the education and working life of each citizen are to be dedicated to the optimal performance of a single craft.[41] If the female guardians were no longer to be defined in relation to particular men, children, and households, it seems that Plato had no alternative but to consider them persons in their own right. If they were to take their place as members of the guardian class, each must share in the functions of that class. Thus Plato had to convince his skeptical audience that women were able to perform tasks very different from those customarily assigned to them.

Socrates first reminds his audience that they have all agreed that each individual should be assigned work that is suited to his or her nature. But, he says, since none of them will claim that there is no difference of nature between the male and the female, they are in danger of contradicting themselves if they argue that the female guardians should do the same work as the male. However, there are many ways in which human beings can differ, and we do not regard all of them as relevant in assigning different functions to different persons. Socrates asserts that we have not yet considered "what form of different and same nature, and applying to what, we were distinguishing when we assigned different practices to a different nature and the same ones to the same."[42] But, he continues, is it not reasonable to consider only those differences and similarities that have some bearing on the activity in question? We do not worry about whether a man is bald or longhaired when assessing his capacity to be a good shoemaker. There is, therefore, no reason to consider the difference in procreative function between the sexes – "that the female bears and the male mounts" – as relevant in deciding whether they should play equal roles in the ruling class. Socrates lays the burden of proof firmly on whoever should claim that it is. He argues, rather, that since the characteristics of the soul determine whether a person is capable of a certain pursuit, and since sex is no more related to the soul than the presence or absence of hair, members of both sexes will be skilled in all the arts, depending on the nature of their individual souls. Thus, though he asserts that women in general are not as capable as men in general, especially in physical strength, individual members of both sexes will be capable of performing all the functions needed by the city, including guardianship and philosophy. The only way to ensure that persons are assigned the jobs for which they are best suited is to assess the merits of each, independently of sex.

This argument, simple as it seems, is unique in the treatment of women by political philosophers, and has revolutionary implications for the female sex. Plato's bold suggestion that perhaps there is no difference between the sexes, apart from their roles in procreation, is possible only because the requirement of unity among the ruling class, and the consequent abolition of private property and the family, entail the abolition of wifehood and the absolute minimization of motherhood. Once the door is open, the possibilities for women are boundless. The annihilation of traditional sex roles among the guardians is total – even the earliest childcare is to be shared by men and women.[43] Plato concludes that, though females as a class are less able, the best of women can share with the best of men in the highest functions involved in ruling the city. The "philosopher monarchs," as they should always have been called, were to include both sexes.[44]

The overwhelming hostility from male scholars to Plato's first wave of paradox is fascinating in its own right, but this is not the place to discuss it. However, one charge that has been laid against him must be dealt with here. Leo Strauss and Allan Bloom have claimed that Plato's arguments for the equality of women depend on his "abstracting from" or "forgetting" the body, and particularly his "abstracting from the difference between the sexes with regard to procreation."[45] Clearly they do not. Plato is very careful to take into account those differences between the sexes that are palpably biological and therefore inevitable – pregnancy, lactation, and a degree of difference in physical strength. These scholars, in the company of millions of other people, mistakenly assume, as Plato very rationally does not, that the entire conventional female sex role follows logically from the single fact that women bear children. The real significance of the treatment of the women question in *Republic* V is that it is one of the very few instances in the history of thought when the biological implications of femaleness have been clearly separated from all the conventional, institutional, and emotional baggage that has usually been identified with them. Plato's elimination of a private sphere from the guardians' lives entailed the radical questioning of all the institutionalized differences between the sexes.

During the argument about the proper education and role of women, Socrates twice indicates directly that these and the abolition of the family are really parts of the same issue. He talks, first, of the "right acquisition and use of children and women" and later of "the law concerning the possession and rearing of the women and children."[46] In addition, the way he introduces the emancipation of the female guardians is in itself significant. Having dropped in an aside the proposal that the guardians will have women and children as well as their other possessions in common, Socrates is challenged, at the beginning of Book V, to justify this important decision. In answer to this challenge, he embarks on his discussion, first, of the equal education and treatment of women and, second, of the communal breeding and rearing arrangements. It seems, then, that having decided to do away with the conventional role of women by doing away with the family, he feels impelled to support this proposal by demonstrating that women are capable of filling many roles outside of their traditional sphere. A brief passage from the *Laws* shows how aware Plato was of the danger of freeing women from their confined, domestic role without giving them an alternative function. He thought the example of the Spartans should be enough to discourage any legislator from "letting the female sex indulge in luxury and expense and disorderly ways of life, while supervising the male sex."[47] Thus it was his dismantling of the family which not only enabled Plato to rethink the question of women and their potential abilities but forced him to do so.

Two additional arguments show clearly that it is the abolition of the family that leads Plato into emancipating the female guardians rather than vice versa. First, no mention is made of the women of the inferior classes. We are told that among these householders and farmers, private land, houses, and other property are to be preserved. The close connection between these things and the private ownership of women and children implies, though we are not specifically told this, that the family too is preserved among the lower classes.[48] Efficiency is no doubt one of Plato's primary aims in the organization of the artisans. But although the argument in Book V about women's talents is just as applicable to the other crafts as to that of governing the city, there is no suggestion of applying it to the women of any class but the guardians. The only possible explanation seems to be that where the family is retained, women continue to be private wives and functional mothers, so that their equality with men in other roles is not considered an open issue.[49]

Second, what happens to women in Plato's second-best city – that depicted in the *Laws* – overwhelmingly confirms our hypothesis. On the subject of women, Plato in the *Laws* is a study in ambivalence. He is caught in a dilemma caused by the impossibility of reconciling his increasingly firm beliefs about the potential of the female sex with the reintroduction of private property and the family into the social structure of his city. On the one hand, having thought about women as individuals with vast unused talents, Plato seems to have been more convinced than ever, by the time he wrote the *Laws*, that existing practice with regard to women was foolish and that they should be educated and used to their greatest capacity. In theory, the radical statements about women from *Republic* V are carried in the *Laws* to new extremes. On the other hand, the *Laws* is a considerably less revolutionary document than the *Republic*; far from being "a pattern laid up in heaven," the second-best city is put forward as a far less utopian construct.[50] The very title of the dialogue, usually translated "Laws," is in fact more accurately rendered as "Tradition." A significant casualty of this "realism" is Plato's conception of the role of women. What is proposed for them in general terms is simply not fulfilled by the details of the society, in which they are again private wives and the functioning mothers of particular children.

Plato's arguments and conclusions in the *Laws* about the natural potential of women are far more radical than those of the *Republic*. He appears to attribute to the different rearing and education of the two sexes practically all differences in their subsequent abilities and achievements. Pointing to the example of the Sarmatian women, who participate in warfare equally with the men, as proof of the potential of the female sex, he argues that the Athenian practice of maintaining rigid sex roles is absurd. Only a legislator's "surprising blunder" could allow the waste of half the state's available resources, by prescribing the "most irrational" practice – "that men and women should not all follow the same pursuits with one accord and with all their might."[51] In addition, a few speeches before these striking assertions are made, Plato prepares the way for them by means of an elaborate metaphor about ambidexterity – a lightly veiled allusion to his belief that men and women, like right and left hands, would be far more equal in ability if they received equal training.[52]

By the time he wrote the *Laws*, then, Plato had clearly come to recognize that female human nature was not fairly represented by the deprived and stunted women of his own society. Indeed, it was as yet unknown, although one could derive some impression of what women were capable of achieving from the example of the female warriors who in other societies held their own with the men in battle. However, in the *Laws*, the statements of general principle about women are far more radical than the actual details of the society as it is drawn up. Having made the general proclamation that the law should prescribe the same education and training for girls as it does for boys and that "the female sex must share with the male, to the greatest extent possible, both in education and in all else" – should "share with men in the whole of their mode of life"[53] – Plato's Athenian legislator fails to apply these precepts, in many of the most crucial instances. In order to understand the inconsistency between the general statements about women and the detailed specifications given for the most important of civic duties, we must turn to the effects on women of the reintroduction of private property and the family.

Though it is clearly a source of regret to Plato, he concedes that the citizens of the second-best city, not being gods or sons of gods, are not capable of holding their property in common. The reinstatement of private property, one of the most far-reaching differences between the *Laws* and the *Republic*, brings with it in the same paragraph the reintroduction of marriage and the family.[54] It is clear from the context that the need for a property-holding man to have an heir requires the disappearance of the communal ownership of women and children simultaneously with that of other property. However, the identification of women and children to-gether with other possessions was so automatic to the Greek mind that, again, no separate justification is felt to be necessary. The failure to achieve communism of property, it seems, entails the private possession of women.

The family, moreover, is the basis of the polity planned in the *Laws*. As Glenn Morrow has noted, "the state is a union of households or families, not a collection of detached citizens," and "the vitality of the family in Plato's state is evident at many points in his legislation."[55] The existence of family shrines, the complexity of marriage and inheritance laws, the family's crucial role in the prosecution of criminal justice, and the denial to sons of the right to defend themselves against their fathers – all these provisions indicate the central and authoritative position of the family.[56] The marriage laws are the first to be drawn up, and their repercussions for the position of women are immediate and extensive. In contrast to the temporary mating system of the *Republic*, in which neither sex had more freedom to choose or refuse a mate than the other, the reintroduction of permanent marriage seems to involve, without any explanation, a very different degree of choice of spouse for women and men. Marriage is to be compulsory for all, since procreation is regarded as a universal duty. But whereas a man, subject to the provision that he seek a partnership that will result in the best offspring for his society, decides whom he will marry, a woman is "given" in marriage.[57] The "right of valid betrothal" of a woman belongs in turn to a long succession of male kindred, and only if she has no close male relatives at all can she have any say in choosing her husband. Ironically, considering this preemption of women's choice, Plato refuses to enforce legally the prohibition of unsuitable marriages, since he considers that to do so, "besides being ridiculous, would cause widespread resentment."[58] Apparently what was to be customary for women was considered intolerable control if applied to men.

The treatment of women by the marriage laws is closely related to the fact that they are virtually excluded from property ownership. Even if she has no brothers, a daughter can participate in the inheritance of the family estate only by serving as the instrument through which the husband her father chooses for her can become her father's heir, if she has no brothers.[59] The *Laws* documents the essential connection of property and inheritance to the marriage system and position of women. When a man owns inheritable property, he must own a wife too, in order to ensure a legitimate heir. The fact that women are private wives entails that in many ways they are treated as property rather than as persons. They themselves cannot inherit real property, which to a large extent defines personhood within the society (a disinherited son must leave the city unless another citizen adopts him as his heir);[60] and they are treated as commodities to be given away by their male relatives. Given these basic features of the social structure of the city, it is not surprising that Plato, in spite of general pronouncements to the contrary, is not able to treat women as the equals of his male citizens. Their status as property seems to prevent the execution of his declared intentions.

Although the legal status of women in Plato's second-best city is an improvement on that in contemporary Athens, it is not one of equality with men. Glenn Morrow has said that "it is certainly Plato's expressed intention (though not fully carried out) to give women a more equal status under the law . . ."[61] The proposed divorce laws, unlike the marriage laws, do treat women considerably more equally than did those of contemporary Athens; the criminal statutes enforce the same punishments for the wounding or murder of wives as of husbands, and they are generally applied without discrimination according to the sex of either plantiff or defendant.[62] The most striking instance of equal treatment before the law is in the case of extramarital intercourse, where the same penalties are extended to offenders of both sexes.[63] This unusual departure from the double standard that one might expect to find in a society so firmly based on monogamy and inheritance can probably be explained by Plato's wish to make all the members of his city as virtuous and temperate as possible. After all, the standards are not relaxed for women, but they are considerably tightened up for men. However, the Athenian concept of women as legal minors is still present in significant ways in the *Laws*. Besides not being eligible to own property, they are not allowed until the age of forty to give evidence in a court of law or to support a plea, and only if unmarried are they allowed to bring an action.[64] Women, especially if married, are still to a large extent *femmes couvertes*.

What begins to be revealed through the denial of important civil and legal rights to women is strongly confirmed by the roles allotted them within the official governmental sphere. In the *Republic*, once we have been told that women of the guardian class are to share with men in every aspect of ruling and guarding, they are not specifically assigned to any particular offices, and there is no implication that they are ineligible for any. The only case where women are specifically mentioned as being eligible for office is at the end of Socrates' account of the philosophers' education. Here, presumably because the very idea must have seemed so outrageous, Plato feels it necessary to remind his audience that everything he has been saying applies equally to all women with the necessary abilities.[65] It is most unlikely that the women guardians, if allowed to compete for the highest rank of all, would have been excluded from any other office.

In the *Laws*, by contrast, in spite of the general pronouncements cited above, Plato both specifies when a certain function, such as the priesthood, is to be performed by persons of both sexes, and makes particular mention of women's holding certain offices, frequently with the strong implication that only women are eligible for them.[66] Thus, it is women who supervise married couples, who look after infants, whose role in the educational system is to provide the children's meals and oversee their games – in short, who perform, in positions not of the highest rank, all those domestic, nurturing, child-oriented tasks to which women have traditionally been assigned. On the other hand, there is no hint of women's participation in the magistracy, or the "divine nocturnal synod," whose role parallels that of the philosophers in the *Republic*.[67] The children are given their lessons by male educational officers; the post of supervisor of education is "by far the most important . . . of the highest offices of State" and must be filled by "that one of the citizens who is in every way the most excellent," and it is explicitly laid down that its occupant be male, for he must be "the father of legitimate children."[68] This qualification adds weight to what is implied throughout the work – that in the second-best city, unless the eligibility of women is plainly mentioned, most offices, and especially high ones, are reserved for men.[69] Even for those in which she can share, a women is not eligible until age 40, whereas a man is eligible from the age of 30.[70]

In spite of his controversial proposal in the *Laws* that, in the interests of order and discipline, even married women should take their meals communally, though segregated from the men, it is clear that Plato was ambivalent about the wisdom, or perhaps the feasibility, of bringing wives out of their domestic seclusion. Thus when he describes the funeral processions for distinguished citizens, women of childbearing age are noticeably omitted from a list in which every other class of citizen has its place. They are similarly omitted from the choral competitions.[71] Most remarkable, however, given his previous insistence that neither gymnastics nor riding are improper for women, and that trained women can perform in the military sphere equally as well as men,[72] is the fact that, once the detailed regulations are being made, he exempts women almost entirely from military service. Young girls are to learn the military arts only "if they agree to it," whereas they are obligatory for the boys.[73] Then, although he makes the general provision that men, women, and children are all to participate in military training at least one day a month, when the details are given, women after the age of marriage (20 at the latest) are again noticeably absent. They are not included either in races or in wrestling, both of which are integral parts of the training. As for horsemanship, it is decreed that "it is not worthwhile to make compulsory laws and rules about their taking part in such sports," but that they may do so "without blame," if they like.[74] It should be noted that Plato was not in the habit of making aspects of his educational systems optional – particularly those relating to the defense of the state.

Finally, whereas the term of military service for men is from the ages of 20 to 60, "for women they shall ordain what is possible and fitting in each case, after they have finished bearing children, and up to the age of fifty, in whatever kind of military work it may be thought right to employ their services."[75] This means that for all the grand assertions about the necessity and rationality of women's being trained equally with men to share in the defense of the state, they are in fact allowed, not compelled, to train up to the age of, at latest, 20, they are then excluded from most military activity until they are past childbearing, and they are subsequently exempted again at 50. In a society in which men had no other condoned sexual outlet than their wives, and contraception was hardly in an advanced state, this could well mean an expectation of five years of military service from adult women. Surely this was no way to produce Amazons.

Despite Plato's professed intention to have the women of the second-best city share equally with the men in all the duties of citizenship, the fact that they are private wives curtails their participation in public life for three reasons. The first is pregnancy and lactation, which is not controlled and predictable as it was in the *Republic*, where the guardians were to mate only at the behest of the rulers. In the *Laws*, since women are permanent wives, they are far less able to time or limit their pregnancies and cannot be held continuously liable for public and, especially, military duties. Second, the reinstitution of the private household makes each wife into the mistress responsible for its welfare, and it is clear that in the *Laws* a mother is to participate far more in early childcare than did the female guardian, who was not even to know which child was hers.[76]

The third reason is that Plato found it inconceivable that women who are "private wives" – the private property of the male citizens – should play the same kind of public and, especially, military roles as the female guardians, who were not defined in terms of a traditional relationship to a man. Whereas the female guardians, like their male counterparts, could exercise naked, the young girls in the *Laws* must be "clad in decent apparel," as if a maiden who was shortly to become the respectable wife and private property of a citizen could hardly be seen naked by the world at large.[77] Plato expresses as much expectation of ridicule for his suggestion in the *Laws* that wives should dine at public, though segregated, tables as he had expressed in the *Republic* for his proposal that all the guardians of both sexes should exercise together naked.[78] Although he thought it even more dangerous to leave women undisciplined than to neglect men and insisted that women too should dine in public, he was well aware that, in the kind of society he was planning, there would be enormous resistance to such an idea. Consequently, although he deplored the fact that even the supposedly trained women of Sparta had panicked and run when an enemy invaded their city, and thought it folly that so important a potential for defense as the entire female sex should be neglected, he seems to have found it impossible to hold to his original proposal that women should participate in military activities equally with men. If the segregated public dining of private wives could cause a general outcry, there was no knowing what revolutions might be provoked by the proposal that men should mingle with other men's private wives on the battlefield. Despite all his professed intentions in the *Laws* to emancipate women and make full use of the talents that he was now convinced they had, Plato's reintroduction of the family has the direct effect of putting them firmly back into their traditional place.

In the *Republic*, because the abolition of property and the family for the guardian class entails the abolition of woman's traditional sphere, the difference between the sexes is reduced to that of their roles in procreation. Since the nature of the women of this class is declared to be the same as that of the men, the radical proposal that their educations and lifestyles are to be identical follows accordingly. Plato has prescribed an androgynous character for all the guardians; both male and female are to be courageous and gentle, and both, because of their education and continued fellowship, will hold precious the good of the entire community. For the purposes of this society, therefore, the abolition of traditional sex roles is declared to be far more in accordance with nature than is the conventional adherence to them.

In the *Laws*, by contrast, the reinstatement of property requires monogamy and private households, and thus restores women to their role of "private wives" with all that this entails. Although his general statements about women's potential are considerably stronger here than in the *Re-*

public, Plato *cannot*, because of the economic and social structure he has prescribed, carry out to any significant extent the revolution in woman's role that would seem to follow from such beliefs. In this society, the "nature" of woman must be different from the "nature" of man. She must be pure and respectable, as befits a private wife who is to ensure the legitimacy of the property owner's heir, while he is to retain the noble and courageous qualities which resemble those of the ideal guardian.

The striking difference between the roles of women in the *Republic* and the *Laws*, then, is not due to a change in Plato's beliefs about the nature and capacities of women. On the contrary, his convictions appear to have changed in exactly the opposite way. The difference is due to the abolition of private property and the family, in the interest of unity, in the former dialogue, and their reinstatement in the latter. When a woman is once again perceived as the privately owned appendage of a man, when the family and its needs define her function, the socialization and regulation prescribed for her must ensure that her "nature" is formed and preserved in accordance with this role.

Notes

1 See, for example, Christine Pierce, "Equality: *Republic* V," *Monist*, 57 (1), January 1973; Anne Dickason, "Anatomy and Destiny: The Role of Biology in Plato's Views of Women," *Philosophical Forum*, 5, (1–2), 1973–4; and, since this paper was written, Arlene Saxonhouse, "The Philosopher and the Female in the Political Thought of Plato," *Political Theory*, 4, (2), May 1976.

2 *The Republic of Plato*, trans. Allan Bloom (New York, 1968), 420b.

3 *Statesman*, trans. H. B. Skemp, in *The Collected Dialogues of Plato*, ed. Edith Hamilton and Huntington Cairns (New York, 1961), 297b. Cf. *Laws*, trans. R. G. Bury (Cambridge, Mass., 1926), 630c, 644–5, 705d–6a, 707d; *Euthydemus*, trans. W. H. D. Rouse, in *Collected Dialogues*, 292b–c; and cf. Sheldon Wolin, *Politics and Vision* (London, 1961), pp. 34–6.

4 *Laws*, 731e.

5 Ibid., 743d–e.

6 Glenn R. Morrow, *Plato's Cretan City* (Princeton, 1960), p. 101; cf. *Laws*, 736e.

7 *Republic*, 372e–3e, and VIII passim.

8 Ibid., 462a–e.

9 Ibid., 462a–e.

10 *Laws*, 739c–40a.

11 *Republic*, 416c–17b.

12 Ibid., 416c–d.

13 Ibid., 417a–b.

14 Ibid., 423e; *Laws*, 739c.

15 *Republic*, 423e.

16 Ibid., 423e, 462, 464; *Laws*, 739c, 807b.

17 The Greeks' basically proprietary attitude towards women is well illustrated by the following statement from Demosthenes' account of the lawsuit, *Against Naera*: "For this is what living with a woman as one's wife means – to have children by her and to introduce the sons to the members of the clan and of the deme, and to betroth the daughters to husbands as one's own. Mistresses we keep for the sake of pleasure, concubines for the daily care of our persons, but wives to bear us legitimate children and to be faithful guardians of our households." Demosthenes, *Private Orations*, Loeb edn, trans. A. T. Murray (Cambridge, Mass., 1939), III: 122. For confirmation that this was a prevalent attitude see Victor Ehrenberg, *Society and Civilization in Greece and Rome* (Cambridge, Mass., 1964), p. 26.

18 Cf. G. M. A. Grube, *Plato's Thought* (London, 1935), p. 89.

19 *Republic*, 464c–d.

20 *Laws*, 805e.

21 *Republic*, 547b, 548a.

22 Ibid., 549c–e.

23 Morrow, *Plato's Cretan City*, n. 13 on p. 102, in which he notes that in Athens custom forbade the alienation of family land. The connection in classical Greek thought and practice between the wife and custody of the household property is amply confirmed in the descriptions of household management given by Xenophon and Aristotle.

24 See, for example, Thucydides, *The Peloponnesian War*, 46; Sophocles, *Ajax*, Loeb edn, trans. F. Storr (Cambridge, Mass., 1913), 291–3; Xenophon, *Oeconomicus*, in *Xenophon's Socratic Discourse*, trans. Carnes Lord, ed. Leo Strauss (Ithaca, 1970), p. 29 and cf. pp. 30–3; Aristotle, *The Politics*, I, xiii, II; Victor Ehrenberg, *The People of Aristophanes*, 2nd rev. edn (Oxford, 1951), pp. 202, 295.

25 M. I. Finley, *The Ancient Greeks* (New York, 1963), pp. 123–4; Ehrenberg, *Society and Civilization*, p. 59.

26 Finley, *Ancient Greeks*, p. 124.

27 *Laws*, for example, 866 and 873e.

28 *Euthyphro*, 4a–b.

29 Grube, *Plato's Thought*, p. 270; cf. A. E. Taylor, *Plato: The Man and His Work* (London, 1926; 7th edn, 1960), p. 278.

30 Leo Strauss, "On Plato's Republic," in *The City and Man* (Chicago, 1964), p. 117.

31 Taylor, *Plato*, p. 278; see also Grube, *Plato's Thought*, p. 270, and Strauss, "On Plato's Republic," p. 117.

32 Jean Ithurriague, *Les idées de Platon sur la condition de la femme* (Paris, 1931), p. 53.

33 Grube, *Plato's Thought*, p. 270.

34 Stanley Diamond, "Plato and the Definition of the Primitive," in *Culture in History*, ed. Diamond (New York, 1960), p. 126.

35 *Timaeus*, trans. Benjamin Jowett (Oxford, 1871), 18c–d.

36 *Republic*, 463c–e.

37 Ibid., 464d–e, 465a–b, 471c–d.

38 Gregory Vlastos, *Platonic Studies* (Princeton, 1973), p. 11.

39 Rousseau, *Emile*, Pléiade edn (Paris, 1914), 4: 699–700 (my translation).

40 For examples of these three positions, see Pierce, "Equality," p. 6; Strauss, "On Plato's Republic," p. 116; Taylor, *Plato*, p. 278.

41 *Republic*, 370; this is graphically illustrated by the assertion at 406d–7a that if one can no longer perform one's task, it is worthless to go on living.

42 Ibid., 454b; cf. 454–6 in general for source of this paragraph.

43 Ibid., 460b.

44 Ibid., 540c.

45 Strauss, "On Plato's Republic," pp. 116–17; Allan Bloom, "Interpretive Essay," in *Republic of Plato*, trans. Bloom, pp. 382–383.

46 *Republic*, 451c, 453d.

47 *Laws*, 806a–c.

48 *Republic*, 417a–b.

49 It is illuminating that in Aristotle's response to the proposals of Book V, once the issue of the family is settled, that of the role of women is not considered an independent one. It is clear that, since Aristotle considers himself to have refuted the proposal for the community of women and children, he does not deem it necessary to argue against Plato's wild ideas about women and their potential as individual persons. Given the family and the private household, women are private wives with domestic duties, and further discussion of the subject would be superfluous. *Politics*, II: 1264b.

50 *Republic*, 592b; *Laws*, 739.

51 *Laws*, 805a–b.

52 Ibid., 794c–d; see also Morrow, *Plato's Cretan City*, p. 329.

53 *Laws*, 805c–d.

54 Ibid., 740a–c.

55 Morrow, *Plato's Cretan City*, pp. 118–19.

56 *Laws*, 866a, 868b–c, 871b, 879c; cf. Morrow, *Plato's Cretan City*, pp. 120–1.

57 *Laws*, 772d–3e, 774e.

58 Ibid., 773c.

59 Ibid., 923e.

60 Ibid., 928e–9a.

61 Morrow, *Plato's Cretan City*, n. 55 on p. 113.

62 *Laws*, 784b, 929e, 930b, 882c; cf. Morrow, *Plato's Cretan City*, p. 121.

63 *Laws*, 784d–e.

64 Ibid., 937a–b.

65 *Republic*, 540c. The fact that Plato's rulers have always been referred to as philosopher kings suggests that the reminder was, and still is, necessary.

66 *Laws*, 741c, 759b, 764c–d, 800b, 813c, 828b, 784a–c, 790a, 794a–b, 795d, 930.

67 Ibid., 961.

68 Ibid., 765d–6b.

69 Ronald Levinson agrees with this conclusion – see *In Defense of Plato* (Cambridge, Mass., 1953), p. 133 – and Morrow notes that Plato gives no hint that women should perform the basic civic function of attending the assembly of the people. See *Plato's Cretan City*, pp. 157–8.

70 *Laws*, 785b.

71 Ibid., 947b–d, 764e.

72 Ibid., 804e–5a, 806b.

73 Ibid., 794c–d.
74 Ibid., 833c–d, 834a, 834d.
75 Ibid., 785b.
76 Ibid., 808a, 808e.
77 Ibid., 833d.
78 Compare *Laws*, 781c–d with *Republic*, 452a–b.

2

Aristotle: Defective Males, Hierarchy and the Limits of Politics

Arlene Saxonhouse

Teleology and Nature

Aristotle was the son of a Greek physician serving at the court of the Macedonian king. Whether or not Aristotle's interest in scientific questions can be traced to the influence of his father, the study of the natural world plays a central role in the development of his thought. The study of the physical world, of which animals are a part, is for Aristotle the study of nature, *physis*; and for him the study of nature is the study of how things grow. The Greek term *physis* derives from the verb *phueo*, which means "to grow." The questions which Aristotle asks as he analyzes the natural world have to do with growth and change over time, according to set patterns of development. We understand living things, according to him, by understanding their patterns of development, whether we are talking about a flower, an earthworm, a woman, a family, or a political community. Growth as we see it in the natural world is not indiscriminate. There are certain patterns of growth in nature for each class of things. A maple sapling does not suddenly become an elephant: if the maple sapling follows the course prescribed by nature, it becomes a maple tree. Every living thing, including ourselves, possesses a certain potential. We have the capacity to grow into something, and it is that something at the end of our growing process that defines what we are – for instance, a human being or a tree.

Aristotle's study of living things is based on the apprehension of the end toward which each thing directs itself. The sapling has the potential to become a maple tree when it has come to the conclusion of its growing process. This process may not be the usual or normal pattern followed by all maple saplings. Indeed, most die. But, according to Aristotle, in order to fulfill its nature, the maple sapling *should* become a maple tree. It is this focus on the normative end that defines Aristotle's work as teleological. Each plant and animal, including the human being, has an end, a *telos*, a point at which it attains its final form, toward which it is directed from the moment of generation – that is, from the moment it is put into motion. If it fails to reach that end, it has not fulfilled its potential, and it has not become what it can become under normal conditions.

There is an end toward which each must aspire by nature. This "must" is implanted by nature, and with the acceptance of nature as an end becomes a moral "must." In order to be good, that end must be pursued. Not to attain that end is a deformity, a deviation from natural patterns of growth. For the human being, that completion is attained when, as a fully grown person, one exercises one's reason to make the right choices concerning good and bad, right and wrong actions. The end for the human being is not a static condition but one of activity, specifically the activity of choices according to reason, which, for Aristotle, is the source of human happiness.

In order to attain this end, the human being must live in the *polis* – that is, the human being is a political animal. The individual must associate with others in the political realm and benefit from the educative processes of the *polis* and its laws. The natural end of the human thus does not come simply from nature. For other animals, the end, their perfection, is determined by nature; if they arrive at the perfection of their nature, they do so whether they chose to or not. If nature succeeds, they reach that point. If nature fails, which is often the case (the sapling dies, the acorns rot), then they do not. But for humans this is not the case. Human actions work with nature. The human being must employ convention, the laws of the city, in order to reach a condition of completion. Life must be ordered through the creation of the *polis* and its law. There must be human activity directed specifically to the creation and preservation of the realm of the city, the realm of reasoned choice, speech, and education.

The human being is different from other living creatures because of the possession of reason (*logos*), a term that in the Greek also entails speech. To exercise our reason-speech is the fulfillment of our natures, but in exercising our reason we must engage in discourse with others, must make choices, and must be able to explain to others the choices we have made. These choices and the grounds we have for making them determine the kinds of lives we shall lead. The difference between the maple sapling and the human being is that the human engages in choice; the maple sapling is influenced by external factors: the weather, the gardener, the soil con-

ditions. The human is self-moving, making decisions and choices concerning
how to live. These choices allow for a certain openness, but they also allow
for mistakes. The plant does not make mistakes.

All natural phenomena can be studied according to Aristotle's model of
growth and teleology. In his biological works he applies this mode of
analysis to the female. When we look at his analysis of the female as a
natural biological creature, however, what we find is not particularly
congenial to our notions of equality. For Aristotle the biologist studying
the generation and the growth of living things, the female of the species,
human or otherwise, is the defective male. She arises when the growth
process is not completed according to its natural pattern.

The duality of the sexes, Aristotle explains, is necessary: "To be is
better than not to be and to live is better than not to live: on account of
these causes there is the generation of animals. Since it is impossible that
the nature of one born is to be everlasting, it is everlasting according to the
way open to it, that is, generation."[1] In order that there be this generation
that keeps specific classes of beings in existence, it is necessary that there
be both the male and the female principle.[2] However, though both are
necessary for generation, Aristotle continues, it is also necessary that the
male and the female be kept separate, "for the better and the stronger are
to be kept apart from that which is inferior."[3]

The male is better in this context because he gives to that which is
generated both the final cause, the *telos*, the reason for existence, and the
form, the shape that being will take when it has reached its completed
state. The female provides only the matter. Aristotle offers an elaborate
comparative analysis of semen and menstrual fluids to support his observations, which include the notion that the female's body is incapable of
concocting the necessary heat, the "pneuma," which transfers to the
generated being both reason and form.[4] He does not deny the necessity of
the female's participation in this process. Both male and female contribute
"residues," the difference being that the male's residue is "concocted"
through the presence of heat, while the female's is not.[5]

Behind his attempts to offer scientific presentations of the processes of
generation lie Aristotle's biological assumptions concerning the physical
inferiority of the female because she cannot "concoct" the "pneuma" that
gives form to matter. This failure on the part of the female comes from a
disruption at the point of conception. Aristotle begins Book IV of *The
Generation of Animals* by noting that the distinctions between male and
female arise while the animals are still incomplete: the female arises when
the male principle, the semen, fails to gain mastery over the female
principle. The case for the weakness of the male principle is the absence of
heat. Aristotle then proceeds to support these speculations with evidence:
young parents produce more female offspring, and more female offspring

are conceived when the wind is in the north or when the moon is waning. All these conditions are characterized by reduced heat and lead to the birth of females and deformed children.[6] The growth pattern of the human being normally leads to the full-grown male; the existence of the female suggests that the pattern was not fully followed. Throughout his work on the generation of animals, Aristotle compares the female to a child or a boy. The female is understood as an infertile male, but whereas the child has the potential to continue to grow and to become the fertile male, the female's growth has already been diverted and she retains no such potential. With analyses such as these from his biological works, Aristotle has easily become the *bête noire* of ancient philosophy, the classic male chauvinist who assumes the natural inferiority of the female, she who failed to become male.

Hierarchy and the Limits of Observation

The world for Aristotle is hierarchically structured. Aristotle's teleology entails an orderly, structured perspective on the universe, and part of this order is the relation of things to one another, specifically in terms of better and worse. For the human being this hierarchy begins on the most basic level: the soul is superior to the body. In an ordered individual, living according to his nature, the soul rules the body. This hierarchy is crucial if life on earth is to continue. The mind must rule the body, or the body could not be fed and clothed and housed. Similarly, according to Aristotle's analysis of the generation of the female as the defective, incomplete male, the male is superior to and should have authority over the female – *if* all works according to nature *and if* the intentions of nature are clearly understood and capable of being implemented.

Reading Aristotle's comments concerning teleology and the processes of generation, and his justification of hierarchy, might easily lead (and has led) to a view of him as a simple supporter of the society of ancient Athens, where the female was indeed considered an inferior being entirely subject to the males around her, incapable of making appropriate choices in marriage or in monetary affairs. But all this would assume that the society of ancient Athens is the society that comes from the natural growth processes that Aristotle emphasized elsewhere in his works, that nothing similar to the absence of heat in the generation of the female hindered Athens's growth, that all the choices entailed in the "growth" of Athens were correctly directed not to the apparent but to the true good.

This was not the case. Athens is not the regime according to nature. At the very end of Book III of the *Politics*, Aristotle tells us that the regime according to nature is that in which the best rules; he who is most able by nature must be left to rule over those who by nature are inferior.[7] However, after ending Book III on this note, Aristotle turns in Book IV to the cities that are possible – especially those he finds in his own time, such as the democracy at Athens or the oligarchy at Chalcis in Euboea; there the best do not rule. Athens as a democracy is one of the defective regimes. It makes equal those who are not and acts in the self-interest of the many against the interest of the rich. Along with the oligarchies found elsewhere, it does not allow for the rule of the best. Indeed, Athens has even instituted ostracism to remove the best from the city.[8]

The disjunction between what is and what should be in a world organized around the principle of the superior having authority over the inferior is particularly apparent in Aristotle's discussion of the problems presented for Greek society by slavery. He begins by noting that the slave is an animate piece of property; the problem, however, occurs when the question is asked as to who is to be this piece of animate property and who is to control it. Can such a relationship between human beings be based on nature? Immediately, what is not sufficient for the subordination of one individual to another is clear: "It is necessary to look to that by nature which obtains according to nature rather than to those [relations] which have been corrupted."[9] In the corruption of Aristotle's society we find slaves who exist in such a condition according to the laws of the society but not necessarily according to nature.

The slaves in Athens are those whose cities have been conquered by the stronger forces of the Athenians. Though some would argue that such strength would justify the enslaving of those conquered, since the stronger are the better by nature, Aristotle does not agree. Nevertheless, even if one were to grant *this* position, Aristotle further argues that we cannot take the children of slaves as slaves as well. The enslaving of the children of slaves assumes that "just as humans are born from humans, and beasts are born from beasts, so too the good are born from the good." Aristotle demurs: "But while nature may wish to do this often, it is not, however, always able to do so."[10]

As a consequence, Aristotle suggests, those who are not worthy by nature to rule over others remain masters while those not worthy by nature to be subjected remain slaves. Force rather than friendship, therefore, is necessary to preserve the hierarchical structure of slavery.[11] The pattern of growth within the city has been perverted, and slavery is but one example of this problem.

What holds for the master–slave relationship may also be true in the case of the male–female relationship. According to nature the male is superior to the female, but in the cases where nature has not fulfilled itself, which are outside or against *physis*, the female may be superior to the male; and when she is, then it is against the natural hierarchy that the male rule over the female. In this case, the inferior rules over the superior. Aristotle does not state that all males are better than all females, only that this is natural. We cannot be assured that nature is in control at all times.

At the end of the first book of his *Politics*, Aristotle discusses fleetingly the relationships within the family. He distinguishes between the rule of the master over the slave and that of the husband and father over the wife and children. The latter two forms of rule he defines as political, while the former is despotic. Rule over the child and the wife is rule over free individuals, though in the case of the child it is rule over one who has not yet reached a condition of completion – that is, the reasoning powers have not matured.

In other words, wife and child are free and to be treated as one treats fellow citizens – or potential fellow citizens. Aristotle's understanding of the political relationships that he attributes to the husband–wife relationship entails the process of a rule among equals, those who are equal in taking their turns to rule. In the case of the wife, though, what he sees around him is that the rule of the male is permanent, whereas in other political relationships the process is one of taking turns to rule and be ruled. Later, he will say of political relationships: "In the largest number of states the ruler and the ruled exchange positions, wishing to be equal in nature and differing in nothing."[12]

Aristotle brings home the ambiguity of the ascription of power according to sex or birth with an allusion to a play by Sophocles. Concerned with the problem of whether the virtues of the ruler and the ruled are the same, he turns to the question of the unity or multiplicity of virtues: is virtue the same for all, ruler and ruled, master and slave, male and female? Aristotle quotes Sophocles to show the common assumption concerning the virtue of the female: "Silence brings orderliness to a woman."[13] These words are spoken by Ajax to his wife Tecmessa in Sophocles' tragedy the *Ajax*. Ajax is angered that Achilles' shield has been given to Odysseus rather than to himself. This brings on his madness, his slaughter of the cattle of the Greeks, which he mistakes for the heroes of the Greek army. Tecmessa tries to calm him, urging him not to put on his armor in his rage.

It is in this context that Ajax speaks the words concerning the appropriateness of silence for women. In this context they are entirely inappropriate, an indication of his madness and failure to see the truth in what she says. Had he listened to her words, he would not have acted so destructively. He would have maintained the order that he claims Tecmessa's silence would preserve. The natural hierarchy of the male over the female has been reversed, and it is the failure of Ajax to recognize this aberration in the natural way of things that leads to disaster. Virtues are not easily assigned to a class of people or things. The context and the particularity of the situation must be taken into account if what is natural is to be preserved. To treat all those who lived in conquered cities as slaves, or all those born female as lacking sense, is to fail to recognize the diversity of nature and to limit oneself to a functionalist perspective.

The problems for women in Aristotle's model of society and sexual relations do not come from their reproductive role, as some have suggested,[14] but from the perception of women as controlled by their emotions rather than their reason (*logos*). In the story of Tecmessa and Ajax, however, it is the male who lets his emotions and his anger rule, while the female retains perspective on the situation. The subordinate position of women comes from their being inferior by nature, but the problem with society – and precisely where Aristotle is critical of the hierarchical relations in the society in which he lived – arises when it is unable to determine when the female, and which females, may have something to offer to the males to whom society has given authority. The failure to recognize such times and such women is a sign of the defects of the society, a sign that it is not ruled by the best.

At the end of Book I, when Aristotle is trying to clarify the differing relationships within the family, he does so at one point with reference to the deliberative power (*to bouleutikon*) of each member of the family. The deliberative power gives each individual the capacity to choose actions and to be able to express in words the justifications for such choices. The activity of the city is deliberative – that is, it debates courses of action as participants justify to each other one policy or another. Therefore, it is in their interest to be the subjects of those who can choose. In a child the deliberative capacity is not yet fully developed, and thus the child must be educated so as to mature into an individual who can make the appropriate choices and be able to justify his actions to others. In the female, the deliberative power, Aristotle maintains, is *akuron*, without authority.

Here there is a problem with translation: often *akuron* is translated as "inferior" and *kuros* as "superior." In the Greek, though, *kuros* is associated with the possession of authority or the right to rule over another. When the male is described as being *kuros* over the female, Aristotle is not saying that he is superior, only that he has authority. Thus, the deliberative power in the female lacks authority. The problem of translation goes further, though: does Aristotle mean authority within the soul, or in the female's relationships with others? If we are meant to take this only as referring to relationships within, then women would appear to be emotional cripples, unable to control their desires through rational choice. On the other hand, if we see *akuron* as referring to relations between people, we can see that Aristotle is suggesting that the female lacks authority with the males around her, who would refuse to listen to the advice of a woman just as Ajax refused to listen to the advice of Tecmessa. The actual meaning of *akuron* here is ambiguous, but this ambiguity is crucial because it leads to an ambiguity concerning who should rule and who should have authority in situations that arise in opposition to nature, such as those in which the female may be more "deliberative" than the passionate male.

The failure of Athenian society to understand when the female *bouleutikon* should and should not have authority leads to the indiscriminate exclusion of the female from all deliberations, and thus fails to take account of the natural (rather than the conventional) hierarchy. The city has had to rely on an inadequate criterion, sex, in order to determine that hierarchy, and thus the actual regimes give precedence to those who are inferior (the many) rather than the superior, just as within the family the Athenians always give authority to the male rather than the female.

The problem arises because the city needs some external standard by which to distinguish between people, by which to decide who shall rule and who shall be ruled, who shall participate in government and who shall not. But a problem arises: virtue resides in the soul, which we cannot see, and thus it is difficult to recognize the goodness of one individual in contrast with another. The problem is particularly acute for Aristotle in the case of the slave.

> Nature wishes to make the bodies of free men and of slaves different, the latter strong for the sake of life's necessities, the former straight and useless for such work, but useful for the political life. . . . but often the opposite happens and slaves have the bodies and souls of free men. Since this is clear, if in body alone men would differ so much as the statues of the gods, then all would agree that those who are inferior are worthy of being enslaved to them. And if this holds concerning the body, then by so much more justly is this said with regard to the soul. But it is not entirely easy to see the beauty of the soul as of the body.[15]

We can't see the souls of the individuals who are placed in a position of authority because nature does not always relate the beauty of the soul to the beauty of the body. The problem of political life, for Aristotle, is how to discover superior and inferior, who should rule and who should be ruled. Nature has not made it easy for us to answer this question, since observations of what exists do not give us information about the worth of the individuals who have power.

The task of politics, for Aristotle, is how to deal with this problem of distortion. The answer is not to install the best in positions of power, since we cannot know the best. Therefore, observing the problems in the society in which he lives – the instability of the political regimes in which men disagree about who should have power, since they cannot see the best – Aristotle turns to the question of stability: "For the good of each thing preserves that thing."[16] It is not simply preservation for preservation's sake, but that stability ensures the leisure that is necessary to pursue the higher things in life. In Book VII he elaborately develops the point that war is for the sake of peace and that the polity, giving us leisure to become full human beings exercising our capacity to make reasoned choices, must be preserved. But how can the political system that is not directed by the best preserve itself? Although much of Book V, on revolutions, is devoted to this question, it is in Book II that we learn how women specifically help or hinder the preservation of order and stability in the political realm.

The Family, the Female, and the Problem of Political Stability

At the beginning of Book I of the *Politics*, Aristotle explains the genesis of the political community and expresses the view that the growth of the city entails the transformation of the human concern with mere life into a concern with the good life. The *polis* provides the condition for the good life, the life of moral choice; but before we can live the good life, the necessities of the body must engage us. We must live in order to live well. Thus, Book I of the *Politics* quickly becomes a compendium of ways to ensure life itself on the most basic levels of reproduction, manual labor, and food gathering. Even on this level, Aristotle assumes social interaction, cooperation between individuals to draw forth from nature that which creates and supports life. He presupposes that there must be families. They exist by nature and are the expression of our most fundamental drives. Even more basic than our life in the *polis* is our life in the family. The move toward the family comes initially from an inclination no different from animals' inclinations to reproduce themselves. There is no choice for animals but, according to Aristotle's conception of the development of human reason, the human being moves beyond simple inclination, to choice.

The attempts of philosophers and lawgivers to envision and create the best political regimes evidence a deep concern with the family. The social organization of the family, unlike the social organization of the ancient city, includes both the female and the male, the slave and the master, the child and the parent. How does the female fit into the society dedicated to the preservation of life, and how does the organization of this association affect the *polis'* problems of stability? If the barbarians ordered their private life incorrectly, what is the right way to order private life?

The answer is clearly not just submission to the husband's authority. Even as defective male, the female is not a slave, nor is the difference between male and female so great as to lead to slavery for women.[17] But where does the difference that does exist lead? What solution is possible? In Book II Aristotle discusses several very different solutions, two of which are presented below. On the one hand, he explains the Spartan answer, license for women of the city: freedom from laws and constraints, and little contact with their husbands. On the other hand, he offers for consideration the solution that Socrates in Plato's *Republic* proposes: a community of wives and children in which anything that is private is destroyed among those, including women, who are to be the rulers in his city.

Freedom for women: the case of Sparta

The freedom given women [in Sparta] is harmful concerning the aims of the regime and the happiness of the city. Just as the man and the woman are a part of the household so it is clear that it is necessary to think of the city as divided into almost two equal parts, that of men and that of women, so that in existing regimes which hold as trifling matters the affairs having to do with women, it is necessary to think of one half of the city as being without laws and legislation. This is what has happened [in Sparta] for the lawgiver wishing to make the entire city strong, has done so clearly among the men, but was unconcerned with the women.[18]

The result in Sparta, according to Aristotle, has been a regime that, though directed toward military superiority, the expression of virile power, is in fact ruled by women. The women, uncontrolled by the traditions and the laws of the society, live a life showing no restraint, dedicated to the pursuit of luxuries. Thus, the regime from which we get our term "spartan" is one that honored wealth. The principles of the Spartan regime had not been directed toward women, and thus the *polis* was divided within itself – on the one hand ascetic and martial in its aims; on the other, luxurious and effete. When Sparta was attacked, Aristotle notes, the women offered no help: they had not been trained in the art of courage, and thus they created more commotion than the enemy did.

In this brief analysis of the Spartan constitution, Aristotle goes against the conventional wisdom of his time, which had commended that constitution for its good laws, its *eunomia*. Tradition had it that these laws had survived 700 years. They had provided for a strong military city considered the model of orderly existence for the Greek world.[19] Aristotle here does not criticize the aim of the regime[20] but, rather, its failure to recognize the distinction it unwittingly made between male and female. The men of the city came to understand the demands of a social life from their experience on military campaigns. There they had learned to submit to the discipline required in a political community. They had thus been willing to submit to the authority of the laws that governed their lives off the battlefield as well as on it. But the women, having been left at home to do as they liked, were free from the exigencies of the military life and did not learn the art of submission to authority. They resisted the restraints of political authority even within the city, and pursued private rather than communal aims.

In his critique of the Spartan regime and its failure to take seriously the political education of women, whether it be through military campaigns or otherwise, Aristotle recognizes the importance of the female in the political life of Greece. Precisely because he recognizes her importance, he rejects the common opinions of the Greeks concerning the virtue of the Spartan regime, a regime not attendant to its women. In the *Rhetoric* he also criticizes the Spartans: "Whoever treats the affairs of women as worthless, as the Spartans do, lacks one half of happiness."[21] He sees not only the license and lack of courage that came from the failure to deal appropriately with the women, but also the avarice of the society as a whole. The women are greedy and, as rulers over their men, they make the city as a whole one that is governed by greed: even as success greeted the male warriors, the seeds of internal decay were growing.

The passage cited at length above, taken out of context, might lead to the view that Aristotle saw women as naturally weak and licentious. Nevertheless, there are two important points to note here: the men were not as weak or as lascivious as the women because they were taken out on military campaigns and thus learned the art of submission, while the women were left free at home; and the problem is not insoluble, for since men had learned to submit to political and military authority, so could the women. The latter were lacking in discipline because the male lawgiver had forgotten them. The female must be part of the city, part of its educative process. The city is to train men to make them part of the community, to make choices that correspond to the needs and the interests of that community; and if it forgets about the education of women, it creates within itself a destabilizing force.

Political life must attend to the problem of stability because it cannot discern who is best; thus, such a disregard for the education of the females in the city undermines the entire political endeavor. Socrates' city in the *Republic*, with its education for women and its inclusion of the female in the city's army, seems to answer Aristotle'a reservations about the Spartan regime. But Socrates adds a community of wives and children, which in Aristotle's mind undermines Socrates' whole endeavor and becomes a destabilizing force.

The community of women: the case of Socrates' city

When a modern reader turns to Plato's *Republic* and the utopian scheme therein, the most striking suggestion for many is the proposal that women be allowed to participate along with men of equal talents in the political and military life of the city. Aristotle, when he evaluates Socrates' proposals, ignores the issue of sexual equality. Rather, he finds the most novel proposal to be the community of wives; the question of equality would arise only if there were such a community. For Aristotle the community of wives assumes the equality of the sexes, while the preservation of the family entails the maintenance of sexual inequality. So long as there continue to be females to keep the race in existence, there will be, for Aristotle, hierarchy, authority, and inequality – the family.

The problem that Aristotle poses for himself as he begins to consider Socrates' city is how much should be held in common in the political association: some, all, or none? Clearly some, since without something held in common there is no city. At the most basic level the land on which the city is located must be shared. But Socrates goes to the other extreme and says that all must be held in common. His arguments for this communism are varied, but behind them all lies the concern with the stability of the political system that comes from unity.

The female and the family exist within a private realm that focuses on what is particular rather than on what is universal; thus they work, as Socrates presents it, in opposition to the interests of the community, which must emphasize a devotion to the universal. By destroying the private realm through the destruction of the family and its particularistic orientation, Socrates aims to leave the self open to the complete devotion to the public.

This had been possible in Socrates' city because Socrates had abstracted from the body, which ties one to the procreative and nutritive aspects of the family. He had worked through education in poetry to train his warriors to scorn their bodies and their bodily needs. The abstraction from the body had removed a concern with the private and the particular. The bodies of Socrates' citizens did not define who they were, and thus the female body could be ignored in the communism of the city and the equality of the sexes introduced at the beginning of Book V.

Aristotle does not abstract from the body; instead, he emphasizes how the body works against Socrates' proposals, how nature turns our attention to our bodies, what is particular about them, and how, by nature, we love our own bodies. Socrates abstracts from difference by avoiding bodies. Aristotle emphasizes bodies and, thus, difference. For instance, he finds support for the ties between children and specific parents in the natural physical resemblances between parent and child. He suggests that the people in Socrates' city would be driven to discover their own relations. "Furthermore, it is not possible to escape some form of guessing about who are brothers, and children, and fathers and mothers."[22] Socrates' citizens will engage in this guessing precisely because it is possible to recognize similarities between children and parents. Our bodies indicate these connections.

Bodies, by revealing these connections, accomplish what intellects,

particularly Socrates' intellect, may wish to ignore. Denying such connections, as Socrates tries to do in the *Republic*, is, according to Aristotle,
to act against nature. Acting against nature leads to unholy and impious
deeds that are offensive even in the contemplation of them. In referring to
such deeds, Aristotle moves from violent acts against one's parents to the
sexual liaisons that would occur between the members of one's own
natural family: fathers with daughters and even, what he considers the
most horrendous and unnatural of all, brothers with brothers. The an-
onymity imposed by Socrates' scheme, and thus the lack of shame to
restrain human actions, opens the door for all these acts against nature.

Aristotle finds further problems with Socrates' city, for it fails to take
account of the natural love of oneself and of what is one's own. "Not in
vain," he says, "does each have a love of oneself. This is according to
nature."[23] We love ourselves and we love what we create. We exist
through activity, and since we love our existence, we love what that
existence has brought into being, be it our children, our handiwork, our
writings. We act in accordance with a love of ourselves and of what we
have created.[24] Socrates' community eliminated that natural love of oneself and one's creative activity. This distortion of our natural drives,
Aristotle claims, will cause instability and lead to the demise of the city.
He uses the example of household slaves to support this point: if too many
slaves are assigned a particular task and no one feels that the accomplishment of that task entails his or her creative activity, the task will not be
performed. The many, having no particular attachments to the task,
having no sense of seeing themselves in the accomplishment of that task,
will leave the work to others. "There is the least concern for what is
common, but the most care for what is private."[25]

The female, as the symbol of what is private, of the home and what is
particular, as the source of children who are one's own and recognized as
such by the city at large, is a vivid expression of the need all humans have
to tie themselves to that which is particular and one's own. To communalize
the female is to destroy the private and to overemphasize the public and
its universalistic aims; for Aristotle this is the same as destroying the
moral and psychological bases of the city. The community of women, so
opposed to the demands of nature, cannot support the city as an institution
arising from the natural drive of men to perfect themselves.

There are other problems with Socrates' city. By removing the family
and ignoring the difference between male and female, Socrates destroys
the diversity, multiplicity, and interdependence at the core of the city.
Aristotle argues that diversity is essential for the city; we need cobblers as
well as doctors. To make the cobblers and the doctors the same, to ignore
what is different about them, and to expect the same expertise from each is
to change the city into an individual. By nature we are different and have

different abilities. Socrates himself had stressed this as he began to found his city in the city of pigs.

By nature the male is not the same as the female. Though in Aristotle's biological works these differences are often expressed in terms of defects, in the "practical" pieces he focuses on the differences in virtues. "The virtues of a youth are moderation and courage in the soul. . . . The virtue of a girl is beauty and greatness of body, and in the soul moderation and a love of work without slavishness."[26] That diversity must be retained on the private level, or the city – lacking cobblers and doctors, men and women – will die. Socrates' abstraction from the private realm casts doubt on the survival of his city. In contrast, on the public level, the realm of political life, there must be an equality, a focus on what unites through similarity. All are citizens, all are capable of ruling and being ruled. The particular differences between individuals defined as equal become irrelevant. But we can reach this state of equality only when the necessities that demand differentiation have been met.

The problem with Socrates' model, as Aristotle sees it, is that Socrates, in proposing sexual equality in the political realm, had done so through ignoring the diversity demanded in the private realm, through ignoring that the public must build up from the private. As shown in Book I of the *Politics*, Aristotle cannot discuss the good life until he has discussed life itself. In Book V of the *Republic*, Socrates tries to ignore life in order to jump headlong into the good life. As a result, as Aristotle understands it, Socrates destroys the potential for both.

Aristotle on the family and the female in the polity

There seems to be a friendship between man and woman by nature. For the human being by nature is more disposed to live in pairs than in the polis, insomuch as the household is prior in time and more necessary than the polis, and the creation of children is more common with other animals. Among other animals, the community extends only this far [to the creation of children], but for the human being, living together is not only for the sake of reproduction, but also for various aspects of their lives. Immediately, the work is divided, and there is one task for men and another for women. So they assist one another, putting their individual talents into the common good. On account of these things, there seems to be both usefulness and pleasure in this sort of friendship. This friendship also exists in accordance with virtue, if they are both good. For there is a virtue of each, and they are pleased by this. . . . It seems that children are a bond, wherefore marriages without children dissolve more quickly. For children are a common good for both and what is common holds them together.[27]

This passage offers a picture of human involvement in the family often forgotten as one turns to the Aristotle of the famed "man is a political animal" quote. Here he portrays the human being as an economic being, in the true sense of the term. We see in this passage a concern with the community that is the family, the pleasure that both members, male and female, derive from a friendship devoted to what is common and their individual talents exercised in their attention to what unites them. The family here is not a dark recess of subordination and domination, but a prepolitical condition incorporating into itself many of the elements of unity and friendship that the actual cities of Greece in Aristotle's time failed to exhibit.

Neither the Spartan lawgiver nor Socrates recognized the special value that Aristotle attributes to the family, a value that takes it far beyond the process of reproduction that ties the human species to other animals. The Spartans with their men at war all the time and Socrates with his communism ignored the family and the female who was a part of it. Aristotle wants to reassess the stature of the family, and his criticism of the utopian and the practical regimes is a major part of that reassessment.

In Socrates' city Aristotle had found a community with no family to educate in a love that goes beyond the self, a community where the door had been opened for the common practice of impiety. Socrates' city left no room for liberality. If one identified the city as being the same as oneself, to act for the city could not be called a liberal act. Thus, the communism of his city destroyed all the potential for virtue. The Spartan regime had failed to educate women in the art of submission to authority that all regimes must entail. The failures of others are captured in Aristotle's attempt to justify and resuscitate the family. The *polis* arises, in his view, to help complete what the family ultimately cannot do successfully: educate the young. It is to continue the process begun in the family, not to make the family irrelevant, as the others had tried to do.

Throughout all the criticisms of Socrates' city and the Spartan regime, Aristotle never focuses on the inherent deformity of the female that had been a part of his work on the biology of animals. His arguments against communism do not come from arguments about the inequality of women, that women need supervision, as does the natural slave. The value of the family for Aristotle is not that it brings about subordination, but that it provides the orderly community of love and friendship, the natural hierarchy whose stability offers the preconditions for the pursuit of virtue. Though the family may not always conform perfectly to the rule of superior over inferior, it appears to order itself naturally, to be founded on a natural hierarchy that the city composed of supposed equals can only pretend to approximate.

Because of the problems with observation noted above, it is difficult within the context of the city to determine who is equal, who should rule, and who should be subject. The justice of the city in distributing offices is artificial rather than complete. It is dependent on an inequality that cannot be secure. All polities depend on this justice. Within the family the hierarchy in operation is closer to the natural way of things. The family is the model of the natural aristocracy. By this Aristotle means an association in which the man rules according to his worth "and about those things that it is necessary for a man to rule, but whatever fits well with a woman, he hands over to her."

If the man chooses to rule in those areas where he is not suited by nature to rule, he transforms the aristocratic relationship into one that is oligarchic, one in which he rules in his own self-interest and not in the interests of the community. A few lines before the passage just cited, Aristotle had suggested that an oligarchy is a regime in which the rulers do not distribute the affairs of the city according to worth, but give all the good things to themselves.[28] The well-structured family recognizes the differences between the members and takes these differences into account as they all work toward the common good. Within the city that is based on equality and a sharing in the process of rule, the differences between those who are citizens must be ignored and each has the same tasks as everyone else. With all citizens determined by artificial criteria of equality, there can be no distribution of offices or tasks according to worth, since all must share in the activities of the political community.

When cities are threatened with revolution and instability, it is because there is disagreement about the meaning of equality, who is to be equal and who is to be subject. In Book V of the *Politics*, Aristotle notes that in all cases, "on account of inequality, there is internal conflict."[29] While men agree that justice is simply distribution according to worth, "they differ nevertheless with some saying that if they are equal according to one attribute, then they are completely equal, while others claim that if they are unequal in one attribute, then they are worthy of unequal treatment."[30] In families in which the difference between the sexes and the generations at the base of the distribution of tasks is more readily observed, the distribution of tasks and authority is more easily accepted.

The city's inequality and equality are not precise. They therefore remain constantly subject to debate and are an incentive for internal strife. The city becomes, in a sense, only an imperfect reflection of the natural hierarchy of the family, and the order of the family is only inadequately captured by men's attempts to set up barriers among themselves, barriers for which nature has offered no clear signposts. Even within the patriarchal household, where differences are more subject to observation, mistakes can occur, as in the case of Ajax and Tecmessa. Thus, even within the smaller unit of the family, true justice is not always at work, because the criterion of differentiation is not always adequate to justify differential treatment.

The portrait of the female within the family may not earn much admiration from contemporary students of women in the social sphere, but Aristotle's analysis of the family, as a cooperative adventure in which the friendship between the members comes from a common concern for the welfare of the unit, goes far beyond the view of the family in ancient Greek society that many have offered to us. Students of the Greek legal system trace a set of relationships in which the female is little more than the instrument for transferring property from one family to another and for giving birth to future protectors of the religious rites of a particular family. Aristotle's understanding of the family goes beyond such "uses" for women and suggests that the family must be understood as a set of associations and relationships from which the grander and more important *polis* derives.

Within the family, the role of the female, that task assigned to her because of her special abilities, is the same one taken up by the statesman within the city – preserving what has been acquired, providing for stability. Nevertheless, however important the female may be in the family, Aristotle never envisions her as part of the public realm of the city. Again this view derives from his understanding of the notions of equality and inequality. The family as a realm of hierarchy stands in contrast with the city as a realm of equality. Within the family the male retains authority over the female, the father over the son, the master over the slave. Inequality of authority or power derives from differences with regard to sex, age, ability.

The family, unlike the city, is characterized by its differences; and in order for it to continue over time, it must incorporate these differences. The male must be different from the female if there is to be sexual reproduction. The master must have the intelligence that the slave lacks, and the slave must have the physical capacity that the master need not develop. The relations of difference within the family maintain the unit. Within the *polis*, the criterion must be one of equality: citizens must be equal in their possession and exercise of reasoned speech, of discourse about the just and the unjust, and they must be equal in their leisure to engage in such speech. Thus, as workers captured by the necessities of existence, lacking the leisure to participate in such discourse, cannot be part of the citizen body, neither can the female, who, because she is nourishing the young with her body, lacks such leisure.

For Aristotle, then, the exclusion of women is based in part on their unequal leisure time, their role as the preservers of the household and the bearers of the young. However, more significant for Aristotle's exclusion of the female from the public realm is the lack of authority of her reasoned discourse. Since the *polis* is to be a realm of activity for the *logos*, the female, in whom that *logos* is not predominant, cannot participate fully.

In being so excluded, women are not alone. Slaves obviously are excluded, but so are workers, not because Aristotle the aristocrat rejects the lower classes, but because his conception of political life requires the participation of those who engage in the reasoned discourse of the complete human being. Workers lack the leisure for this engagement. In contemporary society, where political participation is not defined by the activity of reasoned discourse, the restrictions that Aristotle established appear meaningless or downright unjust, but his concern that the public realm serve as the arena for the highest human activities (after philosophy) led to his demand for such an intellectual engagement.[31]

In the last two books of the *Politics*, Aristotle discusses the city of his dreams.[32] Women figure here only very briefly as he considers the issues of reproduction and the earliest stages of the child's life. The legislator must have the best material with which to work, and that means the healthiest population. To ensure this health, he must attend to the laws governing matrimony and reproduction. Aristotle is particularly concerned that reproduction not begin at too young an age, when deformed offspring (including women) are likely to be born.

But Aristotle slips from these biological considerations to psychological ones. Picking up on the themes in the *Ethics*, he maintains that the legislator must also be concerned with the community that is created within the family and must ensure that there is a compatibility of sexual life for the married couple. This means that the ages of husband and wife must match, so that one will not be able to be reproductively active when the other can no longer function in this capacity. Thus, since he sees 70 as the age for men's declining sexual potency and 50 for women, he suggests that the man be 20 years older at the time of marriage.[33]

Once conception has taken place, the female is to exercise her body, but not her mind, for her body must be strong in order to give strength to the growing child, just as something growing draws from the earth.[34] If we look only at these last words comparing the female to the soil, Aristotle could justly be accused of seeing only the material role of the female. She is the matter out of which the citizens grow, but the earlier comments expressing concern for the compatibility within marriage suggest that Aristotle has a deeper understanding of the female's place in the polity. Though she is not a part of the public community, the private community depends on a nonexploitive, communal relationship between the male and female.

Again, however, the student of Aristotle must go further to understand fully the place of the female in his analyses of the best city. Specifically, one must note the persistent hostility to the city as an armed camp composed of virile warriors, spirited in their desires to acquire dominion. As Aristotle expresses it at the beginning of Book VII, the best city, the one that need not worry about stability, is the one that promotes the individual happiness of its citizens. The task for Aristotle is to explain the conditions that would provide this happiness. The mistake of the many, according to him, is that they equate happiness with what is external, with the excessive accumulation of goods. For these men conquest, war as the means to acquire goods, becomes the source of happiness. Aristotle argues that the city must not be structured to facilitate the continual pursuit of goods, but the limitless pursuit of virtue. And how does one pursue virtue? Not through conquest, but through education, through attention to the arts.

In chapter 7 of Book VII, Aristotle attacks regimes dominated by a spirited love of war. He associates such regimes with the cannibalism practiced by the Cyclops. The most choiceworthy life, with which Aristotle's investigation into the best regime began, is not one of domination – one country over another, the male over the female, the master over the slave, all of which are based ultimately on war and inequality – but one of the processes of ruling over men who are equals.

Thus, Aristotle's analysis of the best regime focuses on the processes of education in moderation, the characteristic that he had previously ascribed to the good woman. The cities of Aristotle's time that catered to a concern with material wealth emphasized the virility that was necessary to pursue domination. The city of Aristotle's dreams exalts the feminine virtue of restraint. While the female herself appears only in her reproductive capacity in these last two books, the feminine, as opposed to the masculine, virtue provides the foundation for the city that offers human beings the truly happy life. The body of the female is not the same as the female soul; and just as those who attend exclusively to what is external are mistaken in their evaluations of the source of happiness, so are those who attend exclusively to the body of the female. Aristotle's books on the best city are incomplete, but in what remains, little is actually said about the public life of the citizen; the focus is on education in moderation. The female is part of that education, and thus part of the true life of the city.

Conclusion

Aristotle is well known in the literature today as the classic misogynist, and his words have often been used to support misogyny throughout the ages.[35] The accusation of misogyny today can condemn an author and relegate him to the scrap heap. In Aristotle's writing there is no hatred of women; rather, there is the attempt, from the perspective of the male, to understand the origins of the female and her role in the male city. The female is a defective male, but so are most of the males whom Aristotle sees around him. Seldom is the true man found, one who combines the physical, intellectual, and moral qualities of the individual who has reached the completion of his growing process.

Aristotle's understanding of the female in the political world leads to a vision of hierarchy, but not submission on all levels. The woman, he steadfastly maintains, is not a slave. Thus he must understand her distinct role in society, and he finds it in her capacity within the structure of the family – a realm in which she not only gives birth but also gives stability, preserves and educates the young of the city. It is a realm in which she can demonstrate her unique virtue.

The Socratic vision in the *Republic* had excluded the private realm. All virtue was public. Aristotle retains the private and encourages the pursuit of excellence and community there. Without that excellence on the part of both the male and the female, there can be excellence nowhere in the life of the city. Cities that ignore the female and her potential for excellence, such as Sparta or Socrates' city, Aristotle warns, are placing themselves in jeopardy of internal conflict, dissolution, and chaos. In no way can we pretend that the female is the central issue in Aristotle's writings, but she raises for him a variety of questions and alternative perspectives with which he must deal before he can complete his presentation of the full political life for the human being.

Notes

1 Aristotle, *The Generation of Animals*, 731b30–33.
2 Ibid., 767b8ff.
3 Ibid., 732a6–7.
4 Ibid., 765b10ff., 766a30ff., and passim.
5 *Aristotle's Generation of Animals*, ed. and trans. A. L. Peck, (Cambridge, Mass.: Harvard University Press, 1943), p. xiv.
6 Aristotle, *Politics*, VII.16 (1335a11–13, 1335a39–1335b2).
7 Ibid., III.17 (1288a26–29); see also I.5 (1254b33–1255a2).
8 Aristotle describes the institution of ostracism in his *Constitution of Athens*, XXII.
9 *Politics*, I.5 (1254a36–37).
10 Ibid., I.6 (1255b1–4).
11 Ibid., (1255b12–15).
12 Ibid., I.12 (1259b4–6).
13 Ibid., I.13 (1260a30).
14 Susan Moller Okin, *Women in Western Political Thought* (Princeton: Princeton University Press, 1979), chapter 4, argues from this perspective.
15 *Politics*, I.5 (1254b27–1255a1).
16 Ibid., II.2 (1261b9).
17 In the *Nicomachean Ethics*, V.6 (1134b8–18), Aristotle distinguishes paternal

and despotic relationships from the marital relationship with regard to justice. There can be no injustice to things that are one's own possessions (slaves) or to children (up to a certain age), since no one can wish to harm oneself. "Wherefore there is more justice towards a wife than towards children and possessions." This he calls household justice in the *Ethics*. Justice is not part of one's relationship with slaves.

18 *Politics*, II.9 (1269b12–22).

19 J. Peter Euben, "Political Equality and the Greek Polis," in *Liberalism and the Modern Polity*, ed. Michael J. Gargas McGrath (New York and Basel: Marcel Dekker, 1978), p. 210.

20 However, see the discussion in Book VII of the *Politics*, where Aristotle explicitly rejects a focus on military achievements as the aim of his best regime, especially chapter 2.

21 *Rhetoric*, I.5 (1361a9–11).

22 *Politics*, II.3 (1262a14–16).

23 Ibid., II.5 (1263a41–1263b1).

24 In the *Nicomachean Ethics*, IX.7 (1168a24–26), Aristotle comments: "On account of these things mothers love their off-spring more [than fathers do]. They suffer in childbirth and know with greater certainty that they [the children] are their own."

25 *Politics*, II.3 (1261b36).

26 *Rhetoric*, I.5 (1361a2–7).

27 *Nicomachean Ethics*, VIII.12 (1162a16–29).

28 Ibid., VIII.10 (1160b35–36).

29 *Politics*, V.1 (1301b26–27).

30 Ibid. (1301b35–39).

31 We might, nevertheless, see in Aristotle's framework a greater potential for an egalitarian, nonhierarchical relationship between males and females than emerges from Plato's thought. If the female could be shown to be the intellectual equal, if her reason could be shown to have authority, and if leisure were hers, participation in the political community could follow. Plato, in contrast, in his works sees the potential for such intellectual capacity, but because of the female's ties to the processes of reproduction, she cannot participate fully. Plato's equality depends on advances in reproductive technology, while the Aristotelian model could incorporate women once their capacity was acknowledged and women were not denied the leisure to engage in the deliberative life.

32 Questions have been raised about the order of these books. For the most recent assessment that would place them after Book III, see Carnes Lord, "The Character and Composition of Aristotle's *Politics*," *Political Theory*, 9, November 1981, pp. 459–78.

33 *Politics*, VII.16 (1335a7–10).

34 Ibid., (1334b19).

35 See Maryanne Cline Horowitz, "Aristotle and Woman," *Journal of the History of Biology*, 9, Fall 1976, pp. 183–213: she traces some of the uses to which Aristotelian quotes about women were put in the Middle Ages.

3

"God Hath Ordained to Man a Helper": Hobbes, Patriarchy and Conjugal Right

Carole Pateman

The decisive moment in the conjuring trick has been made, and it was the very one we thought quite innocent.

L. Wittgenstein, Philosophical Investigations

Most studies of Hobbes have nothing to say about the relation of his political theory to seventeenth-century patriarchalism. Writers who have thought it worthwhile to consider the question have almost all agreed that Hobbes's argument is patriarchal, although more recently the claim has been made that, for example, Hobbes's views were subversive of "patriarchal attitudes," or that his theory is free from patriarchal assumptions.[1] More strongly, in a rational choice interpretation of Hobbes (which shares Hobbes's radical individualism) the implicit assumption is that Hobbes's theory is so far opposed to patriarchalism that his sovereign can be referred to as "she."[2] Despite such differences, political theorists are united on one point; they agree that to argue about patriarchy is to argue about the family and paternal power. Hobbes is assumed to be a patriarchal theorist in the same sense that his adversary Sir Robert Filmer is a patriarchalist; or, conversely, Hobbes is assumed to be opposed to patriarchalism because his theory is antithetical to Filmer's on some crucial issues.

The major debates about patriarchy over the past two decades have been conducted by feminists, not mainstream political theorists, but feminists have paid remarkably little attention to political theory in the controversy over the meaning and usefulness of the term "patriarchy." The predominant assumption among feminists, or, at least, among those engaged in the theoretically informed controversies over patriarchy, is also that patriarchal relations are familial relations and that patriarchal political right is paternal right.[3] To be sure, many feminists also use "patriarchy" to mean the power that men exercise over women more generally – what I shall call masculine right – but, notwithstanding the copious empirical evidence available to support this interpretation, the usage has not yet been given a great deal of theoretical substance. A major reason for this lack of theoretical robustness is feminist neglect of the arguments among political theorists about patriarchy in the seventeenth century. Feminist scholars have undertaken some very revealing and exciting work on the classic texts of political theory, but little attention has been paid to Hobbes, whose writings are of fundamental importance for an understanding of patriarchy as masculine right. Hobbes is a patriarchal theorist – but the possibility that is considered by neither conventional political theorists nor feminists is that he is a patriarchalist who rejects paternal right.

Both feminism and political theory are dogged by a anachronistic, although literal, interpretation of patriarchy as father-right. Patriarchy is assumed to be about fathers and mothers. For example, Di Stefano has argued that Hobbes is a masculinist theorist, but her reading of Hobbes is that his arguments rest on a denial of the mother. His picture of natural, atomized individuals, who spring up like mushrooms – "consider men as if but even now sprung out of the earth, and suddenly, like mushrooms, come to full maturity, without all kind of engagement to each other"[4] – denies any significance to the mother–child relationship and the dependence on the mother that provides the first intersubjective context for the development of human capacities. Di Stefano claims that there is no room for nurture within the family in Hobbes's state of nature; "men are not born of, much less nurtured by, women, or anyone else for that matter."[5] Hobbes's family is certainly very peculiar, but the problem with Di Stefano's argument is that, in the state of nature, mothers, far from being denied, are enthroned. For Hobbes, political right in the natural condition is mother-right. Hobbes goes to great lengths to deny that father-right is the origin of political right, yet he is still seen as a patriarchalist in the same sense as Filmer for whom political and paternal power were one and the same.

A different problem confronts the writers who argue that Hobbes subverts patriarchalism, or merely tacitly assume that the terms "men" and "individual" in Hobbes's texts are used generically; they fail to explain why Hobbes's writings contain so many references to the rightful power of fathers – or why he endorses the subjection of wives to husbands. Commentators on Hobbes, like almost all political theorists of the recent past, see no problems of political interest arising from the subordination of wives to husbands. Conjugal right, the right exercised by men, as husbands, over their wives, is not a matter that falls within their scholarly purview. The standard interpretations of the theoretical battle between the classic contract theorists, including Hobbes, and the patriarchalists of the seventeenth century is that the engagement concerned the political right of fathers and the natural liberty of sons. That the father was a master, exercising jurisdiction over servants and apprentices, is acknowledged, but another inhabitant of the family is usually ignored. The father is also a husband, and as a husband is a master over his wife. In discussions of Hobbes and patriarchy, the position of the *wife* in the family is rarely mentioned. She appears, if at all, in another capacity, as a *mother*. When a problem about women is admitted to exist, it is taken to be that of maternal jurisdiction over children.

The failure to distinguish marriage from the family and to recognize the existence of conjugal right means that the most distinctive aspect of Hobbes's political theory is disregarded. Hobbes is the only contract theorist (and almost the only writer admitted into the "tradition" of Western political theory) who begins from the premise that there is no natural dominion of men over women. In his natural condition female individuals are as free as, and equal to, male individuals. The remarkable starting point of his political theory is usually passed over extremely quickly. Even in discussions that focus on patriarchy no questions are asked or explanations offered about why and how it is, in the absence of sexual dominion in the state of nature, that marriage and the famly take a patriarchal form. Nor is anything odd seen in the fact that Hobbes argues both that women are naturally free and always subject to men through (the marriage) contract.

There are also other problems about Hobbes, patriarchy and contract when "patriarchy" is interpreted literally. Some commentators have noted certain tensions in Hobbes's arguments between contract and patriarchy; one earlier scholar, for instance, took the logical position that if Hobbes is interpreted as a patriarchalist then the original contract is superfluous.[6] Another commentator has attributed a consensual form of patriarchy to Hobbes and argued that his patriarchalism is, therefore, the strongest form – and even a more typically English variety.[7] Hobbes took contract much further than most other classic contract theorists and claimed that even infants (could be said to have) contracted themselves into subjection to mothers. To posit a contract by an infant is to reject outright any suggestion that political subjection is natural and to confirm in the most emphatic possible manner that all dominion is conventional in origin. Yet it was precisely the doctrine of the natural freedom of mankind and its corollary, contract and consent, that Sir Robert Filmer saw as the major cause of sedition and political disorder. Why, then, should a purported advocate of patriarchy as paternal right, and a writer who, in his own way, was as absolutist as his opponent, take so many pains to deny the assumptions of Filmer's theory? More generally, if political right has a natural origin in fatherhood and contract is thus superfluous – and, according to Filmer, politically dangerous – why should Hobbes argue that civil society was created through an original contract?

To remain within the standard, patriarchal interpretation of "patriarchy" as fatherly power is to remain within a patriarchal reading of Hobbes's texts, a reading that ignores the subjection of women. Hobbes's patriarchalism is a new, *specifically modern* form, that is conventional, contractual and originates in conjugal right, or, more accurately, sex-right; that is, in men's right of sexual access to women, which, in its major institutional form in modern society, is exercised as conjugal right (a term also providing a polite locution in, say, a discussion of Adam and Eve). To appreciate the character of Hobbes's patriarchal theory the distinctive features of his natural condition – mother-right and the absence of natural dominion of male over female individuals – have to be taken seriously as fundamental premises of his political theory. In addition, Hobbes's extraordinary conception of the "family" needs to be emphasized. Hobbes did not merely leave no room for nurture or argue that the family was conventional, a political rather than a natural social form. For Hobbes, a "family" was solely composed of a master and servants of various kinds and had its origins in conquest.

I

Before looking in greater detail at Hobbes's arguments it is necessary to say something more about patriarchy and to look again at Filmer's patriarchalism.[8] A good deal of confusion over the term "patriarchy" has arisen because of the failure to distinguish between three different historical forms of patriarchal theory: traditional, classic and modern. Traditional patriarchal argument assimilates all power relations to paternal rule. For centuries the family and the authority of the father at its head provided the model and metaphor for political society and political right. The traditional form is also full of stories, of conjectural histories, about the emergence or creation of political society from the family or the coming together of many families. Such stories are also to be found in the writings of the classic contract theorists, even though they defeated and eliminated the second, shortlived form of classic patriarchalism. Classic patriarchy was formulated and died in the seventeenth century and is exemplified by Sir Robert Filmer's arguments. Schochet shows in *Patriarchalism in Political Thought* that Sir Robert broke with the traditional form by insisting that paternal and political rule were not merely analogous but identical. In the 1680s and 1690s, "the Filmerian position very nearly became the official state ideology."[9] The classic form was a fully developed theory of political right and political obedience and was the first of its kind; "there was no patriarchal theory of obligation prior to 1603."[10] The standard claim in political theory is that patriarchalism was dead and buried by 1700 – but the form that passed away was Filmer's classic patriarchy.

Filmer wrote in response to the challenge posed by the doctrine of the natural freedom of mankind. If men were born free and equal then, necessarily, political right or the dominion of one man over another could be established in one way only; through an agreement (contract) between those concerned that such a relation should be brought into being. According to Filmer, acknowledgement that Adam had been granted monarchical power by God by virtue of his fatherhood cut the ground from under the feet of the contract theorists. At the birth of his first son, Adam became the first king and his political right passed to all subsequent fathers and kings, who were one and the same: all kings ruled as fathers in consequence of their procreative power, and all fathers were monarchs in their families. Sons were born into political subjection to their fathers and hence to the monarch: no such political nonsense as talk of contracts was required to justify political subjection. Filmer's account of the natural origin of political right appears straightforward enough, and no hint is given in discussions of the relation between the theories of Hobbes and Filmer that patriarchy is more complicated.

Paternal right is only one dimension of patriarchy – as Filmer himself reveals. Filmer's apparently straightforward statements obscure the original foundation of political right. Paternal power is not the origin of political right. Father-right is established only after political right has been brought into being. Another act of political genesis is required before a man can acquire the natural right of fatherhood. Sons do not spring up like mushrooms, as Filmer was quick to remind Hobbes. Adam's political title is granted *before* he becomes a father. If he is to be a father, Eve has to become a mother. In other words, *sex-right or conjugal right must necessarily precede the right of fatherhood*. The genesis of political dominion lies in Adam's sex-right, *not* in his fatherhood.

Filmer makes clear that Adam's political right is originally established in his right as a husband over Eve: "God gave to Adam . . . the dominion over the woman," and, citing Genesis 3:16, "God ordained Adam to rule over his wife, and her desires were to be subject to his."[11] (Genesis states that Eve's "desire shall be to thy husband, and he shall rule over thee".)

Adam's desire is to become a father, but in no ordinary sense of "father." He desires to obtain the remarkable powers of a patriarchal father. Filmer briefly mentions Adam's original, divine grant of political right over Eve at various points, but it has a shadowy presence in his writings. In recent (patriarchal) commentaries on his texts, sex-right has completely disappeared. And, to be sure, when reading Filmer from the perspective of only one dimension of patriarchalism, conjugal right is not easy to discern under the cloak of Adam's fatherhood.

The biblical patriarchal image (here in Locke's words) is of "nursing Fathers tender and carefull of the publick weale."[12] The patriarchal story is about the procreative power of a father who is complete in himself, who embodies the creative power of both female and male. His procreative power both gives and animates physical life and creates and maintains political right. Filmer is able to refer to Adam's power over Eve so casually because classic patriarchalism declares women to be procreatively and politically irrelevant. The reason that Adam has dominion over "the woman" is, according to Filmer (here following the patriarchal idea of fatherhood, which is very ancient), that "the man . . . [is] the nobler and principal agent in generation."[13] Women are merely empty vessels for the exercise of men's sexual and procreative power. The original political right that God gives to Adam is the right, so to speak, to fill the empty vessel. Adam, and all men, must do this if they are to become fathers. But men's generative power has a dual aspect. The genesis of new physical life belongs in their hands, not in the empty vessel. Men are the "principal agents in generation," and "generation" includes political creativity. Men's generative power includes the ability to create new political life, or to give birth to political right.

In view of the character of the extraordinary powers that classic patriarchalism arrogates to men, it is appropriate that the powers are contained in the name of "father" and encompassed under the writ of "fatherhood." The presence of conjugal right is very faint in Filmer's writings because (although at one level he must acknowledge it) Adam's original political right is subsumed under the power of fatherhood. For instance, after stating that Eve and her desires are subject to Adam, Filmer continues in the next sentence, "here we have the original grant of government, and the fountain of all power placed in the Father of all mankind." Moreover, Adam is also Eve's father. In the story of the Book of Genesis, Eve is created only after Adam and the animals have been placed on earth. God creates and names the animals and Adam but, we are told in Genesis 2:20, "for Adam there was not found an help meet for him." Eve is then created, but she is not created *ab initio* but *from* Adam, who is, in a sense, her parent, and Adam, not God, gives Eve her name. Filmer is therefore able to treat all political right as the right of a father. Eve is not only under the dominion of Adam, but he is (with God's help) the "principal agent" in her generation. The father in classic patriarchal theory is not just one of two parents – he is *the* parent, and the being able to generate political right.

The greatest story of masculine political birth is the story of an original contract that creates civil freedom and civil society. The classic patriarchalists lost the battle over fathers and sons and the natural origin of political right. Patriarchalism, in the sense of paternal right, ceased to be politically relevant by the end of the seventeenth century. Civil society is constituted by the (ostensibly) universal, conventional bonds of contract not the particular, natural bonds of kinship and fatherhood. However, the standard account of the defeat of patriarchy ignores the fact that the contract theorists had no quarrel with classic patriarchalism over the true origin of political right; they fought against paternal right but had no wish to disturb the other dimension of patriarchy, conjugal right.

The "freedom of mankind" in contract argument means what it says, the freedom of *men*. The victory of contract doctrine over the classic form of patriarchal argument was, rather, the *transformation* of classic patriarchy into a new form. The contract theorists constructed their own, modern patriarchal argument – the third of the historical forms. Modern patriarchy is contractual not natural and embodies masculine right not the right of fatherhood. Hobbes, the most brilliant and bold of contract theorists, is a patriarchal theorist in the modern sense, but his arguments differ in some significant respects from those of his fellow contract theorists and, in the end, it was they, not Hobbes, who provided the necessary theoretical framework for patriarchal civil society.

II

On the face of it, Hobbes's writings seem unequivocally opposed to both dimensions of classic patriarchy. Hobbes's theory rests on mother-right and the absence of natural sexual dominion; how, then, does Hobbes transform natural maternal power and women's natural freedom into patriarchal right, and why have scholars been able to identify so many passages in Hobbes's writings where he apparently falls back on the traditional form of patriarchal argument? The appropriate place to begin to consider the conjuring tricks is with Hobbes's picture of the natural condition. Hobbes's imaginative resolution of civil society into its most fundamental ("natural") parts was much more rigorous than the similar undertakings of the other contract theorists. Hobbes was willing to take the logic of individualism to its most radical conclusions in this as in other respects. When Hobbes reconstitutes natural entities in perpetual motion

into something recognizably human, the result is that humans interact in
a natural condition that can barely be recognized as social. Hobbes's state
of nature is the famous war of all against all, and, in a statement which is
rarely seen as of political significance, Hobbes writes that in the natural
condition there are "no matrimonial laws."[14] Marriage – that is to say, a
long-term relation between the sexes – must be brought about in exactly
the same way as any other relation between the inhabitants of the state of
nature where there is no natural order of dominion, and no politically significant difference in strength or prudence between individuals. Relations
can arise in two ways only: either individuals contract themselves into a
given relationship; or one, by some stratagem, is able to coerce another
into the desired arrangement. This is also true of relations between a man
and a woman. In the natural condition women face men as free equals;
Hobbes writes that "whereas some have attributed the dominion to the
man only, as being of the more excellent sex; they misreckon in it. For
there is not always that difference of strength or prudence between the
man and the woman, as that the right can be determined without war."[15]

   In the state of nature there is no law to regulate marriage – and no
marriage. Marriage does not exist because marriage is a long-term arrangement, and long-term sexual relationships, like other such relationships,
are very difficult to establish and maintain in Hobbes's natural condition.
The boundaries separating the inhabitants one from another are so tightly
drawn by Hobbes that each one can judge the rest only from a subjective
perspective, or from the perspective of pure self-interest. Natural individuals will, therefore, always break an agreement, or refuse to play their
part in a contract, if it appears in their interest to do so. To enter a
contract or to signify agreement to do so is to leave oneself open to
betrayal. Hobbes's natural state suffers from an endemic problem of
keeping contracts and of "performing second"; "If a covenant be made,
wherein neither of the parties perform presently, but trust one another; . . .
upon any reasonable suspicion, it is void: . . . And . . . he which performeth
first, does but betray himself to his enemy."[16] The only contract that an
individual, of his or her own volition, can enter into in safety is one in
which agreement and performance take place at the same time. An agreement to perform an act of coitus provides an example of a contract that
comes close to meeting this criterion, but an agreement to marry, to enter
into a long-term sexual relationship, would founder in the same manner as
contracts to create other relations that endure over time.

   The women and men in Hobbes's state of nature can engage in sexual
intercourse and, therefore, children can be born. A child, however, is born
a long time after any act of intercourse. As Hobbes notes, in the absence of
matrimonial laws proof of fatherhood rests on the testimony of the mother.
Since there is no way of establishing paternity with any certainty, the

child belongs to the mother. Hobbes's argument is all the more striking since he, too, suggests that men are the "principal agents" in generation. Echoing the classic patriarchal view of fatherhood, Hobbes writes that "as to the generation, God hath ordained to man a helper"[17] – but the female "helper" in the state of nature becomes much more than an auxiliary once the birth takes place. Hobbes insists that no man can have two masters and so only one parent can have dominion over the child. In the natural condition the mother, not the father, enjoys this right. In direct contradiction of Sir Robert Filmer and the patriarchal doctrine that political right originates in the father's generative power, Hobbes proclaims that "every woman that bears children, becomes both a *mother* and a *lord*."[18] At birth, the infant is in the mother's power. She makes the decision whether to expose or to nourish the child. To have the power to preserve life is, according to Hobbes, to exercise rightful dominion, whether the subject is a newly born infant or a vanquished adult. If the mother preserves the infant, she thereby becomes a lord; "because preservation of life being the end, for which one man [or infant] becomes subject to another, every man is supposed to promise obedience, to him [or her], in whose power it is to save, or destroy him."[19]

From 1861 for a half century or more (following the publication of Sir Henry Maine's *Ancient Law* and Johann Bachofen's *Mother Right*) another controversy raged about political origins, matriarchy and patriarchy. The proponents were all reluctant to admit that matriarchy in the literal sense – rule by women as mothers – ever existed, even hypothetically.[20] Similarly, some contemporary theorists still find it necessary to take issue with Hobbes's logic on mother-right. The rather amusing objection has been raised that Hobbes is mistaken; a mother "simply does not wield" the power Hobbes ascribes to her.[21] The "helper" herself always requires another helper. In Hobbes's day, the objection continues, the mother was attended by a midwife or male physician, and it is the latter who, at the moment of birth, has power over the child in her or his hands. Hobbes should have concluded that neither fathers nor mothers possessed an original political power in the natural condition, but then his argument against natural paternal right would have been "more absurd still." In his eagerness to combat Filmer, Hobbes "overlooked the defects attached to an argument which would transfer this power to a party – the mother– whom no one supposed ever had a proper right or even opportunity to exercise it (given the establishment of a civil society)."[22] Precisely; in patriarchal civil society, past or present, political theorists rarely are willing to contemplate that mothers (women) could legitimately exercise political right, even in an hypothetical state of nature or as a matter of mere logic. The other social contract theorists, unlike Hobbes, built masculine sexual dominion as a natural fact of human existence into their political theories and so demonstrated in a straightforward fashion that, for all that their arguments are couched in universal terms, equality, freedom and contract are a male privilege – although contemporary political theorists still manage to avoid noticing the fact.[23] Hobbes's logic is impeccable. In his natural condition (whatever the facts of childbirth in the seventeenth century) a pregnant woman would not give herself up as a hostage to fortune by enlisting helpers in her labors; no free, strong woman would place her right of dominion at risk with such assistance.

By nature, a mother is a lord who can do as she wills with her infant. If she decides to "breed him," the condition on which she does so, Hobbes states, is that "being grown to full age he become not her enemy."[24] That is to say, the infant must contract to obey her. The mother's political right over her child originates in contract, and gives her absolute power. A woman can contract away her right over her child to the father, but, when the premise of Hobbes's argument is that women naturally stand as equals to men, there is no reason why a woman should do this, and, least of all, why she should *always* do so. To argue that a tiny infant can contract, or should be regarded as if it had contracted, with its mother is, as Filmer insisted, anthropological nonsense. In terms of Hobbes's understanding of "contract," however, this agreement is as convincing an example of a contract as any other in Hobbes's writings. Scholars have drawn attention to Hobbes's claim that the reasons and circumstances under which agreement are given are irrelevant to the validity of the contract; for Hobbes, it makes no difference whether a contract is entered into after due deliberation or with the conqueror's sword at one's breast. Submission to overwhelming power in return for protection, whether the power is that of the conqueror's sword or the mother's power over her newly born infant, is always a valid sign of agreement for Hobbes. Hobbes's assimilation of conquest to contract, enforced submission to consent, is often remarked upon, but the political significance of his peculiar notion of contract for the origin of the family in the state of nature and for the making of the original pact is less often appreciated.

III

The logical conclusion of Hobbes's resolution of civil society into its natural parts of rational entities in motion, and his reconstitution of the natural condition, is that the sexes come together only fleetingly and that the original political right is mother-right. Yet Hobbes also writes in a passage (cited by Richard Chapman and Gordon Schochet, for example), "that the beginning of all dominion amongst men was in families. In which, . . . the father of the family by the law of nature was absolute lord of his wife and children: [and] made what laws amongst them he pleased."[25] And he also refers to familial government or a "patrimonial kingdom" in which the family:

> if it grow by multiplication of children, either by generation, or adoption; or of servants, either by generation, conquest, or voluntary submission, to be so great and numerous, as in probability it may protect itself, then is that family called a *patrimonial kingdom*, or monarchy by acquisition, wherein the sovereignty is in one man, as it is in a monarch made by *political institution*. So that whatsoever rights be in the one, the same also be in the other.[26]

Moreover, Hobbes also makes statements such as "cities and kingdoms . . . are but greater families,"[27] and "a great family is a kingdom, and a little kingdom a family."[28] He also remarks that Germany, like other countries "in their beginnings," was divided between a number of masters of families, all at war with each other.[29] Such statements have been treated as evidence that Hobbes was a patriarchalist like Filmer and that his natural condition was composed of families not individuals. Such an interpretation leaves unanswered the questions of how the transformation comes about from mother-right to the patriarchal family in the state of nature and how the family is generated.

Chapman has stressed that Hobbes's family is an artificial, political institution rather than a natural social form, but its extraordinary character consists in more than a conventional, political origin. No attention is paid to the most bizarre aspect of Hobbes's account of the family because conjugal right and the position of a wife are ignored. Indeed, the scholars involved in the debate about Hobbes and the family have not paused to wonder how there can be wives in the state of nature where there is no law of matrimony. Nor have they asked how families can come into existence when marriage does not exist and yet marriage is the "origin" of the family. Hobbes's "family" is very curious and has nothing in common with the families of Filmer's pages, the family as found in the writings of the other classical social contract theorists, or as popularly understood today. Consider Hobbes's definition: in *Leviathan* he states that a family "consist[s] of a man and his children; or of a man and his servants; or of a man, and his children, and servants together; wherein the father or master is the sovereign."[30] In *De Cive* we find "a *father* with his *sons* and *servants*, grown into a civil person by virtue of his paternal jurisdiction, is called a *family*."[31] What has happened to the wife and mother? Only in *Elements of Law* does he write that "the father or mother of the family is sovereign of the same."[32] But the sovereign cannot be the mother, given the conjectural history of the origin of the family implicit in Hobbes's argument.

The "natural" characteristics postulated by Hobbes mean that long-term relationships are very unlikely in his state of nature. However,

Hobbes states in *Leviathan* that, in the war of all against all, "there is no man who can hope by his own strength, or wit, to defend himself from destruction, without the help of confederates."[33] But how can such a protective confederation be formed in the natural condition when there is an acute problem of keeping agreements? The answer is that confederations are formed by conquest. If one male individual manages to conquer another in the state of nature the conqueror will have obtained a servant. Hobbes assumes that no one would willfully give up his life, so, faced with the conqueror's sword, the defeated man will make a (valid) contract to obey his victor. Hobbes defines dominion or political right acquired through force as "the dominion of the master over his servant."[34] Conqueror and conquered then constitute "a little body politic, which consisteth of two persons, the one sovereign, which is called the *master*, or lord; the other subject, which is called the *servant*."[35] Hobbes distinguishes a servant from a slave, but his definition of a servant makes it hard to maintain the distinction: "the master of the servant, is master also of all he hath: and may exact the use thereof; that is to say, of his goods, of his labour, of his servants, and of his children, as often as he shall think fit."[36]

The master and his slave-servant form the little body politic of a defensive confederation against the rest of the inhabitants of the state of nature. That is to say, according to Hobbes's definition of a "family," the master and his servant form a family. For Hobbes, the origin of the family is entirely conventional. A "family" is created not through procreation but by conquest, and a family consists of a master and his servants; that is, all those, whatever their age or sex, who fall under his absolute jurisdiction. A "family" composed only of a master and his male servants is a singular institution and it becomes more singular still if this male household contains children. Hobbes remarks at one point that sovereignty can be established "by natural force; as when a man maketh his children, to submit themselves, and their children to his government."[37] Children have again sprung up like mushrooms, ready to submit to (contract with) their fathers. And what of their mothers; how are they included in the "family"? In the natural condition there are two ways only in which sexual relations between free, equal women and men can take place. Either a woman freely contracts to engage in intercourse or she is outwitted and taken by force. There is no reason why a woman should contract of her own free will to enter into a long-term sexual relationship and become a "wife," that is, to be in servitude to – to become the servant (slave) of – a man. In the state of nature a woman is as able as a man to defend herself or to conquer another to form a protective confederation of master and servant. Why then does Hobbes assume that only men become masters of servants?

The answer is that, by the time the original contract is entered into, *all* the women in the natural condition have been conquered by men and become servants. Hobbes is explicit that "dominion amongst men" begins in the defensive confederation or small body politic he calls a family, but he does not spell out that men also gain dominion over women by creating "families." A conjectural history of how this comes about might run as follows. At first, women, who are as strong and as capable as men, are able to ensure that sexual relations are consensual. When a woman becomes a mother and decides to become a lord and raise her child, her position changes; she is put at a slight disadvantage against men, since now she has her infant to defend too. Conversely, a man obtains a slight advantage over her and is then able to defeat the woman he had initially to treat with as an equal. Mothers are lords in Hobbes's state of nature, but, paradoxically, for a woman to become a mother and a lord is her downfall. She has then given an opening for a male enemy to outwit and vanquish her in the ceaseless natural conflict. Mother-right can never be more than fleeting.

The original political dominion of maternal lordship is quickly overcome and replaced by masculine right. Each man can obtain a "family" of a woman servant and her child. Thus mother-right is overturned and the state of nature becomes filled with patriarchal "families." All the women in the natural condition are forcibly incorporated (which for Hobbes, is to say contract themselves) into "families" and become the permanent servants of male masters. The "help" given by women to men in procreation then becomes the unending help of domestic servitude. The "wife" is relegated to the status of a helper too politically insignificant to be worthy of listing as a member of this peculiar protective association. A story along these lines is necessary to explain the existence of patriarchal "families" in the state of nature, and also to explain why a patriarchal law of matrimony is instituted through the original contract.

But it is hard to tell a consistent and convincing story about women's subjection when beginning from the postulate of natural freedom and equality between women and men.[38] The conquest of women would surely take more than one generation. Some women, either by choice or the accident of nature, would be childless and so would remain free. Indeed, once childless women saw the fate of women who decided to exercise maternal lordship they would, as rational beings, choose to remain childless and conserve their natural freedom. Free women would, however, be found only in the first generation in the natural condition. Childless women would die, and all subsequent generations of women would be born into servitude (and so, according to Hobbes's definition of servitude, would be under the jurisdiction of the master). The problem with this version of the conjectural history is that, if there are free childless women in the first generation in the natural condition, there is no reason why they should not form protective confederations of their own by conquering men, or each other, and so obtaining servants. Women and men would then wage the war of all against all as masters of "families" – and who knows who might win in the end? But in Hobbes's theory we do know who wins, and thus there is only one story that can be told. Women must all be conquered in the first generation; there can be no female masters in the state of nature or there will be no original contract and no law of matrimony.

IV

The method through which Hobbes constructed his picture of the state of nature meant that, as a ruthlessly consistent theorist, he had to begin from the logical but shocking premise of an absence of sexual dominion and original mother-right. But Hobbes was well aware, as indicated in the passages that I cited above, that, historically, paternal right and the subjection of wives was the established custom. In the *logical* beginning, all political right is maternal right. In the *historical* beginning, masculine or "paternal" right holds sway. The story of the defeat of women in the state of nature explains how patriarchal "families," incorporating all the women, are formed through conquest and ruled by "fathers." This stage of the history of the natural condition must be reached if men are to enter the original contract, exercise their political creativity and create a new phase of history in the form of modern patriarchal society. Commentators on contract theory generally take it for granted that there are no problems in referring to "individuals" entering into the original contract, so implying that any or all of the inhabitants of the state of nature can participate. Some commentators are more careful, and Schochet, for example, notes that in the seventeenth century fathers of families were assumed to have sealed the original pact. He argues that Hobbes shared this assumption. Despite Hobbes's use of traditional patriarchal language, his "families" are not ruled by men as fathers but by men as masters. Masters of families rule by virtue of contract (conquest) not their paternal, procreative capacity. Men as masters – or as free and equal men – enter into the original contract that constitutes civil society. Women, now in subjection, no longer have the necessary standing (they are no longer free and equal or "individuals") to take part in creating a new civil society.

The civil law of matrimony, which upholds conjugal right, is created through the original pact. Political theorists consistently omit to mention one of the most remarkable features of Hobbes's political theory. Hobbes makes it quite clear that conjugal right is not natural. Conjugal right is created through the original contract and so is a *political* right. The right is deliberately created by the men who bring civil society into being. The other classic contract theorists presuppose that the institution of marriage exists naturally and that conjugal relations are nonpolitical relations, carried over into civil society. In Hobbes's theory, the law of matrimony is created as part of the civil law. Contemporary political theorists, too, take for granted that the structure of the institution of marriage is nonpolitical and so they pay no attention to conjugal right. Hobbes's political theory makes clear what the other classic contract stories, and contemporary commentaries on contract theory, leave implicit: that the original contract is not only a *social* contract that constitutes the civil law and political right in the sense of (state) government; it is also a *sexual* contract that institutes political right in the form of patriarchal – masculine – power, or government by men, a power exercised in large part as conjugal right.

Hobbes states that in civil society the husband has dominion "because for the most part commonwealths have been erected by the fathers, not by the mothers of families."[39] Or again, "in all cities . . . constituted of *fathers*, not *mothers* governing their families, the domestical command belongs to the man; and such a contract, if it be made according to the civil laws, is called matrimony."[40] If free and equal women could enter the original contract there is no reason whatsoever why they would agree to create a civil law that secures their permanent subjection as wives. Matrimonial law takes a patriarchal form because *men* have made the original contract. The fact that the law of matrimony is part of the civil law provides another reason for self-interested individual men to make a collective agreement. In addition to securing their natural liberty, *men as a sex* have an interest in a political mechanism which secures for them collectively the fruits of the conquests made severally by each man in the natural condition. Through the civil institution of marriage they can all lawfully obtain the familiar "helpmeet" and gain the sexual and domestic services of a wife, whose permanent servitude is now guaranteed by the law and sword of Leviathan.

Hobbes had no wish to challenge the law of matrimony of his own day, embodied in the common law doctrine of coverture. The law of coverture was given classic expression by Sir William Blackstone in his *Commentaries on the Laws of England* in the eighteenth century. Under coverture, a wife had no independent juridical existence; she was a civilly dead being, absorbed into the person of her husband. No one, it would seem, could fail to be struck by the legal powers given to husbands, whether in Blackstone's gloss on the law or in marital practice – powers that can only be compared, as they were regularly compared by feminists in the nineteenth century, to those of slave-masters.[41] Yet patriarchy runs so deeply in the contemporary theoretical consciousness that Chapman comments (echoing Blackstone) that "the most striking feature of the common law family is the liabilities attached to the man, particularly regarding the acts of his wife and servants."[42] Now, if women had made the original contract, civil law might well reflect the fact and attach all manner of "liabilities" to men. But we did not make it, and could not have made it, and so "the most striking feature" of coverture is the juridical nonexistence of a wife (just as she disappears in Hobbes's definition of the "family" in the state of nature). The liabilities of the husband that impress Chapman are the other side of the wife's subjection. "Liabilities" are the price the husband pays for being a master, that is, a protector. The most fundamental premise of Hobbes's political theory is that no individual will give up the right of self-protection.[43] In the state of nature women too have this right, but in civil society women as wives have given up (been forced to give up) this right in favour of the "protection" of their husband – and husbands are now protected by the sword of Leviathan.

Students of Hobbes do not usually make a connection between the original overthrow of mother-right and the establishment of Leviathan. The crucial political significance of the conquest of women in the natural condition is that, unless the defeat occurs, Leviathan is impossible to envisage. The conjuror Hobbes is far too clever a wizard for his patriarchal successors and the trick is never remarked on in discussions of his theory. If women took part in the original contract the awesome figure of the mortal god Leviathan could not be created. Leviathan can be brought into being only if participation in his generation is confined to men. The creation of civil society is an act of masculine political birth; men have no need of a "helper" in *political* generation. In the state of nature, individuals are differentiated only by their sex; that is to say, by their bodily form (in strength, rationality and prudence there is no politically significant difference between individuals with female bodies and individuals with male bodies). Hobbes's account of the institution of Leviathan makes sense only if the participants in the original contract all have the same bodily form.

The creation of Leviathan, Hobbes tells us, involves "more than consent, or concord; it is a real unity of them all, in one and the same person."[44] When men cease to be a mere natural multitude and transform themselves through the act of contract into a unified body, or body politic, bound together through the conventional bonds of contract and civil law, their unity is represented in a very literal sense by the person of their (absolute) master and ruler, Leviathan. They create him "to bear their person," and, Hobbes states, "it is the *unity* of the representer, not the *unity* of the represented, that maketh the person *one*."[45] No such unity would be possible if both sexes took part in the constitution of Leviathan – there could be no representative figure who could represent the "person," the bodily form, of both sexes. Men must be represented and their civil unity given literal symbolic personification by one of their own kind. Similarly, "private bodies" are also represented by one person, and Hobbes uses the example of "all families, in which the father, or master ordereth the whole family." Husband and wife cannot govern jointly in the family; there can be one master only, and the husband is the necessary "one person representative" of the family in civil society.[46] An act of masculine political birth creates civil beings and their sovereign in the image of their makers (only Adam, the first man, through the hand of God, could generate a woman). If the representer is to be unified, he must be *he*. To attempt to represent both sexes within the figure of one master would be to dissolve his unity and oneness and to shatter political order.

V

Hobbes turned classic into modern patriarchy but several features of his argument worked against him becoming a founding father of modern patriarchal theory. For example, Hobbes negated Filmer's arguments but that was not sufficient to create the theory required for civil patriarchy. Hobbes turned Filmer's social bonds into their opposite. Filmer saw families and kingdoms as homologous and bound together through the natural, procreative power of the father. Hobbes saw families and kingdoms as homologous, but as bound together through the conventional tie of contract, or, what for Hobbes is the same thing, the force of the sword. Hobbes also agreed with Filmer that sovereignty must be absolute – but sovereignty in the state, not in private bodies. Civil fathers and masters are not miniature Leviathans. Their powers run only so far as permitted by Leviathan's laws and his sword. Leviathan thus enabled Hobbes to offer a solution to the problem that dogged Filmer's classic patriarchalism. Hinton has noted that if fathers were kings then there could be no king with true monarchical power.[47] Hobbes's civil masters cannot detract from the absolute mastery of Leviathan. Hobbes's solution, however, retained absolutism in the state, the form of political right that, as Locke argued, had to be replaced by limited, constitutional government in a properly *civil* order.

The absolute power of Leviathan's sword was not the only problem with Hobbes's patriarchalism. Hobbes was too revealing about civil society. The political character of conjugal right was expertly concealed in Locke's separation of what he called "paternal" power from political power and, ever since, most political theorists, whatever their views about other forms of subordination, have accepted that the powers of husbands derive from nature and, hence, are not political. Not only are a range of important questions about domination and subjection in our own society thus suppressed, but some other important questions about the "origin" of civil society are also neatly avoided. In the past two decades, individualism of a radical, Hobbesian kind has become very influential, although the absolutist conclusions that Hobbes drew from his individualist premises are rejected in favour of a view of the state as a minimal, protective association.[48] The association is held to have a legitimate origin in voluntary transactions between individuals in the state of nature. In the final chapter of *Leviathan*, Hobbes writes that "there is scarce a commonwealth in the world, whose beginnings can in conscience be justified."[49] Hobbes's "beginning" of the original contract between men can only be justified if, as he believed, political order depended on the erection of Leviathan. Without Leviathan, and from Hobbes's starting point of free and equal women and men, a voluntary beginning might be possible. Such a story could not be told by political theorists who acknowledge only half the original contract (the social contract) and thus endorse patriarchal right. The origin of the patriarchal protective state in Hobbes's theory lies in the conquest and servitude of women in the state of nature and in their civil subjection and domestication as wives.

Hobbes's theory is an early version of the argument, presented in the later nineteenth and early twentieth centuries in elaborate detail and with reference to much ethnographic data, that civilization and political society resulted from the overthrow of mother-right and the triumph of patriarchy. The silences and omissions of contemporary political theory and the standard readings of Hobbes's texts do nothing to question that argument. Scholars do not mention the problems about women and the civil order arising from Hobbes's theory and the subsequent development of contract theory. For example, why has conjugal right never been seen as political when every other form of power has been subjected to the closest scrutiny and judgment? Why is women's exclusion from the original pact not mentioned in most discussions of contract theory? If women can take no part in the original contract what is their status as parties to the marriage contract? Has Hobbes's identification of enforced submission with consent (contract) any relevance to present-day sexual relations? By the beginning of the eighteenth century, when, according to political theorists today, patriarchalism had come to an end, Mary Astell asked, "if *all Men are born Free*, how is it that all Women are born Slaves?"[50] Most political theorists have yet to recognize the existence or relevance of Astell's question – or the political significance of the fact that Hobbes did not think that we were so born.

Notes

1 The arguments are those, respectively, of Richard A. Chapman, "*Leviathan Writ Small: Thomas Hobbes on the Family,*" *American Political Science Review,* 69, 1975, p. 77; and John Zvesper, "Hobbes' Individualistic Analysis of the Family," *Politics,* 5, 1985, p. 33. For references to other discussions of Hobbes and patriarchy see Chapman, nn. 2–14 on p. 76.

2 Jean Hampton, *Hobbes and the Social Contract Tradition* (Cambridge: Cambridge University Press, 1986).

3 Contemporary feminist arguments about patriarchy are discussed in Carole Pateman, *The Sexual Contract* (Cambridge: Polity; Stanford: Stanford University Press, 1988), ch. 2.

4 Thomas Hobbes, *Philosophical Rudiments Concerning Government and Society,* the English version of *De Cive,* in *The English Works of Thomas Hobbes of Malmesbury* (London: John Bohn, 1841), vol. 2, ch. 8, p. 109.

5 Christine Di Stefano, "Masculinity as Ideology in Political Theory: Hobbesian Man Considered," *Women's Studies International Forum,* 6, 1983, p. 638.

6 Leslie Stephen in 1904; cited by Gordon Schochet, *Patriarchalism in Political Thought* (Oxford: Basil Blackwell, 1975), p. 234.

7 R. W. K. Hinton, "Husbands, Fathers and Conquerors," *Political Studies,* 16, 1968, p. 57.

8 This section draws on Pateman, *Sexual Contract,* ch. 4.

9 Schochet, *Patriarchalism,* p. 193.

10 Ibid., p. 16.

11 Sir Robert Filmer, *Patriarcha or the Natural Powers of the Kings of England Asserted and Other Political Works,* ed. Peter Laslett (Oxford: Basil Blackwell, 1949), pp. 241, 283. Genesis, too, can be interpreted in more than one way, and equality of men and women in the sight of God is not incompatible with male supremacy in human affairs; e.g. Calvin argued from both the perspective of *cognitio dei* (the eternal, divine perspective in which all things are equal) and the perspective of *cognitio hominis* (the wordly perspective in which humans are hierarchically ordered). See Mary Potter, "Gender Equality and Gender Hierarchy in Calvin's Theology," *Signs,* 11, 1986, pp. 725–39.

12 John Locke, *Two Treatises of Government,* 2nd edn, ed. Peter Laslett (Cambridge: Cambridge University Press, 1967), II, §2.

13 Filmer, *Patriarcha,* p. 245.

14 Hobbes, *Leviathan,* in *English Works,* vol. 3, ch. 20, p. 187.

15 Ibid., pp. 186–7.

16 Ibid., ch. 14, pp. 124–5.

17 Ibid., ch. 20, p. 186.

18 Hobbes, *Philosophical Rudiments,* ch. 9, p. 116.

19 Hobbes, *Leviathan,* p. 188.

20 For an account of the controversy, see Rosalind Coward, *Patriarchal Precedents* (London: Routledge and Kegan Paul, 1983), ch. 2. See also Pateman, *Sexual Contract,* ch. 2.

21 Preston King, *The Ideology of Order* (London: Allen and Unwin, 1974), p. 203.

22 King, *Ideology of Order*, pp. 205, 206. Hobbes's most recent biographer suggests that his argument about mother-right derives from his own experience as a child. Hobbes's views perhaps "owed much to that occasion during those years when the curate [Hobbes's father], possibly long before his disappearance, was forced by his character and circumstances to yield the government to Hobbes' mother." Arnold A. Rogow, *Thomas Hobbes: Radical in the Service of Reaction* (New York and London: W. W. Norton, 1986), p. 132. Hobbes's father, rather fond of drink and neglectful of his parish, fled after being accused of assaulting a rector of a neighboring parish. Ironically Rogow was unable to find any new information about Hobbes's mother. Even her maiden name remains uncertain.

23 The other classic contract theorists are discussed in Pateman, *Sexual Contract*, chs 3 and 4.

24 Hobbes, *Philosophical Rudiments*, ch. 9, p. 116.

25 Thomas Hobbes, *A Dialogue between a Philosopher and a Student of the Common Laws of England*, in *English Works*, vol. 6, p. 147.

26 Thomas Hobbes, *De Corpore Politico, or The Elements of Law*, in *English Works*, vol. 4, ch. 4, pp. 158–9 (Hobbes's emphasis here and below).

27 Hobbes, *Leviathan*, ch. 17, p. 154.

28 Hobbes, *Philosophical Rudiments*, ch. 8, p. 108.

29 Hobbes, *Leviathan*, ch. 10, p. 82.

30 Ibid., ch. 20, p. 191.

31 Hobbes, *Philosophical Rudiments*, ch. 9, p. 121.

32 Hobbes, *De Corpore Politico*, ch. 4, p. 158.

33 Hobbes, *Leviathan*, ch. 15, p. 133.

34 Ibid., ch. 20, p. 189.

35 Hobbes, *De Corpore Politico*, ch. 3, pp. 149–50.

36 Hobbes, *Leviathan*, ch. 20, p. 190.

37 Ibid., ch. 17, p. 159.

38 I am grateful to Peter Morriss for raising the question of generations and for other helpful criticisms.

39 Hobbes, *Leviathan*, ch. 15, p. 187.

40 Hobbes, *Philosophical Rudiments*, ch. 9, p. 118.

41 On the implications of coverture, see Pateman, *Sexual Contract*, chs 5 and 6.

42 Chapman, "*Leviathan* Writ Small," n. 90 on p. 84.

43 Hampton, *Hobbes*, pp. 197–207, argues that his deduction of absolute sovereignty fails precisely because Hobbes makes self-protection an absolute right. But because she takes no account of Hobbes's patriarchalism, she fails to mention that, if the argument about sovereignty in the state is correct, then conjugal sovereignty fails too.

44 Hobbes, *Leviathan*, ch. 17, p. 158.

45 Ibid., ch. 16, p. 151.

46 Ibid., ch. 22, pp. 221–2.

47 R. W. K. Hinton, "Husbands, Fathers and Conquerors," *Political Studies*, 15, 1967, pp. 294, 299.

48 For an argument that absolutist conclusions are ultimately unavoidable, see Carole Pateman, *The Problem of Political Obligation*, 2nd edn (Cambridge: Polity;

Berkeley and Los Angeles: University of California Press, 1985), ch. 3. Hampton, *Hobbes*, interprets Hobbes's commonwealth as a union of slaves within the will of a master.

49 Hobbes, *Leviathan*, part IV, p. 706.

50 Mary Astell, *Some Reflections Upon Marriage*, from the 4th edn of 1730 (New York: Source Book Press, 1970), p. 107 (emphasis in the original).

4

Early Liberal Roots of Feminism: John Locke and the Attack on Patriarchy

Melissa A. Butler

In early seventeenth-century England, patriarchalism was a dominant world view.[1] It was a fully articulated theory which expressly accounted for all social relations – king–subject, father–child, master–servant, etc. – in patriarchal terms. Sir Robert Filmer and other patriarchal writers insisted that the king ruled absolutely, the divinely ordained father of his people. No one was born free; everyone was born in subjection to some patriarchal superior. Each individual human being could find his or her proper place by consulting patriarchal theory. Places were not matters of individual choice but were assigned according to a divinely ordained pattern set down at the Creation.

By the end of the seventeenth century, the patriarchal world view had crumbled. It was replaced by a new understanding of human nature and of social and political organization. Whigs such as Sidney, Tyrrell and Locke grounded political power in acts of consent made by free-born individuals. Contract and individual choice supplanted birth and divine designation as crucial factors in social and political analysis. These changes raised problems concerning the status of women in the new order. At first, liberal theorists resisted the suggestion that the old assigned position of women might have to be abandoned. The champions of consent theory saw no need to secure the consent of women. Yet their critics insisted that excluding women violated the very theory of human nature on which liberalism was based. Eventually, liberals would be forced to bring their views on women into line with their theory of human nature. This changing image of women certainly played a part in that shift in consciousness which paved the way for the sexual revolution.

The Statement of Patriarchy: Sir Robert Filmer

Full-blown patriarchal political theory was occasioned primarily by the turbulence of seventeenth-century English politics, but patriarchal ideas and intimations could be found in political writings long before they received more systematic theoretical expression in the writings of Sir Robert Filmer.[2]

In that era of "divine right kings," the legitimacy of a monarch's claim to absolute rule could be proved if the source of a divine grant of power could be found. Patriarchal political theory satisfied this need. It offered an explanation of the historical origins of the king's political power and of the subject's political obligation. By tracing the king's power back to Adam, the theory provided more than mere historical justification; it provided divine sanction.

The explanation derived its effectiveness from a general awareness of the obvious truth which patriarchalism told.[3] The patriarchal family experience was universal. The family patriarch was a universally-acknowledged authority figure with immense power. By linking the authority of the king with the authority of the father, a theorist could immediately clarify the nature of a subject's political obligations. Moreover, monarchical power grounded in patriarchal power took on the legitimacy of that least challengeable social institution, the family. The linkage of paternal and monarchical power provided a means for transcending any intermediate loyalties a subject might have. Absolute, patriarchal, monarchical power was vested in the king. It was to the king, not to the local nobility, that loyalty and obedience were rightfully owed.

Patriarchalists insisted that God, nature and history were on their side. For proof, one need only consult the Book of Genesis. Not only was Genesis divinely inspired, it was also the oldest possible historical source and the best guide to man's nature.[4] There, in the Genesis account, was the evidence that God had created Adam in His image – patriarch and monarch He created him.

The gradual unfolding of biblical history showed that the basic institution of patriarchy, the patriarchal family, had always been a fundamental feature of society. Throughout Judeo-Christian society, family life, bolstered by marriage and divorce laws, primogeniture and property rules, continued thoroughly patriarchal down to the seventeenth century.[5]

During the English Civil War, both divine right monarchy and the patriarchal theory which helped support it were severely challenged. In reaction to new and dangerous doctrines, Sir Robert Filmer penned the best-known treatises in defense of the patriarchal position, including *The Anarchy of a Limited or Mixed Monarchy* (1648), *The Freeholder's Grand Inquest*

(1648), and *Observations upon Aristotle, Touching Forms of Government* (1652). The work for which he is most remembered, *Patriarcha*, was begun around 1640, but was published posthumously in 1680.[6]

To elaborate his patriarchal theory of politics, Filmer turned to both classical and constitutional sources. But Filmer's most important, most authoritative source was always scripture. The scriptural arguments for monarchy illustrate the most literally patriarchal aspects of Filmer's thought. In brief, his account of the biblical origins and justifications of patriarchy was as follows:

> God created only Adam, and of a piece of him made the woman; and if by generation from them two as parts of them, all mankind be propagated: if also God gave to Adam not only the dominion over the woman and the children that should issue from them, but also over the whole earth to subdue it, and over all the creatures on it, so that as long as Adam lived no man could claim or enjoy anything but by donation, assignation, or permission from him.[7]

Again and again throughout his works Filmer recalled the divine grant of paternal, monarchical power to Adam. Filmer drew upon the Book of Genesis, specifically Genesis 1:28, when he claimed that "the first government in the world was monarchical in the father of all flesh."[8]

As critics from Filmer's own century were only too happy to observe, Sir Robert had erred in his biblical analysis. Filmer had assigned all power to Adam, but God had given dominion to Adam *and* Eve. The divine grant of power in Genesis 1:28 was made to "them," ostensibly the male and female whose creation had been announced in the preceding verse. Sir Robert had to tamper with the text because the original grant of power detailed in Genesis 1:28 was not, as he maintained, an exclusive grant of private monarchical dominion given to Adam, the patriarch. On the contrary, the blessing was given to both the male and the female.

If evidence for the patriarchal theory could not be found in God's blessing, perhaps it could be found in His curse. Filmer could have maintained that the lines of patriarchal authority were established after the Fall. Genesis 3:16 could have been offered as proof: "Thy desire shall be to thy husband, he shall rule over thee."

Indeed, in the *Anarchy*, Filmer did refer to these lines as proof that "God ordained Adam to rule over his wife . . . and as hers so all theirs that should come of her."[9] Nevertheless, Sir Robert preferred the Genesis 1:28 passage. By using that text, he could show that patriarchal order was in accord with man's original nature, not simply with his fallen nature. Filmer hoped to show that the human hierarchy was established in the *very* beginning. Each passing second made monarchical power appear less natural, and shared dominion more legitimate. Consequently, Filmer preferred to insist that Adam was monarch of the world from the very first moment of creation: "By the appointment of God, as soon as Adam was created he was monarch of the world, though he had no subjects; . . . Adam was a King from his creation . . . Eve was subject to Adam before he sinned; the angels who are of a pure nature, are subject to God."[10]

Genesis was not the only biblical source of patriarchal theory. The Decalogue, too, served to support patriarchal political authority, according to Filmer: "The power of the government is settled and fixed by the commandment of 'honour thy father'; if there were a higher power than the fatherly, then this command could not stand and be observed."[11] Filmer's omission is obvious. In service of political patriarchalism, the last half of the fifth commandment was dropped. All honor due to mother was forgotten.

Filmer and the Contract Theorists

Filmer's selective quotation was not overlooked by his critics. In the 1680s Whigs severely attacked *Patriarcha* by dredging up one biblical reference after another to prove Sir Robert had flagrantly abused scriptural texts to support his theory.[12] In the eyes of his fellow Englishmen who shared his world view, the only way Sir Robert could be refuted was by destroying his scriptural base.[13]

In the course of the seventeenth century, standards of evidence and styles of argument changed dramatically. Forms of argument which had been perfectly acceptable in earlier political discourse were rejected in favor of newer "rational" arguments. Although John Locke would champion the new mode of thought, the old form still had a hold on him. Locke took Filmer's biblical arguments seriously, as challenges to be met and overcome. Locke's attack on Filmer, though incomplete, gives the impression that once the biblical criticism was finished, he believed Filmer stood refuted and the attack on contract theory rebutted. This was not necessarily true.[14]

Filmer staunchly insisted that man was not by nature free. Rather, man was born to subjection: "Every man that is born is so far from being free-born that by his very birth he becomes a subject to him that begets him."[15]

By looking to the Garden of Eden, Filmer thought he could demonstrate the truth about natural man and his natural forms of association, but his assertion did not receive its force solely from the scriptural account. Sir Robert also relied on constitutional and classical sources to complement his biblical evidence. More importantly, however, his claims were strengthened by their apparent empirical relevance. The paternal power of the father and of the king was evident to all who would but look about them. So too, paternal power in a kingdom would remain constant: "There is and always shall be continued to the end of the world, a natural right of a supreme Father over every multitude."[16]

There was absolutely no room in patriarchal theory for free-born individuals. Government could not begin with an act of consent made by free and equal individuals in a state of nature. Filmer insisted that such government could be based on no more than myth. Furthermore, he insisted that contract theories which advanced such a myth would be replete with contradictions and logical fallacies.

Filmer offered a theory which was truly comprehensive and coherent, one which provided a place for every individual in society. His opponents, on the other hand, were far less able to provide a satisfactory accommodation for all the individuals and groups which made up seventeenth-century English society. They wished to destroy the patriarchal base of monarchy, and sever the connection between patriarchalism and divine-right politics, yet they were unable to reject less comprehensive forms of patriarchalism as basic organizing principles of government and society. They developed a new theory of human nature, but did not forsee or develop the implications of that theory.

Despite their criticisms of patriarchalism and their arguments based on consent, neither Edward Gee nor Algernon Sidney nor James Tyrrell, nor his friend, John Locke, were willing to allow participation to all comers. Tyrrell, for example, wished to limit participation to male property owners. Locke, as MacPherson argues, would have limited participation to the demonstrably rational (read "acquisitive") classes.[17] But these limitations were swept away by historical actualities over the next two centuries. Rights to political participation were gradually extended to all men and subsequently to all women. Indeed, Filmer rather than Locke or Tyrrell, proved the better predictor of the historical course plotted by the liberal logic when he wrote of government by the people:

> If but one man be excluded, the same reason that excludes one man, may exclude many hundreds, and many thousands, yea, and the major part itself; if it be admitted, that the people are or ever were free by nature, and not to be governed, but by their own consent, it is most unjust to exclude any one man from his right in government.[18]

No one could be excluded from political participation if contract theorists were to remain true to their principles. Filmer understood that in speaking of "the people" and their natural liberty, one had to talk about all mankind.

Though contract theorists came to consider their theories as logical or moral rather than as historical, Filmer used the historical problems of the social contract in an attempt to undermine the logical and moral status of the theory. Filmer insisted that the state of nature and the social contract became logically and historically unacceptable doctrines if "the people" were to be equated with "all mankind." Furthermore, he believed that contract theorists themselves would recoil when faced with the full implications of their theory.

Filmer demanded to know the details of the great meeting where the contract was approved. When did the meeting occur? Who decided the time and place? More importantly, he wanted to know who was invited. Filmer saw these as serious problems for consent theorists since:

> Mankind is like the sea, ever ebbing and flowing every minute one is born another dies; those that are the people this minute are not the people the next minute, in every instant and point of time there is a variation: no one time can be indifferent for all of mankind to assemble; it cannot but be mischevious always at least to all infants and others under the age of discretion; not to speak of women, especially virgins, who by birth have as much natural freedom as any other and therefore ought not to lose their liberty without their consent.[19]

Filmer's attack was no longer simply historical; it was now logical and moral as well. It was clear to him that if the "natural freedom" of mankind was to be taken seriously, obviously the natural freedom of women and children would have to be considered. If women and children were free, they would have to be included in any sort of compact. "Tacit consent" was an impossibility, and was rejected by Filmer as "unreasonable" and "unnatural." Simply to "conclude" the votes of children, for example, in the votes of parents would not be adequate:

> This remedy may cure some part of the mischief, but it destroys the whole cause, and at last stumbles upon the true original of government. For if it be allowed that the acts of the parents bind the children, then farewell the doctrine of the natural freedom of mankind; where subjection of children to parents is natural there can be no natural freedom.[20]

Filmer would probably have agreed that the same line of reasoning could be used to analyze the relationship of women to the social contract.

Filmer's technique in this instance was one of his favorites – *reductio ad absurdum*. His aim was to show the absurdity of the concept "consent of all the people." He insisted that "all the people" must be taken at face value. It must include groups of people generally accounted unfit for such decision making, that is, children, servants and *women*. Each of these groups had been accorded a place within the social and political theory of patriarchy. Each group's place was in accord with a traditional evaluation of its status.

Those who asserted the natural freedom of all mankind upset the applecart. If men were born free and equal, status could not be ascribed at birth, but would have to be achieved in life. If Filmer's opponents were to be consistent, new political roles would have to be opened up for those previously judged politically incompetent. This consequence was never fully clear to Filmer's critics. Though Tyrrell and Sidney criticized Filmer's patriarchalism, they were not ready to break with all the trappings of patriarchy. Consequently, they faced additional difficulties when they tried to account for the political obligation of the politically incompetent.

They maintained that the obligation of disenfranchised groups stemmed from their nurture, from the debt of gratitude owed to the government for their upbringing and education. Members of these groups had no actual voice and were themselves never expected to give free consent to their government. Yet still they were held to be obliged – out of gratitude.

This sort of obligation theory is not far removed from Filmer's. The natural duties of Filmer's king were "summed up in a universal fatherly care of his people."[21] The king preserved, fed, clothed, instructed, and defended the whole commonwealth. Government by contract would do the same things for those who were not part of the contract. In return for these services alone, political nonparticipants owed "a higher Obligation in conscience and gratitude." No participation, no express consent was necessary to put an end to their natural freedom.

A third problem was created for both Filmer and his critics when the questions of participation and monarchical succession were considered together. Filmer did not use patriarchal theory to challenge women's claims to the throne. His critics, especially Sidney, seized upon his silence, protesting that Filmer would allow even women and children to rule as patriarchs. Patriarchal theory enthroned "the next in Blood, without any regard to Age, Sex or other Qualities of the Mind or Body."[22]

Whig theorists did not render Filmer's arguments less damaging to their cause, but they did turn them back on patriarchal theory. To Filmer, contract theory was absurd because it entailed the participation of politically unfit groups in the formation of government and society. To Whigs, the patriarchal position was outrageous because it risked giving a single, similarly incompetent individual absolute unchecked dominion.

To summarize, both Whig and patriarchal theorists used the position of women as a critical tool in evaluating competing theories. Both Whig and patriarchal theorists had to find places for women in their theories. Each criticized the other for the role and status eventually assigned to women.

In effect, Whigs substituted a community of many patriarchs for Filmer's supreme patriarch. Filmer, the patriarch, realized immediately that this simple substitution alone was much less than was required by the doctrine of natural freedom of all mankind. Slowly, over the next two centuries, even liberal thinkers would be drawn to the same conclusion.

Locke's Attack on Patriarchy

While other Whig writers simply declared that their theories necessitated no new roles for women, John Locke treated the problem somewhat differently. He was among the first to sense the inherent contradiction in a "liberalism" based on the natural freedom of mankind, which accorded women no greater freedom than allowed by patriarchalism. New places had to be opened to women. This is not to claim that John Locke planned or even foresaw the feminist movement. It does seem true, however, that Locke took his individualist principles very seriously, even when they entailed an admission that women, too, might have to be considered "individuals."

Clearly Locke was not interested in creating a world in which all were equal; in his view, there would always be differences among individuals. The key question here concerns the extent to which a Lockean society would discriminate on the basis of sex. Would the fact that some are more equal than others necessarily be determined by traditionally assigned sex roles?

Filmer's patriarchal theory included a particular view of the status of women, based on biblical arguments, so Locke's refutation had to deal with that view. Concerning the benediction of Genesis 1:28, Locke noted that it was bestowed on "more than one, for it was spoken in the Plural Number, God blessed *them* and said unto *them*, Have Dominion. God says unto *Adam* and *Eve*, Have Dominion."[23] This argument introduced the possibility that Adam's dominion was not exclusive but was shared with Eve. Further, Eve's subjection to Adam need not have prevented her from exercising dominion over the things of the Earth. Eve, too, might have had property rights.

In the fifth chapter of the *First Treatise*, Locke argued against "Adam's title to Sovereignty by the Subjection of Eve." He took issue with Filmer's use of Genesis 3:16 ("And thy desire shall be to thy Husband and he shall rule over thee"). Those words, Locke objected, were a "punishment laid upon Eve." Furthermore, these words were not even spoken to Adam. The moment after the great transgression, Locke noted, "was not a time when Adam could expect any Favours, any grant of Priviledges from his offended Maker." At most, the curse would "concern the Female Sex only," through Eve, its representative.[24]

Here, Locke argued that Genesis 3:16 offered no evidence of a general grant of power to Adam over all mankind. By limiting the curse to Eve and to women, Locke effectively removed males from the sway of the patriarchal monarch. But he went even further, and suggested that the arguments for the subjection of women based on the Genesis 3:16 passage could be faulty.

First, the subjection of women carried no political import. The curse imposed "no more [than] that Subjection they [women] should ordinarily be in to their Husbands." But even this limit on women's freedom was not immutable and could be overcome:

> There is here no more Law to oblige a Woman to such a Subjection, if the Circumstances either of her Condition or Contract with her Husband should exempt her from it, then there is, that she should bring forth her Children in Sorrow and Pain, if there could be found a remedy for it, which is also part of the same Curse upon her.[25]

Nevertheless, Locke largely accepted the empirical fact of women's inferiority and saw it grounded in nature as ordered by God. He attempted to avoid the conclusion that Adam became Eve's superior or that husbands became their wives' superiors, yet his effort is fairly weak:

> God, in this Text, gives not, that I see, any Authority to Adam over Eve, or to Men over their Wives, but only foretells what should be the Woman's Lot, how by his Providence he would order it so, that she should be subject to her husband as we see that generally the Laws of Mankind and customs of Nations have ordered it so; and there is, I grant, a Foundation in Nature for it.[26]

Locke was principally interested in refuting the idea of a divine grant of authority to Adam. He lived in a world in which the subjection of women was an empirical fact and he willingly yielded to the contemporary view that this fact had some foundation in nature. His tone was hesitant, though. Locke seemed to wish that God had not been responsible for women's inferior status. He tried to cast God in the role of prophet rather than creator. God merely "foretold" what women's lot would be. Locke found it difficult to keep God in the role of innocent bystander, however. Where Locke admitted the use of divine power, he tried to remain tentative: God, in his Providence, "would order" social relations so that wives would be subject to their husbands. But God did not give men any kind of rightful authority over women. Locke implied that God merely suggested one empirical relationship which was subsequently adopted by mankind and reinforced by the laws and customs of nations. That these laws and customs were largely established by males did not, in Locke's opinion, damage the case. It did not seem to bother him that such laws and customs offered proof of the authority which men exercised over women.

Locke simply wished to deny that male authority was exercised by virtue of some divine grant. At this point, he had no need to reject the customary exercise of such authority. It was enough to show only that it was human and not divine in origin.

Peter Laslett notes that "Locke's attitude towards the curse on women in childbearing is typical of his progressive, humanitarian rationalism."[27] But Locke's views on women were also evidence of his individualism. Though Locke believed there was a "foundation in nature" for the limitations on women, he remained faithful to the individualist principles which underlay his theory. In his view, women were free to overcome their natural limitations; each woman was permitted to strike a better deal for herself whenever possible.

In conjunction with his attack on Filmer's use of Genesis 3:16, Locke touched another of patriarchy's soft spots. He sensed the weakness of Filmer's insistence on women's inferiority in a nation where women had worn the crown. Locke made no sustained analysis of this point, but remarked, instead, "[will anyone say] that either of our Queens *Mary* or *Elizabeth* had they Married any of their Subjects, had been by this Text put into a Political Subjection to him? or that he thereby should have had Monarchical Rule over her?"[28]

Locke also accused Sir Robert of performing procrustean mutilations of "words and senses of Authors".[29] This tendency was most evident in Filmer's abbreviation of the fifth commandment. Filmer cited the command throughout his works, always in the same terms, "Honour thy Father." Locke noted this and complained that "and Mother, as Apocriphal Words, are always left out." Filmer had overlooked the "constant Tenor of the Scripture," Locke maintained. To bolster his position, Locke produced over a dozen scriptural citations showing the child's duty to father *and* mother. A mother's title to honor from her children was independent of the will of her husband. This independent right, he argued, was totally inconsistent with the existence of absolute monarchical power vested in the father.[30] Ultimately, Locke denied that the fifth commandment had any political implications at all.[31]

In this analysis, Locke broke with one of patriarchy's strongest traditions. Political obligation had been justified through the fifth commandment. In seventeenth-century sermon literature and catechism texts, the subject's duty of obedience was firmly rooted in this command. Locke refuted these arguments, not by rejecting scriptural evidence, but by analyzing the interpretations supposedly based on that source.

This completed the destructive part of Locke's case. His attack rent the fabric of Filmer's theory. Since patriarchalism represented a complete, integrated theory of society, an adequate successor theory would have to replace all its shattered parts. If all social relations could no longer be

understood through the patriarchal paradigm, how could they be understood? Locke's answer came in the *Second Treatise*. There he made his
positive contribution to the understanding of social relations.

Social Relations in the *Second Treatise*

For Filmer and his sympathizers there was only one type of power:
paternal power. This power was, by its nature, absolute. Filmer's simplistic,
uncluttered view of power fits in perfectly with his analysis of social
relations. Filmer admitted only one kind of social relationship: the paternal
relationship. Each member of society was defined by his or her relation to
the patriarchs of the family and of the nation.

Locke, however, maintained that there were many kinds of power and
many types of social relations. He analyzed several nonpolitical relationships including those of master–servant, master–slave, parent–child, and
husband–wife.[32] Each of these forms of association was carefully distinguished from the political relationship of ruler–subject. Two of the nonpolitical relationships, namely the parental and the conjugal, reveal a
great deal about the status of women in Lockean theory.

From the very outset of the discussion of the parent–child relation,
Locke rejected the terminology of patriarchy, claiming that "[paternal
power] seems so to place the Power of Parents over their Children wholly
in the Father, as if the Mother had no share in it, whereas if we consult
Reason or Revelation, we shall find she hath an equal Title. . . . For
whatever obligation Nature and the right of Generation lays on Children,
it must certainly bind them equal to both the concurrent Causes of it."[33]

The basic argument at the root of his terminological objection was one
familiar from the *First Treatise*. Patriarchal theory could not stand if power
were shared by husband and wife. As Locke argued in the *Second Treatise*,
"it will but very ill serve the turn of those Men who contend so much for
the Absolute Power and Authority of the *Fatherhood*, as they call it, that the
Mother should have any share in it."[34]

Locke's examination of the conjugal relationship demanded a more
extensive analysis of the roles and status of women in society. He described
conjugal society as follows:

> *Conjugal Society* is made by a voluntary Compact between Man and Woman:
> tho' it consist chiefly in such a Communion and Right in one another's
> Bodies, as is necessary to its chief End, Procreation; yet it draws with it
> mutual Support and Assistance, and a Communion of Interest too, as
> necessary not only to unite their Care, and Affection, but also necessary to
> their common Off-spring, who have a Right to be nourished and maintained
> by them, till they are able to provide for themselves.[35]

Conjugal society existed among human beings as a persistent social relationship because of the long term of dependency of the offspring and further because of the dependency of the woman who "is capable of conceiving, and *de facto* is commonly with Child again, and Brings forth too a new Birth long before the former is out of a dependency."[36] Thus the father is obliged to care for his children and is also "under an Obligation to continue in Conjugal Society with the same Woman longer than other creatures."[37]

Though the conjugal relationship began for the sake of procreation, it continued for the sake of property. After praising God's wisdom for combining in man an acquisitive nature and a slow maturing process, Locke noted that a departure from monogamy would complicate the simple natural economics of the conjugal system.[38] Though conjugal society among human beings would be more persistent than among other species, this did not mean that marriage would be indissoluble. Indeed, Locke wondered "why this *Compact*, where Procreation and Education are secured, and Inheritance taken care for, may not be made determinable, either by consent, or at a certain time, or upon certain Conditions, as well as any other voluntary Compacts, there being no necessity in the nature of the thing, nor to the ends of it, that it shall always be for life."[39]

Locke's tentative acceptance of divorce brought him criticism over 100 years later. Thomas Elrington commented that "to make the conjugal union determinable by consent, is to introduce a promiscuous concubinage." Laslett notes that Locke was prepared to go even further and suggested the possibilities of lefthand marriage.[40] In Locke's view, the actual terms of the conjugal contract were not fixed and immutable: "Community of Goods and the Power over them, mutual Assistance and Maintenance, and other things belonging to *Conjugal Society*, might be varied and regulated by that Contract, which unites Man and Wife in that Society as far as may consist with Procreation and the bringing up of Children."[41] Nevertheless, Locke described what he took to be the normal distribution of power in marital relationships: "The Husband and Wife, though they have but one common Concern, yet having different understandings will unavoidably sometimes have different wills, too; it therefore being necessary, that the last Determination, *ie.* the Rule, should be placed somewhere, it naturally falls to the Man's share, as the abler and the stronger."[42] Clearly all forms of patriarchalism did not die with Filmer and his fellows. Here, the subjection of women is not based on Genesis, but on natural qualifications. Nature had shown man to be the "abler and stronger." Locke's patriarchy was limited, though. The husband's power of decision extended only to those interests and properties held in common by husband and wife. Locke spelled out the limits on the husband's power:

[His power] leaves the Wife in the full and free possession of what by Contract is her Peculiar Right, and gives the Husband no more power over her Life, than she has over his. The *Power of the Husband* being so far from that of an absolute monarch that the *Wife* has, in many cases, a Liberty to *separate* from him; where natural Right or their Contract allows it, whether that Contract be made by themselves in the state of Nature or by the Customs or Laws of the Country they live in; and the Children upon such Separation fall to the Father or Mother's lot, as such contract does determine.[43]

In addition, Locke distinguished between the property rights of husband and wife. All property in conjugal society was not automatically the husband's. A wife could have property rights not subject to her husband's control. Locke indicated this in a passage on conquest: "For as to the Wife's share, whether her own Labour or Compact gave her a Title to it, 'tis plain, her Husband could not forfeit what was hers."[44]

There were several similarities between the conjugal and the political relationship. Both were grounded in consent. Both existed for the preservation of property. Yet conjugal society was not political society because it conferred no power over the life and death of its members. In addition, political society could intervene in the affairs of conjugal society. Men and women in the state of nature were free to determine the terms of the conjugal contract. But in civil society these terms could be limited or dictated by the "Customs or Laws of the Country."

The extent to which the participants in the parental and conjugal relationships could also participate in political relationships remains to be considered. We may gain some insight into the matter by following Locke's route, that is, by tracing the origins of political power from the state of nature.

To Locke, the state of nature was a "state of perfect Freedom" for individuals "to order Actions and dispose of their Possessions, and Persons, as they think fit." Furthermore, Locke also described the state of nature as:

A *State* also of Equality, wherein all the Power and Jurisdiction is reciprocal, no one having more than another: there being nothing more evident, than that Creatures of the same species and rank promiscuously born to all the same advantages of Nature and the use of the same faculties should also be equal one amongst another without Subordination or Subjection, unless the Lord and Master of them all should by any manifest Declaration of his Will set one above another.[45]

Because of certain inconveniences, men quit the state of nature to form civil society through an act of consent. It was in criticizing the formation of society by consent that Filmer's theory was most effective. Indeed,

Locke found it difficult to show how free and equal individuals actually formed civil society. Ultimately he was forced to admit that the first political societies in history were probably patriarchal monarchies. He described the historic origins as follows:

> As it often happens, where there is much Land and few People, the Government commonly began in the Father. For the Father having by the Law of Nature, the same Power with every Man else to punish his transgressing Children even when they were Men, and out of their Pupilage; and they were very likely to submit to his punishment, and all joyn with him against the Offender in their turns, giving him thereby power to Execute his Sentence against any transgression . . . [the] Custom of obeying him, in their Childhood made it easier to submit to him rather than to any other.[46]

In this passage, Locke lumped paternal power and natural power together, allowed for the slightest nod of consent, and – presto – civil society emerged. Even in a Lockean state of nature, paternal (parental?) power could be effective. Children growing up in the state of nature were under the same obligations to their parents as children reared in civil society. What of natural freedom and equality? Locke confessed:

> *Children* are not born in this full state of *Equality*, though they are born to it. Their parents have a sort of Rule and Jurisdiction over them when they come into the World, and for some time after, but 'tis but a temporary one. The Bonds of this Subjection are like Swadling Cloths they are wrapt up in and supported by in the weakness of their Infancy. Age and Reason as they grow up, loosen them till at length they drop quite off, and leave a Man at his own free Disposal.[47]

Of course, once children reached maturity in the state of nature they no longer owed obedience to their parents, but were merely required to honor them out of simple gratitude. At this stage, however, Locke introduced another sort of power to support the father's claim to his child's obedience – namely that power which accrued to every man in the state of nature, the power to punish the transgressions of others against him. But the father's power was reinforced by his children's longstanding habit of obedience to him. In the state of nature, the father's commands to his mature children received added weight and legitimacy because he *was* their father. His children would recognize this legitimacy and would join their power to his to make him lawmaker. At this point, it seems, the father's former paternal power and his existing natural power were transformed by consent into political power.

In this discussion, Locke was willing to concede the historical or anthropological case for patriarchalism. He was not ready to concede the moral case, however. Filmer had tied his moral and historical arguments together by using the Book of Genesis as the source of both. Locke split the two cases apart. Locke's biblical criticisms were intended to demonstrate the weakness of the moral conclusions which Filmer had drawn from the Genesis creation account. Thus, at best, Filmer was left with only an historical case. But, Locke insisted, history was not the source of morality. He wrote that "an Argument from what has been, to what should of right be, has no great force."[48] Instead, he broke with history and based his moral theory on a new understanding of human nature. In doing so, however, he reopened questions closed by Filmer's theory. Locke had to deal with the political roles and status of women, children and servants. He was somewhat sensitive to Filmer's criticisms concerning the place of these politically unfit groups within contract theory. He certainly tried to make a consistent explanation of the relationship of children to civil society; "We are *born Free*, as we are born Rational; not that we have actually the Exercise of either: Age that brings one brings with it the other too. And thus we see how natural *Freedom and Subjection to Parents* may consist together and are both founded on the same Principle."[49] No immature child could be expected to take part in the social compact. Yet children's inability to participate in politics would not preclude their right to consent to government when they reached adulthood. Locke indicated the necessity of each person giving consent as a condition of full political rights and full political obligation. Grown sons were free to make their own contract as were their fathers before them. An individual could not be bound by the consent of others but had to make a personal commitment through some separate act of consent.

But what of women? Unlike Tyrrell and Sidney, Locke remained silent on the specific question of their participation in the founding of political society. Of course, it is possible Locke referred to the role of women in the lost section of the *Treatises*. Or, perhaps Locke understood that explicit exclusion of women seriously weakened a theory grounded in the natural freedom of mankind. Yet Locke was also a good enough propagandist to have realized how deeply ingrained patriarchalism was in everyday life. Locke had criticized Filmer's use of the fifth commandment – "Honor thy father" – as a basis for political obligation. If the command were taken seriously, he charged, then "every Father must necessarily have Political Dominion, and there will be as many Sovereigns as there are Fathers."[50] But the audience Locke was addressing was essentially an audience of fathers, household heads and family sovereigns. Locke had freed them from political subjection to a patriarchal superior – the king. He did not risk alienating his audience by clearly conferring a new political status on their subordinates under the patriarchal system, that is, on women. Nevertheless, despite the absence of any sustained analysis of the problem of women, we may draw some conclusions from an examination of Locke's scattered thoughts on women.

Though Locke gave the husband ultimate authority within conjugal society, this authority was limited and nonpolitical. Yet when Locke's account of the husband's conjugal authority was combined with his account of the historical development of political society, several questions occur which were never adequately resolved in Locke's moral theory. Did not the award of final decision-making power to the father and husband (in conjugal society) transform "parental power" into "paternal power"? Was the subsequent development of political power based on paternal power a result of that transformation? What was woman's role in the establishment of the first political society? Since her husband was to be permitted final decisions in matters of their common interest and property, and since political society, obviously, was a matter of common interest, would her voice simply be "concluded" in that of her husband? If so, then Filmer's question recurs – what became of her rights as a free individual? Did she lose her political potential because she was deemed not as "able and strong" as her husband? If this were the case, Locke would have had to introduce new qualifications for political life. ·

Locke portrayed political society as an association of free, equal, rational individuals who were capable of owning property.[51] These individuals came together freely, since none had any power or jurisdiction over others. They agreed to form a civil society vested with power to legislate over life and death, and to execute its decisions in order to protect the vital interests of its members, that is, their lives, liberties and estates. Yet John Locke was certainly no believer in the absolute equality of human beings. Indeed, on that score, he was emphatic:

> Though I have said . . . *That all Men by Nature are equal,* I cannot be supposed to understand all sorts of *Equality; Age* or *Virtue* may give Men a just Precedency: *Excellence of Parts and Merit* may place others above the Common Level; *Birth* may subject some and *Alliance* or *Benefits* others, to pay an Observance to those whom Nature, Gratitude, or other Respects may have made it due.[52]

But these inequalities in no way affect an individual's basic freedom or political capacity, for Locke continued in the same passage:

> yet all this consists with the *Equality* which all Men are in, in respect of Jurisdiction or Dominion one over another, which was the *Equality* I there spoke of, as proper to the Business in hand, being that *equal Right* every Man hath, *to his Natural Freedom,* without being subjected to the Will or Authority of any other Man.[53]

If "Man" is used as a generic term, then woman's natural freedom and equality could not be alienated without her consent. Perhaps a marriage contract might be taken for consent, but this is a dubious proposition. Locke had indicated that a marriage contract in no way altered the political capacity of a queen regnant.[54] While decision-making power over the common interests of a conjugal unit belonged to the husband, Locke admitted that the wife might have interests apart from their shared interests. Women could own separate property not subject to their husbands' control. If a husband forfeited his life or property as a result of conquest, his conquerors acquired no title to his wife's life or property.

Did these capacities entitle women to a political role? Locke never directly confronted the question; nevertheless, it is possible to compare Locke's qualifications for political life with his views of women. Locke used the Genesis account to show that women possessed the same natural freedom and equality as men. Whatever limitations had been placed on women after the Fall could conceivably be overcome through individual effort or scientific advance. Furthermore, women were capable of earning through their own labor, of owning property and of making contracts.

Locke and the Rational Woman

The one remaining qualification for political life is rationality. For Locke's views on the rationality of women it will be necessary to turn to his other writings, notably his *Thoughts on Education*.

In the published version of his advice on education, Locke mentioned that the work had been originally intended for the education of boys; but he added that it could be used as a guide for raising children of either sex. He noted that "where difference of sex requires different Treatment, 'twill be no hard Matter to distinguish."[55]

Locke felt that his advice concerning a gentleman's education would have to be changed only slightly to fit the needs of girls. However, in a letter to a friend, Mrs Edward Clarke, Locke tried to show that his prescriptions were appropriate for her daughter and not unnecessarily harsh.[56] On the whole, Locke believed that except for "making a little allowance for beauty and some few other considerations of the s[ex], the manner of breeding of boys and girls, especially in the younger years, I imagine, should be the same."[57]

The differences which Locke thought should obtain in the education of men and women amounted to slight differences in physical training. While Locke thought that "meat, drink and lodging and clothing should be ordered after the same manner for the girls as for the boys," he did introduce a few caveats aimed at protecting the girls' complexions.[58]

Locke introduced far fewer restrictions in his plan for a young lady's mental development. In a letter to Mrs Clarke he wrote: "Since, therefore I acknowledge no difference of sex in your mind relating . . . to truth, virtue, and obedience, I think well to have no thing altered in it from what is [writ for the son]."[59]

Far from advocating a special, separate and distinct form of education for girls, Locke proposed that the gentleman's education should more closely resemble that of young ladies. For example, he favored the education of children at home by tutors. Modern languages learned through conversation should replace rote memorization of classical grammars. In addition, Locke suggested that young gentlemen as well as young ladies might profit from a dancing master's instruction.

Taken as a whole, Locke's thoughts on education clearly suggest a belief that men and women could be schooled in the use of reason. The minds of both men and women were blank slates to be written on by experience. Women had intellectual potential which could be developed to a high level.

Locke's educational process was designed to equip young men for lives as gentlemen. Since the gentleman's life certainly included political activity, a young man's education had to prepare him for political life. If a young lady were to receive the same education, it should be expected that she, too, would be capable of political activity.

Finally, 300 years ago, Locke offered a "liberated" solution to a controversy which still rages in religious circles – the question of the fitness of women to act as ministers. In 1696 Locke, together with King William, attended a service led by a Quaker preacher, Rebecca Collier. He praised her work and encouraged her to continue in it, writing, "Women, indeed, had the honour first to publish the resurrection of the Lord of Love; why not again the resurrection of the Spirit of Love?"[60] It is interesting to compare Locke's attitude here with the famous remark made by Samuel Johnson on the same subject in the next century: "Sir, a woman's preaching is like a dog's walking on his hindlegs. It is not done well; but you are surprized to find it done at all."[61]

Perhaps a similar conclusion might be reached about the roots of feminism in Lockean liberalism. In a world where political antipatriarchalism was still somewhat revolutionary, explicit statements of more far-reaching forms of antipatriarchalism were almost unthinkable. Indeed, they would have been considered absurdities. Thus, while Filmer had presented a comprehensive and consistent patriarchal theory, many of his liberal opponents rejected political patriarchalism by insisting on the need for individual consent in political affairs but shied away from tampering with patriarchal attitudes where women were concerned. John Locke was something of an exception to this rule. Though his feminist sympathies certainly did not approach the feminism of Mill writing nearly two centuries later, in view of the intense patriarchalism of seventeenth-century England, it should be surprising to find such views expressed at all.

Notes

1 On patriarchalism as a world view, see Gordon J. Schochet, *Patriarchalism and Political Thought* (New York: Basic Books, 1975); also, W. H. Greenleaf, *Order, Empiricism, and Politics* (London: Oxford University Press, 1964)¸ chs 1–5; Peter Laslett's introduction to Sir Robert Filmer, *Patriarcha and other Political Works of Sir Robert Filmer*, ed. Peter Laslett (Oxford: Basil Blackwell, 1949), p. 26; and John W. Robbins, "The Political Thought of Sir Robert Filmer," Ph.D. dissertation, The Johns Hopkins University, 1973.

2 Patriarchal strains may be found in the literature of the sixteenth century including John Knox, *First Blast of the Trumpet Against the Monstrous Regiment of Women* (Geneva, 1558); James I in *The Trew Law of Free Monarchies* (1598); Richard Field, *Of the Church* (1606). Patriarchal theorists among Filmer's contemporaries included John Maxwell who wrote *Sacro-Sancta Regum Majestas or the Sacred and Royal Prerogative of Christian Kings* (Oxford, 1644); and James Ussher, *The Power Communicated by God to the Prince, and the Obedience Required of the Subject* (written ca. 1644, first published 1661, 2nd edn, London, 1683); and Robert Sanderson, in his preface to Ussher's work.

3 Peter Laslett, *The World We Have Lost* (New York: Scribner's, 1965), passim; Greenleaf, *Order, Empiricism and Politics*, pp. 80–94; Peter Zagorin, *A History of Political Thought in the English Revolution* (New York: Humanities, 1966), pp. 198–9.

4 On the use of scripture in historical argument see J. G. A. Pocock, *The Ancient Constitution and the Feudal Law* (Cambridge: Cambridge University Press, 1967), pp. 188–9.

5 See especially Greenleaf, *Order, Empiricism and Politics*, p. 89; also Julia O'Faolain and Lauro Martines, eds, *Not in God's Image* (New York: Harper Torchbooks, 1973), pp. 179–207; and Schochet, *Patriarchalism*, p. 16.

6 See Filmer, *Patriarcha and Other Political Works*, ed. Laslett.

7 Ibid., 241.

8 Ibid., 187.

9 Ibid., 283.

10 Ibid., 289.

11 Ibid., 188.

12 See, for example, Edward Gee, *The Divine Right and Original of the Civil Magistrate from God* (London, 1658); [James Tyrrell], *Patriarcha Non Monarcha* (London: Richard Janeway, 1681); and Algernon Sidney, *Discourses Concerning Government* (London, 1698).

13 Arguments had to be structured to persuade the widest possible audience. For an exploration of this general problem, see Mark Gavre, "Hobbes and his Audience," *American Political Science Review*, 68, December 1974, pp. 1542–56.

14 Laslett concluded that "neither Locke nor Sidney nor any of a host of others who attacked *Patriarcha* ever attempted to meet the force of [Filmer's] criticisms [about political obligation], and that none of them ever realized what he meant by his naturalism." Filmer, *Patriarcha and Other Political Works*, introduction, p. 21.

15 Ibid., 232.

16 Ibid., 62.

17 C. B. MacPherson, *The Political Theory of Possessive Individualism* (London: Oxford University Press, 1962), ch. 5; and MacPherson, "The Social Bearing of Locke's Political Theory," *Western Political Quarterly*, 7 March 1954, pp. 1–22.

18 Filmer, *Patriarcha and Other Political Works*, 211.

19 Ibid., 287.

20 Ibid., 225, 287.

21 Ibid., 63.

22 Algernon Sidney, *Discourses Concerning Government* (London, 1698), p. 4.

23 John Locke, *Two Treatises of Government*, ed. Peter Laslett (Cambridge: Cambridge University Press, 1960), p. 29.

24 *Two Treatises*, I, 45–7.

25 Ibid., I, 47.

26 Ibid.

27 Ibid., ed. Laslett, p. 210n.

28 Ibid., I, 47.

29 Ibid., I, 60.

30 Ibid., I, 63.

31 Ibid., I, 65.

32 See especially R. W. K. Hinton, "Husbands, Fathers, and Conquerors," *Political Studies*, 16 February 1968, pp. 55–67; Geraint Parry, "Individuality, Politics and the Critique of Paternalism in John Locke," *Political Studies*, 12 June 1964, pp. 163–77; and MacPherson, *Possessive Individualism*.

33 Locke, *Two Treatises*, II, 52.

34 Ibid., II, 53.

35 Ibid., II, 78.

36 Ibid., II, 80.

37 Ibid.

38 Ibid.

39 Ibid., II, 81.

40 Ibid., ed. Laslett, p. 364n.

41 Ibid., II, 83.

42 Ibid., II, 82.

43 Ibid.

44 Ibid., II, 183.

45 Ibid., II, 4.

46 Ibid., II, 105.

47 Ibid., II, 55.

48 Ibid., II, 103.

49 Ibid., II, 61.

50 Ibid., I, 65.

51. See MacPherson, *Possessive Individualism*, ch. 5. MacPherson argues that Locke assumed a class differential in the distribution of these qualities. Full membership in political society would be limited to those who fully demonstrated them. The question under consideration here is the extent to which this class differential might also be a sex differential.

52 Locke, *Two Treatises*, II, 54.

53 Ibid.

54 Ibid., I, 47.

55 John Locke, *Some Thoughts Concerning Education*, section 6; also, see Locke to Mrs Clarke, Jan. 7, 1683/4, in *The Correspondence of John Locke and Edward Clarke*, ed. Benjamin Rand (Cambridge: Harvard University Press, 1927).

56 Locke to Mrs Clarke, Jan. 7, 1683/4, in *Correspondence*, ed. Rand, p. 121.

57 Locke to Mrs Clarke, Jan. 1, 1685, in ibid.

58 Locke to Mrs Clarke, in ibid., p. 103.

59 Locke to Mrs Clarke, in ibid., pp. 102–3.

60 Locke to Rebecca Collier, Nov. 21, 1696, reprinted in H. R. Fox Bourne, *The Life of John Locke*, vol. 2 (New York: Harper and Row, 1876), p. 453.

61 E. L. McAdam and George Milne, eds, *A Johnson Reader* (New York: Pantheon Books, 1964), p. 464.

5

Rousseau and Modern Feminism

Lynda Lange

Introduction

Jean-Jacques Rousseau has often been charged with inconsistency, despite his own assertion that all his writing is informed by the same principles.[1] Recently, however, there has been a different sort of charge of inconsistency. It is claimed that his spirited opposition to sexual equality is grossly inconsistent with his defence of equality for all citizens.[2] On the other hand, the conservative Allan Bloom, who claims to detect consistency in his approach to women and men, finds him a stay of contemporary antifeminism.[3] I propose an interpretation of Rousseau which is different from both of these perspectives. In my view, Rousseau is basically consistent in his treatment of men and women, despite a few discrepancies. However, writing as a feminist, I believe his views can be studied to advantage by feminists. Rousseau addresses almost every social issue that contemporary feminism is concerned with, and he does this in a manner which proves on examination to be surprisingly relevant to present problems, whether one agrees with his precise conclusions or not. With regard to sexual equality, it is possible to "turn Rousseau on his head," in a manner of speaking.

The theory of women's nature and their role in society which I shall present has been developed on the basis of ideas and insights found in many works of Rousseau. The years 1756 to 1759, immediately following the writing of the First and Second Discourses, saw Rousseau's production of a large body of work devoted to a great extent to the relations of the sexes and the nature and role of women. His major work on the subject is found in *Julie ou la nouvelle Héloïse*, the *Lettre à M. D'Alembert sur les spectacles*, and *Emile ou de l'éducation,* all written during this period. Book V of *Emile,* on the education of women, was written before the other books of that work, immediately after the *Lettre à M. d'Alembert.* Prior to this period, some footnotes in the Second Discourse, as well as the philosophical anthropology concerning the origin of the family in that work, show that this subject had earlier been of interest to Rousseau as well. In other words, it is not peripheral to his central work as a political philosopher, even from his own point of view.

Rousseau was a severe critic of what he regularly referred to as *la société civile.* It is my view that *la société civile,* as Rousseau pictures it, has the main features of capitalism, or "possessive market society," as it is modelled by C. B. Macpherson.[4] Just as Macpherson demonstrated that the work of Hobbes, Locke, and others had the effect of justifying the crucial features of "possessive market society" by showing that their assumptions and conclusions conformed to that model of society, and not by showing that they had a concept of "possessive market society," I believe that Rousseau's criticism applies to that model, but not that he actually perceived the emergence of capitalism out of feudalism. The view that Rousseau's criticisms are applicable to a certain form of civil society, and not to civil society *per se,* bridges the gap between the vitriolic criticism of "civil society" in the early discourses, and the ideal of a good and legitimate society present later in *Du Contrat Social.*

All the evils of modern civil society, according to Rousseau, are derived ultimately from the fact that personal or particular interest (*l'intérêt personnel, l'intérêt particulier*) is the dominant rationale for action. What is worse, according to Rousseau, is that society is structured in such a way as to make this type of behavior rational in the circumstances. For Rousseau, the incompatibility of this with our authentic interests, and its deeply corrupting effect on our moral character, only appear after a thorough study of nature and history.

Feminist ideas were widely discussed in prerevolutionary France, but Rousseau thought that the idea that the sexes might *both* operate on these modern principles and that women should not be denied the right to advance their particular interests as men do was one of the most absurd and lamentable consequences of this modern philosophy. It is in this area that I find his views insightful and potentially instructive. It has been a theme of feminist criticism that the opposition of interests, exploitation, competition, and so on, endemic to our social and economic system, are, in some sense, male values. Yet because these values *are* endemic, they tend to shape feminism in their mold, and may be perfectly compatible with a lack of social discrimination between the sexes. It is another question, however, whether these individualist principles are ultimately useful to *democratic* feminism. This essay addresses these concerns through an examination of Rousseau's works.

Origins and Foundations of Sexual Inequality

According to Rousseau, and contrary to contractarian theory, the innate drive for self-preservation (*amour de soi*) does not, in itself, suggest any necessary opposition of interests. The gradual development of inter-dependence and entrenched inequality of power and wealth transform the expression of the drive for self-preservation into rational egoism, or *amour propre*. Since all develop these same concerns, their interests are necessarily in constant opposition. It is frequently apparent that Rousseau's views on women are a response to feminist arguments, and he was a severe critic of these arguments, in a manner which was consistent with his general criticism of individualist thought.[5]

In Book V of *Emile*, Rousseau states the following essential difference between the moral potential of men and women:

> The Supreme Being wanted to do honour to the human species in every-thing. While giving man inclinations without limit, He gives him at the same time the law which regulates them, in order that he may be free and in command of himself. While abandoning man to immoderate passions, He joins reason [*la raison*] to these passions in order to govern them. While abandoning woman to unlimited desires, He joins modesty [*la pudeur*] to these desires in order to constrain them.[6]

The functions of these virtues, it may be noted, have a difference that corresponds to the difference in their character. The man "controls" or "governs" (*gouverner*) his own behavior with the use of reason; the woman merely "restrains" hers (*contenir*).[7]

While the man under the sway of *amour propre* may be thought to display his human potential for rationality in a corrupted form, the woman so swayed is sharply deflected from her unique human virtue of modesty. How has Rousseau concluded that there are such great differences between the sexes? It is done, surprisingly enough, in a manner which appears on analysis to be determinedly empiricist. Contrary to expectation, Rousseau does not rely on custom, prejudice, or God's will in the course of his attempt to justify a unique and inferior feminine role for women. It is probably because he uses these modern methods that Rousseau's theories of feminine and masculine social roles have remained influential even to the present.

In the *Discours sur l'origine et les fondements de l'inégalité* (Second Discourse), and in *Emile*, Rousseau's method is that of philosophical anthropology, and he even uses a type of argument found in contemporary evolutionary biology. This putatively scientific approach seems to him to justify the quick inference of a principle with vast consequences. It is one which is only too familiar to the contemporary reader, but by no means evidently true: "the man should be strong and active; the women should be weak and passive."[8] The different biological contributions of the sexes to their common aim (*l'objet commun*) of reproduction dictates this principle, according to Rousseau. Equal strength and self-assertion are inconsistent with the reproductive biology of each sex. This argument concerns *homo sapiens* in the pure state of nature, prior to the development of any specifically human culture or society. From a biological point of view, for procreation to occur, Rousseau writes, "One must necessarily will and be able; it suffices that the other put up little resistance."[9]

In another direct response to feminist debate, he argues that it is scarcely natural that men and women should enter with equal boldness on a course of action that has such very different consequences for each of them.[10] This response, however, presumes that the woman in the state of nature knows the consequences of sexual interaction for herself, which is at least debatable given what Rousseau says about the total inability of *homo sapiens* to formulate ideas or project expectations in the pure state of nature.[11]

Is sheer physical domination of women by men then natural? No. In the pure state of nature men are not very aggressive about anything, including sex, and natural compassion (*pitié*) is undiminished. We may suppose that a rebuff, or flight, or even a display of fear on the part of a woman would probably be sufficient to discourage an unwanted partner in the pure state of nature. Most importantly, honor is not at stake for men. According to Rousseau, the violence and incessant competition commonly attributed to male sexuality are a result of the knowledge and pride of *amour propre* developed in social relations. They are not "natural."

The timidity and weakness of the woman, according to Rousseau, inspire her to be pleasing to a man out of the basic impulse of self-preservation, that is if she is pleasing she is less likely to be violent. Rousseau thinks this behaviour simultaneously makes the man more inclined to remain with her (an important consideration if one has given up one's autonomy). These are the means she is given to supplement her weakness, and therefore, to act to please men is a quality of women directly derivable from nature. Rousseau writes:

> If woman is made to please and to be subjugated, she ought to make herself agreeable to man instead of arousing him. Her own violence is in her charms. . . . From this there arises attack and defence, the audacity of one

sex and the timidity of the other, and finally the modesty and the shame with which nature armed the weak in order to enslave the strong.[12]

However, as we have seen, these responses, based on natural compassion (*pitié*), are corrupted by the individualistic society of *amour propre*. If within civil society the man is stronger and dependent on the women only through desire, as Rousseau claims, whereas she depends on him through desire and need,[13] why should he bother to please her, and refrain from simply exercising his will? Rousseau has provided two answers to this question in *Emile*, concerning women and men in what Rousseau considers a good society.

The first argument is that real violence in sexual relations is contrary to its own ends since it is a declaration of war which may result in death, whereas the goal of sexual relations is the perpetuation of the species. This is clearly a restraint which is based on sophisticated rationality. Rousseau believes that it is reason that restrains masculine sexuality, and it is noteworthy that it is not the mode of rational egoism which is said to be the restraint in question. The goal of sexual relations is here defined as a collective goal of the species, rather than in terms of individual self interest.

The other argument is related to the ultimately conventional character of paternity. It is that "a child would have no father if any man might usurp a father's rights."[14] This is meant to be a consideration that a *man* might use to govern his own behavior, and is once again a collective, rather than a purely individual, motive. However, from a feminist perspective, this is a surprisingly explicit admission of male solidarity opposed to women, rather than of fully social motivation.[15] Here Rousseau tips on his head quite easily!

As we have seen, the male-dominated family is not a purely natural phenomenon for Rousseau, inasmuch as he does not suppose it to be present in the pure state of nature. In the speculative history of the Second Discourse, women are depicted in the state of nature as able to provide for themselves and their dependent children. It is a momentous development for humanity when increasing population drives some to less balmy climates where they are motivated to learn to build permanent shelters. Rousseau writes:

> The habit of living together gave rise to the sweetest sentiments known to men: conjugal love and paternal love. Each family became a little society all the better united because reciprocal affection and freedom were its only bonds; and it was then that the first difference was established in the way of life of the two sexes, which until this time had had but one. Women became more sedentary, and grew accustomed to tend the hut and the children, while the men went to seek their common subsistence.[16]

Though able to meet her own needs when solitary, the woman is assumed to be weaker than the man, so that living together is assumed to result in a division of labor.[17] It also results in more frequent pregnancy, which is thought to entrench the dependence of the woman on the man. The man, though quite insensible to love in the state of nature and utterly ignorant of his connection to children, is thought to become attached to both woman and children through constant association. This response is similar to that of the woman in the state of nature, who is thought to care for her offspring because she grows fond of them "through habit."[18] However, there is a crucial philosophic difference, which is a good example of the way in which thought may be shaped by male bias. The woman's attachment to her dependent offspring is "natural" in the fullest sense of the word: it could be said to be merely instinctive, since it is presumed to occur when human beings live exactly like animals. Paternal affection, however, is said to be a significant development, the result of socialization, and based on a rather abstract knowledge.

As such, paternity is a product of human artifice, based on knowledge and custom, and therefore, according to this philosophy, specifically human in a way that maternal love is not thought to be. Because of this, paternity will not be treated as a disqualification for the highest forms of human artifice, namely, political life and rational discourse. Allegedly natural maternity, on the other hand, is typically treated as such by political theorists, including Rousseau. This difference has important implications for the structure of Rousseau's political philsophy. For the moment, however, we will confine our discussion of this issue to the terms of Rousseau's own theory.

The sexual division of labor which appears as a result of the association of the sexes is not simply the result of practical cooperation for Rousseau, but a reflection of the essential difference between the sexes. The woman is so constituted that passivity and timidity are assets to her "proper purpose" (*leur destination propre*) once social relations have developed. This purpose is to reproduce within a family whose unity depends entirely on her behavior. Natural passivity and timidity in sexual relations, according to Rousseau, form the natural base for modesty (*la pudeur*) which is the specifically feminine virtue in civil society.

Modesty is the virtue which may ensure biological paternity of the children to the man she lives with, and the necessity Rousseau sees for this dictates the retiring and wholly domestic life of good women. "She serves as the link between them and their father; she alone makes him love them and gives him the confidence to call them his own."[19] On account of the artificiality and apparent fragility of the bond of the father to his children, the woman is required to live a life dictated by the necessity to appear respectable, that is, to convince her husband and everyone else that she is sexually monogamous. Nothing less than this degree of certitude, bolstered by public opinion, is thought to be sufficient to induce him to remain attached to that particular family and provide for its support.

> By the very law of nature women are at the mercy of men's judgments, as much for their own sake as for that of their children. It is not enough that they be estimable; they must be esteemed. It is not enough for them to be pretty; they must please. It is not enough for them to be temperate; they must be recognized as such. Their honor is not only in their conduct but in their reputation; and it is not possible that a woman who consents to be regarded as disreputable can ever be decent.[20]

The wholly incompatible bases of masculine and feminine virtue are summed up in the following sentence from *Emile*: "Opinion is the grave of virtue among men and its throne among women."[21]

This abandonment of moral autonomy for women is particularly damning from Rousseau, who considers such autonomy essential not only for citizenship, but even for true humanity.[22] That the male-headed family requires women to abandon moral autonomy functions without alteration as a severe criticism of that institution.

Rousseau does not leave himself completely exposed to empirical refutation concerning the nature of women. In the *Lettre à M. d'Alembert sur les spectacles*, he writes:

> Even if it could be denied that a special sentiment of chasteness was natural to women, would it be any the less true that in society their lot ought to be a domestic and retired life, and that they ought to be raised in principles appropriate to it? If the timidity, chasteness, and modesty which are proper to them are social inventions, it is in society's interest that women acquire these qualities.[23]

Thus although Rousseau does not argue that the male-headed biological family is natural and unaffected by history, he does argue that it is nevertheless a social institution that may be grounded on nature by reason. He writes: "When woman complains on this score about unjust man-made inequality, she is wrong. This inequality is not a human institution – or at least, it is the work not of prejudice but of reason."[24] This type of willingness to come to grips with a "tough necessity" still seems to be bracing to conservative antifeminists!

It is of philosophic significance that virtuous women in civil society are characterized as closer to "nature" than virtuous men. The men must be transformed and denatured in a good society, according to Rousseau.[25] The modest woman appears still as little more than uncorrupted. As such she will form a necessary link between the supreme artifice of the good society on the one hand, and nature, on the other.

The Problem of Female Power

According to Rousseau, the social equality of the sexes poses a serious danger to civic virtue. His view of this danger is based on the critical analysis of modern "civil society," especially the concept of *amour propre*. It is Rousseau's belief that if women attempt to act in society according to the norms of *amour propre*, engaging in constant competition to further their "particular interest," they will inevitably be bested by the men. But this does not signify his admiration for the success of the male within that mode of social interaction.

The basic inequality of Rousseau's approach appears, however, in his belief that the woman who enters public life on the terms of *amour propre* does even more violence to her nature than the man caught up in that mode of interraction.

In the *Lettre à M. d'Alembert*, Rousseau argues at great length that one of the major reasons why there ought not to be a theatre established at Geneva is that this will result in women going out in public in company with men. Because of the very nature of sexual relations, according to Rousseau, the presence of women in public life undermines masculine excellence and exacerbates *amour propre*. The frequent attendance of men and women at public entertainments will focus attention on the natural impulses of the sexes to be pleasing to one another. While this is an expansion of the domain of women, since love is their "empire," it diminishes men. This occurs because the standards of behavior appropriate to love and courtship are inevitably feminine standards, given Rousseau's view of female power. According to Rousseau, men who lead a life of constant association with women become enervated and weak.[26] Such men will be far more prone to turn their learning or talent to the pleasing performance arising from *amour propre*, rather than to the rigorous, or morally challenging, pursuit of truth, since they will inevitably compete with one another for feminine approbation. He writes: "By themselves, the men, exempted from having to lower their ideas to the range of women and to clothe reason in gallantry, can devote themselves to grave and serious discourse without fear of ridicule."[27] Why these "grave and serious" intellectuals should be such an easy prey to ridicule is probably a question best answered by feminists over a few drinks at the faculty club. It does not seem to occur to Rousseau that the importance of the feminine role for the good society is rather dicey if there is this degree of tension between the masculine and feminine spheres. From the perspective he presents, a presumed seductive power of women to impose their standards, on account of the nature of sexual relations, enables women to dominate even in areas which are thought to be ultimately beyond their competence. It appears in the Second Discourse, and in *Emile*, that "love" may have been the original stimulus to the appearance of *amour propre*, even though it quickly lost sight of its origin. At the beginning of the "state of savagery," when people first settled in shelters of their own making, they were soon seduced by the pleasures of social life:

> People grew accustomed to assembling in front of the huts or around a large tree; song and dance, true children of love and leisure, became the amusement or rather the occupation of idle and assembled men and women. Each one began to look at the others and to want to be looked at himself, and public esteem had a value . . . that was the first step toward inequality and, at the same time, toward vice. From these first preferences were born on one hand vanity (*la vanité*)[28] and contempt, on the other shame and envy; and the fermentation caused by these new leavens eventually produced compounds fatal to happiness and innocence.[29]

In civil society, according to Rousseau, the consequences of the combination of *amour propre* and "love" as a value in itself (that is, unconnected to duty) are morally disastrous. According to him, this is an important reason why women should be confined to the sphere of their true competence: childcare, household tasks, and "rest and recreation" for men. Regarding the actual mental capacity of women, Rousseau does what is rare for him – he confuses a social artifact with a natural quality, a lack of education and opportunity for development, with an inherent deficiency.

Much of what Rousseau writes concerning the desirability of a separate feminine sphere centers around the evils to be thus avoided, and the harshness of his strictures are no doubt partly constructed out of his fear of female power. There is, however, a substantive contribution which can be made to the good of society by women, according to Rousseau, one which is an essential feature of a truly legitimate society governed by the general will.

The Foundation of the Good Society is Built out of Women

The contribution women make to a good society by playing a feminine role has ramifications for virtually every issue in moral and political life, according to Rousseau. The scheme he presents also includes a fully developed romantic ideal of the relations of the sexes, presented in a very complete form in *Julie ou la Nouvelle Héloïse*, and to a lesser extent in *Emile* in Book V dealing with the education of women. Nevertheless, the place of the feminine role in Rousseau's political philosophy may be focused around two basic themes. These are:

1 The need for the family and its particular attachments as a natural
   base for patriotism (*amour de la patrie*), and hence as a nursery for good
   citizens; and,
2 The need for certainty of paternity in connection with the requirements
   of the institution of private property.

Regarding the first of these themes, it is apparent that it concerns
education in the widest sense of the term, which is to say, the whole
socialization of citizens. It is not surprising, therefore, that Rousseau
addresses this issue most directly in his work on education, *Emile*. Like
Plato, he puts correct education at the very foundation of the good society.
The contractarian solution to the conflict between individual self-interest
and the existence of the civil state, which is to attempt a logical identification
of the two in the terms of enlightened self-interest, was rejected by Rousseau
as an inadequate foundation of political right.[30]

Rousseau fields a third alternative in which he attempts to sustain the
materialist epistemology which was a philosophically progressive element
in early contractarian theory. It is the injunction not to obey the law
because it is rational (though it ought to be in fact rational), but to love it,
and thus bring into harmony particular and public interest. This emotional
leap is what makes possible the transcendence of *amour propre* required for
the determination of the general will.

It is Rousseau's belief that those who are incapable of loving those near
to them and who have no particular attachments will be even less capable
of the love of their country and its laws or of any sacrifice for the common
good. Particular affective relationships are an essential part of the personal
development of the citizen for Rousseau, and play a foundational role in
civil society. Although the virtue of citizens consists in a conformity of the
individual will to the general will, which may in principle be justified by
reason, Rousseau places a great deal of emphasis on the necessity for
appropriate feeling to make such a civil state possible in fact. Mere
abstract principles, he argues, even if backed by force, will never be
enough to prevent individual self-interest from undermining the state. He
recommends patriotism (*amour de la patrie*) as the most efficacious means of
raising the sights of individuals from self-interest to the good of the state,
for "we willingly want what is wanted by the people we love."[31] Patriotism,
therefore, is not an abstract principle for Rousseau, but an active sentiment which promotes the type of personal development needed to create
citizens.

Even supposing the average citizen were a philosopher, according to
Rousseau, this would not solve the problem of sustaining the general will
in a good state. Reason, because of what it is, is cosmopolitan in its
outlook. Patriotism is therefore ultimately based on a lie, though a "noble

lie," if you will. The shared customs and religion that give a nation cohesion, when regarded dispassionaely and objectively, cannot be shown to be any better in reality than those of any other nation. But each nation, according to Rousseau, needs emotional loyalty from its citizens, rather than mere approval of its authority on the basis of reason.

It is the same with the family. As Allan Bloom puts it, we would think it monstrous if a man neglected his own children in favor of some others he thought superior.[32] The strong claim is that these loyalties are arbitrary – accidents of history. This is why, according to Rousseau, philosophers make poor kinsmen and citizens.

Particular affective relations in the family are therefore a foundation for particular affective relations to a given state. The relation of mother and child is the prototype of particular attachment, whether considered in relation to the philosophic history Rousseau provides in the Second Discourse, or in relation to the development of the individual within the civil state. It is the human relationship that precedes all others, for the species and for the individual. As we have seen, it provides the link between children and artificial paternity. Without a feminine role grounded on motherhood, the family, viewed from within this model, loses its unique quality of being a human artificial institution which incorporates natural relations. Losing that, it can no longer function as a "natural base" for the development of *amour de la patrie* and hence civic virtue.

In addition to the need for a family as a natural base for the development of *amour de la patrie*, Rousseau needs a mechanism to ensure certainty of paternity for the inheritance of property. In spite of Rousseau's criticism of bourgeois individualism, there is no doubt that from Rousseau's point of view private property is an inviolable requirement of civil life. In *Emile* he writes: "The unfaithful woman . . . dissolves the family and breaks all the bonds of nature. In giving the man children which are not his, she betrays both. She joins perfidy (*perfidie*) to infidelity. I have difficulty seeing what disorders and what crimes do not flow from this one." To the husband, a child not his own represents "the plunderer of his own children's property."[33]

Much of the force of this may be traced to the theme already presented – that the family is not a family unless united in the manner described by the woman's playing a correct feminine role. It is only necessary to establish a link between this and property.

In spite of Rousseau's criticism of economic inequality, as well as other forms of inequality, he never moves toward the view that private property ought to be done away with. Whatever other reasons there may be for Rousseau's repeated insistence that private property is a basic, even a "sacred" right, the male-headed private family has a basic inexorable economic requirement: it requires to have its subsistence in the form of private property in control of the male head of the family. This is necessary because the family is not "private" if the mode of acquisition, use, and disposal of its subsistence and surplus do not meet the basic requirements of the institution of private property; and it is not male-headed unless these rights and duties are centered on the husband and father.

The Transformation of Natural Qualities by Social Relations

The Pure State of Nature	The State of War (There may or may not be a bogus social contract)	Legitimate Civil State
Emotional autonomy	*Amour propre*	Moral liberty
Practical autonomy	Master/slave relations	Equality
Self-preservation	Particular or personal interest	Virtue (conformity of the particular will to the general will)
Female weakness and sexual timidity	Sexual manipulation or pseudo-masculinity	Modesty
Male sexual spontaneity	Compulsive and violent sexuality, domination of unsuccessful female manipulators	Male sexual spontaneity, governed by reason and knowledge
Spontaneous compassion (*pitié*)	(All but destroyed)	Patriotism friendship romantic love

It is clear that Rousseau's ideal family is made up of a male provider and a dependent wife and children, so that the basic requirement of privacy is met. Family privacy, because of the way it particularizes the individual's relations to certain others, is necessary, as we have seen, for the particular attachments so important to the early development of citizens and for the provision of a link between nature and social life. On the other hand, an equal distribution of private property among men is seen as necessary for the autonomy of the male head of the family in relation to other males. The particularlity of his relation to his family would collapse if he did not have unique responsibilities and rights in relation to them.

From Nature to Virtue

In his treatment of the nature of the sexes, Rousseau's principles and method are precisely the same as what he exhibits in connection with all his important claims concerning human nature. The structure of his views can be shown to be parallel to that of his views of the natural man and citizen (see table). A natural quality is transformed by social relations. It may be corrupted by bad social relations, a process which occurs as the "golden age" of savagery degenerates into civilized social relations dominated by particular interests and *amour propre*. This process results in the development of a state of war like that of Hobbes, that is, one in which the interests of each individual are opposed to the interests of every other individual. This state, according to Rousseau, may or may not be characterized by a bogus social contract which primarily serves the interests of the rich.[34] Alternatively, a good civil society ruled by the general will would make possible the development of the uniquely human potential of these natural qualities.

Democratic Feminism

Reading Rousseau helps to provoke thoughts as to what sort of social arrangements would be most conducive to sexual equality. In particular, it challenges the liberal individualist view that women's liberation can be furthered primarily by means of the removal of legal and social obstacles to the advancement of individual women.

In a period when political philosophy was still preoccupied with the new ideal of equality before the law, Rousseau leapt ahead to the insight that where there is objective inequality, virtually any law helps the powerful and harms the less powerful.[35] Therefore, no legal system can morally reform the relations of men and women so long as there is social and economic inequality of the sexes, or general social and economic inequality. So long as women are socially and economically unequal to *each other*, and occupy the society of individualism and *amour propre*, relations between the sexes will be either patriarchal, or competitive and manipulative. In view of the differences in physical strength, this would also undoubtedly include continued male violence against women.

Rousseau's analysis of the particular interest and *amour propre* of social inequality reveals the pitfalls of attempting the integration of women, on the same footing as men, into an unequal, competitive, society. Particular interest and the consciousness of *amour propre* militate against the abandonment of male attempts to dominate women, and also against the abandonment of sexual manipulation of men by women. Reading Rousseau makes it clear that in possessive individualist society, it is imprudent to abandon any potential source of power over others. It is therefore very unlikely that moral improvement can occur without basic social change.

Rousseau contended that women who demand equality with men usually do not abandon the feminine wiles that pressupose inequality. They attempt to play two incompatible roles, and as a result succeed at neither.[36] He wrongly thought that the continued inequality of women despite substantial sentiment in favor of their equality was the result of inferior capacity, but the hampering effects of contradictory role-playing remain as Rousseau perceived them.

Despite some substantial sentiment in favour of the equality of women in the present age, and in spite of some legal and economic reforms, for most women, particularly if they want children, dependence on a particular man remains their best option for a livelihood. Sexual monogamy and other adherence to his wishes remains part of the price they pay. If we were to extend Rousseau's philosophy of moral autonomy to women, it appears that these cannot be truly *moral* choices unless and until women have personal autonomy. The male-dominated family is therefore an immoral institution which corrupts its members and is inimical to the development of a good society. It is clear, for example, that men resist reform of the abuses of sexism to a large extent because they do not want to lose their personal privileges based on power over women. At the same time, women are often afraid to resist sexism because of their dependence on men. It also should not be forgotten that the sexual division of labor between public and private spheres is undemocratic even in the relatively narrow, liberal individualist, sense of "democracy," never mind Rousseau's more thoroughgoing sense of egalitarianism. It prevents women from participating in public discourse as autonomous citizens with the freedom to speak out about social reforms.

But so long as women and men live together with any degree of intimacy and privacy, will even economic equality and legal restraint be enough to prevent masculine violence against women from continuing to be a common occurrence? It is suddenly apparent that the lack of opportunity for sharing housework and childcare is not the only reason why women are worse off the more individualistic a society is. More communal ways of life may give women more security and freedom from personal oppression than the social relations of private property and an atomized private life. From the perspective of feminist criticism, Rousseau's theory shows very clearly the links between private property, individualism, and male domination of women. The male head of the family requires private property in order to have a private sphere within which to control the female.

The present law in Western countries concerning masculine violence against women displays a deepseated ambivalence in the political will of its makers. It is against the law for a man to attack a women with whom he lives, yet enforcement is feeble for a number of reasons. One is the lack of genuine autonomy on the part of women, sufficient to be able to make use of legal remedies for harm. Another is the high value placed on the retention of a private sphere, on personal freedom in intimate relations, and on the use and disposal of private property. To make the injunction against masculine violence unambivalent would represent not only a fundamental change in the social relations of the sexes, but also significant social change in general.

Yet many communal societies have exhibited serious sexual inequality. The potential of more communal ways of life is greater enforcement of *desirable* norms in hitherto private areas of life. So the problem, finally, is still the choice of egalitarian norms of sexual and reproductive behavior.

On account of the unique characteristics of the relations between the sexes, democratic feminism is a force for basic social change. But law is only an aspect of this. Law which opposes the physical force of individual men with yet greater force, and which reaches a long arm into the home even as far as the bedroom, is a necessary, but not a sufficient, condition for material sexual equality.

Reading Rousseau serves two functions. First, because he was a modern thinker, he was and still remains useful to antifeminism. For this reason reading him is an exercise in "knowing the enemy." However, he understands very clearly many aspects of the structure of male dominance, which from the critical perspective of feminism function as effective criticisms of that system, often virtually without revision. The second, and larger, message for feminist thinkers in this study is that they cannot afford to do less than examine the whole of the social structure, for any attempt to examine the relations of men and women in isolation from other questions may be very misleading.

Since the early 1980s, grass roots and socialist feminism in North America have suffered marginalization, while liberal individualist feminism has institutionalized itself, and presented itself as if it *is* feminism. Some individual women have made stellar careers for themselves within institutionalized feminism, but women's condition in general has benefited little from it. Considering Rousseau's epigraph to the First Discourse, from Horace, it may also happen to feminists that: "We are deceived by the appearance of right."

Notes

1 "J'ai écrit sur divers sujets, mais toujours dans les même principes." "Lettre à Beaumont" (1762), in Jean-Jacques Rousseau, *Oeuvres Complètes*, ed. B. Gagnebin and M. Raymond (Paris: Editions de la Pleiade, 1959–), vol. 4, p. 928.
2 Work on this subject includes: Susan Moller Okin, *Women in Western Political*

Thought (Princeton, NJ: Princeton University Press, 1979); Nannerl O. Keohane, "But For Her Sex . . . the Domestication of Sophie", and Lynda Lange, "Women and the General Will", both in *Trent Rousseau Papers*, ed. MacAdam, Neumann, Lafrance (Ottawa: University of Ottawa Press, 1980); and Eva Figes, *Patriarchal Attitudes* (London: Panther, 1972), p. 105.

3 Allan Bloom, introduction to Jean-Jacques Rousseau, *Emile: Or, On Education*, trans. and annotated Allan Bloom (New York: Basic Books, 1979).

4 C. B. MacPherson, *The Political Theory of Possessive Individualism* (London: Oxford University Press, 1962), p. 53.

5 My interpretation of Rousseau substantiates the claim of C. E. Vaughan that Rousseau attacked individualism "in its theoretical stronghold." Vaughan, introduction, *Political Writings of Rousseau* (Cambridge: Cambridge University Press, 1915).

6 *Emile*, trans. Bloom, p. 359.

7 Rousseau, *Oeuvres Complètes*, vol. 4, p. 695.

8 *Emile*, trans. Bloom, p. 358.

9 Ibid., p. 358. Compare Sigmund Freud, "Femininity," in his *New Introductory Lectures on Psychoanalysis*, trans. and ed. James Strachey (New York: W. W. Norton, 1965): "it is our impression that more constraint has been applied to the libido when it is pressed into the service of the feminine function . . . And the reasons for this may lie – thinking once again teleologically – in the fact that the accomplishment of the aim of biology has been entrusted to the aggressiveness of men and has been made to some extent independent of women's consent" (pp. 179–80).

10 *Emile*, trans. Bloom, p. 359.

11 Jean-Jacques Rousseau, *Discourse on the Origin and Foundations of Inequality* (Second Discourse), ed. Roger D. Masters, trans. Roger D. and Judith R. Masters (New York: St Martin's Press, 1964), p. 117.

12 *Emile*, trans. Bloom, p. 358.

13 Ibid., p. 364.

14 Ibid., p. 359.

15 These observations of Rousseau appear to be a remarkable substantiation of the theory of reproduction in Mary O'Brien, *The Politics of Reproduction* (Boston and London: Routledge and Kegan Paul, 1981).

16 Second Discourse, trans. Masters, pp. 146–7.

17 The "naturalness" of a sexual division of labor is widely assumed. Even Marx, who infers no "natural" inequality of the sexes as a result, *assumes* this, rather than concluding it after reflection or investigation. See, for example, *Capital*, vol. I, part 4, ch 14, section 4; and *The German Ideology*, part A.

18 Second Discourse, trans. Masters, p. 121.

19 *Emile*, trans. Bloom, p. 361.

20 Ibid., p. 364.

21 Ibid., p. 365.

22 Jean-Jacques Rousseau, *On the Social Contract*, Book I, ch. 8.

23 Jean-Jacques Rousseau, *Politics and the Arts: Letter to M. d'Alembert on the Theatre*, trans. Allan Bloom (Ithaca, NY: Cornell University Press, 1977), p. 87.

24 *Emile*, trans. Bloom, p. 361.

25 "Forced to combat nature or the social institutions, one must choose between making a man or a citizen, for one cannot make both at the same time." Ibid. On the Legislator, essential to the founding of a good society, he writes: "One who dares to undertake the founding of a people should feel that he is capable of changing human nature, so to speak; of transforming each individual . . ." *On the Social Contract*, Book II, ch. 7.

26 *Letter to M. d'Alembert*, trans. Bloom, p. 103.

27 Ibid., p. 105.

28 It is *la vanité*, and not, as yet, *amour propre*. Rousseau, *Oeuvres Complètes*, vol. 3, p. 170.

29 Second Discourse, trans. Masters, p. 149.

30 See, for example, the first version of *Du Contrat Social* (Geneva manuscript), in *On the Social Contract*, ed. Roger D. Masters, trans. Judith R. Masters (New York: St Martins Press, 1978), p. 158.

31 *Political Economy*, in *On the Social Contract*, ed. Masters, p. 218.

32 Interpretative essay, in Plato, *Republic* (New York: Basic Books, 1968), p. 385.

33 *Emile*, trans. Bloom, p. 361.

34 Second Discourse, ed. Masters, pp. 159–60.

35 "Under bad governments, this equality is only apparent and illusory. It serves merely to maintain the poor man in his misery and the rich in his usurpation. In fact, laws are always useful to those who have possession and harmful to those who have nothing." *On the Social Contract*, trans. Masters, p. 58.

36 *Emile*, trans. Bloom, p. 364.

6

"The Oppressed State of My Sex": Wollstonecraft on Reason, Feeling and Equality

Moira Gatens

Still harping on the same subject you will exclaim – How can I avoid it, when most of the struggles of an eventful life have been occasioned by the oppressed state of my sex: we reason deeply when we forcibly feel.

Mary Wollstonecraft, *Letter XIX*, in Janet Todd,
A Wollstonecraft Anthology

Reason and feeling is the governing dichotomy and the source of the major conflicts in Mary Wollstonecraft's work and in her life. It is her concentration on this dichotomy and her obvious faith in the power of reason to reform sociopolitical life that places her firmly within the Enlightenment tradition. Yet, because she is concerned to address the specificity of female social and political existence, her treatment of the reason/feeling distinction inevitably conjures up its partners: the nature/culture and private/public distinctions. Enlightenment philosophers were able to treat man's political possibilities without (explicit) reference to sexuality, reproduction, the family and the domestic sphere because these matters were assumed to fall outside the public realm of politics. Certainly, the political body assumes the private sphere, which underpins public life, but this sphere is taken to be the natural base of political life. Any consideration of women's access to or place in the public sphere necessarily raises the question of their role in the private sphere.

Whereas Enlightenment philosophers argued that political authority is artificial and conventional they assumed that relations between the sexes and within the family are based on natural authority. Wollstonecraft argued against this assumption in favour of a conception of reason as the sole authority in all matters and in all spheres. Her insistence on the role of reason, in all areas of human life, created paradoxes in her application of Enlightenment notions of equality that she was unable to resolve. Eighteenth-century notions of equality were articulated specifically in connection with the public sphere. Men, as husbands/fathers, presumably did not want (or need) to assert the principles of equality in the private sphere since this would, in fact, be acting against their interests. One of Wollstonecraft's major aims is to insist that the power and authority that men wielded in the private sphere was as artificial as the authority of royalty and aristocracy in the sphere of politics. She sees clearly that liberating women from political oppression is not simply a matter of political enfranchisement, since they are also subjected in the private sphere. This makes Wollstonecraft's task far more complex than the task that confronted the political philosophers who were concerned only with men's political rights.

Another major aim of Wollstonecraft's writings is to insist that the natural rights of men are human rights. Therefore women, no less than men, are entitled to political equality and representation. It is in her articulation of this claim that Wollstonecraft strikes paradox after paradox. In her attempt to extend liberal principles of equality to women she neglects to note that these principles were developed and formulated with men as their object. Her attempt to stretch these principles to include women results in both practical and conceptual difficulties. These principles were developed with an (implicitly) male person in mind, who is assumed to be a head of a household (a husband/father) and whose domestic needs are catered for (by his wife). Although the citizen is not explicitly male, the assumed characteristics of the citizen coincide with those of a husband/ father. No matter how strong the power of reason, it cannot alter the fact that male and female embodiment, at least as lived in eighteenth-century culture, involved vastly different social and political consequences. Wollstonecraft did not take sufficient account of these consequences in her call for the realization of the rights of women. Women's (traditional) labor is not even visible in the public sphere. It does not count as socially necessary work and is not acknowledged in any system of public exchange. This point is no less relevant in our contemporary context where the equality that women are entitled to, for example in the sphere of employment, is limited to activities which overlap with male activities. Those aspects of women's lives that bear on female specificity were, until very recently, completely ignored: for example, sexual harassment, maternity, childcare, and so on. Wollstonecraft's tendency to treat the role of wife/mother/ domestic worker as one which follows directly from women's biology raises further problems for a feminist analysis of women's social and political status.

The tendency to conceive of women's bodies as complicit in their social and political oppression has certainly been a feature of much contemporary feminist writing. Wollstonecraft was able to tolerate the paradoxes of liberal theory in a way that contemporary feminist theory, at least from the time of Simone de Beauvoir, cannot. This intolerance has caused a marked rift in feminist responses to women's place in contemporary society. On one side are those like Shulamith Firestone[1] who advocate the use of science to effectively "neuter" the female body. Woman can thus truly become a "rational man." On the other, theorists like Carol McMillan[2] see this corporeal denial as anti-woman and argue that difference does not necessarily involve relations of inferiority/superiority. Men and women, she argues, are different and have necessarily different roles, but these roles are of equal value.

The source from which these two responses flow is clearly present in Wollstonecraft's writings. Both views locate the cause of women's social role in her body. This assumption must be challenged on at least two levels. First, feminists must challenge the notion inherited from Cartesian dualism that human beings are separable into two neat bundles: a neutral, universal mind; and a sexed body. Second, we must challenge the imputed "naturalness" of the form and capacities of the female body along with the idea that this form determines the scope of female social being. The converse proposition – that social and political arrangements curtail or impede the form and capacities of the female body – must also be considered. This must be done not simply in order to allot primacy to the social but rather to bring out the complexity of the relationship between the biological and the social.

In this paper these issues are brought to bear on Wollstonecraft's struggle with the reason/feeling distinction. *A Vindication of the Rights of Woman* and *The Wrongs of Women, or Maria* will be examined in the light of Wollstonecraft's attempts to work through the power of both reason and feeling in women's lives. The progressive sophistication with which Wollstonecraft analyzes the complexities of women's social and political position may be linked to the increasing social and political complexity in the progress of her own life. Various commentators have railed against the legitimacy of referring to Wollstonecraft's personal life in the context of appraising her work. Given the close kinship between her life and her politics, the subject matter of much of her writings and her own lived experience, it seems appropriate to at least indicate the links between her intellectual development and her biography. For one thing this approach allows the contemporary reader to ponder the relation between an eighteenth-century feminist's analysis of her social and political context and the exigencies of a life that was lived in that context. Wollstonecraft's life was certainly a struggle and undeniably eventful. She lived through one of the most turbulent and politically unstable times in our recent past. She was vocal in the movement which sought to restore to "men" their natural rights; she was adamant that women also possessed natural rights and natural equality; and she spent some time in France during the revolution. Wollstonecraft also bore two children, had two significant heterosexual relationships, attempted suicide twice, and wrote prolifically. Much of what she wrote is concerned to expose and remedy the social and political injustices experienced by women. However, her work as a whole displays a passionate rejection of oppression in general, regardless of its specific form.

Her first major work of political importance is *A Vindication of the Rights of Men* (1790). This text carries the distinction of being the first published response to Edmund Burke's *Reflections on the Revolution in France* (1790). The dynamics of her response are governed by the dichotomy of reason and sentiment. Burke's lauding of tradition and hereditary rights and his dogmatic insistence on the conservation of existing rigid political relations are all treated by Wollstonecraft as evidence of his lack of reason. Instead of using his rational capacity – which would reveal to him the natural rights and natural equality of all "men" – he allows his sentiments, his passions and his feeling to dominate his political thinking. For Wollstonecraft it is the preponderance of sentiment in political thought that gives rise to nostalgia and social stagnation, which act to impede the dynamic and progressive nature of sociopolitical life. Moreover, the sentiment displayed by Burke and his kind is riddled with hypocrisy. The romanticism of his conception of a hierarchically ordered political system is belied by the profligacy and corruption of the rich, the degradation of the poor and their appalling conditions of life. It is reason and not sentiment that should dictate the terms of political life and what any person's rational capacities will show is that "The birthright of Man . . . is such a degree of liberty, civil and religious, as is compatible with the liberty of every other individual with whom he is united in a social compact, and the continued existence of that compact."[3] Burke is not only guilty of irrationality, hypocrisy and impeding the progress of civilization, he is also complicit in reneging on the terms of the social compact and so represents a threat to its continuing existence. Wollstonecraft thus relocates the responsibility for political unrest with the conservatives.

The social and political status of women is not central to the concerns of
A Vindication of the Rights of Men. Nevertheless, Wollstonecraft is careful to
insist that women, no less than men, are parties to the social compact.
Their sociopolitical rights and duties are not, however, identical with
those of men. It is the part of the rational woman to "superintend her
family and suckle her children, in order to fulfil her part of the social
compact."[4] This difference between the sexes in fulfilling the compact will
be treated further when we turn to *A Vindication of the Rights of Woman*. At
this stage Wollstonecraft seems content to understand women's rights as
implicit in the genus of men's rights, appending comments which bear on
women's specificity – childbearing, for example – when necessary. Her
naiveté is, perhaps, explicable by the context in which she was then living,
working and thinking. At the time of the writing of *A Vindication of the
Rights of Woman* (1792) Wollstonecraft was single and part of a (predominantly male) intellectual milieu which included William Blake,
Thomas Paine, William Godwin and Henry Fuseli. This group was in-
toxicated with the idea of social reform and exhibited the boundless
optimism typical of the Enlightenment. Yet they, no less than the general
reading public, were inclined to understand the rights of man as being just
that, the rights of men. This is the context in which Wollstonecraft
resolves to write specifically on the question of women's rights.

A Vindication of the Rights of Woman presents an argument for an enlightened
understanding of human nature which stresses that women, no less than
men, share in this nature. The result is a text that is plagued with
contradictions and irresolvable tensions. Again, the overriding tension is
that between reason and sentiment. The tension between these two terms
is present in her treatment of friendship versus sexual passion, the socially
responsible family versus the sensual couple; the respectable mother versus
the degraded concubine. As Cora Kaplan has observed, it is as if Wollstonecraft sees sexuality and pleasure as special dangers to women, as
"narcotic inducements to a life of lubricious slavery."[5] Wollstonecraft's
amulet against the temptations of sensuality is, of course, reason.

A Vindication of the Rights of Woman is not so much an appeal to women's
reason – which she takes to be obscured by a culture which encourages the
exaggerated development of women's sentiment, feeling and passion – as
it is an appeal to men's reason. The addressee, as Anca Vlasopolos
convincingly argues,[6] is male. It is pertinent to recall that *A Vindication of
the Rights of Woman* is dedicated to Charles Talleyrand whose proposal for
free national education (for boys) was then before the French National
Assembly. By dedicating her treatise to Talleyrand, Wollstonecraft hoped
to encourage him to extend his proposal to include girls (needless to say,
he did not). The future strength of the New Republic, she argued, will be

ensured only when children of both sexes are trained to reason. She challenges Talleyrand:

> if women are to be excluded, without having a voice, from a participation of the natural rights of mankind, prove first, to ward off the charge of injustice and inconsistency, that they want reason – else this flaw in your NEW CONSTITUTION will ever shew that man must, in some shape, act like a tyrant, and tyranny, in whatever part of society it rears its brazen front, will ever undermine morality.[7]

Her own analysis of women's social and political status, she tells him, aims "to prove that the prevailing notion respecting a sexual character was subversive of morality."[8] In fact her target is much wider than morality. She also seeks to show that reason has no sex, knowledge has no sex, in short, that the mind itself is sexless.[9] The distinction between the sexes is entirely bodily and of relevance to one issue only: the reproduction of the species. All other human activity, if it is to deserve the title "human," should be governed by the principles of reason which are "the same in all" and appropriate to any task – even, or especially, childrearing.[10] It is to the shame and detriment of the society she addresses that human activity is so infrequently governed by these principles. Rather, it is passions and prejudices that determine social mores and this is nowhere more evident that in the social expectations surrounding women.

Wollstonecraft's social theory is very much dependent on her conception of human being and what it is capable of becoming. A rational society is one which takes account of and founds itself on the character and needs of human nature. That society is most just and rational that allows human beings to actualize, to the highest possible degree, their potentialities. Her opposition to a society which is governed by royalty and aristocracy, or as she calls them, the "pestiferous purple," is grounded in her belief that this kind of society limits the freedom of human beings to improve themselves, which in turn limits the progress of society. A human life is not worth living, is not truly a human life, unless there is opportunity for growth and self-improvement:

> the perfection of our nature and capability of happiness, must be estimated by the degree of reason, virtue, and knowledge, that distinguish the individual, and direct the laws which bind society: and that from the exercise of reason, knowledge and virtue naturally flow, is equally undeniable, if mankind be viewed collectively.[11]

Just as monarchical rule is an irrational basis for society, so too is patriarchal rule. She chastises the enlightened philosophers for not going far enough in their challenge to illegitimate authority. She argues that "the divine right of husbands," like the "divine right of kings," must be contested. If hereditary power amounts to illegitimate authority and is damaging to society then it is damaging in all its forms.

In the presentation of her case for the rights of women, Wollstonecraft most frequently employs the *reductio ad absurdum* form of argument. She repeatedly undermines her opponents' accounts of women's roles and duties by uncovering the inconsistencies in their arguments. The central example, which appears in several guises throughout the text, is the following: men argue that rights and duties assume one another; men deny women their rights; yet, men expect women to honour their duties. Wollstonecraft's own views on rights and duties are complex. She does not deny that much of what has been written about women is easily verified by experience. Some passages in *A Vindication of the Rights of Woman*, which describe the frivolity, vanity and inconstancy of women, are far from flattering. However, rather than judging that social and political rights should not be granted to such weak creatures, she argues that rights are the only remedy for their weaknesses. Women will not become dutiful or rational until they are treated with the same dignity and allowed to share in the same privileges as men. In this context she asks: "Why do men halt between two opinions, and expect impossibilities? Why do they expect virtue from a slave, from a being whom the constitution of civil society has rendered weak, if not vicious?"[12]

In order to answer this question Wollstonecraft turns to a critical reading of Rousseau's *Emile*, which was presented, and widely used, as a handbook for the education of children. She also considers several "popular" books that were influential in the formation of bourgeois expectations of female behavior and manners. These include writings by Dr Gregory, Dr Fordyce and Lord Chesterfield. These four writers are her main opponents in *Rights of Woman*. It is significant that it is mainly the informal "philosophy of manners and customs" that Wollstonecraft is obliged to engage with in her assessment of the dominant social attitudes toward the formation of women's character. It reveals the extent to which the socialization and control of women was a "private" affair.

Wollstonecraft condemns these texts for encouraging "a sexual character to the mind." Since all human beings naturally possess the capacity for reason, and hence for knowledge and virtue, the fact that women often are not rational or virtuous indicates that art has "smothered nature." And women are, for Wollstonecraft, the most artificial of creatures. This artifice, however, is not the invention of women. Wollstonecraft very firmly locates the source of women's corrupt nature in the passions of men. She writes that "all the causes of female weakness, as well as depravity, which I have already enlarged on, branch out of one grand cause – want of chastity in men."[13] She finds Rousseau, and his "philosophy of lasciviousness," particularly culpable. Wollstonecraft traces the many inconsistencies of Rousseau's philosophy to his poorly controlled sexual passions. Fearful of losing the services of an odalisque, men withhold the means whereby women could become free and rational companions. The iniquitous result of this attitude is that it denies women the opportunity to "unfold their own faculties and acquire the dignity of conscious virtue."[14] This "philosophy of manners" limits the possibilities of female understanding by ensuring that it is "always subordinated to the acquirement of some corporeal accomplishment."[15]

In this argument Wollstonecraft is worrying a sensitive spot in Enlightenment discourses. If certain rights are "human" and "inalienable" then how can one consistently deny these rights to women (or "savages", or children)? At certain points the Enlightenment discourse threatens to fall back on its dark Aristotelian and Thomistic past. Is woman a part of mankind? Is she a "lesser" or inferior type of man?[16] There are two, overlapping notions that save the "modern" philosophers from falling back on their fathers. The first is the notion of human progress: different cultures, and so perhaps different sexes, progress at a differential rate. This form of argument was certainly used by the newly formed French Republic to justify the exclusion of women from political participation. One such argument, offered by Amar who was representing the views of the Committee for General Security, goes as follows:

> If we take into account the fact that the political education of men is still at its very beginnings, that all the principles are not yet developed, and that we still stammer over the word "liberty," then how much less enlightened are women, whose moral education has been practically non-existent. Their presence in the *sociétés populaires*, then, would give an active part in government to persons exposed to error and seduction even more than are men. And, let us add that women by their constitution, are open to an exaltation which would be ominous in public life. The interests of the state would soon be sacrificed to all the kinds of disruption and disorder that hysteria can produce.[17]

Wollstonecraft dispenses with this argument by pointing out that if the female body is hysterical it will infect the political body whether it has "a voice" or not. Women's indirect influence on the public sphere, she argues, is pernicious precisely because of its clandestine character. If marriage and the family are the "cement of society," excluding women from the civic sphere does not remove the foundational threat they pose to that sphere. Second, Cartesian dualism was called upon to provide a justification for women's weaker reason. Descartes thought that the mind had no sex. Nevertheless female consciousness may be inhibited in its operations by its association with the female body and its unruly passions.

Wollstonecraft's strategy here is quite ingenious. She shifts the cause of women's weaker reason from the female body to the social environment, in particular to educational practices. She effects a neat inversion of the philosopher's arguments by locating the ultimate cause of female inferiority in the male body and its lasciviousness and in the masculine body politic which denies women access to reason. This, of course, puts a new slant on Rousseau's stricture that it is reason and not prejudice that dictates that women be educated "to please men."[18]

It is with arguments such as these that Wollstonecraft refutes the notion that women's social status is just, natural or necessary. She argues for the improvement of the female mind both for the sake of women and society. The performance of the "peculiar duties which nature has assigned them" will only be improved by the acquisition of reason. These duties are no less human for being peculiarly female. Wollstonecraft's arguments for the rights of women are not restricted to the right of the individual to realize and improve his or her own nature. Her particular conception of the relation between the individual and society is such that to improve (or inhibit) the possibilities of an individual necessarily improves (or inhibits) society in general. She therefore has an additional argument in favor of the "revolution in female manners" which bears on the quality of the social body.

Virtue is the product of reason, it is not relative to situation or sex. The sham virtue that women are encouraged to practice – notably by Rousseau – has public repercussions since "public virtue is only an aggregate of private."[19] The dire consequence of rendering women weak and irrational is that the progress and strength of the human race is thereby endangered. Wollstonecraft makes this point graphically:

> Make them [women] free, and they will quickly become wise and virtuous, as men become more so; for the improvement must be mutual, or the injustice which one half of the human race are obliged to submit to, retorting on their oppressors, the virtue of men will be worm-eaten by the insect whom he keeps under his feet.[20]

This view of social progress makes Wollstonecraft's stress on the necessity for both sexes to be chaste, seem less prudish. The relation between the sexes lies at the core of the body politic. If this core is bad it will, eventually, infect the political body.

Wollstonecraft's recommendations, in *A Vindication of the Rights of Woman*, concerning the improvement of women's character, and so society in general, range from an abstract appeal to men that they allow their reason to show them the importance of chastity and intersexual friendship, to the provision of practical guidelines for the institution of national coeducation.

She also stresses the necessity for women to be granted "the protection of civil laws"; the freedom to follow careers compatible with their "natural" duties (for instance, physicians, nurses, midwives); and even mentions, though with some embarrassment, that women ought to have representatives in the government. These recommendations do not sit very easily with her attitude towards women's "natural" role as childrearer and domestic worker. The sexual division of labor, and its corollary, the public/private split, remain structurally untouched. This reflects Wollstonecraft's enormous faith in the power of reason to bring about the revolution in manners. If we follow reason, the flourishing of sexual fidelity, virtue, friendship and equality between the sexes will be the automatic result.

The uneasiness we may feel with this resolution only increases when she, unselfconsciously, paints a picture of domestic bliss – complete with a female servant:

> I have then viewed with pleasure a woman nursing her children, and discharging the duties of her station with, perhaps, *merely a servnt maid to take off her hands the servile part of the household business.* I have seen her prepare herself and children, with only the luxury of cleanliness, to receive her husband, who returning weary home in the evening found smiling babes and a clean hearth. My heart has loitered in the midst of this group, and has even throbbed with sympathetic emotion, when the scraping of the well known foot has raised a pleasing tumult.[21]

From our perspective, it is interesting to note the extent to which Wollstonecraft seems utterly oblivious to the contradictions implicit in her view. The sexual division of labor lies at the heart of the difficulty and she does not see this division as socially constituted, but rather as dictated by nature. This passage is worrying also for its apparent blindness to class differences between women. These difficulties flaw the basic argument of *Rights of Woman* making its conclusion inevitably paradoxical: "The conclusion which I wish to draw, is obvious; make women rational creatures, and free *citizens*, and they will quickly become good *wives*, and *mothers*; that is – if men do not neglect the duties of husbands and fathers.[22]

This formulation leaves the asymmetry between the citizen/husband/father and the citizen/wife/mother unaddressed. In the eighteenth century, public interest is constructed, both conceptually and practically, in direct opposition to the domestic sphere of women and the family. "Women" and "the family" are almost indistinguishable, both in terms of the way their interests are represented and in terms of their relation to civic and public pursuits. Given the character of liberal social organization it is inappropriate to argue that women are as free as men to occupy the public sphere as "disembodied" rational agents. This ignores the asymmetrical consequences of embodiment for man and woman *within that organization.*[23] For men, the actualization of the option of marriage, parenthood and the establishment of a private familial unit does not intrude on their access to the public sphere. Nor does it deplete their power to act in that sphere; on the contrary, it may enhance their power. The same cannot be said of women. The tensions brought about by the sharp division between the public and the private sphere crystallize around the issue of men's rights and duties and women's rights and duties. Several philosophers (unsuccessfully) attempted to resolve the dilemma by insisting on men's civil and political rights by carefully specifying women's private duties. As Wollstonecraft points out, there is a lacuna in this argument. Human rights and duties seem to be sexually divided: men get the rights and women the duties!

A major problem with the argument of *A Vindication of the Rights of Woman* is its uneasy alliance with the suspect notion of the essential sexual neutrality of the rational agent. Wollstonecraft thinks it is sufficient to overcome social prejudice in order to allow woman to realize her rights and hence her "true nature." This approach simply does not take the structural necessity of women's subordination in liberal society seriously. Yet, limitations on what can be demanded from the public sphere are revealed in Wollstonecraft's own writings. Demands concerning the character and quality of women's lives in the private sphere are inevitably addressed to an individual man, whose own involvement in the private sphere is often marginal, or actually oppositional, to his public activities and interest. In this regard women *qua* women lack a "voice" in the body politic. Their lot seems to be circumscribed by natural, familial or personal arrangements which fall outside the scope of public interest or relevance.

The great difficulty confronting Wollstonecraft in her attempt to resolve the moral and political disjunction between the (female) private sphere and the (male) public sphere is worsened by her acceptance of the idea that it is nature rather than social organization that requires women to assume the responsibility for childcare and home maintenance. This sexual division of labor is inherent in the rationalism of the liberal paradigm. That paradigm is necessarily limited when it comes to consider the question of the social status of women. It may well be that it offers an inconsistent argument, as Wollstonecraft herself recognizes. However, she does not, in *A Vindication of the Rights of Woman*, seem to acknowledge that it is a necessary inconsistency that cannot be resolved within the terms of liberal political theory. While feminists continue to accept the liberal emphasis on the essential neutrality of the mind, sexual discrimination will continue to be "justified" by natural bodily difference. Given the high value placed on the neutrality and universality of mind, it will be female corporeality which is conceived as limiting. The female body will appear as the natural site of women's oppression, turning attention from the sociopolitical organization that can then present itself as an *effect*, rather than a cause.

It is an implicit assumption of modern political theory that men are able to dissociate themselves from sexuality, reproduction and natural passions. Male subjectivity and male sexuality are divorceable conceptually and spatially in a way that female subjectivity and female sexuality are not. As Rousseau puts it, "man is only man now and again, but the female is always a female."[24] Since it is she who has been allotted the role of perpetuating and managing the natural base of culture, she cannot be considered independently of these functions, which coincide, in traditional accounts, with her sexuality. The satisfaction of the needs of "natural man" has become the work of woman. She tends to his natural, corporeal needs while he is transforming himself into rational "social man."

Any attempt to introduce women into the body politic necessarily raises the question of how these "natural" human needs are to be satisfied. The social reduction of woman to her function of satisfying these needs makes it conceptually impossible to consider her social possibilities without also considering, as a social problem, the question of the reproduction and management of the natural base of cultural life.

The liberal paradigm, assumed by Wollstonecraft, is not helpful at this point. Its traditional concern with protecting the individual in his private sphere of thought, personal taste and private relations from the intrusions of the state forecloses the possibility of challenging the "private" arrangements between men and women. The labour, effort and "self" of women are contained in the private sphere – "protected" from public scrutiny and legislation – making structural inequalities between its inhabitants socially and politically invisible.

By the time Wollstonecraft begins her next major piece on women, *The Wrongs of Women, or Maria*, she has obviously become painfully aware of this fact. If *A Vindication of the Rights of Woman* was Wollstonecraft's eulogy to the powers of reason, *Maria* is her diatribe against the bondage of passion. Yet in both cases the reason and the passion are peculiarly masculine. The figure of woman stands in an ambiguous relation to the eighteenth-century Enlightenment ideal of man. She may gain from sharing in masculine rationality but can be ruined by masculine passion. And it is here that the source of the tension in this central dichotomy is bared. Reason, which Wollstonecraft saw as the force of progress, is Janus-faced. *How* such reason is lived in eighteenth-century culture is closely associated with the public/private split. This division is a highly sexualized one: the public or civic sphere is conceptualized as the realm of rational and contractual pursuits and the private sphere as the realm of nature, feeling and the family. Wollstonecraft, in *A Vindication of the Rights of Woman*, hoped to neutralize passion in both spheres, going so far as to argue that "a master and mistress of a family ought not to continue to love each other with passion. I mean to say, that they ought not to indulge those emotions which disturb the order of society."[25]

However, from our present context we must question this neutralization. How dependent is Wollstonecraft's conception of (public) reason on the privatization of passion? Does masculine reason, in the sociopolitical sphere, rest on and assume men's access to the corporeal and passionate via their role as "head" of a familiar body corporate? If the response to these questions is affirmative then how can women have an independent relation to either reason or passion? This cluster of questions was not consciously raised by Wollstonecraft. Her historical placement is such that these questions defy clear articulation. Yet, from our perspective, a parallel reading of *Rights of Woman* and *Maria* displays the problem clearly enough. It is just not the case that reason and passion or reason and feeling are the provinces of men and women, respectively. Rather, women's exclusion from the social contract bars them from the civic sphere of reason and their containment in the private sphere of feeling and the "natural" family does not guarantee their access to either passion or feeling since they are the servicers rather than the consumers even in the private sphere.

What motivated the writing of the novel, *Maria*? Within two years of the publication of *Rights of Woman*, Wollstonecraft had a passionate affair with Gilbert Imlay – who, from most accounts, was an opportunist, an entrepreneur, and a womanizer – had borne a child by him and was abandoned by him. This precipitated her first suicide attempt. Many commentators have seen this episode as evidence of a damning inconsistency between Wollstonecraft's rational recommendations for heterosexual relations in *Rights of Woman* and her irrational behavior with Imlay. There is no good reason for accepting this interpretation. Any inconsistency in this episode should be located in the sociopolitical body and its constitution rather than in Wollstonecraft and her (mental and/or physical) constitution. In fact, Wollstonecraft's life becomes an unfortunate illustration or verification of her analysis of society and women's position within it. It is a testimony to the power of social structures to ensnare (and sometimes destroy) even, or perhaps especially, those who have a reflective grasp of their operations. "Free love," mutual respect and an ethical relationship between the sexes all suppose a sociopolitical context suitable to such relations. The sociopolitical context in which Wollstonecraft wrote and lived not only tolerated but actually encouraged "the tyranny of men."[26] One of Wollstonecraft's letters, written while travelling in Scandinavia, captures not only her personal disappointment with Imlay, but also, by her provocative use of metaphor, something of the general feminine tenor of sexual disenchantment:

Uniting myself to you, your tenderness seemed to make me amends for all my former misfortunes. – On this tenderness and affection with what confidence did I rest! – but I leaned on a spear, that has pierced me to the heart. – You have thrown off a faithful friend, to pursue the caprices of the moment.[27]

Read in its context this letter is, among other things, a complaint concerning the difficulty of assigning a value to friendship in heterosexual relations.

It is tempting to see her next liaison, with Godwin, as the inverse of her relation with Imlay. Godwin is a friend, a comrade in political struggle, a rational companion. Their love is certainly no *grande passion* and in her relation to Godwin it seems clear that Wollstonecraft has forfeited passion/sensuality for "a convenient part of the furniture of a house."[28] Were these the choices for women? If the public/private split ensured that, once wedded and bedded, a woman's access to the public sphere of reason is forfeited for the role of wife/mother, how can she maintain a relation to either reason or feeling? The (male) citizen is certainly differently placed. He straddles the dichotomy and enjoys a spatial split between his civic, rational pursuits and his sensual, sentimental ones. How can woman, in early modern liberal society, achieve this dual role? (How this quandary should be assessed in our contemporary context is not considered here.) Perhaps it was the experience of motherhood which presented these paradoxes of female existence to Wollstonecraft in such stark form. The task of deciding how best to socialize a female child must have presented her with great difficulties. As Wollstonecraft laments in a letter concerning her daughter Fanny: "I dread lest she should be forced to sacrifice her heart to her principles, or principles to her heart . . . I dread to unfold her mind, lest it should render her unfit for the world she is to inhabit."[29]

These reflections on Wollstonecraft's life and intellectual development help to explain why she turns, not to the genre of the political treatise but to the novel in order to explore how the sociopolitical context constructs women as victims of (male) passion and feeling. *The Wrongs of Women, or Maria* is the result. The addressee of this work is not the enlightened (male) social reformer. It reads as a novel designed for the edification and chastening of a culture. In the introduction Wollstonecraft writes: "In writing this novel, I have rather endeavoured to pourtray passions than manners . . ." and "my main object, the desire of exhibiting the misery and oppression, peculiar to women, that arise out of the partial laws and customs of society."[30] She certainly achieves her object. *Maria* is set in an insane asylum, yet none of its characters is insane. The three main figures are Maria, Darnford and Jemima. Maria is a middle-class woman whose husband wastes her fortune, offers her person as payment to a debtor and finally separates Maria from her daughter when he exercises his legal

right of having her committed. Darnford, a middle-class man, functions
mainly as the recipient of Maria's affections. He represents the precarious
possibility of intersexual friendship. Jemima is a lower-class woman who
was born out of wedlock, the issue of a heartless seduction, who is seduced
and abandoned in turn, who became a thief and a prostitute and whose
relative social "respectability" is bought at the ironic price of acting as a
"keeper of the mad." By acting as madhouse attendant, she colludes with
the society that rejects her by guarding those whom, like her, society
wishes to exclude from its ranks. *Maria* was never finished. Wollstonecraft
died from complications arising from childbirth before it could be completed. The outcome of the web of friendships linking this unlikely trio is
thus left open to history, open to our present.

Is there any reason for us to be more optimistic than Wollstonecraft
could have been about the possibility of friendship between women of
different classes or about friendships between men and women? It is at
least possible, in our current context, to raise these questions as meaningful
political and ethical issues. But is there, even now, a basis for ethical
relations between women? The governing ethic between men and women
is still primarily conjugal in that it treats women primarily as wives/
mothers/sexual partners. Perhaps the most important insight we have to
gain from Wollstonecraft's novel is that political and economic reforms
are necessary but not sufficient for women's genuine access to social,
political and ethical life. This inevitably returns us to the "private"
arrangements made between men and women in the shadow of the civic
sphere.[31] We need to bring that relation out of the shadows and examine
it. Claims that it is based on nature, natural desire or necessary reproductive
survival have by now worn thin. We also need to ask how this shadowy
relation effects relations between men and women, and women and women,
in the public sphere. Perhaps it is time to return, with new insight, to
Wollstonecraft's early claim that "The most holy band of society is friendship. It has been well said, by a shrewd satirist, 'that rare as true love is,
true friendship is even rarer.' "[32] This is an issue that feminists should
resist reducing to a question of sexuality or, as is more usual, *heterosexuality*.
The logically prior problem is a problem in ethics: the meaning and value
of friendship.

If the liberal paradigm posits that sexual equality can only be had at the
price of sexual *neutrality* (meaning the "neutering" of women, since men
are already "neutral") then there is a serious problem with the relevance
of this paradigm to women's situation. Part of the problem is that the
liberal notion of "equality" has developed historically with a male bias
towards the public sphere. As Wollstonecraft's writings show, this notion
has great difficulty extending itself to issues relating to sexual difference.
All liberal theory has to offer on the question of sexual equality is that

women are entitled to be treated "like men," or "as if they were men." In order to pinpoint what is wrong with this response, we are compelled to return to a morality that takes account of bodily specificity. The demand for political equality thus spills over into the ethical, because the very terms in which the demand for political equality is made misses the ethical point: to treat all beings as "the same" is to deny some beings the most basic ethical principle, that is, acknowledgement of its specific being.[33] It is on this point that Wollstonecraft, and other liberal feminists, are at their weakest. On their paradigm, fair and equal treatment for women will only apply to those activities which simulate the neutral subject. In those aspects of her being that bear on her specificity, she will be offered little or no protection: for example, rape, domestic violence, enforced pregnancy. These infringements on women's autonomy significantly overlap in that they represent the unwanted use or abuse of her bodily capacities. The ultimate irony of the liberal state, in relation to woman, is revealed. The founding principle of liberal theory, the right and freedom to use one's bodily capacities as one sees fit, is denied to women with regard to the specific character of their bodies.

Rights of Woman and *Maria* are fruitful texts to study in attempting to clarify these two issues of embodiment and ethics. This problem, in all its complexity, can be found there. Wollstonecraft shows, albeit unintentionally, that settling the political question will not settle the ethical one. Perhaps this should not surprise us. The liberal tradition itself was ushered in not simply with a political question but also with an *ethical* one. Is monarchical power legitimate? What would constitute an ethical relation between men? Aspects of Wollstonecraft's work can be read as gesturing toward questions that still have not been satisfactorily addressed. What would constitute an ethical life for women *qua* women? What are the possibilities for women and men sharing a co-authored ethical community? Viewed from the standpoint of present feminist concerns, these unanswered questions are perhaps the most important legacy of Mary Wollstonecraft's life and work.

Notes

My thanks to Mary Lyndon Shanley who offered extensive comments and suggestions on an earlier draft of this essay.

1 Shulamith Firestone, *The Dialectic of Sex* (New York: Bantam, 1971).

2 Carol McMillan, *Women, Reason and Nature* (Oxford: Basil Blackwell, 1982).

3 Mary Wollstonecraft, *A Vindication of the Rights of Men* in Janet Todd, *A Wollstonecraft Anthology* (Bloomington: Indiana University Press, 1977; Cambridge: Polity, 1989), p. 65.

4 Ibid., p. 72.
5 Cora Kaplan, "Wild Nights: Pleasure/Sexuality/Feminism," in *Formations of Pleasure* (London: Routledge and Kegan Paul, 1983), p. 18.
6 Anca Vlasopolos, "Mary Wollstonecraft's Mask of Reason in *A Vindication of the Rights of Woman*," *Dalhousie Review*, 60 (3), 1980.
7 Mary Wollstonecraft, *A Vindication of the Rights of Woman*, ed. C. H. Poston (New York: Norton, 1975), p. 5.
8 Ibid., p. 4.
9 Ibid., p. 42.
10 Ibid., p. 53.
11 Ibid., p. 12.
12 Ibid., p. 47.
13 Ibid., p. 138.
14 Ibid., p. 26.
15 Ibid., p. 23.
16 Cf. ibid., p. 35n.
17 Quoted in J. Abray, "Feminism in the French Revolution," *American Historical Review*, 80, 1975, p. 56.
18 See Jean-Jacques Rousseau, *Emile* (London: Dent, 1972), p. 324, and Moira Gatens, "Rousseau and Wollstonecraft: Nature vs. Reason," *Australasian Journal of Philosophy*, 64 supplement, June, 1986.
19 Wollstonecraft, *Rights of Woman*, p. 192.
20 Ibid., p. 175.
21 Ibid., pp. 142–3 (emphasis added).
22 Ibid., p. 178 (emphasis added).
23 For an interesting discussion of this question see M. Tapper, "Can a Feminist be a Liberal?" *Australasian Journal of Philosophy*, 64 supplement, June, 1986.
24 Rousseau, *Emile*, p. 324.
25 Wollstonecraft, *Rights of Woman*, p. 30.
26 That this was Wollstonecraft's view is obvious from Letter XXXI in *Letters Written During a Short Residence in Sweden, Norway and Denmark*, in Todd, *Wollstonecraft Anthology*.
27 Letter LXVII, in ibid.
28 Letter from Wollstonecraft to Godwin, quoted in R. M. Wardle, *Mary Wollstonecraft* (Lawrence: University of Kansas Press, 1951), p. 296.
29 Letter VI, in Todd, *Wollstonecraft Anthology*.
30 *The Wrongs of Women, or Maria*, in Todd, *Wollstonecraft Anthology* p. 195.
31 See Pateman, *The Sexual Contract* (Cambridge: Polity; Stanford: Stanford University Press, 1988).
32 Wollstonecraft, *Rights of Woman*, p. 30.
33 See L. Irigaray, *L'éthique de la différence sexuelle* (Paris: Minuit, 1984).

7

On Hegel, Women and Irony

Seyla Benhabib

Das Bekannte überhaupt ist darum, weil es bekannt ist, nicht erkannt.

(The well-known is unknown, precisely because it is well-known.)

G. W. F. *Hegel,* Phaenomenologie des Geistes

Some Methodological Puzzles of a Feminist Approach to the History of Philosophy

The 1980s have been named "the decade of the humanities" in the USA. In many institutions of higher learning a debate is underway as to what constitutes the "tradition" and the "canon" in literary, artistic and philosophical works worth transmitting to future generations in the last quarter of the twentieth century. At the center of this debate is the question: if what had hitherto been considered the major works of the Western tradition are, almost uniformly, the product of a specific group of individuals, namely propertied, white, European and North American males, how universal and representative is their message, how inclusive is their scope, and how unbiased their vision?

Feminist theory has been at the forefront of this questioning, and under the impact of feminist scholarship the surface of the canon of Western "great works" has been forever fractured, its unity dispersed and its legitimacy challenged. Once the woman's question is raised, once we ask how a thinker conceptualizes the distinction between male and female, we experience a *Gestalt* shift: we begin to see the great thinkers of the past with a new eye, and in the words of Joan Kelly Gadol "each eye sees a different picture."[1] The vision of feminist theory is a "doubled" one: one eye sees what the tradition has trained it to see, the other searches for what the tradition has told her was not even worth looking for. How is a "feminist reading" of the tradition in fact possible? At the present, I see two dominant approaches, each with certain shortcomings.

I describe the first approach as "the teaching of the good father." Mainstream liberal feminist theory treats the tradition's views of women as a series of unfortunate, sometimes embarrassing, but essentially corrigible, misconceptions. Taking their inspiration from the example of a progressive thinker like John Stuart Mill, these theorists seek in the classical texts for those moments of insight into the equality and dignity of women. They are disappointed when their favorite philosopher utters inanities on the subject, but essentially hold that there is no incompatibility between the Enlightenment ideals of freedom, equality and self-realization and women's aspirations.

The second view I would characterize as "the cry of the rebellious daughter." Agreeing with Lacan that language is the symbolic universe which represents the "law of the father," and accepting that all language has been a codification of the power of the father, these rebellious daughters seek for female speech at the margins of the Western logocentric tradition. If it is impossible to think in the Western logocentric tradition without binary oppositions, then the task of feminist reading becomes the articulation not of a new set of categories but of the transcendence of categorical discourse altogether. One searches not for a new language but for a discourse at the margins of language.

Juxtaposed to these approaches, in this essay I would like to outline a "feminist discourse of empowerment." With the second view, I agree that the feminist challenge to the tradition cannot leave its fundamental categories unchanged. Revealing the gender subtext of the ideals of reason and the Enlightenment compromises the assumed universality of these ideals. Nonetheless, they should not be thrown aside altogether. Instead we can ask what these categories have meant for the actual lives of women in certain historical periods, and how, if women are to be thought of as subjects and not just as fulfillers of certain functions, the semantic horizon of these categories is transformed. Once we approach the tradition to recover from it women's subjectivity and their lives and activities, we hear contradictory voices, competing claims, and see that so-called "descriptive" discourses about the sexes are but "legitimizations" of male power. The traditional view of gender differences is the discourse of those who have won out and who have codified history as we know it. But what would the history of ideas look like from the standpoint of the victims? What ideals, aspirations and utopias of the past ran into a dead-end? Can we recapture their memory from the battleground of history? This essay attempts to apply such a "discourse of empowerment" to G. W. F. Hegel's views of women.

Hegel's treatment of women has received increased attention in recent years under the impact of the feminist questioning of the tradition.[2] This feminist challenge has led us to ask, is Hegel's treatment of women merely a consequence of his conservative predilections? Was Hegel unable to see that he made the "dialectic" stop at women and condemned them to an ahistorical mode of existence, outside the realms of struggle, work and diremption which in his eyes are characteristic of human consciousness as such?[3] Is the "woman question" in Hegel's thought one more instance of Hegel's uncritical endorsement of the institutions of his time, or is this issue an indication of a flaw in the very structure of the dialectic itself? Benjamin Barber, for example, siding with the second option has recently written:

> What this paradox reveals is that Hegel's position on women is neither a product of contingency nor an effect of ad hoc prejudice. Rather, it is the necessary consequence of his belief that the "Prejudices" of his age are in fact *the* actuality yielded by history in the epoch of liberation. Hegel does not have to rationalize them: because they *are*, they are already rational. They need only be encompassed and explained by philosophy. Spirit may guide and direct history, but ultimately, history alone can tell us where spirit means it to go.[4]

Judging, however, where "history alone can tell . . . spirit" it means it to go, requires a more complicated and contradictory account of the family and women's position at the end of the eighteenth and the beginning of the nineteenth century in the German states than either Barber or other commentators who have looked at this issue so far have provided us with. I suggest that to judge whether or not the Hegelian dialectic has stopped at women, we must first attempt to define the "discursive horizon" of competing claims and visions within which Hegel articulated his position. To evaluate the historical options concerning gender relations in Hegel's time, we have to move beyond the methodology of traditional text analysis to the "doubled vision" of feminist theory. In practicing this doubled vision we do not remain satisfied with analyzing textual discourses about women, but we ask where the women themselves were at any given period in which a thinker lived. With one eye we see what stands in the text, and with the other, what the text conceals in footnotes and in the margins. What then emerges is a "discursive space" of competing power claims. The discursive horizon of Hegel's views of women and the family are defined on the one hand by the rejection of political patriarchy (which

mixes the familial with the political, the private with the public), and on
the other by disapproval of and antagonism toward efforts of early female
emancipation.

This essay is divided into two parts: by using the traditional method of
text analysis in the first part I explore *the logic of oppositions* according to
which Hegel develops his views of gender relations and of female subordination. In particular I focus on the complex relationship between
reason, nature, gender and history. Second, having outlined Hegel's views
of women in his political philosophy, I situate his discourse within the
context of historical views on women and the family at the turn of the
eighteenth century. I read Hegel against the grain; proceeding from
certain footnotes and marginalia in the texts, I move toward recovering
the history of those which the dialectic leaves behind.

Women in G. W. F. Hegel's (1770–1831) Political Thought

In many respects Hegel's political philosophy heralds the end of the
traditional doctrine of politics, and signals its transformation into social
science. *Geist* which emerges from nature, transforms nature into a second
world; this "second nature" comprises the human, historical world of
tradition, institutions, laws, and practices (*objektiver Geist*), as well as the
self-reflection of knowing and acting subjects upon objective spirit, which
is embodied in works of art, religion, and philosophy (*absoluter Geist*). *Geist*
is a transindividual principle that unfolds in history, and whose goal is to
make externality into its "work." *Geist* externalizes itself in history by
appropriating, changing, and shaping the given such as to make it correspond to itself, to make it embody its own subjectivity, that is, reason and
freedom. The transformation of substance into subject is attained when
freedom and rationality are embodied in the world such that "the realm of
freedom" is actualized, and "the world of mind [is] brought forth out of
itself like a second nature." The social world is *Substance*, that is, it has
objective existence for all to see and to comprehend;[5] it is also *subject*, for
what the social and ethical world is can only be known by understanding
the subjectivity of the individuals who compose it.[6] With Hegel's concept
of objective spirit, the object domain of modern social science, that is,
individuality and society, make their appearance.

Does his concept of *Geist* permit Hegel to transcend the "naturalistic"
basis of gender conceptions in the modern period, such as to place the
relation between the sexes in the social, symbolic, historical, and cultural
world? Hegel, on the one hand, views the development of subjectivity and
individuality within the context of a human community; on the other
hand, in assigning men and women to their traditional sex roles, he

codifies gender-specific differences as aspects of a rational ontology that is said to reflect the deep structure of *Geist*. Women are viewed as representing the principles of particularity (*Besonderheit*), immediacy (*Unmittelbarkeit*), naturalness (*Natürlichkeit*), and substantiality (*Substanzialität*), while men stand for universality (*Allgemeinheit*), mediacy (*Vermittlung*), freedom (*Freiheit*), and subjectivity (*Subjektivität*). Hegel develops his rational ontology of gender within a logic of oppositions.

The thesis of the "natural inequality" of the sexes

On the basis of Hegel's observations on the family, women, and the rearing of children, scattered throughout the *Lectures on the Philosophy of History*, I conclude that he was well aware that differences among the sexes were culturally, symbolically, and socially constituted. For example, in the section on Egypt, Hegel refers to Herodotus' observatations "that the women urinate standing up, while men sit, that the men wear one dress, and the women two; the women were engaged in outdoor occupations, while the men remained at home to weave. In one part of Egypt polygamy prevailed; in another, monogamy. His general judgment on the matter is that the Egyptians do the exact opposite of all other peoples."[7]

Hegel's own reflections on the significance of the family among the Chinese, the great respect that is shown to women in this culture, and his comment on the Chinese practice of concubinage again indicate an acute awareness that the role of women is not naturally but culturally and socially defined.[8]

These passages show a clear awareness of the cultural, historical, and social variations in family and sexual relations. Nevertheless, although Hegel rejects that differences between "men" and "women" are naturally defined, and instead sees them as part of the spirit of a people (*Volksgeist*), he leaves no doubt that he considers only one set of family relations and one particular division of labor between the sexes as rational and normatively right. This is the monogamic sexual practice of the European nuclear family, in which the woman is confined to the private sphere and the man to the public. To justify this arrangement, Hegel explicitly invokes the superiority of the male to the female while acknowledging their *functional complementarity* in the modern state.

The "superiority" of the male

The most revealing passages in this respect are paragraphs 165 and 166 of the *Philosophy of Right* and the additions to them. In the Lasson edition of the *Rechtsphilosophie*, Hegel writes that "The natural determinacies of both sexes acquire through its reasonableness *intellectual* as well as *ethical* significance."[9] This explicit reference to the "natural determinacies of the sexes" is given an ontological significance in the next paragraph:

> Thus one sex is mind in its self-diremption into explicit self-subsistence and the knowledge and volition of free universality, i.e. the self-consciousness of conceptual thought and the volition of the objective final end. The other sex is mind maintaining itself in unity as knowledge and volition in the form of concrete individuality and feeling. In relation to externality, the former is powerful and active, the latter passive and subjective. It follows that man has his actual substantive life in the state, in learning, and so forth, as well as in labour and struggle with the external world and with himself so that it is only out of his diremption that he fights his way to self-subsistent unity with himself. In the family he has a tranquil intuition of this unity, and there he lives a subjective ethical life on the plane of feeling. Woman, on the other hand, has her substantive destiny in the family, and to be imbued with family piety is her ethical frame of mind.[10]

For Hegel men's lives are concerned with the state, science, and work in the external world. Dividing himself (*sich entzweiend*) from the unity of the family, man objectifies the external world and conquers it through activity and freedom. The woman's "substantial determination," by contrast, is in the family, in the unity and piety (*Pietät*) characteristic of the private sphere. Hegel suggests that woman are not *individuals*, at least, not in the same measure and to the same extent as men are. They are incapable of the spiritual struggle and diremption (*Entzweiung*) which characterize the lives of men. In a passage from the *Phänomenologie* concerned with the tragedy of Antigone, he indicates that for the woman "it is not *this* man, not *this* child, but *a man* and *children in general*" that is significant.[11] The man by contrast, individuates his desires, and "since he possesses as a citizen the self-conscious power of universality, he thereby acquires the right of desire and, at the same time, preserves his freedom in regard to it."[12]

Most significant is the fact that those respects in which Hegel considers men and women to be spiritually different are precisely those aspects that define women as "lesser" human beings. Like Plato and Aristotle, Hegel not only assigns particularity, intuitiveness, passivity to women, and universality, conceptual thought, and "the powerful and the active" to men, but sees in men the characteristics that define the species as human. Let us remember that *Geist* constitutes second nature by emerging out of its substantial unity into *bifurcation* (*Entzweiung*), where it sets itself over and against the world. The process through which nature is humanized and history constituted is this activity of *Entzweiung*, followed by *external-ization* (*Entäusserung*), namely the *objectification* (*Vergegenständlichung*) of human purposes and institutions in a world such that the world becomes a home for human self-expression. Women, since they cannot overcome unity and emerge out of the life of the family into the world of *universality*, are excluded from history-constituting activity. Their activities in the private realm, namely, reproduction, the rearing of children, and the satisfaction of the emotional and sexual needs of men, place them outside the world of *work*. This means that women have no history, and are condemned to repeat the cycles of life.

The family and political life

By including the family as the first stage of ethical life (*Sittlichkeit*), alongside "civil society" and "the state," Hegel reveals how crucial, in his view, this institution is to the constitution of the modern state. The family is significant in Hegel's political architectonic because it is the sphere in which the right of the modern individual to particularity (*Besonderheit*) and subjectivity (*Subjektivität*) is realized.[13] As Hegel often notes, the recognition of the "subjective moment" of the free individual is the chief strength of the modern state when compared to the ancient *polis*. In the family the right to particularity is exercised in love and in the choice of spouse, whereas the right to subjectivity is exercised in the concern for the welfare and moral well-being of other family members.

The various Additions to the section on the family, particularly in the Griesheim edition of the *Philosophy of Right*,[14] reveal that Hegel is concerned with this institution, not like Aristotle in order to discipline women, nor like Rousseau to prepare the true citizens of the future, but primarily from the standpoint of the freedom of the male subject in the modern state. Already in the *Philosophy of History*, Hegel had observed that the confusion of familial with political authority resulted in *patriarchalism*, and in China as well as in India this had as consequence the suppression of the freedom of the will through the legal regulation of family life and of relations within it. The decline of *political patriarchy* also means a strict separation between the private and the public, between the moral and intimate spheres, and the domain of public law. The legal system stands at the beginning and at the end of family; it circumscribes it but does not control its internal functioning or relations. It recognizes and administers, along with the church, the marriage contract as well as legally guaranteeing rights of inheritance when the family unit is dissolved. In this context, Hegel allows women certain significant legal rights.

He radically criticizes Kant for including women, children, and domestic servants under the category of *jura realiter personalia* or *Personen-Sachen-*

Recht.[15] Women are persons, that is, legal-juridical subjects along with men. They are free to choose their spouse;[16] they can own property, although once married, the man represents the family "as the legal person against others."[17] Nevertheless, women are entitled to property inheritance in the case of death and even in the case of divorce.[18] Hegel is against all Roman and feudal elements of the law that would either revert family property back to the family clan (*die Sippe*), or that would place restrictions on its full inheritance and alienability.[19]

The legal issue besides property rights that most concerns Hegel is that of divorce. Divorce presents a particular problem because, as a phenomenon, it belongs under two categories at once. On the one hand, it is a legal matter just as the marriage contract is; on the other hand, it is an issue that belongs to the "ethical" sphere, and more specifically to the subjectivity of the individuals involved. Hegel admits that because the bodily-sensual as well as spiritual attraction and love of two particular individuals form the basis of the marriage contract, an alienation between them can take place that justifies divorce; but this is only to be determined by an impersonal third-party authority, for instance, a court.[20] Finally, Hegel justifies monogamy as the only form of marriage that is truly compatible with the *individuality* of personality, and the subjectivity of feeling. In an addition to this paragraph in the Griesheim lectures he notes that monogamy is the only marriage form truly compatible with the equality of men and women.[21]

Contrary to parroting the prejudices of his time, or ontologizing them, as Benjamin Barber suggests, with respect to the right of the free choice of spouse, women's property and divorce rights, Hegel is an Enlightenment thinker, who upholds the transformations in the modern world initiated by the French Revolution and the spread of the revolutionary Code Civil. According to the Prussian *Das Allgemeine Landrecht* of 1794, the right of the free choice of spouse and in particular marriage among members of the various *Stände* – the feudal stratas of medieval society – was strictly forbidden. It was legally stipulated "that male persons from the nobility . . . could not enter into marriage . . . with female persons of peasant stock or the lesser bourgeoisie (*geringerem Bürgerstand*)."[22] If such marriages nonetheless occurred, they were declared "null" and the judges "were not empowered to accept their continuation."[23] To avoid social dilemmas, the lawgivers then distinguished between "the lesser" and "the higher bourgeoisie."

Hegel's position on this issue, by contrast, follows the revolutionary proclamations of the French Assembly which, codified as the "Code Civil" in 1804, were also adopted in those parts of Germany conquered by Napoleon.[24] Social strata differences are irrelevant to the choice of spouse and must not be legally regulated: the free will and consent of two adults (as well as of their parents), as long as they are legally entitled to marriage (that is, have not been married before or otherwise have falsified their civil status), is the only relevant point of view.

Yet Hegel inserts an interesting detail in considering this issue, which is wholly characteristic of his general attitude towards modernity. Distinguishing between the extremes of arranged marriages and the wholly free choice of spouse, he argues that: "The more ethical way to matrimony may be taken to be the former extreme or any way at all whereby the decision to marry comes first and the inclination to do so follows, so that in the actual wedding both decision and inclination coalesce."[25] Presumably this decision can also involve such relevant "ethical" considerations as the social background and appropriateness of the spouses involved. Consideration of social origin and wealth are now no longer legal matters to be regulated, as they were in feudal society, but personal and ethical criteria to be kept in view by modern individuals, aware of the significance, as the British Hegelian Bradley named it, of "my station and its duties."

While Hegel certainly was ahead of the Prussian legal practices of his time, and endorsed the general transformations brought about by the French Revolutionary Code Civil, he was, as always, reluctant to follow modernity to its ultimate conclusion and view the choice of spouse as a wholly individual matter of love and inclination between two adults. Hegel's views on love and sexuality, when placed within the larger context of changes taking place at this point in history, in fact reveal him to be a counter-Enlightenment thinker. Hegel surreptitiously criticizes and denigrates attempts at early women's emancipation and seeks to imprison women once more within the confines of the monogamous, nuclear family which they threatened to leave.

The Question of Free Love and Sexuality: The Thorn in Hegel's Side

Hegel's 1797–8 "Fragment on Love" reflects a more romantic conception of love and sexuality than the tame and domesticized view of marriage in the *Rechtsphilosophie*. Here love is given the dialectical structure of spirit; it is unity in unity and separateness; identity in identity and difference. In love, lovers are a "living" as opposed to a "dead" whole; the one aspect of dead matter that disrupts the unity of love is property. Property separates lovers by making them aware of their individuality as well as destroying their reciprocity. "True union or love proper exists only between living beings who are alike in power and thus in one another's eyes living beings from every point of view . . . This genuine love excludes all oppositions."[26]

Yet the discussion of the family in the *Philosophy of Right* is in general more conservative and criticizes the emphasis on free love as leading to libertinage and promiscuity. One of the objects of Hegel's greatest ire is

Friedrich von Schlegel's *Lucinde*, which Hegel names "Die romantische Ab-
wertung der Ehe" ("the romantic denigration of love").[27] To demand free
sexuality as proof of freedom and "inwardness" is in Hegel's eyes sophistry,
serving the exploitation of women. Hegel, in smug bourgeois fashion, observes:

> Friedrich v. Schlegel in his *Lucinde*, and a follower of his in the *Briefe eines
> Ungennanten*, have put forward the view that the wedding ceremony is
> superfluous and a formality which might be discarded. Their reason is that
> love is, so they say, the substance of marriage and that the celebration
> therefore detracts from its worth. Surrender to sensual impulse is here
> represented as necessary to prove the freedom and inwardness of love – an
> argument not unknown to seducers.

And he continues:

> It must be noticed in connexion with sex-relations that a girl in surrendering
> her body loses her honour. With a man, however, the case is otherwise,
> because he has a field for ethical activity outside the family. A girl is
> destined in essence for the marriage tie and for that only; it is therefore
> demanded of her that love shall take the form of marriage and that the
> different moments in love shall attain their true rational relation to each
> other.[28]

Taking my cue from this footnote in the text, I want to ask what this
aside reveals and conceals at once about Hegel's true attitudes toward
female emancipation in this period. The seemingly insignificant reference
to Friedrich Schlegel's *Lucinde* is extremely significant in the context of the
struggles for early women's emancipation at this time.

Remarking on the transformations brought about by the Enlightenment
and the French Revolution, Mary Hargrave has written:

> The close of the eighteenth and the beginning of the nineteenth centuries
> mark a period of Revolution for men and Evolution for women. The ideas of
> the French Revolution, that time of upheaval, of revaluing of values, of
> imperious assertion of the rights of the individual, swept over Europe like a
> quickening wind and everywhere there was talk of Liberty, Equality, Fra-
> ternity, realised (and perhaps only realisable) in that same order of
> precedence. . . .
>
> The minds of intellectual women were stirred, they became more conscious
> of themselves, more philosophic, more independent . . . France produced a
> writer of the calibre of Madame de Staël, England a Mary Sommerville, a
> Jane Austen; and Germany, although the stronghold of the domestic ideal,
> also had her brilliant intellectual women who, outside their own country,
> have perhaps not become as widely known as they deserve.[29]

In this work devoted to *Some German Women and their Salons*, Mary
Hargrave discusses Henriette Herz (1764–1847) and Rahel Varnhagen

(1771–1833), both Jewesses, Bettina von Arnim (1785–1859), and Caroline Schlegel (1763–1809), among others. Of particular importance in this context is also Karoline von Günderode (1780–1806), the most significant woman German poet of the Romantic era, in love with Hegel's high-school friend, Hölderlin. These women, through their lives and friend-ships, salons and contacts, and in some cases through their letters, publica-tions and translations, were not only forerunners of the early women's emancipation, but also represented a new model of gender relations, aspiring to equality, free love and reciprocity.

Definitive for Hegel's own contact with these women and their ideals, was the so-called Jenaer Kreis, the Jena circle, of the German Romantics, Friedrich and August Wilhelm Schlegel, Novalis, Schleiermacher, and Schelling. The journal *Athenäum* (1798–1800) was the literary outlet of this circle, frequented by Goethe as well as Hegel after his arrival in Jena in 1801. The "Jena circle" had grown out of friendship and literary cooperation among men but counted Caroline Schlegel among its most influential members. She had extraordinary impact on the Schlegel brothers, and was the inspiration for many of Friedrich Schlegel's literary characters as well as for his views on women, marriage and free love.[30] It is widely believed that Caroline Schlegel was the model for the heroine in the novel *Lucinde*.

Born as Caroline Albertina Michaelis, in Göttingen, as the daughter of a professor of Old Testament, Caroline was brought up in an intellectual household.[31] Following traditional patterns, in 1784 she married a young country doctor Georg Böhmer and moved from Göttingen to Clausthal, a mining village in the Hartz mountains. Although she suffered from the narrowness of her new surroundings and from the lack of intellectual stimulation, she remained here until suddenly her husband died in 1788. Caroline, who was then mother of three, lost two of her children after her husband's death. With her daughter Auguste Böhmer, she returned to the parental city. At Göttingen she met August Wilhelm Schlegel, six years her junior, who fell in love with her. In 1792 she left Göttingen for Mainz, the home now of her childhood friend Teresa Forster, born Heym. In December 1792 the city fell to the French under General Custine; the aristocrats fled and the republic was proclaimed. Teresa's husband, Forster, who was an ardent republican, was made president of the Jacobin Club. His wife, no longer in sympathy with his views, left him but Caroline stayed on and worked with revolutionary circles. In the spring of the following year, 1793, a German army mustered from Rheinisch principal-ities, retook Mainz. Caroline was arrested and with her little daughter Auguste was imprisoned in a fortress. After some months, her brother petitioned for her release, offering his services as an army surgeon in return, and August Wilhelm Schlegel exercised what influence he could to obtain her freedom.

Caroline was freed, but was banned from the Rheinisch provinces; even Göttingen, her home town, closed its doors to her. She was now pregnant, expecting the child of a French soldier, and August Wilhelm arranged for her to be put under the protection of his brother, Friedrich, then a young student in Leipzig. A lodging outside the city had to be found for her; here a child was born, but it did not live. In 1796, urged by her family and realizing the need for a protector, Caroline agreed to become August Schlegel's wife and settled with him in Jena. She never really loved Schlegel, and with the appearance of the young Schelling on the scene in 1798 a new love started in her life. Caroline's daughter, Auguste, died in July 1800. Schlegel settled in Berlin in 1802, and the increasing estrangement between them was resolved by a divorce in 1803. A few months later, she and Schelling were married by his father, a pastor, and they lived in Jena until her death in 1809.

Hegel lived in the same house with Caroline and Schelling from 1801 to 1803, and certainly the presence of this remarkable woman, an intellectual companion, a revolutionary, a mother, and a lover, provided Hegel with a flesh and blood example of what modernity, the Enlightenment and the French Revolution could mean for women. And Hegel did not like what he saw. Upon her death, he writes to Frau Niethammer: "I kiss a thousand times over the beautiful hands of the best woman. God may and shall preserve her as befits her merit ten times longer than the woman of whose death we recently learned here [Caroline Schelling], and of whom a few here have enunciated the hypothesis that the Devil had fetched her."[32] A damning and unkind remark, if there ever was one!

Whether Hegel should have liked or approved of Caroline, who certainly exercised a caustic and sharp power of judgment over people, making and remaking some reputations in her circle of friends – Schiller's for example – is beside the point. The point is that Caroline's life and person provided an example, and a very close one at that, of the kinds of changes that were taking place in women's lives at the time, of the possibilities opening before them, and also of the transformation of gender relations. In staunchly defending women's place in the family, in arguing against women's education except by way of learning the necessary skills to run a household, Hegel was not just "falling prey to the prejudices of his time." "His time" was a revolutionary one, and in the circles closest to Hegel, that of his Romantic friends, he encountered brilliant, accomplished and nonconformist women who certainly intimated to him what true gender equality might mean in the future. Hegel saw the future, and he did not like it. His eventual critique of Romantic conceptions of free love is also a critique of the early Romantics' aspirations to gender equality or maybe some form of androgyny.

Schlegel's novel *Lucinde* was written as a eulogy to love as a kind of union to be enjoyed both spiritually and physically. In need of neither religious sanction – Lucinde is Jewish – nor formal ceremony, such true love was reciprocal and complete.[33] In the Athäneums-Fragment 34, Schlegel had defined conventional marriages as "concubinages" to which a "marriage à quatre" would be preferable.[34] *Lucinde* is a critical text, juxtaposing to the subordination of women and the duplicitous sexual conduct of the times a utopian ideal of true love as completion between two independent beings. Most commentators agree, however, that *Lucinde*, despite all noble intentions, is not a text of female emancipation: Lucinde's artistic pursuits, once they have demonstrated the equality of the lovers, cease to be relevant. The letters document Julius's development as a man, his *Lehrjahre*, his movement from sexual desire dissociated from respect and equality to his attainment of the ultimate companionship in a spiritually and erotically satisfying relationship. Women are idealized journey-mates, accompanying the men on this spiritual highway. "Seen on the one hand as the complementary opposites of men, embodying the qualities their counterparts lack, they are on the other, complete beings idealized to perfection."[35] Although in a section of the novel called "A dithyrambic fantasy on the loveliest situation in the world,"[36] there is a brief moment of reversal of roles in sexual activity which Julius sees as "a wonderful . . . allegory of the development of male and female to full and complete humanity,"[37] in general in the *Lucinde*, the spiritual characteristics of the two genders are clearly distinguished.

In his earlier essays such as "Über die weiblichen Charaktere in den griechischen Dichtern" and "Über die Diotima" (1793–4), composed after meeting Caroline Schlegel Schelling, and being enormously influenced by her person, Friedrich Schlegel had developed the thesis – to be echoed later by Marx in the *1844 Manuscripts* – that Greek civilization decayed or flourished in proportion to the degree of equality it accorded to women. In particular, Schlegel emphasized that inequality between men and women, and the subordination of women, led to a bifurcation in the human personality, whereby men came to lack "innocence, grace and love," and women "independence." As opposed to the crudeness of male–female relations in Homer, Sophocles in Schlegel's eyes is the poet who conceives his male and female characters according to the same design and the same ideal. It is Antigone who combines the male and female personality into an androgynous ideal: she "desires only the true Good, and accomplishes it without strain," in contrast to her sister, Ismene, the more traditional feminine, who "suffers in silence."[38] Antigone transcends these stereotypes and represents a blending of male and female characteristics; she "is the Divine."

Read against the background of Schlegel's views, Hegel's generally celebrated discussion of Antigone in the *Phenomenology of Spirit* reveals a different message. In Hegel's version of Antigone, she and Creon respectively stand for "female" and "male" virtues, and forms of ethical reality. Antigone represents the "hearth," the gods of the family, of kinship and of the "nether world."[39] Creon stands for the law, for the city, human law and the dictates of politics that are of "this world". Their clash is a clash between equal powers; although through her acknowledgement of guilt, Antigone presents that moment in the dialectic of action and fate which Hegel considers necessary, it is eventually through the decline of the family and the "nether world" that Spirit will progress to the Roman realm of law and further to the public light of the Enlightenment. Spiritually, Antigone is a higher figure than Creon, although even the most sympathetic commentators have to admit that what Hegel has accomplished here is "an apologia for Creon."[40]

Ironically, Hegel's discussion of the *Antigone* is more historically accurate in terms of the condition of Greek women, their confinement to the home, and the enormous clash between the newly emerging order of the *polis* and the laws of the extended family on which Greek society until the sixth and seventh centuries had rested than was Schlegel's.[41] But in his version of Antigone, Hegel was not simply being historically more accurate than Schlegel; he was robbing his romantic friends of an ideal, of a utopian vision. If Antigone's greatness derives precisely from the fact that she represents the ties of the "hearth and blood" over and against the *polis*, notwithstanding her grandeur, the dialectic will sweep Antigone in its onward historical march, precisely because the law of the city is public as opposed to private, rational as opposed to corporal, promulgated as opposed to intuited, human as opposed to divine. Hegel's narrative envisages no future synthesis of these pairs of opposites as did Schlegel's; whether on a world-historical scale or on the individual scale, the female principle must eventually be expelled from public life, for "Womankind – the everlasting irony (in the life) of the community – changes by intrigue the universal end of the government into a private end."[42] Spirit may fall into irony for a brief historical moment, but eventually the serious transparency of reason will discipline women and eliminate irony from public life. Already in Hegel's discussion of Antigone, that strain of restorationist thought, which will celebrate the revolution while condemning the revolutionaries for their actions, is present. Hegel's Antigone is one without a future; her tragedy is also the grave of utopian, revolutionary thinking about gender relations. Hegel, it turns out, is women's gravedigger, confining them to a grand but ultimately doomed phase of the dialectic, which "befalls mind in its infancy."

What about the dialectic then, that locomotive of history rushing on its onward march? There is no way to disentangle the march of the dialectic in Hegel's system from the bdoy of the victims on which it treads. Historical necessity requires its victims, and women have always been among the numerous victims of history. What remains of the dialectic is what Hegel precisely thought he could dispense with: irony, tragedy and contingency. He was one of the first to observe the ironic dialectic of modernity: freedom that could become abstract legalism or selfish pursuit of economic satisfaction; wealth that could turn into its opposite and create extremes of poverty; moral choice that would end in a trivial project of self-aggrandizement; and an emancipated subjectivity that could find no fulfillment in its "other." Repeatedly, the Hegelian system expunges the irony of the dialectic: the subject posits its opposite and loses itself in its other, but is always restored to selfhood via the argument that the "other" is but an extension or an exteriorization of oneself. Spirit is infinitely generous, just like a woman; it gives of itself; but unlike women, it has the right to call what it has contributed "mine" and take it back into itself. The vision of Hegelian reconciliation has long ceased to convince: the otherness of the other is that moment of irony, reversal and inversion with which we must live. What women can do today is to restore irony to the dialectic, by deflating the pompous march of historical necessity – a locomotive derailed, as Walter Banjamin observed – and by giving back to the victims of the dialectic like Caroline Schlegel Schelling their otherness, and this means, in true dialectical fashion, their selfhood.

Notes

Some of the material in this essay formerly appeared as Seyla Benhabib and Linda Nicholson, "Politische Philosophie und die Frauenfrage," in Iring Fetscher and Herfried Münkler, eds, *Pipers Handbuch der politischen Ideen*, vol. 5 (Munich/Zurich: Piper Verlag, 1987), pp. 513–62. I would like to thank Linda Nicholson for her agreement to let me use some of this material in the present article.

1 Joan Kelly Gadol, "Some Methodological Implications of the Relations Between the Sexes," *Women, History and Theory* (Chicago: University of Chicago Press, 1984), pp. 1ff.
2 Cf. Genevieve Lloyd, *The Man of Reason: "Male" and "Female" in Western Philosophy* (Minneapolis: University of Minnesota Press, 1984); Patricia J. Mills, *Woman, Nature and Psyche* (New Haven: Yale University Press, 1987); Benjamin Barber, "Spirit's Phoenix and History's Owl," *Political Theory*, 16 (1), 1988, pp. 5–29.
3 Cf. Heidi Ravven, "Has Hegel Anything to Say to Feminists?", *The Owl of Minerva*, 19 (2), 1988, pp. 149–68.
4 Barber, "Spirit's Phoenix and History's Owl," p. 20. Emphasis in the text.
5 Hegel, *Hegel's Philosophy of Right*, trans. and ed. T. M. Knox (Oxford: Oxford University Press, 1973), para. 144, p. 105.
6 Ibid., para. 146, pp. 105–6.
7 G. W. F. Hegel, *Vorlesungen über die Philosophie der Weltgeschichte*, in *Hegels*

Sämtliche Werke, ed. G. Lasson, vol. 8 (Leipzig, 1923), p. 471. English translation by J. Sibree, *The Philosophy of History* (New York: Dover, 1956), p. 205. Since Sibree's translation diverged from the original in this case, I have used my translation of this passage.

8 *Philosophy of History*, trans. Sibree, pp. 121–2.

9 I have revised the Knox translation of this passage in *Hegel's Philosophy of Right*, para. 165, p. 114, in accordance with Hegel, *Grundlinien der Philosophie des Rechts*, ed. Lasson, para. 165, p. 144. Emphasis in the text.

10 *Hegel's Philosophy of Right*, ed. Knox, para. 166, p. 114.

11 G. W. F. Hegel, *Phänomenologie des Geistes*, ed. J. Hoffmeister, Philosophische Bibliothek, vol. 114 (Hamburg, 1952), p. 326. English translation by A. V. Miller, *Hegel's Phenomenology of Spirit* (New York: Oxford University Press, 1977), p. 274. Emphasis in the text.

12 Ibid.

13 *Hegel's Philosophy of Right*, ed. Knox, paras. 152, 154, p. 109.

14 Cf. the excellent edition by K. H. Ilting, prepared from the lecture notes of K. G. v. Griesheim (1824–5), *Philosophie des Rechts* (Stuttgart: Klet-Cotta, 1974), vol. 6.

15 *Hegel's Philosophy of Right*, ed. Knox, para. 40 Addition, p. 39; cf. also Griesheim edition, para. 40 Z, pp. 180–1.

16 *Hegel's Philosophy of Right*, ed. Knox, para. 168, p. 115.

17 Ibid., para. 171, p. 116.

18 Ibid., para. 172, p. 117.

19 The one exception to this rule is the right of primogeniture, that is, that the oldest son among the landed nobility receives the family estate. It has long been observed that here Hegel indeed supported the historical interests of the landed Prussian gentry against the generally bourgeois ideology of free and unencumbered property and commodity transactions, which he defended in the rest of his system. However, on this issue as well Hegel is a modernist insofar as his defense of primogeniture among the members of the landed estate is justified not with reference to some family right but with reference to securing an independent income for the eldest son of the family, who is to function as a political representative of his class. Cf. *Hegel's Philosophy of Right*, ed. Knox, para. 306 and Addition, p. 293.

20 Ibid., para. 176, p. 118.

21 *Philosophie des Rechts*, Griesheim edition, para. 167 Z, p. 446.

22 Hans Ulrich Wehler, *Deutsche Gesellsachftsgeschichte* (Darmstadt: C. H. Verlag, 1987), vol. 1, p. 147.

23 Ibid.

24 Emil Friedberg, *Das Recht der Eheschliessung* (Leipzig: Bernhard Tauchnitz, 1865), pp. 593ff.

25 *Hegel's Philosophy of Right*, ed. Knox, para. 162, p. 111.

26 G. W. F. Hegel, "Love," in his *Early Theological Writings*, trans. T. M. Knox (Philadelphia: University of Pennsylvania Press, 1971, p. 304).

27 *Hegel's Philosophy of Right*, ed. Knox, para. 164 Addition, p. 263; cf. Griesheim edition, p. 436.

28 *Hegel's Philosophy of Right*, ed. Knox, para. 164, p. 263.

29 Mary Hargrave, *Some German Women and their Salons* (New York: Brentano, n.d.), p. viii.

30 Cf. ibid., pp. 259ff; Kurt Lüthi, *Feminismus und Romantik* (Vienna: Harmann Böhlaus Nachf., 1985), pp. 56ff.

31 Cf. ibid., pp. 251ff.

32 G. W. F. Hegel, *The Letters*, trans. Clark Butler and Christiane Seiler (Bloomington: Indiana University Press, 1984), p. 205.

33 Friedrich Schlegel, *Friedrich Schlegel's Lucinde and the Fragments*, trans. and intro. Peter Frichow (Minneapolis: University of Minnesota Press, 1971); cf. Sara Friedrichsmeyer, *The Androgyne in Early German Romanticism*, Stanford German Studies, vol. 18 (New York: Peter Lang, 1983), pp. 151ff.

34 Schlegel, *Lucinde and the Fragments*, p. 165.

35 Friedrichsmeyer, *Androgyne*, p. 160; cf. also, Lüthi, *Feminismus und Romantik*, pp. 95ff.

36 Schlegel, *Lucinde and the Fragments*, pp. 46ff.

37 Ibid., p. 49.

38 Cited in Friedrichsmeyer, *Androgyne*, p. 120.

39 Hegel, *Phenomenology of Spirit*, p. 276.

40 George Steiner, *Antigones* (New York: Oxford University Press, 1984), p. 41.

41 Hegel's reading of Antigone is more inspired by Aeschylus, who in his *Oresteia* exposed the clash between the early and the new orders as a clash between the female power of blood and the male power of the sword and the law. The decision to speak Orestes free of the guilt of matricide is signalled by an astonishingly powerful statement of the clash between the maternal power of birth and the paternal power of the law. Athena speaks on behalf of Orestes: "It is my task to render final judgement: / this vote which I possess / I will give on Orestes' side / For no mother had a part in *my* birth; / I am entirely male, with all my heart, / except in marriage; I am entirely my father's. / I will never give precedence in honor / to a woman who killed her man, the guardian of her house. / So if the votes are but equal, Orestes wins." Aeschylus, *The Oresteia*, trans. David Grene and Wendy O'Flaherty (Chicago: University of Chicago Press, 1989), pp. 161–2.

42 Hegel, *Phenomenology of Spirit*, p. 288.

8

Masculine Marx

Christine Di Stefano

We set out from real, active men, and on the basis of their real-life process we demonstrate the development of the ideological reflexes and echoes of this life process.
Marx and Engels, The German Ideology

A Personal Introduction: Confessions of a Former Marxist

I want to begin on a personal note, a note of appreciation for the theorist scheduled for critical scrutiny in this essay. Like many students who came of age in the United States during the late 1960s and early 1970s, my early attraction to political theory was made possible by the work of Karl Marx and those teachers and writers who gave him a sympathetic and expanded reading. Thanks to Marx, political theory came alive as an intellectual enterprise that might contribute to the minimization of oppression and human misery, to the creation of an improved and far better world. Next to Marx, the figures of Plato, Machiavelli, Hobbes and even Rousseau paled in comparison. Classroom discussions about the *polis* seemed irrelevant; Machiavelli bore a disturbing resemblance to Henry Kissinger; and Rousseau was simply impossible to pin down. Marx held out the possibility of theory that could be simultaneously rigorous, systematic, elegant, passionate, critical, utopian, and revolutionary. Feminist theory followed close on the heels, and sometimes directly in the footprints, of academic Marxism. Marx's youthful call for "a ruthless criticism of everything" was taken to heart by many feminists as they worked to expose the historically contingent dimensions of women's sexually differentiated experience and exploitation. Socialist-feminist theory is a significant testament to the intimate, if unstable and unsettling, alliance between Marxism and Western feminism.

Today, my disillusionment with Marxism, as a theory and as a politics, is profound, as this essay will reveal. But the countervailing strength of my indebtedness to Marx cannot be denied. An important measure of this indebtedness is the fact that Marx himself frequently provides the very tools and insights of his subsequent and often immanent criticism by feminists. I like to imagine that Marx would be pleased with and honored by his feminist fate, although this fantasy may imbibe the very ontology of masculinist transcendence of which he now stands accused. That is, it may demand a suprahistorical form of cognitive and empathetic achievement on the part of an imagined contemporary Marx. On the other hand, this fantasy (including my own complicity in the transcendent ontology that I will be criticizing, as well as my need to imagine the father's approval) conveniently captures the disconcerting sense of relation I have tried to convey here: in a word, ambivalence.

Gender Theory and the Critique of Masculinity

Feminist rereadings and criticisms of Marx now abound. These many and excellent studies focus attention on the explanatory inadequacies of orthodox Marxism.[1] There is general agreement among feminists that the Marxist categories of "production," "reproduction," "labor," "exploitation," and "class" fail to capture important dimensions of women's lives. As such, orthodox Marxism is also found lacking as a strategic theory of social change for women. In this essay, I will take a different approach. My interest lies not with the question of descriptive and explanatory relevance or adequacy, but rather with the background conditions of this now well-documented failure. An appraisal of these background conditions, in turn, underscores and intensifies the judgment that Marxist-feminism is a misguided, if not impossible or self-refuting, hybrid. For Marx's theory, as I will argue, is profoundly embedded within a masculine horizon of meaning and sensibility. As such, it is not merely inadequate; rather, it is part and parcel of a misogynous configuration of values, meanings, and practices to which feminism stands opposed.

The links between masculinity and misogyny are detailed and explored within gender theory, a contemporary offshoot of psychoanalytic theory.[2] "Gender" refers to apparent representations of sexual difference and identity which are in fact imposed on human subjects, and social and natural phenomena. In most cultures, gender is patterned in dualistic, dichotomous, and hierarchical modes which promote male privilege and female subordination. Nevertheless, the actual contents of gendered representations carry enormous cross-cultural variability. The implication is that gender is simultaneously a ubiquitous feature of culture, and that it has no fixed, transcultural or trans-historical contents. In short, it is best understood as a complex convention. Leaving aside the difficult and important issue of just how pervasive gender is in cross-cultural terms, it is now unquestionably the case that modern Western culture is and has been profoundly gendered. Humanistic pretensions of the Enlightenment and liberal political discourse notwithstanding, modern Western peoples inhabit a politicized cultural universe elaborately carved out and apportioned in terms of presumed meaningful sexual differences.[3] The key terms of this difference, which are partly but also significantly constitutive of modern subjectivities, and currently in a process of social change and radical assessment, are "femininity" and "masculinity."

In broad, if not coarse, outline, contemporary gender theory suggests that identity formation for males and females is enacted according to asymmetrical, although sometimes complementary, gender scripts. These scripts are first played out during the early months and years of an individual's life (the pre-oedipal period) and the central characters are two: mother (or female caretaker) and child. The net effect of female caretaking is that the mother figure comes to be heavily invested with the ambivalent feelings of her charges. As Isaac Balbus describes this:

> she is at once the being with whom the child is initially indistinguishably identified and the one who enforces the (never more than partial) dissolution of this identification. Thus it is the mother who becomes the recipient of the unconscious hostility that accumulates in children of both sexes as the result of this inescapably painful separation. This mother who is loved is also necessarily the mother who is hated.[4]

In societies where all mothers are female and where most females face likely destinies as mothers, the initial ambivalence towards the mother is easily and subsequently transferred to women in general.

But the ambivalence itself comes to be further differentiated in gender-specific terms. In effect, it becomes heightened for the boy child in his subsequent struggle for a specifically gendered identity, which is the only kind of identity "offered" to him by the culture at large. This is where aspects of separation and individuation take on special and different significance for boys and girls. Coppélia Kahn summarizes the difference, explicated most extensively by Nancy Chodorow and Dorothy Dinnerstein, this way:

> For though [the girl] follows the same sequence of symbiotic union, separation and individuation, identification, and object love as the boy, her femininity arises in relation to a person of the *same* sex, while his masculinity arises in

relation to a person of the *opposite* sex. Her femininity is reinforced by her original symbiotic union with her mother and by the identification with her that must precede identity, while masculinity is threatened by the same union and the same identification. While the boy's sense of *self* begins in union with the feminine, his sense of *masculinity* arises against it.[5]

This account suggests that the critical threat to masculinity is not castration, as orthodox psychoanalysis suggests, but rather the threat of maternal reengulfment. Masculine identity requires a massive repudiation of identification with that all-satisfying/all-terrifying maternal source. The basic ambivalence of male and female children towards the mother is intensified for boys because of the need to define masculinity in *contrast* to maternal femininity. An important feature of masculine development, as outlined in this psychoanalytic literature, is the *negative* articulation of masculine selfhood *vis à vis* the pre-posited maternal-feminine presence. (As a boy, I am that which is *not*-mother). The rudimentary building blocks of the boy's struggle to understand what it is that makes him a "boy" and a future "man," a masculine subject and agent in a gender-differentiated world, consist of negative counterfactuals garnered through comparison with the all-too-proximate mother. This prototypical process of masculine individuation and identity formation is susceptible to a process of "false differentiation" whereby the (m)other is unrealistically objectified in split versions rather than accommodated as a more complex entity. In effect, false differentiation is implicated in the inability/refusal to tolerate ambivalence and to acknowledge difference.[6] Nancy Chodorow sums up her reconstruction of the origins and ramifications of masculinity in a manner that bears directly on these themes:

> The division of labor in childrearing results in an objectification of women – a treating of women as others, or objects, rather than subjects, or selves – that extends to our culture as a whole. Infantile development of the self is explored in opposition to the mother, as primary caretaker, who becomes the other. Because boys are of opposite gender from their mothers, they especially feel a need to differentiate and yet find differentiation problematic. The boy comes to define his self more in opposition than through a sense of his wholeness or continuity. He becomes the self and experiences his mother as the other. The process also extends to his trying to dominate the other in order to ensure his sense of self. Such domination begins with mother as the object, extends to women, and is then generalized to include the experience of all others as objects rather than subjects. This stance in which people are treated and experienced as things, becomes basic to male Western culture.[7]

The literature on gender formation and acquisition suggests that there are ways in which masculine experience yields certain cognitive proclivities, tendencies which structure perception.[8] Such cognitive proclivities may comprise or contribute to intellectual frameworks implicitly organized around the ontological and epistemological primacy of the masculine subject, and include several among the following elements: a combative brand of dualistic thinking, a persistent and systematic amplification of the primal Self–Other oppositional dynamic; the creation of dichotomized polarities by which to describe and evaluate the events, objects, and processes of the natural and social worlds; the need for and privileging of singular identity and certainty with respect to one's "own" identity and that of other "objects" in the environment; the denial or refusal of related-ness, to fellow human beings and to nature; a fear and repudiation of natural contingency, including those limits imposed by the body and the natural surround; an identification of such contingency with the feminine; versions of a solitary subject immersed in a hostile and dangerous world; detailed expressions and descriptions of radical or heroic individualism; preoccupation with themes of freedom, autonomy and transcendence; accounts of knowledge-as-opposition and knowledge-as-struggle, based on a distanced relation between the subject and object of knowledge; attitudes of fear, denigration and hostility towards whatever is identified as female or feminine; idealization and glorification of the feminine. This last set of seemingly incompatible attitudes would recapitulate the effects of false differentiation from the maternal object, the (m)other.

Marx was, of course, a brilliant and acute analyst of the very objectifying stance that Nancy Chodorow and others have identified as basic to male Western culture. To what extent is he exempt from or implicated in the masculine configuration of sensibility and meaning briefly detailed above? I explore this question in the remainder of this essay, with special reference to Marx's style and selected substantive areas of his theory.

Marx's Style

Students of Marx are well aware of the intimate relationship between the substance and style of his work. Critics and disciples of Marx would agree that his characteristic polemical style was an aggressive one, which involved "marking out his own position by eliminating former or potential colleagues from it."[9] Marx's approach to an issue was invariably one that proceeded over the toppled remains of existing, would-be and sometimes fabricated opponents, some of whom began as friends, teachers, and mentors. "From his student days to the time of *Capital*," writes Jerrold Seigel, "Marx's characteristic mode of defining himself was by opposition, excluding others from the personal space he occupied."[10] It would seem that Marx could only create a discursive space for himself by invading and re-appropriating the territory of displaced and vanquished others. In this sense, Marx evinces a combative, heroic, and hence, masculine style.[11]

In speculating on the possible sources of this aggressive style, Seigel has suggested that Marx's mother may provide a clue. He argues that Marx's style might have been a reaction against Henriette Marx's intrusive and dominating nurture style. This interpretation is problematic on several counts, although it contains an important measure of insight.

First, we simply do not know enough about Henriette Marx or her relationship to Karl to characterize her as an overbearing mother.[12] However, we might well ask, when is maternal nurturance within the bourgeois, nuclear family *not* intrusive and dominating? Seigel slides into the tendency of "blaming the mother," whereas the real issue here is a more structural one. That is, the kind of family in which Karl Marx was reared is precisely that modern, intensely affective, socially isolated nuclear configuration in which children are likely to perceive their mothers as intrusive beings, regardless of the particular activities and attitudes of specific mothers. These perceptions, in turn, are likely to be retained in adulthood, often in unconscious, elaborated and/or disguised forms. Marx's estranged adult relationship with his mother, coupled with his inflated-romantic courtship to Jenny von Westphalen, suggest that he suffered from an unresolved ambivalence toward the primal, pre-oedipal (m)other. This ambivalence, as we will see, carries over into his analysis of women's labor under capitalism. But it has precious little to do with the actual woman who mothered him.

A second problem with Seigel's analysis of Marx's aggressive style is that it proceeds as if this style is simply an individual personality quirk. That is, Seigel pays little attention to the intellectual discursive tradition within which Marx was embedded. An adversarial, aggressive style is a significant feature of the Western philosophical tradition;[13] furthermore, this style may have found in dialectics a particularly hospitable environment, since the dialectical conversational form has assumed combative, as well as dialogic, features. Marx's aggressive intellectual style should be recast in terms which acknowledge a pre-existing legacy for which he was temperamentally suited, if not gifted.

Finally, we can augment Seigel's treatment of Marx's style by noting that the aggressive, adversarial mode partakes of a masculine cognitive structure. This style (which Marx shares with other political theorists of notable rhetorical skill, such as Hobbes) may be understood, in part, to recapitulate, at the level of adult intellectual practice, the prior process of struggle for a location and identity *vis à vis* the pre-oedipal (m)other. The echoes of this earlier struggle ramify in distinctive ways on Marx's polemical style, which flourishes in hostile territory and will brook no contenders. Ironically, the radical theorist of species-being and communism embodied an intellectual stance and style which contradicted his social ontology.[14]

Seigel's analysis is vindicated, then, with the proviso that we substitute the fantasized mother of Marx's primary process memory and early experience for his "real" mother, and that we go on to acknowledge that mothers of the former sort lurk within the stylistic tradition of adversarial intellectual discourse and have "helped" (as projections of the masculine imagination) to shape the style and subtext of that tradition.[15]

A Tale of Post-embeddedness

At first glance, Marx seems to elude, if not overtly contest, the masculine scheme of meaning outlined above and initially detected in Marx's polemical style. Modern dialectics, for example, is a methodological attempt to transcend the dichotomies which Cartesian-inspired epistemologies promote. Initially, it would seem, dialectics is more closely allied with a feminine epistemological orientation, most especially in its relational and dialogic orientation. The materialist aspect of Marx's method also bears some apparent affinity with feminist critiques of idealist or rationalist presumptions which elevate the (male) brain at the expense of the (female) body. Yet, in spite of these potential affinities between Marxism and feminism, the actual rendition and deployment of dialectics and materialism found in Marx's work play into and out of a specifically masculinist frame of reference and meaning.

"Marx's procedure was in fact to set out from men's labor and to ignore the specificity of women's labor," writes Nancy Hartsock.[16] This invisibility of women's labor is implicated in important ways with Marx's account of "human" labor. Given Marx's ontological and materialist stress on the laboring activities of human beings and the preconditions for certain forms of distinctively "human" activity, the invisibility of women (and especially of women as caretakers and as mothers) is notably striking and problematic.

In *The German Ideology* Marx and Engels discuss the history of the division of labor and locate its first primordial instance in the sexual division of labor in the family. They go on to categorize familial relations, including the sexual division of labor, as "natural" relations. Adding insult to injury, they dismiss the significance of the familial sexual division of labor by stating that a "real" division only emerges with the (presumably distinct and subsequent) distinction between manual and mental labor.[17] Given Marx's insistence that social relations be analyzed as historically determined and specific outcomes rather than as eternal verities, this is especially troublesome. What Marx and Engels subsequently miss in their focus on the division between "brain" and "hand" is what Hilary Rose refers to as the "heart":

Women's work is of a particular kind – whether menial or requiring the sophisticated skills involved in child care, it always involves personal service. Perhaps to make the nature of this caring, intimate, emotionally demanding labor clear, we should use the ideologically loaded term "love." For without love, without close interpersonal relationships, human beings, and it would seem especially small human beings, cannot survive. This emotionally demanding labor requires that women give something of themselves to the child, to the man. The production of people is thus qualitatively different from the production of things. It requires caring labor – the labor of love.[18]

It seems more reasonable to locate the first materialist premise of human existence in the phenomenon of birth; to acknowledge that some woman has "labored" to bring me into the world. On this view, the second premise is that we will be cared for during our early years of biological and emotional vulnerability. And this second premise calls on, but is not exhausted by, Marx and Engels's first: the production of the means to satisfy our needs for nourishment, shelter, and protection. To this premise we should also add the human neonate's need for social intercourse.

Strangely enough, reproduction enters the scene for Marx and Engels as the third premise of history: "men, who daily remake their own life, begin to make other men, to propagate their kind: the relationship between man and woman, parents and children, the family."[19] The sense of historical sequence here is strangely, but familiarly, skewed. For the starting point of their analysis of the premises of history-making men is the already born and nurtured human being. Not only do mothers not make an appearance until the third act, but mothers and fathers enter the Marxian historical scene simultaneously. History and common sense suggest, however, that "mothers" predated "fathers." Feminist history also suggests that fathers have gone to extensive lengths to eradicate this threatening knowledge. In this sense, *The German Ideology* is thoroughly complicitous with patriarchal history and ideology.

This fanciful historical account saturates Marx's economic framework of description and explanation, in which women's gender-specific labor vanishes and we are left with "a gender-biased account of social production and an incomplete account of the life-processes of human beings."[20] The issue here is not simply one of nominal exclusion, which could be rectified by including women and their labor in the theory. Marx's failure to acknowledge and theorize reproductive and caring labor directly influences his understanding of "human" labor, most artfully captured in his comparison of the architect and the bee in *Capital*. While this comparison rightly emphasizes the creative and self-conscious aspects of human labor, it errs in postulating an idealized and over-voluntarist image of unalienated labor emancipated from the realm of necessity:

> In fact, the realm of freedom begins *only where labor which is determined by*
> *necessity and mundane considerations ceases*; thus in the very nature of things it lies
> beyond the sphere of actual material production. . . . Freedom in this field
> can only consist in socialized men, the associated producers, rationally
> regulating their interchange with Nature, *bringing it under their common control*,
> instead of being ruled by it as the blind forces of Nature; and achieving this
> with the least expenditure of energy and under conditions most favorable to,
> and worthy of, their human nature. (Emphasis added)[21]

Necessity – that ultimately ineradicable foe – must be diminished as much as possible for a truly "human" history to flourish. Nature and humanity are thus, in a significant sense, opposed. On this level, Marx shares a similar orientation towards nature with an unlikely ally, J. S. Mill.[22] This vision of freedom is intimately tied up with Marx's sense of history, especially with his sense of progress as a steadily expanding control over nature. The material and technological conditions for such control are necessary, if not sufficient, guarantors of human self-realization. Marx's youthful anticipated "reconciliation" of humanity and nature in *The Economic and Philosophical Manuscripts* thus takes place at the dialectical expense of nature controlled.

Isaac Balbus argues that Marx's concept of production entails the domination of nature because it requires an "instrumental relationship between humans and their surrounding world."[23] As the substance of "necessity," nature is humanity's adversary in its quest for self-creative, self-sufficient freedom. When we approach nature on these instrumental terms, we must assume that it "has no intrinsic worth, no dignity of its own," and therefore that it makes no normative claims on humanity.[24] William Petty's analogy – quoted approvingly by Marx in *Capital* – that "labour is the father of the material world, the earth is its mother," reinforces the notion that nature provides the inert material substratum for "productive" labor, as it associatively plays on the sexist depiction of women as passive, natural, and therefore less-than-fully human creatures. While the young Marx was obviously groping for some means of reconciliation between humanity and nature, his subsequent vision of communism effectively renders the "humanization" of nature as its sadistic domination by human beings:

> Communism . . . treats *all* natural premises as the creatures of hitherto
> existing men, *strips* them of their natural character and *subjugates* them to the
> power of the united individuals . . . . The reality, which communism is
> creating, is precisely the true basis for rendering it impossible that *anything*
> *should exist independently of individuals*, insofar as reality is *only* a product of the
> preceding intercourse of individuals themselves. (Emphasis added)[25]

The subjugation of natural premises is, in turn, implicated in the act of self-affirmation and self-creation. This agenda for self-creation as the achieved solution to and victory over the threat of uncontrolled natural forces parallels the masculine invention of identity against the (m)other.

If Marx had stopped seriously to consider the labor of female caretakers and mothers, he would have been forced in one of two directions: either to characterize such labor as less than human because it is bound to nature and necessity; or to rethink his account of labor to accommodate reproductive and emotional labor, which is complexly constituted by biology and messy necessity, as well as by culture and history. (If he had done this, he would also have had to recast his historical narrative, which is less obviously "progressive" for women.) Implicitly, the former characterization prevails in his analysis of labor. Explicitly, the laboring mother is conveniently ignored. In short, what we have here is another case of the missing mother in Western political theory.

Mary O'Brien's comparison of the mother and the architect introduces some of the more stubborn and interesting features of maternal labor which Marx avoided. They are worth considering in some detail:

> Biological reproduction . . . is not an act of rational will. No one denies a motherly imagination, which foresees the child in a variety of ways . . . . Female reproductive consciousness knows that a child will be born, knows what a child is, and speculates in general terms about this child's potential. Yet mother and architect are quite different. The woman cannot realize her visions, cannot make them true, by virtue of the reproductive labor in which she involuntarily engages, if at all. Unlike the architect, her will does not influence the shape of her product. Unlike the bee, she knows that her product, like herself, will have a history. Like the architect, she knows what she is doing; like the bee, she cannot help what she is doing.[26]

At issue here are fundamental questions concerning control, the human relationship to nature, and the characterization of identifiably human activities as exclusively rational and self-generative. Stressing the planned, conscious, and purposive dimensions of human labor, Marx counterposes such labor to the realm of Necessity (Nature) and so is constitutionally unable to see women's reproductive labor and its derivatives as human labor. The fact that "productive" labor as such would be impossible without reproductive and caring labor makes this blindspot all the more problematic. Marx has failed to fully specify the preconditions for "human" labor as he defines it. At this point, we could well ask Marx a feminist-inspired version of the question that he put to liberal psychological theories that ignored the history of industry and production in their pronouncements on the psychological life of "man": "What should one think of a science [Marxism] whose preconceptions disregarded this large field of man's [sic] labour [maternal labor] and which is not conscious of its incompleteness . . . ?"[27]

Marx has essentially *denied* and then *reappropriated* the labor of the mother in his historical and labor-based account of self-created man.[28] What is wrong with this familiar account of independence, self-creation and self-sufficiency, within which we can discern a strong dose of modernist sensibility? First, it relies on an overly, but only apparently, "plastic" conception of human nature. That is, plasticity is not the open or unencumbered account of human nature that it claims to be. Secondly, it is arrogant and in keeping with problematic Enlightenment notions concerning the status of nature. Thirdly, it is implicated in the denial of the mother.

Marx provided a significant and much-needed critique of the presocial individual monad of liberal theory who is constituted as a subject prior to the society in which he lives. However, his substitute notion of the individual as "the ensemble of social relations" creates a good many problems. Robert Heilbroner has been especially acute in describing the hazards of a plastic conception of human nature:

> There is a severe price to be paid for a view of the human being as without any definition other than that created by its social setting. For the individual thereupon becomes the expression of social relations binding him or her together with *other* individuals who are likewise nothing but the creatures of their social existences. We then have a web of social determinations that has no points of anchorage other than in our animal bodies.[29]

And our animal bodies, within the frame of Marx's antinaturalist analysis, can't tell us very much about ourselves. Dennis Wrong's identification of a theoretical partnership between an oversocialized view of man and an over-integrated view of society is substantiated in the fate of politics within Marx's theory and the political history of successful Marxist movements.[30] Marx's collapsed vision of a complementary and trouble-free relationship between the individual and communist society is too seamless to admit political struggle and dialogue over society's means, ends, limits, and possibilities. That the theorist *par excellence* of struggle and contradiction should end up with this kind of static vision is rather incredible. Or is it? Perhaps Marx himself embodies a human-all-too-human limit for living with perpetual conflict. Intense, dichotomously framed, do-or-die conflict engenders its opposite: pure, yet false, reconciliation.

An exaggerated emphasis on man's self-creative abilities is also arrogant. It denies our natural embeddedness and promotes resentment against a nature that (like a mother) has not made us godlike. It pits the "human" essence against the "natural" backdrop of limitations. And it actually anticipates a state of "post-embeddedness," where according to Jeremy Shapiro's favorable commentary: "the individual has ceased to become the object of uncontrolled forces and is instead entirely self-created, ceaselessly going beyond its own limits by means of its creativity, and continuously participating in the movement of its own becoming."[31]

Post-embeddedness is a dangerous and arrogant fiction. It is also masculinist and misogynous. It is dangerous because it elicits the revolt of nature. It is masculine because it issues out of a configuration of perceptions and needs rooted in a gendered identity fashioned out of opposition to the maternal world. It is misogynous because it perpetuates a fear of and consequent need to dominate naturalized, and hence, "dangerous" women. The domination of nature issues in a longing to return to it. This return, as Silvia Bovenschen argues, is negotiated through the female: "The biological-natural moments of human existence only appear to have been fully expunged from masculine everyday life: that relationship to inner [and outer] nature which has not yet been mastered is projected onto women, so that women must pay for the dysfunctionality of man's natural drives."[32]

Marx's systematic and related failures to accommodate nature and women within his grand scheme of explanation may help to explain a central tension at the heart of his theory, that between humanistic voluntarism ("man makes himself") and sociostructural determinism ("life is not determined by consciousness, but consciousness by life"). For while this tension may be artfully combined, as we find in *The Eighteenth Brumaire*, it also threatens to erupt in onesided formulations. Humanity's domination over nature promises a human omnipotence which is eternally threatened. Notice that the capitalist version of this threat, analyzed by Marx under the rubrics of "accumulation" and "reproduction," takes on vitalistic, naturelike, and even female capacities, including dynamically regenerative ones. In effect, the mother banished from the realms of history and labor reappears in Marx's portrayal of a fecund capitalism that reproduces and augments itself, while his own intellectual efforts are cast as the contributions of a midwife helping to shorten the birth pangs of an eventual or incipient revolution.[33]

An exaggerated emphasis on self-creation denies that we were born and nurtured. It denies the biosocial basis for species-continuity and projects it exclusively on to the arena of "labor." And it promotes a view of communism as severing "the umbilical cord [!] of the individual's natural connection with the species."[34] These themes help us to ponder Mary O'Brien's suggestion that "underlying the doctrine that man makes history is the undiscussed reality of why he must."[35]

When we deny our first biosocial relationship we deny our own natural embeddedness as physical, vulnerable, animal creatures. We also deny the origins and ground of our sociability as a species. Philosophers such as Marx who wish to articulate and promote this important aspect of human life without reference to maternal or parental labor are forced to ground it in activities which postdate (by a long shot) our first experience of sociability. Small wonder that the theory comes out sounding "utopian" and unrealistic. When we deny maternal labor and women's labors of caring love, which tend to be more aware of a noninstrumental, cooperative and also difficult relationship with nature, we construct a deficient view of "specifically human labor" and of "species life."[36] Without some retrospective appreciation for our biosocial origins, we are all the more likely to join Marx in viewing the past as a mere and disgusting pile of "muck."

This denial of the mother in Marx's theory – which is also central to the social acquisition, definition, and defense of masculinity – helps to maintain the domination of women and the domination of nature. Hence, Marxist social theory may be perpetuating problems – some of which it would like to solve, others of which it is unaware – that involve not only half of the human species, but our literal survival as a species.

Yet there are intimations in Marx (especially the young Marx) of yearning for a genuine, mutually reciprocal relationship between humanity and nature, men and women.[37] A more generous reading than I have offered here would locate him in the tension between the recognition of nature and its domination, within the complex contrariness of his thinking.[38] Such a reading would take issue with Isaac Balbus's argument that Marx is unredeemable because his conception of production is "the ultimate possible expression of" the " 'hubris of domination.' "[39] It would be more in keeping with Nancy Hartsock's suggestion that Marx needs to be (and can be) transplanted to a new epistemological terrain, one that is gender-sensitive, inclusive of a larger subject of history, and explicitly feminist.

Is Marx's theory the "ultimate" in modernist, Enlightenment-inspired attempts to dominate nature? This is a difficult question, one that I am inclined to answer negatively because of Marx's latent intimations of an alternative dialectical interplay between humanity and nature. If we take Marx's failure to consist of "his inability to [maintain and] extend his splendid insight into the epistemological validity of sensuous experience and the sensuousness of the 'man/nature' relationship expressed in labor,"[40] then the terms of his failure, at least, are preferable to those of others.

On the other hand, we had better think twice before we attempt to transplant Marx to new epistemological ground, as Nancy Hartsock suggests. For Marx's theoretical universe is bound up with an ontological habitat that is profoundly masculine. And the knowledge which issues out of and is produced by this framework is limited and damaging, not simply in its inability to "see" aspects of gender-differentiated experience and knowledge, but also in the very action and substance of its interpretive horizon. Marx's epistemological commitment to the arena of "production" commits him to an ontological reality which is detectably masculine, not merely male. As such, it lacks a reflexive appreciation of its own material and ideological roots which, within the Marxian view, is the prerequisite of a genuinely rigorous critical theory. To a great extent, the "root" that Marx unwittingly grasped was gender-specific modern man.

Conclusion

Marx's "real connections" to his social world reflect, in significant measure, the introjected connections of a masculine subject. We find masculinity at work in Marx's need to clear the ground for his intellectual and polemical endeavors. But more significantly, Marx has "successfully" banished the mother from his overall account of social relations. (In this respect, he is not so different from the majority of modern political theorists.) This enables a number of crucial and distinctive turns in his theory: a view of history as forward-moving progress; a dichotomous account of antagonistic class relations; a cataclysmic theory of historical change; and a view of human labor as ultravoluntarist. The missing mother underwrites the Marxian account of labor by helping to subsume nonvoluntarist dimensions of human laboring practices. The voluntarist account of labor, in turn, is a key component of Marx's objectification of nature, for it conveniently promotes a view of nature as the (feminized) passive substratum of (hu)manly active efforts. The inverse relationship between freedom and necessity informs and issues out of the voluntarist conception of labor, and it parallels the antagonistic relationship between son and (m)other, (hu)manity and nature. Post-embeddedness is the inevitably "utopian" endpoint of such a scheme. What it recapitulates at the level of social and political theory is a yearning and fantasy embedded in the deep psychology of masculine identity: clean and ultimate release from the (m)other.

Notes

For generous comments, criticisms, and editorial help, I would like to thank Susan Hekman, Mary Shanley, Katherine Teghtsoonian, and Diane Wolf.

1 It would be impossible to do full justice to this literature in a single note. What follows is a selective list derived primarily from the socialist-feminist genre. Christine Delphy, *Close to Home: A Materialist Analysis of Women's Oppression* (Amherst: University of Massachusetts Press, 1984); Zillah Eisenstein, ed., *Capitalist Patriarchy and the Case for Socialist Feminism* (New York: Monthly Review Press, 1979); Nancy C. M. Hartsock, *Money, Sex, and Power: Toward a Feminist Historical Materialism* (New York and London: Longman, 1983); Alison Jaggar, *Feminist Politics and Human Nature* (Totowa, NJ: Rowman and Allanheld, 1983; Sussex: The Harvester Press, 1983); Mary O'Brien, *The Politics of Reproduction* (Boston and London: Routledge and Kegan Paul, 1981); Juliet Mitchell,

Woman's Estate (New York: Random House, 1973); Lydia Sargent, ed., *Women and Revolution* (Boston: South End Press, 1981); Hilda Scott, *Does Socialism Liberate Women?* (Boston: Beacon Press, 1974); Eli Zaretsky, *Capitalism, the Family, and Personal Life*, revised and expanded edn (New York: Harper and Row, 1986). An excellent recent contribution to the debate concerning the relationship between feminism and Marxism, which extends into postmodern theoretical territory, is the collection of essays edited and introduced by Seyla Benhabib and Drucilla Cornell, *Feminism as Critique* (Cambridge: Polity; Minneapolis: University of Minnesota Press, 1987).

2 Again, it is impossible to do justice to this literature in one note. A helpful review and summary of object relations theory, which often provides the theoretical starting point for American feminist gender theory, is Jay R. Greenberg and Stephen A. Mitchell, *Object Relations in Psychoanalytic Theory* (Cambridge, Mass., and London: Harvard University Press, 1983). Influential works in this feminist object relations genre are: Nancy Chodorow, *The Reproduction of Mothering* (Berkeley: University of California Press, 1978) and Dorothy Dinnerstein, *The Mermaid and the Minotaur* (New York: Harper and Row, 1976). The more orthodox defense and utilization of psychoanalytic theory for feminist analysis is exemplified in Juliet Mitchell, *Psychoanalysis and Feminism* (New York: Random House, 1975) and "Introduction I," to Juliet Mitchell and Jaqueline Rose, eds, *Feminine Sexuality: Jacques Lacan and the École Freudienne* (New York: Norton, 1982). For an influential feminist criticism of psychoanalytic gender theory, see Luce Irigaray, *This Sex Which Is Not One*, trans. Catherine Porter (Ithaca: Cornell University Press, 1985) and *Speculum of the Other Woman*, trans. Gillian C. Gill (Ithaca: Cornell University Press, 1985). For an influential application of Chodorow and Dinnerstein to models of moral development, see Carol Gilligan, *In a Different Voice* (Cambridge, Mass., and London: Harvard University Press, 1982). A similarly influential application of object relations theory to the history and philosophy of science is Evelyn Keller, *Reflections on Gender and Science* (New York and London: Yale University Press, 1985).

3 For important contemporary discussions of the theoretical and political status of gender differences, see the following edited anthologies: Seyla Benhabib and Drucilla Cornell, eds, *Feminism as Critique*; Hester Eisenstein and Alice Jardine, eds, *The Future of Difference* (Boston: G. K. Hall, 1980); Alice Jardine and Paul Smith, eds, *Men in Feminism* (New York and London: Methuen, 1987); Linda Nicholson, ed., *Feminism/Postmodernism* (New York and London: Routledge, 1990).

4 Isaac Balbus, "Disciplining Women: Michel Foucault and the Power of Feminist Discourse," in Benhabib and Cornell, eds, *Feminism as Critique*, pp. 110–27, especially p. 112.

5 Coppélia Kahn, *Man's Estate: Masculine Identity in Shakespeare* (Berkeley: University of California Press, 1981), p. 10.

6 See Jessica Benjamin, "The Bonds of Love: Rational Violence and Erotic Domination," *Feminist Studies*, 6, spring 1980, pp. 144–74.

7 In Judith Lorber, Rose Laub Coser, Alice S. Rossi and Nancy Chodorow, "On *The Reproduction of Mothering*: A Methodological Debate," *Signs: Journal of Women in Culture and Society*, 6, spring 1981, pp. 482–513, especially pp. 502–3.

8 It may also be said that feminine experience yields distinct cognitive proclivities. However, feminine experience has not, until very recently, been systematically articulated in literate form, nor generalized into universalizing statements and theories about humanity, society and social inquiry. Given the contemporary instability of gender in conceptual as well as phenomenological terms, it is unlikely that "femininity" – or feminism, for that matter – will ever imitate or appropriate masculinity's hegemonic achievement.

9 Jerrold Seigel, *Marx's Fate: The Shape of a Life* (Princeton: Princeton University Press, 1978).

10 Ibid., p. 182.

11 On the links between heroism and masculinity, see the following: Christine Di Stefano, "Masculinity as Ideology in Political Theory: Hobbesian Man Considered," *Women's Studies International Forum*, 6, 1983, pp. 633–44; Hartsock, *Money, Sex and Power*, ch. 8; Marina Warner, *Joan of Arc: The Image of Female Heroism* (New York: Random House, 1981).

12 The little evidence that we do have of Henriette Marx's relationship to her son is one letter (reproduced in Seigel, *Marx's Fate*, p. 49) wherein she is solicitous of her son's health and well-being. We also know that she subsequently became critical of his inability to support himself and his family. The record also suggests that Marx showed little affection for her during his adult years and that he visited her infrequently, and then primarily to request money.

13 See Janice Moulton, "A Paradigm of Philosophy: The Adversary Method," in Sandra Harding and Merrill B. Hintikka, eds, *Discovering Reality* (Dordrecht: D. Reidel, 1983), pp. 149–64.

14 For helpful discussions of Marx's ontology, see the following: Norman Geras, *Marx and Human Nature: Refutation of a Legend* (London: New Left Books, 1983); Carol C. Gould, *Marx's Social Ontology: Individuality and Community in Marx's Theory of Social Reality* (Cambridge, Mass., and London: MIT Press, 1978); Bertell Ollman, *Alienation: Marx's Conception of Man in Capitalist Society* (Cambridge: Cambridge University Press, 1971).

15 For an original and helpful discussion of maternal subtexts, see Coppélia Kahn, "Excavating 'Those Dim Minoan Regions': Maternal Subtexts in Patriarchal Literature," *Diacritics: A Review of Contemporary Criticism*, 12, 1982, pp. 32–41.

16 Hartsock, *Money, Sex, and Power*, p. 146.

17 Karl Marx and Frederick Engels, *The German Ideology*, part I, ed. C. J. Arthur (New York: International Publishers, 1970), pp. 43–4, 51–2.

18 Hilary Rose, "Hand, Brain, and Heart: A Feminist Epistemology for the Natural Sciences," *Signs: Journal of Women in Culture and Society*, 9, autumn 1983, pp. 73–90, especially p. 75.

19 Marx and Engels, *The German Ideology*, p. 57.

20 Hartsock, *Money, Sex and Power*, p. 148.

21 *Capital*, vol. III (New York: International Publishers, 1967), p. 820.

22 See J. S. Mill, "Nature," in Marshall Cohen, ed., *The Philosophy of John Stuart Mill: Ethical, Political and Religious* (New York: Random House, 1961).

23 Isaac Balbus, *Marxism and Domination*, (Princeton: Princeton University Press, 1982), p. 269.

24 Ibid., p. 271.

25 Marx and Engels, *German Ideology*, 86.

26 O'Brien, *Politics of Reproduction*, pp. 37–8.

27 Karl Marx, *Economic and Philosophic Manuscripts*, in *Karl Marx: Selected Writings*, ed. David McLellan (Oxford: Oxford University Press, 1977), p. 93.

28 Consider the following passages from the *Economic and Philosophic Manuscripts*: "For socialist man what is called world history is nothing but the creation of man by human (sic) labor and the development of nature for man . . ." "Socialist man . . . has the observable and irrefutable proof of his self-creation and the process of his origin." "A being only counts itself as independent when it stands on its own two feet and it stands on its own two feet as long as it owes its existence to itself." Ibid., pp. 94, 95.

29 Robert Heilbroner, *Marxism: For and Against* (New York and London: Oxford University Press, 1980), p. 163.

30 Dennis Wrong, "The Oversocialized Conception of Man in Modern Sociology," *American Sociological Review*, 26, April 1961, pp. 183–93.

31 Jeremy Shapiro, "The Slime of History: Embeddedness in Nature and Critical Theory," in *On Critical Theory*, ed. John O'Neill (New York: Seabury Press, 1976), pp. 145–63, especially p. 149.

32 Silvia Bovenschen, "The Contemporary Witch, the Historical Witch, and the Witch Myth," *New German Critique*, 15, fall 1978, pp. 83–119, especially p. 117. The "revolt of nature" was theorized by Theodor Adorno and Max Horkheimer in *Dialectic of Enlightenment*. It has subsequently been reinvoked and extended by feminists seeking to articulate a critical theory of feminist ecology. What Adorno and Horkheimer saw in the trajectory of Enlightenment thought and practice was a steady "progress" in the domination of internal and external nature that was necessarily accompanied by social and affective regression. They were also attuned to the gendered dimensions of this dialectic. Women, as Adorno argued in another essay, were "not yet in the grasp of society" (that is, not in a position of power). Furthermore, they were implicated in the dialectic as beings thought to be more "natural" than men; and "where the mastery of nature is the true goal, biological inferiority remains a glaring stigma, the weakness imprinted by nature as a key stimulus to aggression." In other words, "uncivilized" aggression is unleashed by "civilized" men against "naturalized" women, nature, and other "others." Horkehimer and Adorno, *Dialectic of Enlightenment* (New York: Seabury Press, 1972), p. 248.

33 For explorations of the male appropriation of female reproductive powers, see the following: Azizah al-Hibri, "Reproduction, Mothering and the Origins of Patriarchy," in *Mothering: Essays in Feminist Theory*, ed. Joyce Trebilcot (Totowa, NJ: Rowman and Allanheld, 1983), pp. 81–93; Eva Feder Kittay, "Womb Envy: An Explanatory Concept," in the same collection, pp. 94–128; O'Brien, *Politics of Reproduction*.

34 Marx, *Capital*, quoted in Shapiro, "Slime of History," p. 148.

35 O'Brien, *Politics of Reproduction*, p. 53.

36 See Ulrike Prokop, "Production and the Context of Women's Daily Life," *New German Critique*, 13, winter 1978, pp. 18–33; and Sara Ruddick, "Maternal Thinking," in *Rethinking the Family: Some Feminist Questions*, ed.

Barrie Thorne and Marilyn Yalom (New York and London: Longman, 1982), pp. 76–94.

37 The following passage from the *Economic and Philosophical Manuscripts* is especially provocative in this regard: "The infinite degradation in which man exists for himself is expressed in his relationship to woman. . . . In this natural [sic] relationship of the sexes man's relationship to nature is immediately his relationship to man, and his relationship to man is immediately his relationship to nature . . . Thus, from this relationship the whole cultural level of man can be judged." In *Karl Marx: Selected Writings*, ed. McLellan, p. 62.

38 I want to thank Sara Lennox for this suggestion, even though I do not pursue it.

39 Balbus, *Marxism and Domination*, p. 269.

40 Mary O'Brien, "Between Critique and Community" (review of Nancy Hartsock's *Money, Sex, and Power*), *The Women's Review of Books*, 1, April 1984, p. 9.

9

Marital Slavery and Friendship: John Stuart Mill's *The Subjection of Women*

Mary Lyndon Shanley

John Stuart Mill's essay *The Subjection of Women* was one of the nineteenth century's strongest pleas for opening to women opportunities for suffrage, education, and employment. Although hailed by women's rights activists in its own day, it was rarely treated with much seriousness by Mill scholars and political theorists until feminists, beginning in the 1970s, demonstrated the centrality of its themes for feminist theory and political thought. Many feminists have, however, been ambivalent about the legacy of *The Subjection of Women*, seeing in it a brief for "equal rights," and questioning the efficacy of merely striking down legal barriers against women as the way to establish equality between the sexes. Mill's failure to extend his critique of inequality to the division of labor in the household, and his confidence that most women would choose marriage as a "career," in this view, subverted his otherwise egalitarian impulses.[1]

While fully acknowledging the limitations of "equal rights feminism," I argue in this essay that *The Subjection of Women* was not solely about equal opportunity for women. It was also, and more fundamentally, about the corruption of male–female relationships and the hope of establishing friendship in marriage. Such friendship was not only desirable for emotional satisfaction, it was crucial if marriage were to become, as Mill desired, a "school of genuine moral sentiment."[2] The fundamental assertion of *The Subjection of Women* was not that equal opportunity would ensure the liberation of women, but that male–female equality, however achieved, was essential to marital friendship and to the progression of human society.

Mill's vision of marriage as a locus of sympathy and understanding between autonomous adults not only reforms our understanding of his feminism, but also draws attention to an often submerged or ignored aspect of liberal political thought. Liberal individualism is attacked by Marxists and neo-conservatives alike as wrongly encouraging the disintegration of affective bonds and replacing them with merely self-interested economic and contractual ties. Mill's essay, however, emphasizes the value of noninstrumental relationships in human life. His depictions of both corrupt and well-ordered marriage traces the relationship of family order to right political order. His vision of marriage as a locus of mutual sympathy and understanding between autonomous adults stands as an unrealized goal for those who believe that the liberation of women requires not only formal equality of opportunity but measures which will enable couples to live in genuine equality, mutuality, and reciprocity.

The Perversion of Marriage by the Master–Slave Relationship

Mill's reconstruction of marriage on the basis of friendship was preceded by one of the most devastating critiques of male domination in marriage in the history of Western philosophy. In *The Subjection of Women* Mill repeatedly used the language of "master and slave" or "master and servant" to describe the relationship between husband and wife. In the first pages of the book, Mill called the dependence of women on men "the primitive state of slavery lasting on."[3] Later he said that despite the supposed advances of Christian civilization, "the wife is the actual bond-servant of her husband: no less so, as far as legal obligation goes, than slaves commonly so called."[4] Still later he asserted that "there remain no legal slaves, except the mistress of every house."[5] The theme of women's servitude was not confined to *The Subjection of Women*. In his speech on the Reform Bill of 1867, Mill talked of that "obscure feeling" which members of parliament were "ashamed to express openly" that women had no right to care about anything except "how they may be the most useful and devoted servants of some man."[6] To Auguste Comte he wrote comparing women to "domestic slaves" and noted that women's capacities were spent "seeking happiness not in their own life, but exclusively in the favor and affection of the other sex, which is only given to them on the condition of their dependence."[7]

But what did Mill mean by denouncing the "slavery" of married women? How strongly did he wish to insist on the analogy between married women and chattel slaves? While middle-class Victorian wives were clearly not subject to the suffering of chattel slaves, Mill chose the image quite deliberately to remind his readers that by marriage a husband assumed legal control of his wife's property and her body.[8] The social and economic system gave women little alternative except to marry; once married, the legal personality of the woman was subsumed in that of her husband; and the abuses of human dignity – including rape– permitted by custom and law within marriage were egregious.

In Mill's eyes, women were in a double bind: they were not free within marriage, and they were not truly free not to marry.[9] What could an unmarried woman do? Even if she were of the middle or upper classes, she could not attend any of the English universities, and thus she was barred from a systematic higher education. If somehow she acquired a professional education, the professional associations usually barred her from practicing her trade. "No sooner do women show themselves capable of competing with men in any career, than that career, if it be lucrative or honorable, is closed to them."[10] Mill's depiction of the plight of Elinor Garrett, sister of Millicent Garrett Fawcett, the suffrage leader, is telling:

> A young lady, Miss Garrett, . . . studied the medical profession. Having duly qualified, she . . . knocked successively at all the doors through which, by law, access is obtained into the medical profession. Having found all other doors fast shut, she fortunately discovered one which had accidentally been left ajar. The Society of Apothecaries, it seems, had forgotten to shut out those who they never thought would attempt to come in, and through this narrow entrance this young lady found her way into the profession. But so objectionable did it appear to this learned body that women should be the medical attendants even of women, that the narrow wicket through which Miss Garrett entered has been closed after her.[11]

Working-class women were even worse off. In the *Principles of Political Economy*, Mill argued that their low wages were due to the "prejudice" of society which "making almost every woman, socially speaking, an append-age of some man, enables men to take systematically the lion's share of whatever belongs to both." A second cause of low wages for women was the surplus of female labor for unskilled jobs. Law and custom ordained that a woman has "scarcely any means open to her of gaining a livelihood, except as a wife and mother."[12] Marriage was, as Mill put it, a "Hobson's choice" for women, "that or none."[13]

Worse than the social and economic pressure to marry, however, was women's status within marriage. Mill thoroughly understood the stipulations of the English common law which deprived a married woman of a legal personality independent of that of her husband. The doctrine of coverture or spousal unity, as it was called, was based on the Biblical notion that "a man [shall] leave his father and his mother, and shall cleave to his wife, and they shall be one flesh" (Genesis 2:24). If "one flesh," then, as Blackstone put it, "by marriage, the husband and wife are one person in law." And that "person" was represented by the husband. Again Blackstone was most succinct: "The very being or legal existence of the woman is suspended during the marriage, or at least is incorporated and consolidated into that of the husband."[14] One of the most commonly felt injustices of the doctrine of spousal unity was the married woman's lack of ownership of her own earnings. As the matrimonial couple was "one person," the wife's earnings during marriage were owned and controlled by her husband.[15] During his term as a member of parliament, Mill supported a Married Women's Property Bill, saying that its opponents were men who thought it impossible for "society to exist on a harmonious footing between two persons unless one of them has absolute power over the other," and insisting that England has moved beyond such a "savage stage."[16] In *The Subjection of Women* Mill argued that the "wife's position under the common law of England [with respect to property] is worse than that of slaves in the laws of many countries: by the Roman law, for example, a slave might have his peculium, which to a certain extent the law guaranteed to him for his exclusive use."[17] Similarly, Mill regarded the husband's exclusive guardianship over the married couple's children as a sign of the woman's dependence on her husband's will.[18] She was, in his eyes, denied any role in life except that of being "the personal body-servant of a despot."[19]

The most egregious aspects of both common and statute law, however, were those which sanctioned domestic violence. During the parliamentary debates on the Representation of the People Bill in 1867, Mill argued that women needed suffrage to enable them to lobby for legislation which would punish domestic assault:

> I should like to have a Return laid before this House of the number of women who are annually beaten to death, or trampled to death by their male protectors; and, in an opposite column, the amount of sentence passed.
> . . . I should also like to have, in a third column, the amount of property, the wrongful taking of which was . . . thought worthy of the same punishment. We should then have an arithmetical value set by a male legislature and male tribunals on the murder of a woman.[20]

But the two legal stipulations which to Mill most demonstrated "the assimilation of the wife to the slave" were her inability to refuse her master "the last familiarity" and her inability to obtain a legal separation from her husband unless he added desertion or extreme cruelty to his adultery. Mill was appalled by the notion that no matter how brutal a tyrant a husband might be, and no matter how a woman might loathe him, "he can claim from her and enforce the lowest degradation of a human being," which was to be made the instrument of "an animal function contrary to her inclination."[21] A man and wife being one body, rape was by definition a crime which a married man could not commit against his own wife. By law a wife could not leave her husband on account of this offense without being guilty of desertion, nor could she prosecute him. The most vicious form of male domination of women according to Mill was rape within marriage; it was particularly vicious because it was legal. Mill thus talked not of individual masters and wives as aberrations, but of a legally sanctioned system of domestic slavery which shaped the character of marriage in his day.[22]

Mill's depiction of marriage departed radically from the majority of Victorian portrayals of home and hearth. John Ruskin's praise of the home in *Sesame and Lilies* reflected the feelings and aspirations of many: "This is the true nature of home – it is the place of Peace; the shelter, not only from all injury, but from all terror, doubt, and division. . . . It is a sacred place, a vestal temple, a temple of the hearth watched over by Household Gods."[23] Walter Houghton remarked that the title of Coventry Patmore's poem, *The Angel in the House*, captured "the essential character of Victorian love," and reflected "the exaltation of family life and feminine character" characteristic of the mid-nineteenth century.[24] James Fitzjames Stephen, who wrote that he disagreed with *The Subjection of Women* "from the first sentence to the last," found not only Mill's ideas but his very effort to discuss the dynamics of marriage highly distasteful. "There is something – I hardly know what to call it; indecent is too strong a word, but I may say unpleasant in the direction of indecorum – in prolonged and minute discussions about the relations between men and women, and the character of women as such."[25]

The Subjection of Women challenged much more than Victorian decorum, however; it was a radical challenge to one of the most fundamental and preciously held assumptions about marriage in the modern era, which is that it was a relationship grounded on the consent of the partners to join their lives. Mill argued to the contrary that the presumed consent of women to marry was not, in any real sense, a free promise, but one socially coerced by the lack of meaningful options. Further, the laws of marriage deprived a woman of many of the normal powers of autonomous adults, from controlling her earnings, to entering contracts, to defending her bodily autonomy by resisting unwanted sexual relations. Indeed, the whole notion of a woman "consenting" to the marriage "offer" of a man implied from the outset a hierarchical relationship. Such a one-way offer did not reflect the relationship which should exist between those who were truly equal, among beings who should be able to create together by free discussion and mutual agreement an association to govern their lives together.

In addition, Mill's view of marriage as slavery suggested a significantly more complicated and skeptical view of what constituted a "free choice" in society than did either his own earlier works or those of his liberal predecessors. Hobbes, for example, regarded men as acting "freely" even when moved by fear for their lives. Locke disagreed, but he in turn talked about the individual's free choice to remain a citizen of his father's country, as if emigration were a readily available option for all. In other of his works Mill himself seemed overly sanguine about the amount of real choice enjoyed, for example, by wage laborers in entering a trade. Yet Mill's analysis of marriage demonstrated the great complexity of establishing that any presumed agreement was the result of free volition, and the fatuousness of presuming that initial consent could create perpetual obligation. By implication, the legitimacy of many other relationships, including supposedly free wage and labor agreements and the political obligation of enfranchised and unenfranchised alike, was thrown into question. *The Subjection of Women* exposed the inherent fragility of traditional conceptualizations of free choice, autonomy, and self-determination so important to liberals, showing that economic and social structures were bound to limit and might coerce any person's choice of companions, employment, or citizenship.

Mill did not despair of the possibility that marriages based on true consent would be possible. He believed that some individuals even in his own day established such associations of reciprocity and mutual support. (He counted his own relationship with Harriet Taylor Mill as an example of a marriage between equals.)[26] But there were systematic impediments to marital equality. To create conditions conducive to a marriage of equals rather than one of master and slave, marriage law itself would have to be altered, women would have to be provided equal educational and employment opportunity, and both men and women would have to become capable of sustaining genuinely equal and reciprocal relationships within marriage. The last of these, in Mill's eyes, posed the greatest challenge.

The Fear of Equality

Establishing legal equality in marriage and equality of opportunity would require, said Mill, that men sacrifice those political, legal, and economic advantages they enjoyed "simply by being born male." Mill therefore supported such measures as women's suffrage, the Married Women's Property Bills, the Divorce Act of 1857, the repeal of the Contagious Diseases Acts, and the opening of higher education and the professions to women. Suffrage, Mill contended, would both develop women's faculties through participation in civic decisions and enable married women to protect themselves from male-imposed injustices such as lack of rights to child custody and to control of their income. Access to education and jobs would give women alternatives to marriage. It would also provide a woman whose marriage turned out badly some means of self-support if separated or divorced. The Divorce Act of 1857, which established England's first civil divorce courts, would enable women and men to escape from intolerable circumstances (although Mill rightly protested the sexual double standard ensconced in the Act by which men might divorce their wives for adultery, but women had to prove their husbands were guilty of incest, bigamy or cruelty as well as adultery). And for those few women with an income of their own, a Married Women's Property Act would recognize their independent personalities and enable them to meet their husbands more nearly as equals.

However, Mill's analysis went further. He insisted that the subjection of women could not be ended by law alone, but only by law and the reformation of education, of opinion, of social inculcation, of habits, and finally of the conduct of family life itself. This was so because the root of much of men's resistance to women's emancipaton was not simply their reluctance to give up their position of material advantage, but many men's fear of living with an equal. It was to retain marriage as "a law of despotism" that men shut all other occupations to women, Mill contended.[27] Men who "have a real antipathy to the equal freedom of women" were at bottom afraid "lest [women] should insist that marriage be on equal conditions."[28] One of Mill's central assertions in *The Subjection of Women* was that "[women's] disabilities [in law] are only clung to in order to maintain their subordination in domestic life: *because the generality of the male sex cannot yet tolerate the idea of living with an equal*" (emphasis added).[29] The public discrimination against women was a manifestation of a disorder rooted in family relationships.

Mill did not offer any single explanation or account of the origin of men's fear of female equality. Elsewhere, he attributed the general human resistance to equality to the fear of the loss of privilege, and to apprehensions concerning the effect of levelling on political order.[30] But these passages on the fear of spousal equality bring to a twentieth-century mind the psycho-analytic works about human neuroses and the male fear of women caused by the infant boy's relationship to the seemingly all-powerful mother, source of both nurturance and love and of deprivation and punishment.[31] Mill's own account of the fear of equality was not psychoanalytic. He did, however, undertake to depict the consequences of marital inequality both for the individual psyche and for social justice. The rhetorical purpose of *The Subjection of Women* was not only to convince men that their treatment of women in law was unjust, but also that their treatment of women in the home was self-defeating, even self-destructive.

Women were those most obviously affected by the denial of association with men on equal footing. Women's confinement to domestic concerns was a wrongful "forced repression."[32] Mill shared Aristotle's view that participation in civic life was an enriching and ennobling activity, but Mill saw that for a woman, no public-spirited dimension to her life was possible. There was no impetus to consider with others the principles which were to govern their common life, no incentive to conform to principles which defined their mutual activity for the common good, no possibility for the self-development which comes from citizen activity.[33] The cost to women was obvious; they were dull or petty, or unprincipled.[34] The cost to men was less apparent but no less real; in seeking a reflection of themselves in the consciousness of these stunted women, men deceived, deluded, and limited themselves.

Mill was convinced that men were corrupted by their dominance over women. The most corrupting element of male domination of women was that men learned to "worship their own will as such a grand thing that it is actually the law for another rational being."[35] Such self-worship arises at a very tender age, and blots out a boy's natural understanding of himself and his relationship to others.

A boy may be "the most frivolous and empty or the most ignorant and stolid of mankind," but "by the mere fact of being born a male" he is encouraged to think that "he is by right the superior of all and every one of an entire half of the human race: including probably some whose real superiority he has daily or hourly occasion to feel."[36] By contrast, women were taught "to live for others" and "to have no life but in their affections," and then further to confine their affections to "the men with whom they are connected, or to the children who constitute an additional indefeasible tie between them and a man."[37] The result of this upbringing was that what women would tell men was not, could not be, wholly true; women's sensibilities were systematically warped by their subjection. Thus the reflections were not accurate and men were deprived of self-knowledge.

The picture which emerged was strikingly similar to that which Hegel described in his passages on the relationship between master and slave in *The Phenomenology of Mind.*[38] The lord who sees himself solely as master, wrote Hegel, cannot obtain an independent self-consciousness. The master thinks he is autonomous, but in fact he relies totally upon his slaves, not only to fulfill his needs and desires, but also for his identity: "Without slaves, he is no master." The master could not acquire the fullest self-consciousness when the "other" in whom he viewed himself was in the reduced human condition of slavery: to be *merely* a master was to fall short of full self-consciousness, and to define himself in terms of the "thing" he owns. So for Mill, men who have propagated the belief that all men are superior to all women have fatally affected the dialectic involved in knowing oneself through the consciousness others have of one. The present relationship between the sexes produced in men that "self-worship" which "all privileged persons, and all privileged classes" have had. That distortion deceives men and other privileged groups as to both their character and their self-worth.

No philosopher prior to Mill had developed such a sustained argument about the corrupting effects on men of their social superiority over and separation from women. Previous philosophers had argued either that the authority of men over women was natural (Aristotle, Grotius), or that while there was no natural dominance of men over women prior to the establishment of families, in any civil society such preeminence was necessary to settle the dispute over who should govern the household (Locke), or the result of women's consent in return for protection (Hobbes), or the consequence of the development of the sentiments of nurturance and love (Rousseau).[39] None had suggested that domestic arrangements might diminish a man's ability to contribute to public debates in the *agora* or to the rational governing of a democratic republic. Yet Mill was determined to show that the development of the species was held in check by that domestic slavery produced by the fear of equality, by spousal hierarchy, and by a lack of the reciprocity and mutuality of true friendship.

The Hope of Friendship

Mill's remedy for the evils generated by the fear of equality was his notion of marital friendship. The topic of the rather visionary fourth chapter of *The Subjection of Women* was friendship, "the ideal of marriage."[40] That ideal was, according to Mill, "a union of thoughts and inclinations" which created a "foundation of solid friendship" between husband and wife.[41]

Mill's praise of marital friendship was almost lyrical, and struck resonances with Aristotle's, Cicero's, and Montaigne's similar exaltations of the pleasures as well as the moral enrichment of this form of human intimacy. Mill wrote:

> When each of two persons, instead of being a nothing, is a something; when they are attached to one another, and are not too much unlike to begin with; the constant partaking of the same things, assisted by their sympathy, draws out the latent capacities of each for being interested in the things . . . by a real enriching of the two natures, each acquiring the tastes and capacities of the other in addition to its own.[42]

This expansion of human capacities did not, however, exhaust the benefits of friendhsip. Most importantly, friendship developed what Montaigne praised as the abolition of selfishness, the capacity to regard another human being as fully as worthy as oneself. Therefore friendship of the highest order could only exist between those equal in excellence.[43] And for precisely this reason, philosophers from Aristotle to Hegel had consistently argued that women could not be men's friends, for women lacked the moral capacity for the highest forms of friendship. Indeed, it was common to distinguish the marital bond from friendship not solely on the basis of sexual and procreative activity, but also because women could not be part of the school of moral virtue which was found in friendship at its best.

Mill therefore made a most significant break with the past in adopting the language of friendship in his discussion of marriage. For Mill, no less than for any of his predecessors, "the true virtue of human beings is the fitness to live together as equals." Such equality required that individuals "[claim] nothing for themselves but what they as freely concede to every one else," that they regard command of any kind as "an exceptional necessity," and that they prefer whenever possible "the society of those with whom leading and following can be alternate and reciprocal."[44] This picture of reciprocity, of the shifting of leadership according to need, was a remarkable characterization of family life. Virtually all of Mill's liberal contemporaries accepted the notion of the natural and inevitable complimentariness of male and female personalities and roles. Mill, however, as early as 1833 had expressed his belief that "the highest masculine and the highest feminine" characters were without any real distinction.[45] That view of the androgynous personality lent support to Mill's brief for equality within the family.

Mill repeatedly insisted that his society had no general experience of "the marriage relationship as it would exist between equals," and that such marriages would be impossible until men rid themselves of the fear of equality and the will to domination.[46] The liberation of women, in other words, required not just legal reform but a reeducation of the passions. Women were to be regarded as equals not only to fulfill the demand for individual rights and in order that they could survive in the public world of work, but also in order that women and men could form ethical relations of the highest order. Men and women alike had to "learn to cultivate their strongest sympathy with an equal in rights and in cultivation."[47] Mill struggled, not always with total success, to talk about the quality of such association. For example, in *On Liberty*, Mill explicitly rejected von Humbolt's characterization of marriage as a contractual relationship which could be ended by "the declared will of either party to dissolve it." That kind of dissolution was appropriate when the benefits of partnership could be reduced to monetary terms. But marriage involved a person's expectations for the fulfillment of a "plan of life," and created "a new series of moral obligations . . . toward that person, which may possibly be overruled, but cannot be ignored."[48] Mill was convinced that difficult though it might be to shape the law to recognize the moral imperatives of such a relationship, there were ethical communities which transcended and were not reducible to their individual components.

At this juncture, however, the critical force of Mill's essay weakened, and a tension developed between his ideal and his prescriptions for his own society. For all his insight into the dynamics of domestic domination and subordination, the only specific means Mill in fact put forward for the fostering of this society of equals was providing equal opportunity to women in areas outside the family. Indeed, in *On Liberty* he wrote that "nothing more is needed for the complete removal of [the almost despotic power of husbands over wives] than that wives should have the same rights and should receive the same protection of law in the same manner, as all other persons."[49] In the same vein, Mill seemed to suggest that nothing more was needed for women to achieve equality than that "the present duties and protective bounties in favour of men should be recalled."[50] Moreover, Mill did not attack the traditional assumption about men's and women's different responsibilities in an ongoing household, although he was usually careful to say that women "chose" their role or that it was the most "expedient" arrangement, not that it was theirs by "nature."

Mill by and large accepted the notion that once they marry, women should be solely responsible for the care of the household and children, men for providing the family income: "When the support of the family depends . . . on earnings, the common arrangement, by which the man earns the income and the wife superintends the domestic expenditure, seems to me in general the most suitable division of labour between the two persons."[51] He did not regard it as "a desirable custom, that the wife should contribute by her labour to the income of the family."[52] Mill indicated that women alone would care for any children of the marriage; repeatedly he called it the "care which . . . nobody else takes," the one vocation in which there is "nobody to compete with them," and the occupation which "cannot be fulfilled by others."[53] Further, Mill seemed to shut the door on combining household duties and a public life: "like a man when he chooses a profession, so, when a woman marries, it may be in general understood that she makes a choice of the management of a household, and the bringing up of a family, as the first call upon her exertions . . . and that she renounces . . . all [other occupations] which are not consistent with the requirements of this."[54]

Mill's acceptance of the traditional gender-based division of labor in the family has led some critics to fault Mill for supposing that legal equality of opportunity would solve the problem of women's subjection, even while leaving the sexual division of labor in the household intact. For example, Julia Annas, after praising Mill's theoretical arguments in support of equality, complains that Mill's suggestions for actual needed changes in sex roles are "timid and reformist at best. He assumes that most women will in fact want only to be wives and mothers."[55] Leslie Goldstein agrees that "the restraints which Mill believed should be imposed on married women constitute a major exception to his argument for equality of individual liberty between the sexes – an exception so enormous that it threatens to swallow up the entire argument."[56] But such arguments, while correctly identifying the limitations of antidiscrimination statutes as instruments for social change, incorrectly identify Mill's argument for equal opportunity as the conclusion of his discussion of male–female equality.[57] On the contrary, Mill's final prescription to end the subjection of women was not equal opportunity but spousal friendship; equal opportunity was a means whereby such friendship could be encouraged.

The theoretical force of Mill's condemnation of domestic hierarchy has not yet been sufficiently appreciated. Mill's commitment to equality in marriage was of a different theoretical order than his acceptance of a continued sexual division of labor. On the one hand, Mill's belief in the necessity of equality as a precondition to marital friendship was a profound theoretical tenet. It rested on the normative assumption that human relationships between equals were of a higher, more enriching order than those between unequals. Mill's belief that equality was more suitable to friendship than inequality was as unalterable as his conviction that democracy was a better system of government than despotism; the human spirit could not develop its fullest potential when living in absolute subordination to another human being or to government.[58] On the other hand, Mill's belief that friendship could be attained and sustained while women bore nearly exclusive responsibility for the home was a statement which might be modified or even abandoned if experience proved it to be wrong. In this sense it was like Mill's view that the question of whether socialism was preferable to capitalism could not be settled by verbal argument alone but must "work itself out on an experimental scale, by actual trial."[59] Mill believed that marital equality was a moral imperative; his view that such equality might exist where married men and women moved in different spheres of activity was a proposition subject to demonstration. Had Mill discovered that managing the household to the exclusion of most other activity created an impediment to the friendship of married women and men, *The Subjection of Women* suggests that he would have altered his view of practicable domestic arrangements, but not his commitment to the desirability of male–female friendship in marriage.

The most interesting shortcomings of Mill's analysis are thus not found in his belief in the efficacy of equal opportunity, but rather in his blindness to what other conditions might hinder or promote marital friendship. In his discussion of family life, for example, Mill seemed to forget his own warning that women could be imprisoned not only "by actual law" but also "by custom equivalent to law."[60] Similarly, he overlooked his own cautionary observation that in any household "there will naturally be more potential voice on the side, whichever it is, that brings the means of support."[61] And although he had brilliantly depicted the narrowness and petty concerns of contemporary women who were totally excluded from political participation, he implied that the mistresses of most households might content themselves simply with exercising the suffrage (were it to be granted), a view hardly consistent with his arguments in other works for maximizing the level of political discussion and participation whenever possible. More significantly, however, Mill ignored the potential barrier between husband and wife which such different adult life experiences might create, and the contribution of shared experience to building a common sensibility and strengthening the bonds of friendship.

Mill also never considered that men might take any role in the family other than providing the economic means of support. Perhaps Mill's greatest oversight in his paean of marital equality was his failure to entertain the possibilities that nurturing and caring for children might provide men with useful knowledge and experience, and that shared parenting would contribute to the friendship between spouses which he so ardently desired. Similarly, Mill had virtually nothing to say about the positive role which sex might play in marriage. The sharp language with which he condemned undesired sexual relations as the execution of "an animal function" was nowhere supplemented by an appreciation of the possible enhancement which sexuality might add to marital friendship. One of the striking features of Montaigne's lyrical praise of friendship was that it was devoid of sensuality, for Montaigne abhorred "the Grecian license," and he was adamant that women were incapable of the highest forms of friendship. Mill's notion of spousal friendship suggested the possibility of a friendship which partook of both a true union of minds and of a physical expression of the delight in one's companion, a friendship which involved all of the human faculties. It was an opportunity which (undoubtedly to the relief of those such as James Fitzjames Stephen) Mill himself was not disposed to use, but which was nonetheless implicit in his praise of spousal friendship.[62]

One cannot ask Mill or any other theorist to "jump over Rhodes" and address issues not put forward by conditions and concerns of his own society.[63] Nevertheless, even leaving aside an analysis of the oppression inherent in the class structure (an omission which would have to be rectified in a full analysis of liberation), time has made it clear that Mill's prescriptions alone will not destroy the master–slave relationship which he so detested. Women's aspirations for equality will not be met by insuring equal civic rights and equal access to jobs outside the home. To accomplish that end would require a transformation of economic and public structures which would allow wives and husbands to share those

domestic tasks which Mill assigned exclusively to women. In their absence
it is as foolish to talk about couples choosing the traditional division of
labor in marriage as it was in Mill's day to talk about women choosing
marriage: both are Hobson's choices, there are no suitable alternatives
save at enormous costs to the individuals involved.

Mill's feminist vision, however, transcends his own immediate prescriptions for reform. *The Subjection of Women* is not only one of liberalism's most
incisive arguments for equal opportunity, but it embodies as well a belief
in the importance of friendship for human development and progress. The
recognition of individual rights is important in Mill's view because it
provides part of the groundwork for more important human relationships
of trust, mutuality and reciprocity. Mill's plea for an end to the subjection
of women is not made, as critics such as Gertrude Himmelfarb assert, in
the name of "the absolute primacy of the individual," but in the name of
the need of both men and women for community. Mill's essay is valuable
both for its devastating critique of the corruption of marital inequality,
and for its argument, however incomplete, that one of the aims of a liberal
polity should be to promote the conditions which will allow friendship, in
marriage and elsewhere, to take root and flourish.

Notes

1 Contemporary authors who criticize Mill's analysis of equal opportunity for
women as not far-reaching enough are Julia Annas, "Mill and the Subjection of
Women," *Philosophy*, 52, 1977, pp. 179–94; Leslie F. Goldstein, "Mill, Marx,
and Women's Liberation," *Journal of the History of Philosophy*, 18, 1980, pp. 319–
34; Richard Krouse, "Patriarchal Liberalism and Beyond: From John Stuart
Mill to Harriet Taylor," in *The Family in Political Thought*, ed. Jean Bethke
Elshtain (Amherst: University of Massachusetts Press, 1982), pp. 145–72;
Susan Moller Okin, *Women in Western Political Thought* (Princeton: Princeton
University Press, 1979). From a different perspective, Gertrude Himmelfarb,
On Liberty and Liberalism: The Case of John Stuart Mill (New York: Alfred Knopf,
1974) criticizes Mill's doctrine of equality as being too absolute and particularly
takes issue with modern feminist applications of his theory.
2 J. S. Mill, *The Subjection of Women* (1869) in *Essays on Sex Equality*, ed. Alice Rossi
(Chicago: University of Chicago Press, 1970), ch. 2, p. 173.
3 Ibid., ch. 1, p. 130.
4 Ibid., ch. 2, p. 158.
5 Ibid., ch. 4, p. 217.
6 Hansard, *Parliamentary Debates*, series 3, vol. 187 (May 20, 1867), p. 820.
7 Letter to August Comte, October, 1843, in *The Collected Works of John Stuart
Mill*, vol. XIII, *The Earlier Letters*, ed. Francis C. Mineka (Toronto: University
of Toronto Press, 1963), p. 609, my translation.
8 For an assessment of black slave women's possession by their masters, see

Jacqueline Jones, *Labor of Love, Labor of Sorrow: Black Women, Work, and the Family from Slavery to the Present* (New York: Basic Books, 1985).

9 Mill's analysis of women's choice of marriage as a state of life reminds one of Hobbes's discussion of some defeated soldier giving his consent to the rule of a conquering sovereign. Women, it is true, could decide which among several men to marry, while Hobbes's defeated yeoman had no choice of master. But what could either do but join the only protective association available to each?

10 Hansard, vol. 187 (May 20, 1867), p. 827.

11 Ibid. In the United States, one well-documented case in which a woman was prohibited from practicing law was *Bradwell v Illinois*, 83 US (16 Wall) 130 (1873).

12 J. S. Mill, *The Principles of Political Economy* (1848) in *Collected Works*, vol. II, p. 394, and vol. III, pp. 765–6.

13 *Subjection of Women*, ch. 1, p. 156. Tobias Hobson, a Cambridge carrier commemorated by Milton in two Epigraphs, would only hire out the horse nearest the door of his stable, even if a client wanted another. *Oxford English Dictionary*, II, p. 369.

14 William Blackstone, *Commentaries on the Laws of England* (4 vols, Oxford: Clarendon Press, 1765–69), Book I, ch. XV, p. 430.

15 The rich found ways around the common law's insistence that the management and use of any income belonged to a woman's husband, by setting up trusts which were governed by the laws and courts of equity. A succinct explanation of the law of property as it affected married women in the nineteenth century is found in Erna Reiss, *Rights and Duties of Englishwomen* (Manchester: Sheratt and Hughes, 1934), pp. 20–34.

16 Hansard, vol. 192 (June 10, 1868), p. 1371. Several Married Women's Property Bills, which would have given married women possession of their earnings, were presented in parliament beginning in 1857, but none was successful until 1870.

17 *Subjection of Women*, ch. 2, pp. 158–9.

18 Ibid., p. 160.

19 Ibid., p. 161.

20 Hansard, vol. 187 (May 20, 1867), p. 826.

21 *Subjection of Women*, ch. 2, pp. 160–1.

22 For a full discussion of the legal disabilities of married women in Mill's day see Mary Lyndon Shanley, *Feminism, Marriage and the Law in Victorian England, 1850–1895* (Princeton: Princeton University Press, 1989).

23 John Ruskin, "Of Queen's Gardens," in *Works*, ed. E. T. Cook and A. D. C. Wedderburn (39 vols. London: G. Allen, 1902–12), vol. XVIII, p. 122.

24 Walter E. Houghton, *The Victorian Frame of Mind* (New Haven: Yale University Press, 1957), p. 344.

25 James Fitzjames Stephen, *Liberty, Equality, Fraternity* (New York: Henry Holt, n.d.), p. 206.

26 On the relationship between John Stuart Mill and Harriet Taylor see F. A. Hayek, *John Stuart Mill and Harriet Taylor; Their Correspondence and Subsequent Marriage* (Chicago: University of Chicago Press, 1951); Michael St. John Packe, *The Life of John Stuart Mill* (New York: Macmillan, 1954); Alice Rossi,

"Sentiment and Intellect," in *Essays on Sex Equality*, ed. Rossi; and Himmelfarb, *On Liberty and Liberalism*, pp. 187–238.

27 *Subjection of Women*, ch. 1, p. 156.

28 Ibid.

29 Ibid., ch. 3, p. 181.

30 For a discussion of Mill's views on equality generally, see Dennis Thompson, *John Stuart Mill and Representative Government* (Princeton: Princeton University Press, 1976), pp. 158–73.

31 For a reading of Mill from this perspective which challenges my own, see Christine Di Stefano, "Rereading J. S. Mill: Interpolations from the (M)Otherworld," in *Discontented Discourses: Feminism/Textual Intervention/Psychoanalysis*, ed. M. Barr and R. Feldstein (Urbana: University of Illinois Press, 1989). See also Linda Zerilli, *"Women" in Political Theory: Agents of Culture and Chaos* (Madison: University of Wisconsin, 1990).

32 *Subjection of Women*, ch. 1, p. 148.

33 See also Mill's *Considerations on Representative Government* (1861), in *Collected Works*, vol. XIX, pp. 399–400, 411. During his speech on the Reform Bill of 1867, Mill argued that giving women the vote would provide "that stimulus to their faculties . . . which the suffrage seldom fails to produce." Hansard, vol. 189 (May 20, 1867), p. 824.

34 *Subjection of Women*, ch. 2, p. 168, and ch. 4, p. 238.

35 Ibid., ch. 2, p. 172.

36 Ibid., ch. 4, p. 218.

37 Ibid., ch. 1, p. 141.

38 G. W. F. Hegel, *The Phenomenology of Mind*, trans. J. B. Baillie (New York: Harper and Row, 1969). This paragraph is indebted to the excellent study of the *Phenomenology* by Judith N. Shklar, *Freedom and Independence* (Cambridge: Cambridge University Press, 1976), from which the quote is taken, p. 61. Mill's analysis also calls to mind Simone de Beauvoir's discussion of "the Other" and its role in human consciousness in *The Second Sex*, trans. H. M. Parshley (New York: Random House, Vintage Books, 1974), pp. xix ff.

39 For studies of the views of each of these authors on women (except for Grotius) see Okin. Grotius' views can be found in his *De Juri Belli et Pacis Libri Tres* (*On the Law of War and Peace*) (1625), trans. Francis W. Kelsey (Oxford: Clarendon Press, 1925), Book II, ch. 5, section i, p. 231.

40 *Subjection of Women*, ch. 4, pp. 233, 235.

41 Ibid., pp. 231, 233.

42 Ibid., p. 233.

43 Montaigne's essay, "Of Friendship" in *The Complete Works of Montaigne*, trans. Donald M. Frame (Stanford: Stanford University Press, 1948), pp. 135–44.

44 *Subjection of Women*, ch. 4, pp. 174–5.

45 Letter to Thomas Carlyle, October 5, 1833, in *Collected Works*, vol. XII, *Earlier Letters*, p. 184.

46 Letter to John Nichol, August 1869, in *Collected Works*, vol. XVII, *The Later Letters*, ed. Francis C. Mineka and Dwight N. Lindley (Toronto: University of Toronto Press, 1972), p. 1634.

47 *Subjection of Women*, ch. 4, p. 236.

48 *Collected Works*, vol. XVIII, p. 300. Elsewhere Mill wrote, "My opinion on Divorce is that . . . nothing ought to be rested in, short of entire freedom on both sides to dissolve this like any other partnership." Letter to an unidentified correspondent, November 1855, *Collected Works*, vol. XIV, *Later Letters*, p. 500. But against this letter was the passage from *On Liberty*, and his letter to Henry Rusden of July 1870 in which he abjured making any final judgments about what a proper divorce law would be "until women have an equal voice in making it." He denied that he advocated that marriage should be dissoluble "at the will of either party," and stated that no well-grounded opinion could be put forward until women first achieved equality under the laws and in married life. *Collected Works*, vol. XVII, *Later Letters*, pp. 1750–1.

49 *Collected Works*, vol. XVIII, p. 301.

50 *Subjection of Women*, ch. 1, p. 154.

52 Ibid., ch. 2, p. 179.

53 Ibid., ch. 2, p. 178; ch. 3, p. 183; ch. 4, p. 241.

54 Ibid., ch. 1, p. 179.

55 Annas, "Mill and the Subjection of Women," p. 189.

56 Goldstein, "Mill, Marx and Women's Liberation," p. 328.

57 Richard Krouse points out that Mill's own "ideal of a reformed family life, based upon a full nonpatriarchal marriage bond," requires "on the logic of his own analysis. . . [the] rejection of the traditional division of labor between the sexes." Krouse, "Patriarchal Liberalism," p. 39.

58 *Considerations on Representative Government*, in *Collected Works*, vol. XIX, pp. 399–403.

59 *Chapters on Socialism* (1879), in *Collected Works*, vol. V, p. 736.

60 *Subjection of Women*, ch. 4, p. 241.

61 Ibid., ch. 2, p. 170.

62 Throughout his writings Mill displayed a tendency to dismiss or deprecate the erotic dimension of life. In his *Autobiography* he wrote approvingly that his father looked forward to an increase in freedom in relations between the sexes, freedom which would be devoid of any sensuality "either of a theoretical or of a practical kind." His own 20-year friendship with Harriet Taylor before their marriage was "one of strong affection and confidential intimacy only." *Autobiography of John Stuart Mill* (New York: Columbia Unviersity Press, 1944), pp. 75, 161. In *The Principles of Political Economy* Mill remarked that in his own day "the animal instinct" occupied a "disproportionate preponderance in human life." *Collected Works*, vol. III, p. 766.

63 G. W. F. Hegel, *The Philosophy of Right*, ed. T. M. Knox (London: Oxford University Press, 1952), p. 11, quoted in Krouse, "Patriarchal Liberalism," p. 40.

10

John Rawls: Justice as Fairness –
For Whom?

Susan Moller Okin

Theories of justice are centrally concerned with whether, how, and why persons should be treated differently from each other. Which initial or acquired characteristics or positions in society, they ask, legitimize differential treatment of persons by social institutions, laws and customs? In particular, how should beginnings affect outcomes? Since we live in a society in whose past the innate characteristic of sex has been regarded as one of the clearest legitimizers of different rights and restrictions, both formal and informal, the division of humanity into two sexes would seem to provide an obvious subject for such inquiries. But the deeply entrenched social institutionalization of sexual difference, which I will refer to as "the gender system" or simply "gender," has rarely been subjected to the tests of justice. When we turn to the great tradition of Western political thought with questions about the justice of gender in mind, it is to little avail.[1] Except for rare exceptions, such as John Stuart Mill, those who hold central positions in the tradition almost never questioned the justice of the subordination of women. When we turn to contemporary theories of justice, however, we might expect to find more illuminating and positive contributions to the subject of gender and justice. In this essay, I turn to John Rawls's extremely influential *A Theory of Justice*, to see not only what it says explicitly on the subject but also what undeveloped potential it has as we try to answer the question "How just is gender?"[2]

There is little indication throughout most of *A Theory of Justice* that the modern liberal society to which the principles of justice are to be applied is deeply and pervasively gender structured. Thus an ambiguity runs throughout the work, which is continually noticeable to anyone reading it from a feminist perspective. On the one hand, as I shall argue below, a consistent and wholehearted application of Rawls's liberal principles of justice can lead us to challenge fundamentally the gender system of our society. On the other hand, in his own account of his theory, this challenge is barely hinted at, much less developed. The major reason is that throughout most of the argument, it is assumed (as throughout almost the entire liberal tradition) that the appropriate subjects of political theories are not all adult individuals, but heads of families. As a result, although Rawls indicates on several occasions that a person's sex is a morally arbitrary and contingent characteristic, and although he states initially that the family itself is one of those basic social institutions to which the principles of justice must apply, his theory of justice develops neither of these convictions.

Rawls, like almost all political theorists until very recent years, employs in *A Theory of Justice* supposedly generic male terms of reference.[3] "Men," "mankind," "he" and "his" are interspersed with gender-neutral terms of reference such as "individual" and "moral person." Examples of inter-generational concern are worded in terms of "fathers" and "sons," and the difference principle is said to correspond to "the principle of fraternity."[4] This linguistic usage would perhaps be less significant if it were not for the fact that Rawls is self-consciously a member of a long tradition of moral and political philosophy that has used in its arguments either such supposedly generic male terms, or even more inclusive terms of reference ("human beings," "persons," "all rational beings as such"), only to exclude women from the scope of the conclusions reached. Kant is a clear example.[5] But when Rawls refers to the generality and universality of Kant's ethics, and when he compares the principles chosen in his own original position to those regulative of Kant's kingdom of ends, "acting from [which] expresses our nature as free and equal rational persons,"[6] he does not mention the fact that women were not included in that category of "free and equal rational persons" to which Kant meant his moral theory to apply. Again, in a brief discussion of Freud's account of moral development, Rawls presents Freud's theory of the formation of the male super-ego in largely gender-neutral terms, without mentioning the fact that Freud considered women's moral development to be sadly deficient, on account of their incomplete resolution of the Oedipus complex.[7] Thus there is a certain blindness to the sexism of the tradition in which Rawls is a participant, which tends to render his terms of reference even more ambiguous than they might otherwise be. A feminist reader finds it difficult not to keep asking: "Does this theory of justice apply to women, or not?"

This question is not answered in the important passages listing the characteristics that persons in the original position are not to know about themselves in order to formulate impartial principles of justice. In a subsequent article, Rawls has made it clear that sex *is* one of those morally irrelevant contingencies that are hidden by the veil of ignorance.[8] But throughout *A Theory of Justice*, while the list of things unknown by a person in the original position includes "his place in society, his class position or social status . . . his fortune in the distribution of natural assets and abilities, his intelligence and strength, and the like . . . his conception of the good, the particulars of his rational plan of life, [and] even the special features of his psychology . . ."[9] "his" sex is not mentioned. Since the parties also "know the general facts about human society,"[10] presumably including the fact that it is gender structured both by custom and still in some respects by law, one might think that whether or not they knew their sex might matter enough to be mentioned. Perhaps Rawls means to cover it by his phrase "and the like," but it is also possible that he did not consider it significant.

The ambiguity is exacerbated by the statement that those free and equal moral persons in the original position who formulate the principles of justice are to be thought of not as "single individuals," but as "heads of families" or "representatives of families."[11] Rawls says that it is not necessary to think of the parties as heads of families, but that he will generally do so. The reason he does this, he explains, is to ensure that each person in the original position cares about the well-being of some persons in the next generation. These "ties of sentiment" between generations, which Rawls regards as important in the establishment of his just savings principle, would otherwise constitute a problem, because of the general assumption that the parties in the original position are mutually disinterested.[12] In spite of the ties of sentiment *within* families, then, "as representatives of families their interests are opposed as the circumstances of justice imply."[13]

The head of a family need not necessarily, of course, be a man. Certainly in the US, at least, there has been a striking growth in the proportion of "female-headed households" during the last several decades. But the very fact that, in common usage, the term "female-headed household" is used *only* in reference to households without resident adult males implies the assumption that any present male takes precedence over a female as the household or family head. Rawls does nothing to contest this impression when he says of those in the original position that "imagining themselves to be fathers, say, they are to ascertain how much they should set aside for their sons by noting what they would believe themselves entitled to claim of their fathers."[14] Although the "heads of families" assumption is made in order to address the issue of intergenerational justice, and is presumably not intended to be sexist, Rawls is effectively trapped by it into the traditional mode of thinking that life within the family and relations between the sexes are not properly to be regarded as part of the subject matter of a theory of social justice.

Before I go on to argue this, I must first point out that Rawls, for good reason, states at the outset of his theory that the family *is* part of the subject matter of a theory of social justice. "For us," he says, "the primary subject of justice is the basic structure of society . . . the political constitution and the principle economic and social arrangements." These are basic because "taken together as one scheme, [they] define men's rights and duties and influence their life prospects, what they can expect to be and how well they can hope to do. The basic structure is the primary subject of justice because its effects are so profound and present from the start."[15] Rawls specifies "the monogamous family" as an example of such major social institutions, together with the political constitution, the legal protection of essential freedoms, competitive markets, and private property. This initial inclusion of the family as a basic social institution to which the principles of justice should apply, although a break with earlier liberal thought, seems unavoidable given the stated criteria for inclusion in the basic structure. Different family structures, and different distributions of rights and duties within families, clearly affect men's "life prospects, what they can expect to be and how well they can hope to do," and even more clearly affect the life prospects of women. There is no doubt, then, that in Rawls's initial definition of the sphere of social justice, the family is included. However, it is to a large extent ignored, though assumed, in the rest of the theory.[16]

The two principles of justice that are derived and defended in part 1 – the principle of equal basic liberty, and the difference principle combined with the requirement of fair equality of opportunity – are intended to apply to the basic structure of society. They are "to govern the assignment of rights and duties and to regulate the distribution of social and economic advantages."[17] Whenever in these basic institutions there are differences in authority, in responsibility, in the distribution of resources such as wealth or leisure, these differences must be both to the greatest benefit of the least advantaged, and attached to positions accessible to all under conditions of fair equality of opportunity.

In part 2, Rawls discusses at some length the application of his principles of justice to almost all of the major social institutions listed at the beginniing of the book. The legal protection of liberty of thought and conscience is defended, as are democratic constitutional institutions and procedures; competitive markets feature prominently in the discussion of the just distribution of income; the issue of the private or public ownership of the means of production is explicitly left open, since Rawls argues that his principles of justice might be compatible with certain versions of either.

But throughout all these discussions, he never raises the question of whether the monogamous family, in either its traditional or any other form, is just. When he announces that "the sketch of the system of institutions that satisfy the two principles of justice is now complete,"[18] Rawls has still paid no attention at all to the internal justice of the family. In fact, apart from passing references, the family appears in *A Theory of Justice* in only three contexts: as the link between generations necessary for the just savings principle; as an obstacle to fair equality of opportunity – on account of the inequalities among families; and as the first school of moral development. It is in the third of these contexts that Rawls first specifically mentions the family as a just institution. He mentions it, however, not to *consider* whether the family "in some form" is just, but to *assume* it.[19]

Clearly, however, by Rawls's own reasoning about the social justice of major social institutions, this assumption is unwarranted, and this has serious significance for the theory as a whole. The central tenet of the theory, after all, is that justice as fairness characterizes institutions whose members could hypothetically have agreed to their structure and rules from a position in which they did not know which place in the structure they were to occupy. The argument of the book is designed to show that the two principles of justice are those that individuals in such a hypothetical situation would agree to. But since those in the original position are only the heads or representatives of families, they are *not in a position to determine questions of justice within families.*[20] As far as children are concerned, Rawls makes a convincing argument from paternalism for their temporary inequality. But wives (or whichever adult member[s] of a family are *not* its "head") go completely unrepresented in the original position. If families are just, as is assumed, then they must become just in some different way (unspecified by Rawls) than other institutions, for it is impossible to see how the viewpoint of their less advantaged members ever gets to be heard.

There are two occasions when Rawls seems either to depart from his assumption that those in the original position are "family heads," or to assume that a "head of a family" is equally likely to be a woman as a man. In the assignment of the basic rights of citizenship, he argues, favoring men over women is "justified by the difference principle . . . only if it is to the advantage of women and acceptable from their standpoint."[21] Later, he seems to imply that the injustice and irrationality of racist doctrines are also characteristic of sexist ones.[22] But in spite of these passages, which appear to challenge formal sex discrimination, the discussions of institutions in part 2 implicitly rely, in a number of respects, on the assumption that the parties formulating just institutions are (male) heads of (fairly traditional) families, and are therefore not concerned with issues of just distribution within the family or between the sexes. Thus the "heads of families" assumption, far from being neutral or innocent, has the effect of banishing a large sphere of human life – and a particularly large sphere of most women's lives – from the scope of the theory.

One example of this occurs during the discussion of the distribution of wealth. Here Rawls seems to assume that all the parties in the original position expect, once the veil of ignorance is removed, to be participants in the paid labor market. Distributive shares are discussed in terms of household income, but reference to "individuals" is interspersed into this discussion as if there were no difference between the advantage or welfare of a household and that of an individual.[23] This confusion obscures the fact that wages are paid to employed members of the labor force, but that in societies characterized by gender (all current societies) a much larger proportion of women's than men's labor is unpaid, and is often not even acknowledged to be labor. It obscures the fact that the resulting disparities in the earnings of men and women, and the economic dependence of women on men, are likely to affect power relations within the household, as well as access to leisure, prestige, political power, and so on, among its adult members. Any discussion of justice *within* the family would have to address these issues.

Later, too, in his discussion of the obligations of citizens, Rawls's assumption that justice is agreed on by heads of families in the original position seems to prevent him from considering an issue of crucial importance to women – their exemption from the draft. He concludes that military conscription is justifiable in the case of defense against an unjust attack on liberty, so long as institutions "try to make sure that the risks of suffering from these imposed misfortunes are more or less evenly shared by all members of society over the course of their life, and that there is no avoidable *class* bias in selecting those who are called for duty."[24] However, the issue of the complete exemption of women from this major interference with the basic liberties of equal citizenship is not even mentioned.

In spite of two explicit rejections of the justice of formal sex discrimination in part 1, then, Rawls seems in part 2 to be so heavily influenced by his "family heads" assumption that he fails to consider as part of the basic structure of society the greater economic dependence of women and the sexual division of labor within the typical family, or any of the broader social ramifications of this basic gender structure. Moreover, in part 3, where he *assumes* the justice of the family "in some form" as a given, he does not discuss any alternative forms, but sounds very much as though he is thinking in terms of traditional, gendered family structure and roles. The family, he says, is "a small association, normally characterized by a definite hierarchy, in which each member has certain rights and duties." The family's role as moral teacher is achieved partly through parental expectations of "the virtues of a good son or a good daughter."[25] In the family and in other associations such as schools, neighborhoods, and peer groups, Rawls continues, one learns various moral virtues and ideals, leading to those adopted in the various statuses, occupations, and family positions of later life: "The content of these ideals is given by the various conceptions of a good wife and husband, a good friend and citizen, and so on."[26] Given these unusual departures from the supposedly generic male terms of reference used throughout the rest of the book, it seems likely that Rawls means to imply that the goodness of daughters is distinct from the goodness of sons, and that of wives from that of husbands. A fairly traditional gender system seems to be assumed.

However, despite this, not only does Rawls "assume that the basic structure of a well-ordered society includes the family *in some form*"; he adds to this the comment that "in a broader inquiry the institution of the family might be questioned, and other arrangements might indeed prove to be preferable."[27] But why should it require a broader inquiry than the colossal task engaged in *A Theory of Justice* to raise questions about the institution and the form of the family? Surely Rawls is right at the outset when he names it as one of those basic social institutions that most affects the life chances of individuals. The family is not a private association like a church or a university, which vary considerably in type and in degree of commitment expected, and which one can join and leave voluntarily. For although one has some choice (albeit a highly constrained one) about marrying into a gender-structured family, one has no choice at all about whether to be born into one. Given this, Rawls's failure to subject the structure of the family to his principles of justice is particularly serious in the light of his belief that a theory of justice must take account of "how [individuals] get to be what they are" and "cannot take their final aims and interests, their attitudes to themselves and their life, as given."[28] For the gendered family, and female parenting in particular, are clearly crucial determinants in the different socialization of the two sexes – in how men and women "get to be what they are."

If Rawls were to assume throughout the construction of his theory that all human adults are participants in what goes on behind the veil of ignorance, he would have no option but to require that the family, as a major social institution affecting the life chances of individuals, be constructed in accordance with the two principles of justice. I shall develop this positive potential of Rawls's theory in the final section of this essay. But first I shall turn to a major problem for the theory that results from its failure to address the issue of justice within the family – its placing in jeopardy Rawls's account of how one develops a sense of justice.

Gender, the Family, and the Development of a Sense of Justice

Apart from being briefly mentioned as the link between generations necessary for Rawls's "savings principle," and as an obstacle to fair equality of opportunity, the family appears in Rawls' theory in only one context – albeit one of considerable importance – as the earliest school of moral development. Rawls argues, in a much neglected section of part 3 of *A Theory of Justice*, that a just, well-ordered society will be stable only if its members continue to develop a sense of justice – "a strong and normally effective desire to act as the principles of justice require."[29] He specifically turns his attention to the question of childhood moral development, aiming to indicate the major steps by which a sense of justice is acquired.

It is in the context of early moral development, in which families play a fundamental role, that Rawls *assumes* that they are just. In these supposedly just families, the love of parents for their children, coming to be reciprocated in turn by the child, is important in the development of a sense of self-worth. By loving the child and being "worthy objects of his admiration . . . they arouse in him a sense of his own value and the desire to become the sort of person that they are."[30] Next, Rawls argues that healthy moral development in early life depends on love, trust, affection, example and guidance.[31]

Later in moral development, at the stage he calls "the morality of association," Rawls perceives the family, which he describes in gendered and hierarchical terms, as the first of many associations in which, by moving through a sequence of roles and positions, our moral understanding increases. The crucial aspect of the sense of fairness that is learned during this stage is the capacity to take up the points of view of others and to see things from their perspectives. We learn to perceive from what they say and do what other people's ends, plans and motives are. Without this experience, Rawls says, "we cannot put ourselves into another's place and find out what we would do in his position," which we need to be able to do in order "to regulate our own conduct in an appropriate way by reference to it."[32] Participation in different roles in the various associations of society leads to the development of a person's "capacity for fellow feeling" and to "ties of friendship and mutual trust."[33] Rawls says that, just as in the first stage certain natural attitudes develop towards the parents, "so here ties of friendship and confidence grow up among associates. In each case certain natural attitudes underlie the corresponding moral feelings: a lack of these feelings would manifest the absence of these attitudes."[34]

This whole account of moral development is strikingly unlike that of Kant, whose ideas are so influential in other respects on Rawls's thinking about justice. For Kant, any feelings that did not follow from independently established moral principles were morally suspect.[35] But Rawls clearly acknowledges the importance of feelings, first nurtured within supposedly just families, in the development of the capacity for moral thinking. In accounting for his third and final stage of moral development, where persons are supposed to become attached to the principles of justice themselves, Rawls says that "the sense of justice is continuous with the love of mankind."[36] At the same time, he allows for the fact that we have particularly strong feelings about those to whom we are closely attached, and says that this is rightly reflected in our moral judgements: even though "our moral sentiments display an independence from the accidental circumstances of our world . . . our natural attachments to particular persons and groups still have an appropriate place."[37] He indicates clearly that empathy, or imagining oneself into the place of others, plays a major role in moral development, and he turns from Kant to other philosophers – such as Adam Smith and Elizabeth Anscombe – who have paid more attention to such aspects of moral learning, in developing his ideas about the moral emotions or sentiments.[38]

Rawls believes that three psychological laws of moral development help account for the development of a sense of justice. The three laws, Rawls says, are: "not merely principles of association or of reinforcement . . . [but] assert that the active sentiments of love and friendship, and even the sense of justice, arise from the manifest intention of other persons to act for our good. Because we recognize that they wish us well, we care for their well-being in return. . ."[39] Each of the laws of moral development, as set out by Rawls, depends on the one before it, and the first assumption of the first law is: "given that family institutions are just. . ." Thus Rawls frankly admits that the whole of moral development rests at base on the loving ministrations of those who raise small children from the earliest stages, and on the moral character – in particular the *justice* – of the environment in which this takes place. At the foundation of the development of the sense of justice, then, are an activity and a sphere of life that – though by no means necessarily so – have throughout history been predominantly the activity and the sphere of women.

Rawls does not explain the basis of his assumption that family institutions are just. If gendered family institutions are *not* just, but are, rather, a relic of caste or feudal societies in which roles, responsibilities and resources are distributed not in accordance with the two principles of justice, but in accordance with innate differences that are imbued with enormous social significance, then Rawls's whole structure of moral development seems to be built on uncertain ground. Unless the households in which children are first nurtured and see their first examples of human interaction are based on equality and reciprocity rather than on dependence and domination, how can whatever love they receive from their parents make up for the injustice they see before their eyes in the relationship between these same parents? How, in hierarchical families in which sex roles are rigidly assigned, are we to learn to "put ourselves into another's place and find out what we would do in his position"? Unless they are parented equally by adults of both sexes, how will children of both sexes come to develop a sufficiently similar and well-rounded moral psychology to enable them to engage in the kind of deliberation about justice that is exemplified in the original position? Rawls's neglect of justice within the family is clearly in tension with his own theory of moral development, which *requires* that families be just.

What Can Rawls's Theory of Justice Contribute to Feminism?

The significance of Rawls's central, brilliant idea, the original position, is that it forces one to question and consider traditions, customs, and institutions from all points of view, and ensures that the principles of justice are acceptable to everyone, regardless of what position "he" ends up in. The critical force of the original position is clear from the fact that some of the most creative critiques of Rawls's theory have resulted from others interpreting the original position more radically or broadly than he did.[40] For feminist readers, the problem of the theory as stated by Rawls himself is encapsulated in that ambiguous "he." While Rawls briefly rules out formal, legal discrimination on the grounds of sex, he fails entirely to address the justice of the gender system, which, with its roots in the sex roles of the family, is one of the fundamental structures of our society. If, however, we read Rawls in such a way as to take seriously both the notion that those behind the veil of ignorance are sexless persons, and the requirement that the family and the gender system, as basic social institutions, are to be subject to scrutiny, then constructive feminist criticism of these contemporary institutions follows. So also, however, do hidden difficulties for the application of a Rawlsian theory of justice in a gendered society.

Both the critical perspective and the incipient problems of a feminist reading of Rawls can be illuminated by a description of a cartoon I saw a few years ago. Three elderly, robed male justices are depicted looking down with astonishment at their very pregnant bellies. One says to the others, without further elaboration: "Perhaps we'd better reconsider that decision." This illustration points to several things. First, it graphically demonstrates the importance, in thinking about justice, of a concept like Rawls's original position, which makes us adopt the positions of others – especially positions that we ourselves could never be in. Second, it suggests that those thinking in such a way might well conclude that more than formal legal equality of the sexes is required if justice is to be done. As we have seen in recent years, it is quite possible to institutionalize the formal legal equality of the sexes and at the same time to enact laws concerning pregnancy, abortion, maternity leave, and so on, that in effect discriminate against women, not as women *per se*, but as "pregnant persons."[41] One of the virtues of the cartoon is its suggestion that one's thinking on such matters is likely to be affected by the knowledge that one might become "a pregnant person." Finally, however, the illustration suggests the limits of our abilities to think ourselves into the original position as long as we live in a gender-structured society. While the elderly male justices can, in a sense, imagine *themselves* pregnant, what is much more difficult is whether, in constructing principles of justice, they can imagine themselves *women*. This raises the question whether, in a society structured by gender, sex *is* a morally irrelevant and contingent characteristic.

Let us first assume that sex is contingent in this way, though I shall later question this assumption. Let us suppose that it is possible, as Rawls clearly considers that it is, to hypothesize the moral thinking of representative human beings who are ignorant of their sex. Although Rawls does not do so, we must consistently take the relevant positions of both sexes into account in formulating and applying principles of justice. In particular, those in the original position must take special account of the perspective of women, since their knowledge of "the general facts about human society" must include the knowledge that women have been and continue to be the less advantaged sex in a great number of respects. In considering the basic institutions of society, they are more likely to pay special attention to the family than virtually to ignore it, since its customary unequal assignment of responsibilities and privileges to the two sexes and its socialization of children into sex roles make it, in its current form, a crucial institution for the perpetuation of sex inequality.

In innumerable ways, the principles of justice that Rawls arrives at are inconsistent with a gender-structured society and with traditional family roles. The critical impact of a feminist application of Rawls's theory comes chiefly from his second principle, which requires that inequalities be both "to the greatest benefit of the least advantaged" and "attached to offices and positions open to all."[42] This means that if any roles or positions analogous to our current sex roles, including those of husband and wife, mother and father, were to survive the demands of the first requirement, the second requirement would prohibit any linkage between these roles and sex. Gender, with its ascriptive designation of positions and expectations of behavior in accordance with the inborn characteristic of sex, could no longer form a legitimate part of the social structure, whether inside or outside the family. Three illustrations will help to link this conclusion with specific major requirements that Rawls makes of a just or well-ordered society.

First, after the basic political liberties, one of the most essential liberties is "the important liberty of free choice of occupation."[43] This liberty is obviously compromised by the customary expectation, central to our gender system, that women take far greater responsibility for housework and childcare, whether or not they also work for wages outside the home. In fact, both the assignment of these responsibilities to women – resulting in their economic dependence on men – and also the related responsibility of husbands to support their wives, compromise the liberty of choice of occupation of both sexes. But the current roles of the two sexes inhibit women's choices over the courses of a lifetime far more severely than those of men; it is much easier to switch from being a wageworker to a domestic role than to do the reverse. While Rawls has no objection to some aspects of the division of labor, he asserts that in a well-ordered society, "no one need be servilely dependent on others and made to choose between monotonous and routine occupations which are deadening to human thought and sensibility"; work can and should be "meaningful for all."[44] These conditions are far more likely to be met in a society that does not assign family responsibilities in a way that makes women into a marginal sector of the paid workforce and renders likely their economic dependence on men.

Second, the abolition of gender seems essential for the fulfillment of Rawls's criterion for political justice. For he argues that not only would equal formal political liberties be espoused by those in the original position, but that any inequalities in the *worth* of these liberties (for example, the effects on them of factors like poverty and ignorance) must be justified by the difference principle. Indeed, "the constitutional process should preserve the equal representation of the original position to the degree that this is practicable."[45] While Rawls discusses this requirement in the context of *class* differences, stating that those who devote themselves to politics should be "drawn more or less equally from all sectors of society,"[46] it is just as clearly and importantly applicable to sex differences. The equal political representation of women and men, especially if they are parents, is clearly inconsistent with our gender system.[47]

Finally, Rawls argues that the rational moral persons in the original position would place a great deal of emphasis on the securing of self-respect or self-esteem. They "would wish to avoid at almost any cost the social conditions that undermine self-respect," which is "perhaps the most important" of all the primary goods.[48] In the interests of this primary value, if those in the original position did not know whether they were to be men or women, they would surely be concerned to establish a thoroughgoing social and economic equality between the sexes that would preserve either from the need to pander to or servilely provide for the pleasures of the other. They would be highly motivated, for example, to find a means of regulating pornography that did not seriously compromise freedom of speech, and would be unlikely to tolerate basic social institutions that asymmetrically either forced or gave strong incentives to members of one sex to serve as sex objects for the other.

There is, then, implicit in Rawls's theory of justice a potential critique of gender-structured social institutions which can be developed by taking seriously the fact that those formulating the principles of justice do not know their sex. At the beginning of my brief account of this feminist critique, however, I made an assumption that I said would later be questioned – that a person's sex is, as Rawls at times indicates, a contingent and morally irrelevant characteristic, such that human beings really can hypothesize ignorance of this fact about them. First, I shall explain why, unless this assumption is a reasonable one, there are likely to be further feminist ramifications for a Rawlsian theory of justice in addition to those I have just sketched out. I shall then argue that the assumption is very probably not plausible in any society that is structured along the lines of gender. The conclusion I reach is that not only is gender incompatible with the attainment of social justice, in practice, for members of both sexes, but that the disappearance of gender is a prerequisite for the *complete* development of a nonsexist, fully human *theory* of justice.

Although Rawls is clearly aware of the effects on individuals of their different places in the social system, he regards it as possible to hypothesize free and rational moral persons in the original position who, temporarily freed from the contingencies of actual characteristics and social circumstances, will adopt the viewpoint of the "representative human being." He is under no illusions about the difficulty of this task, which requires a great shift in perspective from the way we think about fairness in everyday life. But with the help of the veil of ignorance, he believes that we can "take up a point of view that everyone can adopt on an equal footing," so that "we share a common standpoint along with others and do not make our judgments from a personal slant."[49] The result of this rational impartiality or objectivity, Rawls argues, is that – all being convinced by the same arguments – agreement about the basic principles of justice will be unanimous.[50] He does not mean that those in the original position will agree about *all* moral or social issues – "ethical differences are bound to remain" – but that complete agreement will be reached on all basic principles, or "essential understandings."[51] However, it is a crucial assumption of this argument for unanimity that all the parties have similar motivations and psychologies (for example, he assumes mutually disinterested rationality and an absence of envy), and that they have experienced similar patterns of moral development, and are thus presumed capable of a shared sense of justice. Rawls regards these assumptions as the kind of "weak stipulations" on which a general theory can safely be founded.[52]

The coherence of Rawls's hypothetical original position, with its unanimity of representative human beings, however, is placed in doubt if the kinds of human beings we actually become in society not only differ in respect of interests, superficial opinions, prejudices, and points of view that we can discard for the purpose of formulating principles of justice, but also differ in our basic psychologies, conceptions of the self in relation to others, and experiences of moral development. A number of feminist theorists have argued in recent years that in a gender-structured society the different life experiences of females and males from the start in fact affect their respective psychologies, modes of thinking, and patterns of moral development in significant ways.[53] Special attention has been paid to the effects on the psychological and moral development of both sexes of the fact that children of both sexes are primarily reared by women. It has been argued that the experience of individuation – of separating oneself from the nurturer with whom one is originally psychologically fused – is a very different experience for girls than for boys, leaving the members of each sex with a different perception of themselves and of their relations with others. In addition, it has been argued that the experience of *being* primary nurturers (and of growing up with this expectation) also affects the psychological and moral perspective of women, as does the experience of growing up in a society in which members of one's sex are in many ways subordinate to the other. Feminist theorists' scrutiny and analysis of the different experiences that we encounter as we develop, from our actual lived lives to our absorption of their ideological underpinnings, have in valuable ways filled out de Beauvoir's claim that "one is not born, but rather becomes, a woman."[54]

What is already clearly indicated by these studies, despite their incompleteness so far, is that *in a gender-structured society* there is such a thing as the distinct standpoint of women, and that this standpoint cannot be adequately taken into account by male philosophers doing the theoretical equivalent of the elderly male justices in the cartoon. The very early formative influence on children of female parenting, especially, seems to suggest that sex different in a gendered society is more likely to affect one's thinking about justice than, for example, racial difference in a society in which race has social significance, or class difference in a class society. The notion of the standpoint of women (while not without its own problems) suggests, first, that a fully human moral or political theory can be developed only with the full participation of both sexes. At the very least, this will require that women take their place with men in the dialogue in approximately equal numbers and in positions of comparable influence. In a society structured along the lines of gender, this cannot happen.

In itself, moreover, this is insufficient for the complete development of a fully human theory of justice. For if principles of justice are to be adopted unanimously by representative human beings ignorant of their particular characteristics and positions in society, they must be persons whose psychological and moral development is in all essentials identical. This means that the social factors influencing the differences presently found between the sexes – from female parenting to all the manifestations of female subordination and dependence – would have to be replaced by genderless institutions and customs. Only when men participate equally in what have been principally women's realms of meeting the daily material and psychological needs of those close to them, and when women participate equally in what have been principally men's realms of larger scale production, government, and intellectual and creative life, will members of both sexes be able to develop a more complete *human* personality than has hitherto been possible. Whereas Rawls and most other philosophers have assumed that human psychology, rationality, moral development and so on are completely represented by the males of the species, this assumption itself has now been exposed as part of the male-dominated ideology of our gendered society.

It is not feasible to consider here at any length what effect the consideration of women's standpoint might have on Rawls's theory of justice. I would suggest, however, that it might place in doubt some assumptions and conclusions, while reinforcing others. For example, the discussion of rational plans of life and primary goods might be focussed more on relationships and less exclusively on complex activities if it were to encompass the traditionally more female parts of life.[55] On the other hand, those aspects of Rawls's theory, such as the difference principle, that require a far greater capacity to identify with others than is normally characteristic of liberal theory might well be strengthened by reference to conceptions of relations between self and others that seem in gendered society to be more predominantly female, but that would in a gender-free society be more or less evenly shared by members of both sexes.[56]

The arguments of this essay, while critical of some aspects of Rawls's theory of justice, suggest the potential usefulness of the theory from a feminist viewpoint. Rawls himself neglects gender and, despite his initial inclusion of the family in the basic structure, he does not consider issues having to do with justice *within* the family. In recent work, moreover, he suggests that the family belongs with those "private" and therefore non-political associations for which the principles of justice are not appropriate. He does this, moreover, despite the fact that his own theory of moral development rests centrally on the early experience of persons within a

196 *Susan Moller Okin*

family environment that is both loving and just. Thus the theory as it stands contains an internal paradox. Because of his assumptions about gender, he has not applied the principles of justice to the realm of human nurturance which is so crucial for the achievement and the maintenance of justice.

On the other hand, I have argued that the feminist *potential* of Rawls's method of thinking and his conclusions is considerable. The original position, with the veil of ignorance hiding from its participants their sex as well as their other particular characteristics, their talents, circumstances and aims, is a powerful concept for challenging the gender structure. In particular – notwithstanding the difficulties for those socialized in a gendered society of thinking in the original position – it provides a viewpoint from which we can think about how to achieve justice within the family.

Notes

1　I have analyzed some of the ways in which theorists in the tradition have avoided considering the justice of gender, in "Are Our Theories of Justice Gender Neutral?" in *The Moral Foundations of Civil Rights*, ed. Robert Fullinwider and Claudia Mills (Totowa, NJ: Rowman and Littlefield, 1986), pp. 125–43).

2　John Rawls, *A Theory of Justice* (Cambridge, Mass.: Harvard University Press, 1971).

3　This is no longer the case in his most recent writings. See for example "Justice as Fairness: Political not Metaphysical," *Philosophy and Public Affairs*, 14(3), summer 1985, pp. 223–51.

4　Rawls, *Theory*, pp. 105–6, 208–9, 288–9.

5　See my "Women and the Making of the Sentimental Family," *Philosophy and Public Affairs*, 11(1), winter 1982, pp. 65–88, at pp. 78–82; Carole Pateman, *The Sexual Contract* (Stanford: Stanford University Press, 1988), pp. 168–73.

6　Rawls, *Theory*, pp. 251, 256. See also "Kantian Constructivism in Moral Theory," *The Journal of Philosophy*, 77(9), September 1980, pp. 515–72.

7　*Theory*, p. 459.

8　John Rawls, "Fairness to Goodness," *Philosophical Review*, 84, 1975, p. 537.

9　*Theory*, p. 137; see also p. 12.

10　Ibid. Numerous commentators on *Theory* have pointed out how controversial some of these "facts" are.

11　Ibid., pp. 128, 146.

12　As I have argued elsewhere, this assumption has frequently been misinterpreted by those of Rawls's critics who consider it in isolation from other crucial components of the original position, especially the veil of ignorance. See my "Reason and Feeling in Thinking about Justice," *Ethics*, 99(2), January 1989, pp. 229–49.

13　*Theory*, p. 128; see also p. 292.

14 Ibid., p. 289.
15 Ibid., p. 7.
16 It is noteworthy that in a subsequent paper on the subject of why the basic structure is the primary subject of justice, Rawls does *not* mention the family as part of the basic structure. See "The Basic Structure as Subject," *American Philosophical Quarterly*, 14(2), April 1977, p. 159. More significantly, whereas at the beginning of *Theory* he explicitly distinguishes the institutions of the basic structure from other "private associations," "less comprehensive social groups," and "various informal conventions and customs of everyday life" (p. 8), for which he suggests the principles of justice might be less appropriate or relevant, in two recent papers he classifies the family as belonging *with* such private, nonpolitical associations. See "Justice as Fairness," at p. 245; "The Priority of Right and Ideas of the Good," *Philosophy and Public Affairs*, 17(4), fall 1988, pp. 251–76, at p. 263.
17 *Theory*, p. 61.
18 Ibid., p. 303.
19 Ibid., pp. 463, 490. See Deborah Kearns, "A Theory of Justice – and Love; Rawls on the Family," *Politics (Australasian Political Studies Association Journal)*, 18(2), November 1983, pp. 36–42, at pp. 39–40, for an interesting discussion of the significance for Rawls's theory of moral development of his failure to address the justice of the family.
20 As Jane English says, "By making the parties in the original position heads of families rather than individuals, Rawls makes the family opaque to claims of justice." "Justice between Generations," *Philosophical Studies*, 31(2), 1977, pp. 91–104, at p. 95.
21 *Theory*, p. 99.
22 Ibid., p. 149.
23 Ibid., pp. 270–4, 304–9.
24 Ibid., pp. 380–1 (emphasis added).
25 Ibid., p. 467.
26 Ibid., p. 468.
27 Ibid., p. 463 (emphasis added).
28 Rawls, "Basic Structure as Subject," p. 160.
29 *Theory*, p. 454.
30 Ibid., p. 465.
31 Ibid., p. 466.
32 Ibid., p. 469.
33 Ibid., p. 470.
34 Ibid., p. 471.
35 See Okin, "Reason and Feeling."
36 *Theory*, p. 476.
37 Ibid., p. 475.
38 Ibid., pp. 479ff.
39 Ibid., p. 494; see also pp. 490–1.
40 Charles Beitz, for example, argues that there is no justification for not extending its application to the population of the entire world, which would lead to challenging virtually everything that is currently assumed in the dominant

"statist" conception of international relations. *Political Theory and International Relations* (Princeton: Princeton University Press, 1979).

41 The US Supreme Court decided in 1976, for example, that "an exclusion of pregnancy from a disability benefits plan . . . providing general coverage is not a gender-based discrimination at all." *General Electric v. Gilbert*, 429 US 125 (1976).

42 *Theory*, p. 302.

43 Ibid., p. 274.

44 Ibid., p. 529.

45 Ibid., p. 222; see also pp. 202–5, 221–8.

46 Ibid., p. 228.

47 The paltry numbers of women in high political office is an obvious indication of this. As of 1987, 41 out of the 630 members of the British House of Commons were women. Since 1789, over 10,000 men have served in the US House of Representatives, but only 107 women; some 1,140 men have been senators, compared with 15 women.

48 *Theory*, pp. 440, 396; see also pp. 178–9.

49 Ibid., pp. 516–17.

50 Ibid., pp. 139–41.

51 Ibid., p. 517.

52 Ibid., p. 149.

53 Major works contributing to this thesis are Jean Baker Miller, *Toward a New Psychology of Women* (Boston: Beacon Press, 1976); Dorothy Dinnerstein, *The Mermaid and the Minotaur* (New York: Harper and Row, 1977); Nancy Chodorow, *The Reproduction of Mothering* (Berkeley: University of California Press, 1978): Carol Gilligan, *In a Different Voice* (Cambridge, Mass.: Harvard University Press, 1982); Nancy Hartsock, *Money, Sex, and Power* (New York: Longmans, 1983). Important individual papers are Jane Flax, "The Conflict between Nurturance and Autonomy in Mother–Daughter Relationships and within Feminism," *Feminist Studies*, 4(2), summer 1978; Sara Ruddick, "Maternal Thinking," *Feminist Studies*, 6(2), summer 1980. Summaries and/or analyses are presented in Alison Jaggar, *Feminist Politics and Human Nature* (Totowa, NJ: Rowman and Allenheld, 1983), ch. 11; Jean Grimshaw, *Philosophy and Feminist Thinking* (Minneapolis: University of Minnesota Press, 1986), chs 5–8; Susan Moller Okin, "Thinking Like a Woman," in Deborah Rhode, ed., *Theoretical Perspectives on Sexual Difference* (New Haven: Yale University Press, 1990); Joan Tronto, "Women's Morality: Beyond Gender Difference to a Theory of Care," *Signs*, 12(4), summer 1987, pp. 644–63.

54 Simone de Beauvoir, *The Second Sex*, trans. H. M. Parshley (New York: Vintage Books, 1952), p. 301.

55 Brian Barry has made a similar, though more general, criticism of Rawls's focus on complex and challenging practices – the "Aristotelian Principle" – in *The Liberal Theory of Justice* (Oxford: Oxford University Press, 1973), pp. 27–30.

56 I have developed this argument in "Reason and Feeling."

11

Simone de Beauvoir and Women: Just Who Does She Think "We" Is?

Elizabeth V. Spelman

The critics often repeat in new contexts versions of the old assumptions they set out to contest.

Martha Minow

In *The Second Sex*, Simone de Beauvoir explores the many ways in which men have depicted women as ruled by forces in human nature that men can neither fully accept nor fully deny.[1] *The Second Sex* is a landmark work in contemporary feminist thought (even though for many years de Beauvoir apparently resisted being identified as a feminist).[2] She attempted to give an account of the situation of women in general and to include proposals for the conditions that would have to change if women were to become free. Although not all feminists subsequent to de Beauvoir referred to her work, or even necessarily knew about it, there is hardly any issue that feminists have come to deal with that she did not address. Indeed, she touched on issues such as attitudes towards lesbianism that some later feminists didn't dare to think about.[3]

De Beauvoir explicitly recognized that we live in a world in which there are a number of forms of oppression, and she tried to locate sexism in that context. In her work, we have all the essential ingredients of a feminist account of "women's lives" that would not conflate "woman" with a small group of women – namely, white middle-class heterosexual Christian women in Western countries. Yet de Beauvoir ends up producing an account which does just that. Here I shall explore how both de Beauvoir's theoretical perspective and her empirical observations lend themselves to a far richer account of "women's nature" than she herself ends up giving. (I am not going to argue about the strengths or weaknesses of her theory or the accuracy of her observations, but rather raise some questions about why she took them to lead in one direction rather than another.) Then I want to suggest reasons for the serious discrepancy between the potential broad scope of her views and the actual narrow focus of her position. De Beauvoir is a thinker of great perspicacity, so to explain the discrepancy simply in terms of a kind of race and class privilege that makes it easy for her to think of her own experience as representative of the experience of others is not enough. We need to ask what it might be in the language or methodology or theory employed by de Beauvoir that enables her to disguise from herself the assertion of privilege she so keenly saw in women of her own position.

I

Human beings aren't satisfied merely to live, de Beauvoir insists: we aspire to a meaningful existence.[4] But much about our constitution con-spires against the possibility of such an existence: our being creatures of the flesh entails the ever-present possibility that our grand projects will be mocked. It is not only the facts of our birth and death that give the lie to our being pure, unembodied, immortal spirit. Our bodies need tending to each day, and there is nothing meaningful in the many activities involved in this tending. The feeding and cleaning of bodies, the maintenance of shelter against the powerful vagaries of the natural world, are necessary if we are to live. But if that is all we did, or all we thought we could do, we wouldn't find anything valuable about human life. As de Beauvoir says, unless we can engage in activities that "transcend [our] animal nature," we might as well be brute animals: "On the biological level a species is maintained only by creating itself anew; but this creation results only in repeating the same Life in more individuals. But man assures the repetition of Life while transcending Life through Existence; by this transcendence he creates values that deprive pure repetition of all value."[5]

"Existing," as opposed to merely "living," is best expressed in those aspects of life that are the function of "the loftiest human attitudes: heroism, revolt, disinterestedness, imagination, creation."[6] Only "exist-ing" gives any reason for life; mere living "does not carry within itself its reasons for being, reasons that are more important than life itself."[7] To exist is to be a creative subject, not a passive object of the forces of nature; it is to be molding a new future through the power of one's intelligence, rather than being at the play of the repetitive rhythms of one's animal nature. Existing is as different from living as consciousness is from matter, will from passivity, transcendence from immanence, spirit from flesh.[8]

But life is necessary for existence, and we must preserve life even while we struggle against its demands. Descent into life is possible because of the never fully eradicated allure of dumbness and unfreedom, the ever-present possibility of forgoing (or seeming to forgo) the responsibilities, uncertainties, and risks of intelligence and freedom. Men, de Beauvoir says, make women the repository of the multiform threats to a life of transcendence, agency, freedom, spirit; woman remains "in bondage to life's mysterious processes," "doomed to immanence."[9] Her life "is not directed towards ends: she is absorbed in producing or caring for things that are never more than means, such as food, clothing, and shelter. These things are inessential intermediaries between animal life and free existence."[10] Though woman is no less capable of real "existence" than man, it is in her corporeality rather than his own that man sees palpable and undeniable reminders of his own animal nature, of his own deeply regrettable and undignified contingency. Desirous of seeing no part of himself in her, he regards her as thoroughly Other, or as thoroughly Other as he can, given that he nevertheless needs her as a companion who is neither merely an animal nor merely a thing: "Man knows that to satisfy his desires, to perpetuate his race, woman is indispensable."[11]

Although women are constitutionally no less desirous or capable than men of "existing" rather than merely "living," historically most women have not resisted men's definition of them as embodying mysterious, dumb forces of nature. They have done little to try to undermine the economic, social, and political institutions that reinforce and are reinforced by such attitudes. In this, de Beauvoir says, women are unlike other oppressed groups – for example, Blacks, Jews, workers.

There are two reasons for this. First, women are spread throughout the population, across racial, class, ethnic, national, and religious lines, and this presents huge obstacles to their working together politically. They don't share the same economic and social position, nor do they have a shared consciousness. Moreover, "the division of the sexes is a biological fact, not an event in human history."[12] In all other cases of oppression, she claims, both the oppressors and the oppressed have taken their relative positions to be the result of historical events or social change and hence in principle capable of alteration: "A condition brought about at a certain time can be abolished at some other time, as the Negroes of Haiti and others have proved." Similarly, "proletarians have not always existed, whereas there have always been women."[13]

De Beauvoir's point here presumably is not that whites never have taken racial differences to be biological; rather she seems to be pointing out that the idea that biological differences entitle whites to dominate

Blacks has been undermined in theory (to the extent that differences between Black and white are held to be less significant than their similarities as human beings) and nullified in political struggles (through which Blacks make clear their capacity to regard themselves as "subjects" and whites as "others").[14] De Beauvoir seems to be saying here that owing to a deep and apparently unbridgeable biological divide, women constitute for men the Other, whereas Blacks or the proletariat, for example, have not always constituted an Other for those by whom they may be dominated.

At the same time, despite these differences among women and between women and other oppressed groups, women do share something in common – but what they share paradoxically works against any possible solidarity. They "identify with each other" but do not communicate, as men do, "through ideas and projects of personal interest," and are only "bound together by a kind of immanent complicity."[15] By this de Beauvoir means that women are aware of inhabiting a special domain separate from men – in which they discuss recipes, frigidity, children, clothing – but nevertheless they regard each other as rivals for the attention of the masculine world. They are capable of ceasing to be Other. Despite what men find it convenient to believe, the difference between men and women is no more a biological given and historical necessity than the difference between bourgeoisie and proletariat. There is, however, a difference between the biological condition of being female and the social condition of being woman. So despite the differences among women, their different social and political locations, they could join in resisting the domination of men. But they haven't.[16]

And why haven't they? Sometimes de Beauvoir suggests that it is because being a "true woman" is inseparable from being the Other, so that it is logically impossible both to be a real woman and to be a subject, while there is no definitional problem, whatever other problems there are, in being a Black, or a worker, or a Jew, and also a subject. But this does not explain why women don't refuse to be "true women." And indeed sometimes de Beauvoir suggests that women simply choose to take the less arduous path: "No doubt it is more comfortable to submit to a blind enslavement than to work for liberation"; to "decline to be the Other, to refuse to be a party to the deal – this would be for women to renounce all the advantages conferred upon them by their alliance with the superior caste."[17]

Hence sometimes when she says that economic independence is the necessary condition of women's liberation, there is the suggestion that only if women are forced by circumstance to provide for themselves will they embrace their transcendence rather than fall into their immanence, see themselves as subjects rather than objects, as Self rather than Other. Women recognize the imporance and value of transcendence, but only enough to search for men whose creative and productive flights will rub off on them, metaphysically speaking. Women want what men have, but only in wanting the men who have it. What we need, de Beauvoir is saying, is a world in which if women are to get it at all, they must do it on their own.

In short, de Beauvoir argues that there are at least three things that help to explain the fact of women's domination by men:

1 Men's having the attitudes they do toward women;
2 the existence of economic, social, and political institutions through which such attitudes are expressed, enforced and perpetuated;
3 women's failure to resist such attitudes and institutions.

II

Differences among women

As noted above, de Beauvoir more than once remarks on class, racial, and national differences among women and how such differences bear on the economic, social, and political positions of women thus variously situated. Her comments on the lack of a sense of shared concerns among women are quite arresting: "If [women] belong to the bourgeoisie, they feel solidarity with men of that class, not with proletarian women; if they are white, their allegiance is to white men, not to Negro women."[18] The housewife is hostile toward her "servant [and toward] the teachers, governesses, nurses and nursemaids who attend to her children."[19] "Freed from the male, [the middle-class woman] would have to work for a living; she felt no solidarity with workingwomen, and she believed that the emancipation of bourgeois women would mean the ruin of her class."[20] De Beauvoir, then, is saying that the women least prepared to have their status changed have been white middle-class women, who are willing to keep the sexual status quo in return for the privileges of their class and race.

In all such examples, she cites the unwillingness of women with race or class privileges to give them up as the main obstacle to women's all doing something together to resist the domination of men. That is, what prevents a white middle-class woman from attacking sexism is her awareness that if she undermines sexism she will thereby undermine her race and class privilege. This ties in with de Beauvoir's point about the difference class makes to privilege based on sex. She argues that the less class privilege men and women enjoy, the less sexual privilege men of that class have; the more extreme class oppression is, the less extreme sex oppression is. So according to de Beauvoir sexism and classism are deeply intertwined. An important way in which class distinctions can be made is in terms of male–female relationships: we can't describe the sexism women are subject to without specifying their class; nor can we understand how sexism works without looking at its relation to class privilege. What makes middle-class women dependent on men of their class is the same as what distinguishes them from working-class women.[21]

But de Beauvoir does not heed her own insights here. On the contrary, she almost always describes relations between men and women as if the class or race or ethnic identity of the men and women made no difference to the truth of statements about "men and women." This poses some very serious difficulties for her attempt to give a general account of "woman." On her own terms it ought to be misleading to say, as she does, that we live "in a world that belongs to men,"[22] as if all differences between princes and paupers, masters and slaves, can be canceled out by the fact that they are all male.[23] In describing the psychological development of girls, she remarks on the ways in which everything in a girl's life "confirms her in her belief in masculine superiority."[24] And yet she later makes clear that a white girl growing up in the United States hardly believes that Black men are superior to her: "During the War of Secession no Southerners were more passionate in upholding slavery than the women." She describes ways in which girls of the upper classes are taught to believe in their superiority to working-class men: "In the upper classes women are eager accomplices of their masters because they stand to profit from the benefits provided. . . . The women of the upper middle classes and the aristocracy have always defended their class interests even more obstinately than have their husbands."[25] Whether or not de Beauvoir is entirely accurate in her descriptions of some women's passionate insistence on preserving privilege – were they really more fierce about it than the men of their race and class?[26] – the point is that these descriptions undermine her claims elsewhere about the common position of women.

De Beauvoir's perceptiveness about class and race inequality should make us wonder about her account of the "man" as "citizen" and "producer" with "economic independence" and all "the advantages attached to masculinity" in contrast to the "woman," who is "before all, and often exclusively, a wife," "shut up in the home," enjoying "vast leisure," and entertaining at tables "laden with fine food and precious wines."[27]

> Since the husband is the productive worker, he is the one who goes beyond family interest to that of society, opening up a future for himself through cooperation in the building of the future: he incarnates transcendence. Woman is doomed to the continuation of the species and the care of the home – that is, to immanence.[28]

Here de Beauvoir, despite evidence she provides to the contrary, makes it look as if racism, for example, had never existed and never affected the conditions under which a man can "incarnate transcendence." Here and elsewhere when she points to the role women play in reproducing family and species – "the oppression of woman has its cause in the will to perpetuate the family and to keep the patrimony intact"[29] – she chooses to ignore questions about legitimacy even while alluding to them elsewhere. She quotes Demosthenes: "We have hetairas for the pleasures of the spirit, concubines for sensual pleasure, and wives to give us sons";[30] and her argument implies among other things that human beings typically do not "continue the species" randomly or without regard to what kinds of beings will populate the future. Both Plato and Aristotle were concerned about joining the right kind of men with the right kind of women to produce philosopher-rulers and citizens of the *polis*. De Beauvoir surely was aware of the extent to which racial, class, and religious conventions dictate what comprises appropriate sexual behavior and "legitimate" reproduction. Indeed, as we shall see below, she explicitly points out but does not consider the implications of the fact that everything she says about sexual privilege only works when the man and woman belong to the same race and class.[31]

De Beauvoir sabotages her insights about the political consequences of the multiple locations of women in another way: she frequently compares women to other groups – in her language, "Jews, the Black, the Yellow, the proletariat, slaves, servants, the common people." For example, she asks us to think about the differences between the situation of women, on the one hand, and, on the other "the scattering of the Jews, the introduction of slavery into America, the conquests of imperialism." She discusses with considerable appreciation Bebel's comparison of "women and the proletariat." She remarks that some of what Hegel says about "master and slave" better applies to "man and woman." In reflecting on slavery in the United States, she says that there was a "great difference" between the case of American Blacks and that of women: "the Negroes submit with a feeling of revolt, no privileges compensating for their hard lot, whereas woman is offered inducements to complicity." She speaks of the role of religion in offering "women" and "the common people" the hope of moving out of immanence: "When a sex or a class is condemned to immanence, it is necessary to offer it the mirage of some form of transcendence." She compares the talk of women about their husbands to conversations "of domestics talking about their employers critically in the servants' quarters."[32]

I bring up these comparisons not in order to assess their historical accuracy but to note that in making them de Beauvoir obscures the fact that half of the populations to whom she compares women consists of women. This is particularly puzzling in light of her recognition of the ways in which women are distributed across race, class, religious, and ethnic lines. She sometimes contrasts "women" to "slaves," sometimes describes women as "slaves,"[33] but she never really talks about those women who according to her own categories belonged to slave populations – for example, Black female slaves in the United States. She does say at one point that "there were women among the slaves, to be sure, but there have always been free women"[34] and then she proceeds to make clear that it is free women whom she will examine. She also says that in "classes in which women enjoyed some economic independence and took part in production . . . women workers were enslaved even more than the male workers."[35] But in contrasting "women" to a number of other groups, and in choosing not to pay attention to the women in those other groups, she expresses her determination to use "woman" only in reference to those females not subject to racism, anti-Semitism, classism, imperialism.

Perhaps she is aware at some level that this is the price she must pay for consistency: for where she does describe briefly the situation of females who belong to the groups she contrasts to "women," what she says does not follow from her account of "women." For example, she claims that in the Middle Ages peasant men and women lived on a "footing of equality," and that "in the working classes economic oppression nullified the inequality of the sexes."[36] If she believes this, then of course she has to restrict her use of the word "woman" to those females not subject to the other forms of oppression she refers to; otherwise her large claims about the subordination of women to men would be undermined by her own account. And yet at the same time, she subjects them to question, which we see as we turn to a third way in which de Beauvoir fails to pay attention to her own significant insights.

Toward the end of *The Second Sex*, de Beauvoir acknowledges that the differences in privilege and power between men and women she has been referring to are "in play" only when men and women are of the same class and race.[37] This is a logical conclusion for someone who holds, as we have seen she does, that the wives of white slaveowners in the United States fought even harder than their husbands to preserve the privileges of race; since she thought of "slaves" as male, she could hardly maintain that men who were slaves dominated women who were not. But there is a problem even in the way she signals here that claims about privilege based on sex apply only within the same class or race. For that suggests that sexism within one class or race is just like that within any other class or race. If so, her claims do have a kind of generality after all – for example, what characterizes relations between white men and white women would also characterize those between Black men and Black women. But we've seen that de Beauvoir also holds that sexual oppression is essentially nullified when men and women are subject to other forms of oppression. In that case, her claim is not really that the sexism she describes operates only when class and race are constant, but rather that she is talking about the sexism in effect only when the men and women involved are not subject to class or racial oppression. She herself leads us to the conclusion that the sexism she is concerned with in *The Second Sex* is that experienced by white middle-class women in Western countries.

The creation of women

"One is not born, but rather becomes, a woman". This opening sentence from Book 2 of *The Second Sex* has come to be the most often cited and perhaps most powerful of de Beauvoir's insights. Among other things it offers a starting point for the distinction between sex and gender. It is one thing to be biologically female, quite another to be shaped by one's culture into a "woman" – a female with feminine qualities, someone who does the kinds of things "women," not "men," do, someone who has the kinds of thoughts and feelings that make doing these things seem an easy expression of one's feminine nature.

If being a woman is something one can become, then it also is something one can fail to become. De Beauvoir insists that while being or not being female is a biological matter, becoming or not becoming a woman is not. "Civilization as a whole" produces women. In the absence of other humans, no female would become a woman; particular human "intervention in her destiny is fundamental" to who and what she becomes: "Woman is determined not by her hormones or by mysterious instincts, but by the manner in which her body and her relation to the world are modified through the action of others than herself." In particular, "in men's eyes – and for the legion of women who see it through men's eyes – it is not enough to have a woman's body nor to assume the female function as mistress or mother in order to be "true woman."[38] What she has to do to become a "true woman" is to be seen and to see herself as Other in contrast to the Self of the male, as inessential in contrast to the essential, as object in contrast to the subject. Females of the species don't come created in this way; they are made this way by the concerted efforts of men and women.

Moreover, de Beauvoir insists that humans create whatever significance is attached to having a body and more particularly to having a male or female body. She directs us to thinking about "the body as lived in by the subject" as opposed to the body as described by the biologist. The conscious-ness one has of one's body in this way is acquired "under circumstances dependent upon the society of which [one] is a member" or indeed even upon the class one belongs to. De Beauvour suggests, for example, that the physical event of having an abortion is experienced differently by con-ventional middle-class women and by those "schooled by poverty and misery to disdain bourgeois morality." Along similar lines, she claims that the biological changes that take place during menopause are experienced differently by those "true women" who have "staked everything on their femininity" and by "the peasant woman, the work man's wife," who, "constantly under the threat of new pregnancies, are happy when, at long last, they no longer run this risk."[39]

Biology is not destiny in at least two senses, according to de Beauvoir. First, being female is not the same thing as being a "woman"; nor does it determine whether and how one will become a "woman." Second, different women experience biological events associated with being female differently, depending on how their bodies are otherwise employed and their beliefs about what are the proper things to do with or to their bodies. But de Beauvoir doesn't take this insight as far as she might in the directions to which her own comments lead. She seems to be saying that there is no particular significance that must be given to biological facts about our bodies, that whether or how a female becomes a "woman" depends upon human consciousness and human action. But she is well aware of the fact that in many ways human consciousness and human action take quite different forms in different societies. We get a hint of this in her comment quoted above about how a woman's consciousness of femininity is dependent on the society in which she lives, as well as in her reminder that the intervention of others is so crucial a factor in the creation of a "woman" out of a female that "if this action took a different direction, it would produce a quite different result."[40]

This surely points to the variability in the creation of "women" across and within cultures. Here is where de Beauvoir's lack of attention to females belonging to the populations she contrasts to "women" is particularly disappointing. She doesn't reflect on what her own theoretical perspective strongly suggests and what her own language mirrors: namely, that different females are constructed into different kinds of "women"; that under some conditions certain females count as "women," others don't.

Moreover, de Beauvoir's analysis of racial oppression, cursory as it is, tells us that she believes people have attached different significance to racial differences at different times. She counts as successful social change those economic and political reversals in which a people once regarded as Other no longer are regarded as such by those who formerly dominated them. When she comments, early in the book, on the change of status of Blacks in Haiti after the revolution,[41] and much later on how Black suffrage helped to lead to the perception of Blacks as worthy of having the vote,[42] she is alluding to changes in the significance attached by whites to what they take to be biological differences between whites and Blacks. If we follow up her insistence that we pay attention to "the body as lived in by the subject," we might begin to ask not only about living in a male or female body in the context of sexism but also about living in a black or white or brown or yellow or red body in the context of racism. Though de Beauvoir refers to the variability in ideals of feminine beauty[43] and, as we've seen, is certainly aware of racial oppression, she does not speak at length about women subject to racism and so does not talk about the ways in which notions of beauty are racially coded. While she certainly is aware of the significance attached to skin color, she does not join that to her point about the distinction between other physical differences among human bodies (i.e., sexual differences) and what humans make of those differences.

The real and the ideal woman

A third promising ingredient of de Beauvoir's analysis is her attack on the discrepancy between the reality of actual women and a static ideal of "woman." The latter is not an empirical generalization based on observations of specific women but a male myth about the nature of femininity:

> As against the dispersed, contingent, and multiple existences of actual women, mythical thought opposes the Eternal Feminine, unique and changeless. If the definition provided for this concept is contradicted by the behavior of flesh-and-blood women, it is the latter who are wrong; we are told not that Femininity is a false entity, but that the women concerned are not feminine.[44]

De Beauvoir believes that this mythical ideal reaches deep into the idea of woman as Other, and as we've seen, she sometimes speaks as if men's treatment of women as Other is inevitable. But on the other hand, it is clear that she thinks that if political and economic conditions change in the right direction, women will be seen in their historical specificity – that is, women might come to be truly known by men rather than being the occasion for men's projection of a mythic ideal of femininity.

> It is noteworthy that the feminine comrade, colleague, and associate are without mystery [being "mysterious" is one version of the mythic ideal]; on the other hand, if the vassal is male, if, in the eyes of a man or a woman who is older, or richer, a young fellow, for example, plays the role of the inessential object, then he too becomes shrouded in mystery. And this uncovers for us a substructure under the feminine mystery which is economic in nature.[45]
>
> The more relationships are concretely lived, the less they are idealized. The fellah of ancient Egypt, the Bedouin peasant, the artisan of the Middle Ages, the worker of today has in the requirements of work and poverty relations with his particular woman companion which are too definite for her to be embellished with an aura either auspicious or inauspicious.[46]

De Beauvoir seems to be making a brief here for establishing a set of conditions under which people can see each other as they actually are. The liberation of women depends upon establishing economic and political conditions under which men won't simply project their notion of "woman" onto women but will look at who women in fact are, observing "the behavior of flesh-and blood women." De Beauvoir has high regard for what she refers to as "knowledge," "empirical law," "laws of nature," "scientific explanation."[47] Though she does not explain exactly what she means by these terms, it is clear that she accuses men of not being very scientific in their claims about women. Men are right to look for universally true statements about women, but they don't realize that the only solid grounds for such claims are empirical óbservations. Clear thinking about women would lead to universally true statements about them.

De Beauvoir has not of course laid out a full-blown epistemology here, but the hints of one point to the potential richness of her account of women. As we have noted on several occasions, de Beauvoir at one level is quite aware of the diverse historical, economic, and political situations of women, of the differences class and race make to women's relationships with men and to their relationships with other women. She likens the notion of the "Eternal Feminine" to a Platonic "Idea, timeless, unchangeable." As an existentialist, she has no truck with the idea of an "essence" of anything – of humanity, of man, of woman. We are not who or what we by by virtue of being particular instances of some transcendental entity; rather, "an existent *is* nothing other than what he does . . . he is to be measured by his acts."[48]

De Beauvoir suggests that a search for some essence of "woman" is deeply misplaced: we would look in vain for some metaphysical nugget of pure womanhood that defines all women as women. We have to look at what women do to find out who they are. This means that we cannot decide prior to actual investigation of women's lives what they do or do not have in common; and this means that we cannot assume that what we find to be true about the lives of women of one class or race or nationality or historical period will be true about the lives of other women. De Beauvoir warns us against any inclination to assume that the lives of women of one race or class are representative of the lives of all other women. Both existentialism and "scientific thinking" tell us we have to look and see what women are really like.

But at the same time, de Beauvoir also warns, neither existentialism nor "scientific reasoning" will lead us to the viewpoint of "woman," who "lacks the sense of the universal" and takes the world to be "a confused conglomeration of special cases." So while we can't assume, ahead of time, that any particular universal truth about "humanity" or "men" or "women" will be true, we can assume that investigation of women's lives will lead to such a truth or truths about women. Women's isolation from one another – the very isolation that de Beauvoir cites as one reason for their not constituting a likely political class – accounts in large part for their lacking "the sense of the universal": "She feels she is a special case because she is isolated in her home and hence does not come into active contact with other women."[49] If she had the opportunity to know about other women's lives, she might come to see the grounds for universal truths in the similarities in cases she earlier had taken to be special, unique, *sui generis*.

De Beauvoir has a lively concern that views about women be based neither on the assumption that women necessarily share some metaphysical essence nor on the assumption that women share nothing at all. Yet the universal truths she claims to be noting about "women" do not follow from the observations she makes about differences among women.

III

What might explain the contradictory pulls in de Beauvoir's account of women? The point of asking this is not to exonerate her from the charge of inconsistency or of misrepresenting the situation of white middle-class women as that of "women in general." The point, rather, is to see where white middle-class privilege has to lodge in order to make itself resistant to observations and theoretical perspectives that tell against it.

Certain strands of de Beauvoir's thought lead inexorably in the direction of a central focus on white middle-class women to illuminate the condition of "woman." As we've seen, at least some of the time she holds the following conditions to be true:

1 If one is not a "man," one is either a woman or a Black, a woman or Jewish, a woman or a poor person, etc.
2 Sexism is different from racism and other forms of oppression: sexism is the oppression women suffer as women, racism the oppression Blacks, for example, suffer as Blacks.
3 Sexism is most obvious in the case of women not otherwise subject to oppression (i.e., not subject to racism, classism, anti-Semitism, etc.).

Now insofar as de Beauvoir takes these conditions to be true, it is quite logical for her to take the examination of white middle-class women to be the examination of all women. Indeed, anyone who assumes the truth of these three conditions will take it to be the most logical thing in the world for feminists to focus on white middle-class women. De Beauvoir certainly is not alone in this position. To the degree that conditions 1, 2, and 3 seem logical, we ought to think of the white middle-class privilege her work expresses, not as a personal quirk in de Beauvoir, but as part of the intellectual and political air she and many of us breathe.

There are two important features of what we might call the 1–2–3 punch. First, it has the status of near truism: points 1 and 2 may appear to be true by definition (de Beauvoir, as we saw it, at times took them utterly for granted), and 3 may seem just to be a matter of common sense, something not even needing the confirmation of historical inquiry (aren't the effects of sexism on women more distinct and hence easier to investigate when other forms of oppression don't affect the women in question?). Second, it leads to the focus on white middle-class women *without mentioning white middle-class women.*

These two features are crucial to the way in which white middle-class privilege works in feminist theory and hence crucial to understanding why we would miss a golden opportunity if we simply dismissed de Beauvoir's focus as an individual expression of her privilege and left it at that. (Indeed, it would also be an expression of that privilege to mention its presence but not bother to explore and expose its depth and pervasiveness.) Privilege cannot work if it has to be noted and argued for. For someone to have privilege is precisely *not* to have to beg for attention to one's case. For feminist theory to express white middle-class privilege is for it to ensure that white midle-class women will automatically receive attention. How can it ensure this without making explicit what it is doing? Conditions 1–3 do the trick, by making the default position of feminist inquiry an examination of white middle-class women: unless otherwise noted, that's who we are going to be talking about.

De Beauvoir was very attuned to the expression of privilege in women's behavior: as we saw, she took note of the desire of white slaveowners' wives to preserve the racial status quo; she talked about the hostile treatment of female domestic workers by their middle- and upper-class female employers. But privilege, we well know, can lodge almost anywhere, and since it works best when it is least obvious, it is not surprising that we should find it reflected in what appear to be axioms of her inquiry into the condition of "women."

Insofar as any of us agree to points 1–3 (and the agreement is likely to be implicit, not explicit), we are not likely to give much weight to those strands in de Beauvoir's thought that might give us reason to question their status. For example, we aren't likely to be struck by the fact that if, as de Beauvoir claims, one of the reasons women don't seem to form a natural political class is that we are found in every population, then, contra 1, it is very odd to contrast women with Blacks, Jews, the poor. Nor are we likely to notice the force of de Beauvoir's saying that we ought always to ask about the race and class of any men and women we are talking about, since claims about sexual hierarchy hold only when race and class are kept constant: if this is so, the sexism women are subject to will vary in accordance with their race and class privilege. But in that case, contra 2, there is no simple form of sexism the same for all women as women. Thus even if, as condition 3 claims, sexism is easier to track in the case of women not otherwise subject to oppression, it doesn't mean the sexism one finds is just like the sexism one would find in the case of women who are subject to other forms of oppression. We have to be very careful: the oppression white middle-class women are subject to is not the oppression women face "as women" but the oppression white middle-class women face. Their race and class are not irrelevant to the oppression they face even though they are not oppressed on account of their race and class.

IV

We have been trying to see what might explain the discrepancy between the implicit complexity of de Beauvoir's assessment of the lives of women and the oversimplification in her explicit rendering of "woman's situation" and of gender relations. We've suggested that while it is true that such oversimplification expresses the privileged tunnel vision of someone of de Beauvoir's race and class, we must also take the task of unmasking privilege seriously by trying to locate the places it finds a home, rather than simply noting that it must be at work. Since de Beauvoir herself was highly attuned to and bothered by the presence of such privilege, we honor her work by asking how such privilege functions in her own thinking.

There's no doubt that the case de Beauvoir makes about "woman" would be less compelling, at least to many of her readers, if she were to wonder aloud whether there is any difficulty posed for her account by the fact that there are women among the populations she contrasts to "woman"; if she were to say, "Notice, by the way, that the account I give of relations between middle-class men and women is not the same one I give of relations between working-class men and women"; if she did not hide away on page 605 of a 689-page book the reminder that any time we speak of male–female relations we must make sure that the men and women are of the same race and class.[50]

Such explicit musings would produce a less forceful argument for anyone who thinks that if we cannot talk about "woman" or about "women in general," then no case can be made about the injustice done to women, no strategy devised for the liberation of women. According to this line of thinking, a coherent feminist political analysis and agenda requires that we be able to talk about the history of the treatment of all women, as women. In order to be taken seriously, feminists have to make a case that they are speaking about more than a small group of people and that those referred to have been mistreated. So, for example, a group of white middle-class women would not claim that harm has come to them for being white or middle-class, but for being women. And they might well believe that not only would it be irrelevant to refer to being white and middle-class, but it would suggest that the group is not as representative as it otherwise would appear. So were de Beauvoir to make more explicit than she does who "woman" refers to in her analysis, she would defuse its potential impact: the case would not be that of "woman" but of particular women.

Furthermore, as we've seen, de Beauvoir thinks women lack a "sense of the universal." This has been a crucial part of their failure to resist the domination of men: not caring to notice the similarities in their experiences, each one given to "overestimat[ing] the value of her smile" because "no one has told her that all women smile." They fail to "sum . . . up in a valid conclusion" the many instances that ground claims about the conditions of "woman's" existence. Until women see beyond their own individual cases, they will not "succeed in building up a solid counter-universe whence they can challenge the males."[51] De Beauvoir may well regard it as a kind of weakness on her part were she to resist generalizing from the case of a woman like herself.

But it is one thing to urge women to look beyond their own cases; it is quite another to assume that if one does one will find a common condition or a common hope shared by all women. Perhaps there is a common condition or hope, but de Beauvoir's own work speaks against it. Given her insistence on the different social and economic positions occupied by women, she suggests not that similarities among women's various conditions are there to be found, but rather that they need to be created.

Notes

1 Simone de Beauvoir, *The Second Sex*, trans. and ed. H. M. Parshley (New York: Knopf, 1953).

2 See, for example, Judith Okely, *Simone de Beauvoir* (London: Virago, 1986).

3 This is not to say that feminists have not found reason to disagree with her. For a recent extended critique, see Mary Evans, *Simone de Beauvoir: A Feminist Mandarin* (London and New York: Tavistock, 1985).

4 Though de Beauvoir's terminology is certainly different from Aristotle's, there are echoes here of his distinction between a group of cattle grazing and a vibrant human *polis*.

5 *Second Sex*, pp. 58, 59.

6 Ibid., p. 588.

7 Ibid., p. 59. The translator here renders *l'existence* as "existing" and *la vie* as

"living." "Living" carries more weight for contemporary English speakers than mere "existing."

8 Ibid., p. 134.
9 Ibid., pp. 72, 68.
10 Ibid., p. 569.
11 Ibid., p. 74.
12 Ibid., p. xix.
13 Ibid., p. xviii.
14 Ibid.
15 Ibid., pp. 513, 511.
16 De Beauvoir does say quickly in passing that only feminists have done this. Ibid., pp. xviii–xix.
17 Ibid., pp. 246, xx. But she also insists for example, that "woman's 'character' [is] to be explained by her situation" (p. 588).
18 Ibid., p. xix; cf. pp. 103, 566, 590.
19 Ibid., p. 513.
20 Ibid., p. 103.
21 The idea that white middle-class women might be more reluctant than other women to battle sexism – if doing so is to cost them the privileges they have over white working-class women and all women of color – appears to conflict with what has become a historical truism: that the nineteenth- and twentieth-century women's movements in England, Europe, and the United States were founded and maintained by white middle-class women. Two questions immediately arise. Did they perceive their activity to be something that would involve giving up race or class privilege? Was what they were fighting for in fact something that would lead to loss of privilege whether or not they so perceived it? Were white female abolitionists actually fighting to end race privilege? Did they think it could be ended without ending sex privilege in the white population? In any event, if middle-class women were as reluctant as de Beauvoir says, what might this tell us about those middle-class women who were not reluctant?
22 *Second Sex*, pp. xx, 512, 563.
23 Contemporary feminists now stick in the qualifying adjective "white," as if that took care of the problem. But if it matters whether a man is white, it surely also matters – even if not in the same way – that a woman is white.
24 *Second Sex*, p. 38.
25 Ibid., pp. 566, 590.
26 On this see Ann Firor Scott, *The Southern lady: From Pedestal to Politics* (Chicago: University of Chicago Press, 1971).
27 *Second Sex*, pp. 430, 443, 497, 508, 663.
28 Ibid., p. 404.
29 Ibid., p. 82.
30 Ibid., p. 81.
31 Ibid., p. 605.
32 Ibid., pp. xviii, 49, 59, 278, 585, 579.
33 For instance, ibid., pp. 454, 569.
34 Ibid., p. 131.

35 Ibid., pp. 119–20.
36 Ibid., pp. 94, 96.
37 Ibid., p. 605.
38 Ibid., pp. 249, 682, 245.
39 Ibid., pp. 33, 44, 461, 542.
40 Ibid., p. 682.
41 Ibid., pp. xviii–xix.
42 Ibid., p. 686.
43 Ibid., p. 146.
44 Ibid., p. 237.
45 Ibid., pp. 241–2.
46 Ibid., p. 244.
47 Ibid., pp. 237, 580.
48 Ibid., pp. 237, 241.
49 Ibid., p. 580.
50 As Margaret Simons has pointed out, the English translation of *The Second Sex* does not include all of the original French version. See "The Silencing of Simone de Beauvoir: Guess What's Missing from *The Second Sex*," *Women's Studies International Forum*, 6, 1983, pp. 559–64.
51 *Second Sex*, pp. 580–1.

12

Foucault and Feminism: Toward a Politics of Difference

Jana Sawicki

The beginning of wisdom is in the discovery that there exist contradictions of permanent tension with which it is necessary to live and that it is above all not necessary to seek to resolve.

André Gorz, Farewell to the Proletariat

It is not difference which immobilizes us, but silence. And there are so many silences to be broken.

Audre Lorde, Sister Outsider, *p. 44*

The question of difference is at the forefront of discussions among feminists today.[1] Of course, theories of difference are certainly not new to the women's movement. There has been much discussion concerning the nature and status of women's differences from men (for instance, biological, psychological, cultural). Theories of sexual difference have emphasized the shared experiences of women across the divisions of race, class, age or culture. In such theories the diversity of women's experiences is often lumped into the category "women's experience," or women's caste, presumably in an effort to provide the basis for a collective feminist subject.

More recently, however, as a result of experiencing conflicts at the level of practice, it is the differences among women (for instance, differences of race, class, sexual practice) that are becoming the focus of theoretical discussion. To be sure, Marxist feminists have consistently recognized the significance of class differences among women, but other important differences cry out for recognition. The question arises: do the differences and potential separations between women pose a serious threat to effective political action and to the possibility of theory?

Perhaps the most influential and provocative ideas on the issue of difference in feminism are to be found in the writings of black, lesbian feminist poet and essayist Audre Lorde. In her work, Lorde describes the ways in which the differences among women have been "misnamed and misused in the service of separation and confusion."[2] As a lesbian mother and partner in an inter-racial couple, she has a unique insight into the conflicts and divided allegiances which put into question the possibility of a unified women's movement. She has experienced the way in which power utilizes difference to fragment opposition. Indeed this fragmentation can occur not only within groups but also within the individual. Hence, Lorde remarks: "I find I am constantly being encouraged to pluck out some one aspect of myself and present this as the meaningful whole, eclipsing or denying the other parts of self."[3]

Lorde claims that it is not the differences among women which are the source of separation but rather our "refusal to recognize those differences, and to examine the distortions which result from our misnaming them and their effects upon human behavior and expectation."[4] Thus, she appears to be saying that difference is not necessarily counter-revolutionary. She suggests that feminists devise ways of discovering and utilizing their differences as a source for creative change. Learning to live and struggle with many of our differences may be one of the keys to disarming the power of the white, male, middle-class norm which we have all internalized to varying degrees.

In what follows I shall elaborate on the notion of difference as resource and offer a sketch of some of the implications that what I call a "politics of difference" might have for "revolutionary" femininist theory.[5] In order to elucidate these implications I shall turn to the writings of the social philosopher and historian Michel Foucault. It is my contention that despite the androcentrism in his own writings he too has recognized the ambiguous power of difference in modern society; that is, he recognizes that difference can be the source of fragmentation and disunity as well as a creative source of resistance and change.

My aim in this paper is two-fold: (1) to turn to Foucault's work and method in order to lay out the basic features of a politics of difference; and (2) to show how such a politics might be applied in the feminist debate concerning sexuality. In order to accomplish these aims I shall begin by contrasting Foucault's politics with two existing versions of revolutionary feminism, namely, Marxist and radical feminism. I have selected these two feminist frameworks because they contain the elements of traditional revolutionary theory which Foucault is rejecting.[6] Other Foucauldian feminisms are developed by Morris and Martin.[7]

Foucault's Critique of Revolutionary Theory

It will be helpful to contrast Foucault's approach with Marxism, on the one hand, and radical feminism, on the other. Both Marxism and radical feminism conceive of historical process as a dialectical struggle for human liberation. Both have turned to history to locate the origins of oppression, and to identify a revolutionary subject. Yet radical feminists have criticized Marxism for its inability to give an adequate account of the persistence of male domination. They identify patriarchy as the origin of all forms of oppression. Hence, they view the struggles of women as a sex/class as the key to human liberation.

The recent intensification of feminist attention to the differences among women might be understood as a reaction to the emergence of a body of feminist theory which attempts to represent women as a whole on the basis of little information about the diversity of women's experiences, to develop universal categories for analyzing women's oppression, and, on the basis of such analysis, to identify the most important struggles. When Audre Lorde and others speak of the importance of preserving and re-defining difference, of discovering more inclusive strategies for building theory, and of the need for a broad based, diverse struggle, they are calling for an alternative to a traditional revolutionary theory in which forms of oppression are either overlooked or ranked and the divisions separating women exacerbated. The question is: are there radical alternatives to traditional revolutionary theory? As I have indicated, it is in the writings of Foucault that we find an attempt to articulate an alternative approach to understanding radical social transformation.

Foucault's is a radical philosophy without a theory of history. He does not utilize history as a means of locating a single revolutionary subject, nor does he locate power in a single material base. Nevertheless, historical research is the central component of his politics and struggle a key concept for understanding change. Accordingly, in order to evaluate the usefulness of Foucault's methods for feminism we must first understand the historical basis for his critique of traditional revolutionary theory.

Foucault's rejection of traditional revolutionary theory is rooted in his critique of the "juridico-discursive" model of power on which it is based. This model of power underpins both liberal theories of sovereignty (that is, legitimate authority often codified in law and accompanied by a theory of rights) and Marxist theories which locate power in the economy and the state as an arm of the bourgeoisie. The juridico-discursive model of power involves three basic assumptions:

1   power is possessed (for instance, by individuals in the state of nature, by a class, by the people);
2   power flows from a centralized source from top to bottom (for instance, law, the economy, the state); and
3   power is primarily repressive in its exercise (a prohibition backed by sanctions).

Foucault proposes that we think of power outside the confines of state, law or class. This enables him to locate forms of power which are obscured in traditional theories. Thus, he frees power from the political domain in much the same way as radical feminists did. Rather than engage in theoretical debate with political theorists, Foucault gives historical descriptions of the different forms of power operating in the modern West. He does not deny that the juridico-discursive model of power describes one form of power. He merely thinks that it does not capture those forms of power which make centralized, repressive forms of power possible, namely, the myriad of power relations at the microlevel of society.

Foucault's own model of power differs from the traditional model in three basic ways:

1   power is exercised rather than possessed;
2   power is not primarily repressive, but productive; and
3   power is analyzed as coming from the bottom up.

In what follows I will give Foucault's reasons for substituting his own view of power for the traditional one.

1   Foucault claims that thinking of power as a possession has led to a preoccupation with questions of legitimacy, consent and rights. (Who should possess power? When has power overstepped its limits?) Marxists have problematized consent by introducing a theory of ideology, but Foucault thinks this theory must ultimately rest on a humanistic notion of authentic consciousness as the legitimate basis of consent. Furthermore, the Marxist emphasis on power as a possession has resulted in an effort to locate those subjects in the historical field whose standpoint is potentially authentic, namely, the proletariat. Foucault wants to suspend any reference to humanistic assumptions in his own account of power because he believes that humanism has served more as an ideology of domination than liberation.

For the notion that power is a possession Foucault substitutes a relational model of power as exercised. By focusing on the power relations themselves, rather than on the subjects related (sovereign–subject, bourgeois–proletarian), he can give an account of how subjects are constituted by power relations.

2   This brings us to the productive nature of power. Foucault rejects the repressive model of power for two reasons. First, he thinks that if power were merely repressive, then it would be difficult to explain how it has gotten such a grip on us. Why would we continue to obey a purely repressive and coercive form of power? Indeed, repressive power represents power in its most frustrated and extreme form. The need to resort to a show of force is more often evidence of a lack of power. Second, as I have indicated, Foucault thinks that the most effective mechanisms of power are productive. So, rather than develop a theory of history and power based on the humanistic assumpton of a presocial individual endowed with inalienable rights (the liberal's state of nature) or based on the identification of an authentic human interest (Marx's species being), he gives accounts of the ways in which certain institutional and cultural practices have produced individuals. These are the practices of a disciplinary power which he associates with the rise of the human sciences in the nineteenth century.

Disciplinary power is exercised on the body and soul of individuals. It increases the power of individuals at the same time as it renders them more docile (for instance, basic training in the military). In modern society disciplinary power has spread through the production of certain forms of knowledge (the positivistic and hermeneutic human sciences) and through the emergence of disciplinary techniques which facilitate the process of obtaining knowledge about individuals (techniques of surveillance, examination, discipline). Thus, ways of knowing are equated with ways of exercising power over individuals. Foucault also isolates techniques of individualization such as the dividing practices found in medicine, psychiatry, criminology and their corresponding institutions, the hospital, asylum and prison. Disciplinary practices create the divisions healthy/ill, sane/mad, and legal/delinquent, which, by virtue of their authoritative status, can be used as effective means of normalization and social control. They may involve the literal dividing off of segments of the population through incarceration or institutionalization. Usually the divisions are experienced in the society at large in more subtle ways, such as in the practice of labeling one another or ourselves as different or abnormal.

For example, in *The History of Sexuality* Foucault gives an historical account of the process through which the modern individual has come to see herself as a sexual subject. Discourses such as psychoanalysis view sexuality as the key to self-understanding and lead us to believe that in order to liberate ourselves from personality "disorders," we must uncover the truth of our sexuality. In this way dimensions of personal life are psychologized, and thus become a target for the intervention of experts. Again, Foucault attempts to show how these discourses, and the practices based on them, have played more of a role in the normalization of the modern individual than they have in any liberatory processes. He calls for a liberation from this "government of individualization," for the discovery of new ways of understanding ourselves, new forms of subjectivity.

3   Finally, Foucault thinks that focusing on power as a possession has led to the location of power in a centralized source. For example, the Marxist location of power in a class has obscured an entire network of power relations "that invests the body, sexuality, family, kinship, knowledge, technology. . ."[8] His alternative is designed to facilitate the description of the many forms of power found outside these centralized loci. He does not deny the phenomenon of class (or state) power, he simply denies that understanding it is more important for resistance. As I have indicated, Foucault expands the domain of the political to include a heterogeneous ensemble of power relations operating at the microlevel of society. The practical implication of his model is that resistance must be carried out in local struggles against the many forms of power exercised at the everyday level of social relations.

Foucault's "bottom-up" analysis of power is an attempt to show how power relations at the microlevel of society make possible certain global effects of domination (such as class power, patriarchy). He avoids using universals as explanatory concepts at the start of historical inquiry in order to prevent theoretical overreach. He states:

> One must rather conduct an ascending analysis of power starting, that is, from its infinitesimal mechanisms, which each have their own history, their own trajectory, their own tactics, and then see how these mechanisms of power have been – and continue to be – invested, colonized, utilized, involuted, transformed, displaced, extended, etc., by even more general mechanisms and by forms of global domination. It is not that this global domination extends itself right to the base in a plurality of repercussions. . . .[9]

In other words, by utilizing an ascending analysis Foucault shows how mechanisms of power at the microlevel of society have become part of dominant networks of power relations. Disciplinary power was not invented by the dominant class and then extended down into the microlevel of society. It originated outside this class and was appropriated by it once it revealed its utility. Foucault is suggesting that the connection between power and the economy must be determined on the basis of specific historical analyses. It cannot be deduced from a general theory. He rejects both reductionism and functionalism insofar as the latter involves locating forms of power within a structure or institution which is self-regulating. He does not offer causal or functional explanations but rather historical descriptions of the conditions which make certain forms of domination possible. He identifies the necessary but not sufficient conditions for domination.

In short, Foucault's histories put into question the idea of a universal binary division of struggle. To be sure, such divisions do exist, but as particular and not universal historical phenomena. Of course, the corollary of his rejection of the binary model is that the notion of a subject of history, a single locus of resistance, is put into question.

Resistance

Despite Foucault's neglect of resistance in *Discipline and Punish*, in *The History of Sexuality* he defines power as dependent on resistance.[10] Moreover, emphasis on resistance is particularly evident in his more recent discussions of power and sexuality.[11]

In recent writings Foucault speaks of power and resistance in the following terms:

> Where there is power, there is resistance, and yet, or rather consequently, this resistance is never in a position of exteriority in relation to power.[12]

> I'm not positing a substance of resistance facing a substance of power. I'm simply saying: as soon as there's a relation of power there's a possibility of resistance. We're never trapped by power; it's always possible to modify its hold, in determined conditions and following a precise strategy.[13]

There are two claims in the above remarks. The first is the weaker claim that power relations are only implemented in cases where there is resistance. In other words, power relations only arise in cases where there is conflict, where one individual or group wants to affect the action of another individual or group. In addition, sometimes power enlists the resistant forces into its own service. One of the ways it does this is by labeling them, by establishing norms and defining differences.

The second claim implied in Foucault's description of power is the stronger claim that wherever there is a relation of power it is possible to modify its hold. He states: "Power is exercised only over free subjects and only insofar as they are free."[14] Free subjects are subjects who face a field of possibilities. Their action is structured but not forced. Thus, he does not define power as the overcoming of resistance. When resistant forces are overcome, power relations collapse into force relations. The limits of power have been reached.

So, while Foucault has been accused of describing a totalitarian power from which there is no escape, he denies that "there is a primary and fundamental principle of power which dominates society down to the smallest detail.[15] At the same time he claims that power is everywhere. He describes the social field as a myriad of unstable and heterogeneous relations of power. It is an open system which contains possibilities of domination as well as resistance.

Foucault describes the social and historical field as a battlefield, a field of struggle. Power circulates in this field and is exercised on and by individuals over others as well as themselves. When speaking of struggle, he refuses to identify the subjects of struggle. When asked the question: "Who is struggling against whom?" he responds:

> This is just a hypothesis, but I would say it's all against all. There aren't immediately given subjects of the struggle, one the proletariat, the other the bourgeoisie. Who fights against whom? We all fight against each other. And there is always within each of us something that fights something else."[16]

Depending on where one is and in what role (for instance, mother, lover, teacher, anti-racist, anti-sexist) one's allegiances and interests will shift. There are no privileged or fundamental coalitions in history, but rather a series of unstable and shifting ones.

In his theory of resistant subjectivity Foucault opens up the possibility of something more than a history of constructions or of victimization. That is, he opens the way for a historical knowledge of struggles. His genealogical method is designed to facilitate an "insurrection of subjugated knowledges." These are forms of knowledge or experience which "have been disqualified as inadequate to their task, or insufficiently elaborated: naive knowledges, located low down in the hierarchy, beneath the required level of cognition or scientificity."[17] They include the low-ranking knowledge ("popular knowledge") of the psychiatric patient, the hysteric, the imprisoned criminal, the housewife, the indigent. Popular knowledge is not shared by all people, "but it is, on the contrary, a particular, local, regional knowledge, a *differential* knowledge incapable of unanimity."[18]

The question whether some forms of resistance are more effective than others is a matter of social and historical investigation and not of a priori theoretical pronouncement. The basis for determining which alliances are politically viable ought not to be an abstract principle of unity, but rather historical and contextual analysis of the field of struggle. Thus feminism can mobilize individuals from diverse sites in the social field and thereby use differences as a resource.[19]

Genealogy as a form of resistance

Foucault introduces genealogical critique as his alternative to traditional revolutionary theory. He attempts to liberate us from the oppressive effects of prevailing modes of self-understanding inherited through the humanist tradition. As one commentator suggests, for Foucault, "Freedom does not basically lie in discovering or being able to determine who we are, but in rebelling against those ways in which we are already defined, categorized and classified."[20] Moreover, the view that the purpose of a theory of history is to enable us to control history, is part of the Enlightenment legacy from which Foucault is attempting to "free" us. For him, there is no theory of global transformation to formulate, no revolutionary subject whose interest the intellectual or theoretician can represent. He recommends an alternative to the traditional role for the intellectual in modern political struggles. He speaks of the "specific intellectual" in contrast to the "universal intellectual," that is, the "bearer of universal values" who is the enlightened consciousness of a revolutionary subject.

The specific intellectual operates with a different conception of the relation between theory and practice: "Intellectuals have gotten used to working, not in the modality of the 'universal,' the 'exemplary,' the 'just-and-true-for all,' but within specific sectors, at the precise points where their own conditions of life or work situate them (housing, the hospital, the asylum, the laboratory, the university, family and social relations).[21] Focusing attention on specific situations may lead to more concrete analyses of particular struggles and thus to a better understanding of social change. For example, Foucault was involved in certain conflicts within medicine, psychiatry and the penal system. He facilitated ways for prisoners to participate in discussions of prison reform and wrote a history of punishment in order to alter our perspectives on the assumptions which inform penal practices.

In part, Foucault's refusal to make any universal political, or moral, judgments is based on the historical evidence that what looks like a change for the better may have undesirable consequences. Since struggle is continual and the idea of a power-free society is an abstraction, those who struggle must never grow complacent. Victories are often overturned; changes may take on different faces over time. Discourses and institutions are ambiguous and may be utilized for different ends.

So Foucault is in fact pessimistic about the possibility of controlling history. But this pessimism need not lead to despair. Only a disappointed traditional revolutionary would lapse into fatalism at the thought that much of history is out of our control. Foucault's emphasis on resistance is evidence that he is not fatalistic himself, but merely skeptical about the possibilities of global transformation. He has no particular utopian vision. Yet, one need not have an idea of utopia in order to take seriously the injustices in the present. Furthermore, the past has provided enough examples of theoretical inadequacy to make Foucault's emphasis on provisional theoretical reflection reasonable.

In short, genealogy as resistance involves using history to give voice to the marginal and submerged voices which lie "a little beneath history," that is, the mad, the delinquent, the abnormal, the disempowered. It locates may discontinuous and regional struggles against power both in the past and present. These voices are the sources of resistance, the creative subjects of history.[22]

Foucault and Feminism: Toward a Politics of Difference

What are the implications of Foucault's critique of traditional revolutionary theory, his use of history and his analysis of power for feminism? I have called Foucault's politics a politics of difference because it does not assume that all differences can be bridged. Neither does it assume that difference must be an obstacle to effective resistance. Indeed, in a politics of difference, difference can be a resource insofar as it enables us to multiply the sources of resistance to particular forms of domination and to discover distortions in our understandings of each other and the world. In a politics of difference, as Audre Lorde suggests, redefining our differences, learning from them, becomes the central task.

Of course, it may be that Lorde does envision the possibility of some underlying commonality, some universal humanity, which will provide the foundation for an ultimate reconciliation of our differences. Her own use of the concept of the "erotic" might be understood as an implicit appeal to humanism.[23] As we have seen, Foucault's method requires a suspension of humanistic assumptions. Indeed, feminists have recognized the dangers of what Adrienne Rich refers to as "the urge to leap across feminism to 'human liberation.' "[24] What Foucault offers to feminism is not a humanist theory, but rather a critical method which is thoroughly historical and a set of recommendations about how to look at our theories. The motivation for a politics of difference is the desire to avoid dogmatism in our categories as well as the elision of difference to which such dogmatism can lead.

In conclusion, I want to illustrate the value and limitations of Foucault's politics of difference by bringing it to bear on a recent discussion of difference within feminism, namely, the sexuality debate. This debate has polarized American feminists into two groups, radical and libertarian feminists.[25] The differences being discussed threaten to destroy communications between them. Hence, an understanding of their differences is crucial at this conjuncture in American feminism.

Radical feminists condemn any sexual practices involving the "male" ideology of sexual objectification which, in their view, underlies both male sexual violence and the institutionalization of masculine and feminine roles in the patriarchal family. They call for an elimination of all patriarchal institutions in which sexual objectification occurs, such as pornography, prostitution, compulsory heterosexuality, sadomasochism, cruising, adult/child and butch/femme relations. They substitute an emphasis on intimacy and affection for the "male" preoccupation with sexual pleasure.

In contrast, libertarian feminists attack radicals for having succumbed to sexual repression. Since radicals believe that sex as we know it is male, they are suspicious of any sexual relations whatsoever. Libertarians stress the dangers of censoring any sexual practices between consenting partners and recommend the transgression of socially acceptable sexual norms as a strategy of liberation.

What is remarkable about these debates from the perspective of a politics of difference is the extent to which the two camps share similar views of power and freedom. In both camps, power is represented as centralized in key institutions which dictate the acceptable terms of sexual expression, namely, male-dominated heterosexual institutions whose elements are crystallized in the phenomenon of pornography on the one hand, and all discourses and institutions which distinguish legitimate from illegitimate sexual practice (including radical feminism) thereby creating a hierarchy of sexual expression, on the other. Moreover, both seem to regard sexuality as a key arena in the struggle for human liberation. Thus, for both, understanding the truth about sexuality is central for liberation.

In addition, both operate with repressive models of power. Radical feminists are in fact suspicious of all sexual practices insofar as they view sexual desire as a male construct. They think male sexuality has completely repressed female sexuality and that we must eliminate the source of this repression, namely, all heterosexual male institutions, before we can begin to construct our own. Libertarians explicitly operate with a repressive model of power borrowed from the Freudo-Marxist discourses of Wilhelm Reich and Herbert Marcuse. They recognize that women's sexual expression has been particularly repressed in our society and advocate women's right to experiment with their sexuality. They resist drawing any lines between safe and dangerous, politically correct and politically incorrect, sex. Radical feminists accuse libertarians of being male identified because they have not problematized sexual desire; libertarians accuse radicals of being traditional female sex-prudes.

There are other similarities between the two camps. In the first place, as Ann Ferguson has pointed out, both involve universalist theories of sexuality, that is, they both reify "male" and "female" sexuality and thus fail to appreciate that sexuality is a historically and culturally specific construct.[26] This is problematic insofar as it assumes that there is some essential connection between gender and sexual practice. An historical understanding of sexuality would attempt to disarticulate gender and sexuality and thereby reveal the diversity of sexual experiences across gender as well as other divisions. For example, Rennie Simpson suggests, Afro-American women's sexuality has been constructed differently from white women's.[27] They have a strong tradition of self-reliance and sexual self-determination. Thus, for American black women, the significance of the sexuality debates may be different. Indeed, the relationship between violence and sexuality takes on another dimension when viewed in the light of past uses of lynching to control black male sexuality. And consider the significance of black women's emphasis on issues such as forced sterilization or dumping Depo Provera on third world countries over that of white American feminists on abortion on demand.[28] Yet radical feminists still tend to focus on dominant culture and the victimization of women. Ann Snitow and Carol Vance clearly identify the problem with this approach when they remark:

> To ignore the potential for variations (in women's sexual expression) is inadvertently to place women outside the culture except as passive recipients of official systems of symbols. It continues to deny what mainstream culture has always tried to make invisible – the complex struggles of disenfranchised groups to grapple with oppression using symbolic as well as economic and political resistance.[29]

Rather than generalize on the basis of the stereotypes provided by "dominant culture," feminists must explore the meaning of the diversity of sexual practices to those who practice them, to resurrect the "subjugated knowledge" of sexuality elided within dominant culture.

Secondly, both radicals and libertarians tend to isolate sexuality as the key cause of women's oppression. Therefore, they locate power in a central source and identify a universal strategy for seizing control of sexuality (for instance, eliminate pornography, transgress sexual taboos by giving expression to sexual desire). Both of these analyses are simplistic and reductionist. While it is important, sexuality is simply one of the many areas of everyday life in which power operates.

In sum, the critique of the sexuality debates developed out of a politics of difference amounts to (1) a call for more detailed research into the diverse range of women's sexual experiences, and (2) avoiding analyses which invoke universal explanatory categories or a binary model of oppression and thereby overlook the many differences in women's experience of sexuality. Although a politics of difference does not offer feminists a morality derived from a universal theory of oppression, it need not lapse into a form of pluralism in which anything goes. On the basis of specific theoretical analyses of particular struggles, one can make generalizations, identify patterns in relations of power and thereby identify the relative effectiveness or ineffectiveness, safety or danger of particular practices. For example, a series of links have been established between the radical feminist strategy of antipornography legislation and the New Right's efforts to censor any sexual practices which pose a threat to the family. This is not to suggest that the antipornography movement is essentially reactionary, but rather that at this time it may be dangerous. Similarly, one ought not to assume that there is any necessary connection between transgression of sexual taboos and human liberation. Denying that censorship is the answer is not tantamount to endorsing any particular form of transgression as liberatory.

In a feminist politics of difference, theory and moral judgements would be geared to specific contexts. This need not preclude systematic analysis of the present, but would require that our categories be provisional. As Snitow and Vance point out: "We need to live with the uncertainties that arise along with the change we desire."[30] What is certain is that our differences are ambiguous; they may be used either to divide us or to enrich our politics. If we are not the ones to give voice to them, then history suggests that they will continue to be either misnamed and distorted, or simply reduced to silence.

Notes

1 See Cherrie Moraga and Gloria Anzaldúa, eds, *This Bridge Called My Back: Writings of Radical Women of Color* (Boston: Persephone Press, 1981); Bonnie Thornton Dill, "Race, Class, and Gender: Prospects for an all inclusive Sisterhood," *Feminist Studies*, 9(1), 1983, pp. 131–50; Floya Anthias and Nira Yuval-Davis, "Contextualizing Feminism – Gender, Ethnic, and Class Divisions," *Feminist Studies*, 15, 1983, pp. 62–74.

2 Audre Lorde, *Sister Outsider*, (New York: Crossing Press, 1984).

3 Ibid., p. 120.

4 Ibid., p. 115.

5 "Revolutionary" feminisms are those which appeal to the notion of a "subject of history" and to the category of a "social totality" in their analyses of the theory and practice of social transformation.

6 Socialist feminism is an obvious alternative to the ones that I have chosen. It represents a theoretical development in feminism which is closest to embodying the basic insights of a politics of difference. See for example the work of Linda Nicholson, *Gender and History: The Limits of Social Theory in the Age of the Family* (New York: Columbia University Press, 1986).

7 Meaghan Morris and Paul Patton, eds, *The Pirate's Fiancée: Michel Foucault: Power, Truth, and Strategy* (Sydney: Feral, 1979) and Biddy Martin, "Feminism, Criticism and Foucault," *New German Critique*, 27, 1982, pp. 3–30.

8 Michel Foucault, introduction to *Herculin Barbarin: Being the Recently Discovered*

Memoirs of a Nineteenth Century French Hermaphrodite (New York: Pantheon, 1980), p. 122.

9	Ibid., p. 99.

10	One feminist critic charges that Foucault's institutionalist theory of sexuality results in a picture of the "one-dimensional" containment of sexuality by objective forces beyond our control. She claims that it obscures the "continuous struggles of women against . . . patriarchy. . ." Yet her criticism begs the question since it assumes that an emancipatory theory must rest on the notion of a continuous revolutionary subject. Foucault, after all, is attempting to displace the problem of the subject altogether. See Jacqueline Zita, "Historical Amnesia and the Lesbian Continuum," in *Feminist Theory: A Critique of Ideology*, ed. Nannerl Keohane, Michèlle Z. Rosaldo, and Barbara C. Gelpi (Chicago: Chicago University Press, 1982), p. 173.

11	See Foucault's reproduction of the memoirs of a hermaphrodite for an example of his effort to resurrect a knowledge of resistance. This memoir is an account of the despair experienced by Herculine (formerly Alexina) once a male sexual identity is imposed upon her in her "happy limbo of non-identity." This occurs at a time when the legal and medical profession has become interested in the question of sexual identity and has decided that every individual must be either male or female. Foucault, *Herculin Barbarin*.

12	Michel Foucault, *The History of Sexuality, 1: An Introduction* (New York: Pantheon, 1978), p. 95.

13	Michel Foucault, "The History of Sexuality: An Interview," trans. Geoff Bennington, *Oxford Literary Review*, 4(2), 1980, p. 13.

14	Michel Foucault, "The Subject and Power," afterword, in Hubert Dreyfus and Paul Rabinow, *Michel Foucault: Beyond Structuralism and Hermeneytics*, (Chicago: University of Chicago Press, 1982–3), p. 221.

15	Ibid., p. 224.

16	Foucault, *Herculin Barbarin*, p. 208.

17	Ibid., p. 82.

18	Ibid., emphasis added.

19	For a similar argument against ahistorical criteria of effective resistance see Kathryn Pyne Addelson, "Words and Lives," in *Feminist Theory*, ed. Keohane et al.

20	John Rajchman, "The Story of Foucault's History," *Social Text*, 8, 1984, p. 15.

21	Foucault, *Herculin Barbarin*, p. 126.

22	Linda Nicholson describes an explicitly historical feminism in which the search for origins (genealogy) involves an attempt to deconstruct (give an account of the process of construction of) our present categories (e.g. "personal," "public") and thereby free us from a rigid adherence to them. Foucault's genealogies serve the same function. See Nicholson, *Gender and History*.

23	Lorde, *Sister Outsider*, pp. 53–9.

24	Adrienne Rich, "Toward a Woman-centered University," in *On Lies, Secrets and Silence: Selected Prose 1966–1978*, (New York: W. W. Norton, 1979), p. 134.

25	Ann Ferguson, "Sex War: The Debate between Radical and Libertarian Feminists," *Signs*, 10(1), 1984, pp. 106–12.

26	Ibid., p. 110.

27 Rennie Simpson, "The Afro-American Male," in *The Powers of Desire: The Politics of Sexuality*, ed. Ann Snitow, Christine Stansell, and Sharon Thompson (New York: Monthly Review Press, 1983), pp. 229–35.

28 Valerie Amos and Pratibha Parmer, "Challenging Imperial Feminism," *Feminist Review*, 17, 1984, pp. 1–19.

29 Ann Snitow and Carol Vance, "Towards a Conversation about Sex in Feminism: A Modest Proposal," *Signs*, 10(1), 1984, p. 132.

30 Ibid., p. 133.

13

Hannah Arendt and Feminist Politics

Mary G. Dietz

Hannah Arendt, perhaps the most influential female political philosopher of the twentieth century, continuously championed the *bios politikos* – the realm of citizenship – as the domain of human freedom. In her major work, *The Human Condition*, Arendt appropriated the Aristotelian distinction between "mere life" and "the good life" in order to characterize the crisis of the contemporary age in the West. What we are witnessing, she argued, is the eclipse of the public realm of participatory politics and the emergence of an atomized society bent on sheer survival. Arendt's political vision was decisively Hellenic: the classical Greek *polis* of male citizens was her model of the public; Pericles, the Athenian statesman, was her exemplary citizen-hero; and the quest for freedom as glory was her political ideal.

A political theory so indebted to a culture of masculinity and hero worship was bound to meet with resistance in the feminist writings of the 1970s and 1980s, as feminists began to pursue a woman-centered theory of knowledge, and debunk the patriarchal assumptions of "male-stream" Western political thought. Thus Arendt was not spared the critical, anti-canonical gaze of feminist theory. For Adrienne Rich and Mary O'Brien, *The Human Condition* was simply another attempt to discredit "women's work," to deny the value of reproductive labor, and to reassert the superiority of masculinity. Pulling few punches, Rich argued that Arendt's work "embodies the tragedy of a female mind nourished on male ideologies"; and O'Brien called Arendt "a woman who accepts the normality and even the necessity of male supremacy."[1] For both Rich and O'Brien, Arendt's sins were not simply those of omission. By elevating politics and "the common world of men," they contended, she reinforced the legitimacy of "paterfamilias on his way to the freedom of the political realm," and denied the truly liberatory potential of the female realm of reproduction and mothering.[2]

Other scholars, however, drew some distinctively feminist dimensions from Arendt's political thought. In *Money, Sex, and Power*, Nancy Hartsock noted the significance of Arendt's concept of power as collective action, and her appreciation of "natality" or beginning anew, as promising elements for a feminist theory "grounded at the epistemological level of reproduction."[3] Hanna Pitkin observed that *The Human Condition* is located within "a framework of solicitude for the body of our Earth, the Mother of all living creatures"; so Arendt could hardly be described as hostile in principle to women's concerns.[4] More recently, Terry Winant found in Arendt's work, "the missing element in recent attempts to address the problem of grounding the feminist standpoint."[5]

These differing feminist interpretations of Arendt's political theory serve as the organizational framework of this essay. With the critical attacks of Rich and O'Brien in mind, I argue that *The Human Condition* does, in fact, exhibit a gender blindness that renders it a far less powerful account of politics and human freedom than it otherwise might have been had Arendt been attentive to women's place in the human condition. Unlike Rich and O'Brien, however, I am not ready to dismiss *The Human Condition* as hopelessly "male-stream"; nor do I think "the necessity of male supremacy" follows from Arendt's theoretical presuppositions. This essay also contends, then – in line with Hartsock and others – that Arendt's work has much to offer feminist thought, especially in its attempts to articulate a vision of politics and political life. Unlike Hartsock, however, I argue that an "Arendtian feminism" must continue to maintain an analytical distinction between political life on the one hand, and reproduction on the other, and also recognize the problematical nature of a feminist politics grounded in reproductive processes. Before proceeding to these arguments, it is necessary to outline in brief Arendt's understanding of the *vita activa* – labor, work, and action – which is the core of her theory in *The Human Condition* and the subject of so much feminist debate.

Labor, Work, and Action

Arendt begins *The Human Condition* by distinguishing among three "general human capacities which grow out of the human condition and are permanent, that is, which cannot be irretrievably lost so long as the human condition itself is not changed."[6] The three capacities and their "corresponding conditions" are labor and life, work and worldliness, and action and plurality; together they constitute the *vita activa*.[7] Arendt envisions labor, work, and action not as empirical or sociological generalizations about what people actually do, but rather as existential categories intended to distinguish the *vita activa* and reveal what it means to be human and "in the presence of other human beings" in the world.[8] These "existentials," however, do more than disclose that human beings cultivate, fabricate, and organize the world. In an expressly normative way, Arendt wants to judge the human condition, and to get us, in turn, "to think what we are doing" when we articulate and live out the conditions of our existence in particular ways.[9] Underlying *The Human Condition* is the notion that human history has been a story of continuously shifting "reversals" within the *vita activa* itself. In different historical moments from the classical to the contemporary age, labor, work, and action have been accorded higher or lower status within the hierarchy. Arendt argues that some moments of human experience – namely those in which "action" has been understood as the most meaningful human activity – are more glorious and free than those in which either "the labor of our body or the work of our hands" is elevated within the *vita activa*.[10] Hence her reverence for the age of Socrates and the public realm of the Greek *polis*, and her dismay over the ensuing events within Western culture and political thought (including liberalism and Marxism), as citizen-politics is increasingly lost and the world of action is displaced by the primacy of labor and work. The critique of the modern world that *The Human Condition* advances rests on the claim that we are now witnessing an unprecedented era in which the process-driven activity of labor dominates our understanding of human achievement. As a result, we live in and celebrate a world of automatically functioning jobholders, having lost all sense of what constitutes true freedom and collective public life.

When Arendt calls "life" the condition of labor, "worldliness" the condition of work, and "plurality" the condition of action, she means to associate a corresponding set of characteristics with each. Labor (*animal laborans*) corresponds to the biological process of the human body and hence to the process of growth and decay in nature itself. Necessity defines labor, insofar as laboring is concentrated exclusively on life and the demands of its maintenance. Labor takes place primarily in the private realm, the realm of the household, family, and intimate relations. The objects of labor – the most natural and ephemeral of tangible things – are the most consumed and, therefore, the least worldly. They are the products of the cyclical, biological, life process itself, "where no beginning and no end exist and where all natural things swing in changeless, deathless, repetition."[11] *Animal laborans* is also distinguished by a particular mentality or mode of thinking-in-the-world. It cannot conceive of the possibility of breaking free or beginning anew; "sheer inevitability" and privatization dominate it. Hence, Arendt refers to the "essential worldly futility" of the life process and the activity of *animal laborans*.[12]

In contrast to labor, work (*homo faber*) is the activity that corresponds to the "unnaturalness" of human existence. If "life" and the private realm locate the activity of *animal laborans*, then "the world" locates *homo faber*. Work is, literally, the working up of the world, the production of things-in-the-world. If *animal laborans* is caught up in nature and in the cyclical movement of the body's life processes, then *homo faber* is, as Arendt puts it, "free to produce and free to destroy."[13] The fabrication process, with its definite beginning and predictable end, governs *homo faber* activity. Repetition, the hallmark of labor, may or may not characterize work; at least it is not inherent in the activity itself. The objects of this activity, unlike those of labor, are relatively durable, permanent endproducts. They are not consumed, but rather used or enjoyed. The "fabrications" of *homo faber* have the function of "stabilizing" human life and they bear testimony to human productivity.[14]

Insofar as they are all *homo faber*, human beings think in terms of gaining mastery over nature, and approach the world itself as a controllable object, the "measure of man." This tendency to objectify things and persons in the world is a foreboding of, in Arendt's words, "a growing meaninglessness, where every end is transformed into a means," and even those things not constructed by human hands lose their value and are treated as instruments at the behest of the "lord and master of all things."[15] The corresponding mentality of *homo faber*, then, is a rational-instrumental attitude concerned with the usefulness of things and with the "sheer worldly existence" made possible through human artifice. Understood as an existential "type," *homo faber* is that aspect of human beingness that places its confidence in the belief that "every issue can be solved and every human motivation reduced to the principle of utility."[16]

What Arendt calls "action" stands in sharp contrast with, but is not unrelated to the activities of labor and work. In order to act, human beings must first have satisfied the demands of life, have a private realm for solitude, and also have a stable world within which they can achieve "solidity" and "retrieve their sameness . . . their identity."[17] At the same time, human beings possess extraordinary capabilities that neither labor nor work encompass. They can disclose themselves in speech and deed, and undertake new beginnings, thereby denying the bonds of nature and moving beyond the means–end confines of *homo faber*.[18] Without action to bring new beginnings (natality) into the play of the world, Arendt writes, there is nothing new under the sun; without speech, there is no memorialization, no remembrance.[19] Unlike either labor or work, action bears no corresponding singular Latin synonym, perhaps because Arendt means for it to capture an aspect of human life that is essentially collective, rather than solitary or distinguished by the "separateness" of persons. This collective condition, where speech and action materialize, Arendt calls "the human condition of plurality."[20]

Plurality is perhaps the key concept in Arendt's understanding of action. She uses it to explore the situation humans achieve when they "gather together and act in concert," thus finding themselves enmeshed within a "web of relationships."[21] In general terms, plurality is the simultaneous realization of shared equality and distinctive, individual differences. Arendt calls it "the basic condition of both action and speech."[22] Without equality, individuals would not be able to comprehend each other or communicate, and without distinctiveness, they would have no need or reason to communicate, no impetus to interject themselves as *unique* selves into the shared world. Plurality, then, is the common condition in which human beings reveal their "unique distinctiveness." Arendt presents this in terms of a paradox: "Plurality is the condition of human action because we are all the same, that is, human, in such a way that nobody is ever the same as anyone else who ever lived, lives, or will live."[23] Thus, plurality promotes the notion of a politics of shared differences.

Because Arendt introduces plurality as a political and not a metaphysical concept, she also locates this common condition in a discernible space which she calls "the public" or "the space of appearances."[24] The public exists in stark contrast to the private realm; it is where the revelation of individuality amidst collectivity takes place. The barest existence of a public realm "bestowed upon politics a dignity," Arendt writes, "that even today has not altogether disappeared."[25]

Arendt's concept of plurality as the basic condition of action and speech allows her to reconceptualize politics and power in significant ways. Put simply, politics at its most dignified is the realization of human plurality – the activity that simply *is* the sharing of the world and exemplary of the human capacity for "beginning anew" through mutual speech and deed.[26] Power, which Arendt understands as "acting together," maintains the space of appearances; as long as it persists, the public realm is preserved.[27] Politics is the activity that renders us something more than just the *animal laborans*, subject to the cyclicality of human biological processes, or the *homo faber*, artificer of the world. When Arendt characterizes action as the only activity entirely dependent on "being together" and "the existence of other people," she intends to posit the existential difference between politics on the one hand, and labor and work on the other. She also wants to use action as a way of getting us to consider yet one other dispositional capacity we possess – something she variously calls common sense, judging insight, or "representative thinking."[28] Representative thinking can be distinguished from both the process logic of *animal laborans* and the instrumentalism of *homo faber* insofar as it is guided by a respect for persons as distinctive agents, as "speakers of words and doers of deeds." In order to flourish, the public realm requires this way of thinking; it proceeds from the notion that we can put ourselves in the place of others, in a manner that is open, communicative, and aware of individual differences, opinions, and concerns.

Without question, Arendt understands politics as existentially superior to both labor and work. Thus she has often been interpreted as devaluing the latter, or worse, as having contempt for the lives of the poor and working classes – in her own words, "the vast majority of humankind."[29] Here it is worth repeating that Arendt presents labor, work, and action *not* as constructs of class or social relations, but rather as properties of the human condition which are within the range of every human being. Likewise, our "world alienation" is not a matter of rising masses or threatened aristocracies, but has to do with the fact that, as *humans*, we are rapidly losing our collective capacity for exercising power through shared word and deed, and succumbing ever more steadily to an existence governed by the instrumental calculations of *homo faber* and the process mentality of *animal laborans*. Freedom is fast disappearing in the face of the sheer survivalism and automatic functioning that is the condition of the modern world.

Women and the Human Condition

The feminist critic who approaches *The Human Condition* for the first time is likely to conclude that Arendt's *magnum opus*, with its generic male terms of reference, its homage to the canon of Western political thought, and its silences about women, reads like another contribution to a long line of political works in the tradition. Inconceivable as it may sound to contemporary feminists, Arendt mentions women only twice (aside from a few footnotes) in her lengthy discussion of the classical conception of labor and work, public and private. She observes, without comment, that in the sphere of the Greek household, men and women performed different tasks, and she acknowledges, briefly, that women and slaves "belonged to the same category and were hidden away" because their lives were devoted to bodily functions.[30] Her scholarly development of a conceptual history of labor and work is remarkably silent on the sexual division of labor in the family and on the way in which gender informed traditional understandings of labor and work in both classical and modern thought. Also missing from *The Human Condition* is any sustained discussion of women's systematic exclusion from the public realm throughout occidental history. Not only does Arendt seem to be trading in abstract, ahistorical categories; she also seems to have little awareness of the gender assumptions that underlie and complicate them.

Nevertheless, the feminist critic is well advised to give *The Human Condition* a second look. For, not unlike many other supposedly "male-stream" texts in political thought, Arendt's work is an enriching, not simply a frustrating, site for feminist criticism. Partly this is because of its scope and complexity; as the various feminist accounts mentioned earlier reveal, *The Human Condition* admits of no definitive interpretive conclusions. Moreover, Arendt herself offers some promising directions for feminist speculation concerning labor, work, and action. In this sense, although a feminist analysis never emerges in *The Human Condition*, the materials for one are always threatening to break out. What these materials are, and how they might enrich a feminist political theory despite Arendt's neglect of women and gender, is what I explore below. What I want to argue is that, from one possible feminist perspective, *The Human Condition* is *both* flawed and illuminating.

Although Arendt has been accused of romanticizing the public realm and ignoring the brutality and patriarchalism that attends politics, she is, in fact, not wholly inattentive to the historically grounded relationships that have structured the activities she posits as fundamental to the human condition.[31] From the beginning, she argues, some have sought ways to ease the burden of life by forcibly assigning to others the toil of *animal laborans*. Those who have been regularly reduced to the status of "world-less specimens of the species mankind," have made it possible for others to transcend "the toil and trouble of life" by standing on the backs of those they subordinate.[32] In the modern age, this subordination is most vividly revealed within the working class. The activity of *homo faber* has lost its worldly character and is now performed by a mass of workers who are bent upon sheer survival and reduced to little more than servants of mechanized processes. (Work of this kind brings *homo faber* ever closer to *animal laborans*.) Arendt is also aware that the freedom of the "man of action" – the speaker of words and doer of deeds in the public realm – is made possible because of others who labor, fabricate, and produce. The man of action, as citizen, thus "remains in dependence upon his fellow men."[33] She does not press the sociological analysis of labor, work, and action along the lines of master and slave, elite and mass, privileged and oppressed, nearly as far as she could. But she is not completely unconcerned with the coercive and oppressive aspects of human experience that have allowed the privileged alone to enjoy the benefits of action in the public realm.

Likewise, Arendt cannot be accused of completely overlooking the manifestations of patriarchal power within the historical development of the public and private realm. Although she literally renders the discussion as footnotes, she provides in small print some illuminating insights into various dimensions of our patriarchal history. She tells us, for instance, that the terms *dominus* and *paterfamilias* were synonymous throughout "the whole of occidental antiquity."[34] The realm of the ancient household was, literally, a miniature *patria* – a sphere of absolute, uncontested rule exercised by the father over women, children, and slaves. Only in the public realm did the *paterfamilias* shed his status as ruler, and become one among equals, simultaneously ruling and ruled. Only he was able to move between public and private as both citizen among citizens, and ruler over those not fit for admission to the public realm.

In her subtext discussion of the Greek distinction between labor and work (*ponos* and *ergon*), Arendt notes that Hesiod considered labor an evil that came out of Pandora's box. Work, however, was the gift of Eris, the goddess of good strife.[35] Earlier she also tells us that, for Aristotle, "the life of woman" is called *ponetikos* – that is, women's lives are "laborious, driven by necessity, and devoted, by nature, to bodily functions.[36] Following the poet and the philosopher, our patriarchal history begins by counting painful labor (*ponon alginoenta*) as "the first of the evils plaguing man," and by assigning to women and slaves the inevitable and ineliminable task of carrying out this labor, according to their respectively less rational and irrational natures.[37] These are the tasks that, for the Greeks, occupied and defined the private realm and were forced into hiding within the interior (*megaron*) of the house. Here Arendt observes that the Greek *megaron* and the Latin *atrium* have a strong connotation of darkness and blackness.[38] Thus the realm of women and slaves is, for the ancients, a realm of necessity, painful labor, and blackness. In its toil and trouble, the private realm symbolizes the denial of freedom and equality, and the deprivation of being heard and seen by others. In its material reality, it makes possible the Greek male's escape from the "first evil" into the life of the public.

As Arendt implies, then, for the realm of freedom and politics to exist and take on meaning, it needed an "other" – a realm of necessity and privacy against which it could define and assert itself.[39] That this realm of the other and the human practices that distinguish it came to be conceptualized in terms of the female and made the domain of women's lives is something feminist theorists have brought to light in powerful detail. In *The Human Condition*, Arendt presents even more evidence for this argument, but it is evidence she does not utilize in her own theorizing of the human condition. Indeed, despite numerous instances in which she comes close to something like a nascent "gender insight" in her analysis of the public and private realm, and the activity of labor and work, Arendt never fully develops this insight or incorporates it systematically into her theory of the human condition.

Nowhere, perhaps, is Arendt's failure to develop her evidence about gender more striking than in her discussion of the character and conditions of *animal laborans*. It is the most illuminating example of how the materials

for a feminist analysis are present in *The Human Condition*, but in the end
are left unplumbed by Arendt herself. Consider again some of the characteristics that distinguish the life of *animal laborans*, as Arendt presents
them: enslavement by necessity and the burden of biological life, a primary
concern with reproduction, absorption with the production of life and its
regeneration, and a focus on the body, nature, and natural life processes.
Labor assures "not only individual survival, but the life of the species,"
and, finally, there is the elemental happiness that is tied to laboring, to the
predictable repetition of the cycle of life and from just "being alive."[40] As
Arendt writes:

> The blessing or joy of labor is the human way to experience the sheer bliss of
> being alive which we share with all living creatures, and it is even the only
> way men, too, can remain and swing contentedly in nature's prescribed
> cycle . . . with the same happy and purposeless regularity with which day
> and night and life and death follow each other.[41]

The reference to "men" in this last passage sounds especially odd
because the laboring Arendt has captured so vividly is more readily
recognizable for the feminist reader as that associated with women's
traditional activities as childbearers, preservers, and caretakers within the
household and family.[42] Yet the activity of "world-protection, world-
preservation, world-repair" that Arendt encompasses in her category
"labor" is not acknowledged in *The Human Condition* as indicative of
women's practices and activities.[43] But surely being "submerged in the
over-all life process of the species," and identified with nature has been
women's lot; being tied to biological processes has been women's destiny;
facing the "essential worldly futility" of the lifecycle, within the darkness
of the private realm, has been women's challenge. The cyclical, endlessly
repetitive processes of household labor – cleaning, washing, mending,
cooking, feeding, sweeping, rocking, tending – have been time-honored
female ministrations, and also conceived of and justified as appropriate to
women. Since the Greeks, the cyclical, biological processes of reproduction
and labor have been associated with the female, and replicated in a
multitude of historical institutions and practices. It is indeed curious that
Arendt never makes this central feature of the human condition an integral
part of her political analysis. Let us speculate nonetheless: what if *The
Human Condition* had explored the category *animal laborans* as a social
construction of "femaleness"? What else might we learn? A number of
lessons emerge.

First, an Arendtian analysis enlightened by gender reveals that the
"permanent capacities" of labor, work, and action are neither antiseptic
analytical categories, nor "generic" human activities but rather social
practices that have been arranged according to socially constituted and

deeply entrenched sex differences. From Aristotle on, women have been systematically constructed as *animal laborans*, and deemed neither capable nor worthy of location with in the "space of appearances" that is action. Moreover, even when they are in the guise of *homo faber* – in the workplace of the "artificer" – women have carried out the routinized tasks of stoop labor on assembly lines, and as cleaners, cooks, and clericals. The mechanisms of institutionalized sexism have assigned to women unpaid, devalued, monotonous work, both within the private realm and within the world outside. Nominally *homo faber*, they are really *animal laborans*, transported from life into worldliness. It seems, then, that the fundamental existentials Arendt designates have actually been lived out as either male or female *identities*. *Animal laborans*, the "reproducer," has been structured and experienced as if it were natural to the female, and *homo faber* the "fabricator," has been constructed as if it were natural to the male. Once we see this, we can no longer understand the *vita activa* as a neutral stage on which male and female players appear in modes of laboring, working, or acting. These activities have, from the start, been "cordoned off" according to sex, and women have been consistently relegated – both materially and symbolically – to the lowest dimension of the *vita activa*, to the life or world of labor.

Second, and following from the above, an Arendtian analysis informed by gender allows us to see that the disappearance of the public world, and the loss of freedom, has been a reality for only one small part of humanity. Just as "citizen" is an identity until recently granted to (some) men alone, so the "lost treasure" of political freedom, as Arendt calls it, has in fact been the historical possession of only (some) men. The feminist reader who shares Arendt's regret over the disappearance of freedom in the modern world is also aware that the treasure was never women's to lose.[44] The most emancipatory aspect of human experience as Arendt presents it – the collective determination of human community through shared speech and deliberation in the public sphere – is not a central aspect of female experience. Thus the human condition must be assessed not only for what it has lost, but for what it has done – for how it has systematically subordinated a portion of the human race, and refused them, on Arendt's telling, the most meaningful experience of human freedom.

Finally, an Arendtian analysis informed by gender, and the recognition of women's exclusion from the public, amplifies our conception of the relationship between public and private, and of freedom itself. Even if we were to recover the public realm Arendt so vividly imagines, no society could count itself free so long as women were refused admittance to the space of appearances or confined to gendered institutions within the private realm. But the admission of women into the public raises other questions, not the least of which is "who will tend to the private?" Or, as a graduate student I know puts it wryly, "Every citizen needs a wife."[45]

Thus, if we are to have a truly emancipated *human* condition, we must inquire after both the arrangements that constitute the public, and the conditions of the realm of necessity, without which the public world of citizens cannot flourish. Susan Okin acknowledges this when she writes:

> Only when men participate equally in what have been principally women's realms of meeting the daily material and psychological needs of those close to them, and when women participate equally in what have been principally men's realms of larger scale production, government, and intellectual and creative life, will members of both sexes develop a more complete *human* personality than has hitherto been possible.[46]

Notice that this formulation does not require the abandonment of a conception of public and private, or a refusal of the distinction between labor, work, and action. But it does require us, in both theory and practice, to disconnect gender from these conceptions and reconceptualize them accordingly, as genderless realms and genderless activities. By "genderless" I do not mean "androcentric," but rather relations and realms unfettered by roles assigned according to perceived "natural" differences between the sexes. As Hanna Pitkin writes: "Women should be as free as men to act publicly; men should be as free as women to nurture . . . A life confined entirely to personal and household concerns seems . . . stunted and impoverished, and so does a life so public or abstracted that it has lost all touch with the practical, everyday activities that sustain it."[47]

Arendt's failure to recognize, much less develop, the issues that surround the constitution of women as *animal laborans* is readily apparent. Her failure to integrate these issues into *The Human Condition* is particularly serious given her belief that we must "think what we are doing," lest we lose forever our understanding of those "higher and more meaningful activities" for the sake of which our release from the bonds of necessity deserves to be won."[48] Had she recognized that "thinking what we are doing" entails not just a reconsideration of the *vita activa*, but also an account of how gender is implicated in the *vita activa* itself, *The Human Condition* would have been a far more emancipatory project. For all her attentiveness to the relationship between public and private, however, Arendt's gender blindness prevents her from seeing these realms as domains that have historically enforced women's subordination. For all her concern for freedom, she seems not to consider the exclusion of women from the public world at all informative of her analysis of the alienation of the contemporary age. In these respects, the androcentrism of Arendt's political theory diminishes her account of the very human condition she wishes us to comprehend.

Feminist Theory and the Public Realm

To the extent that *The Human Condition* fails to acknowledge the problem of women's subordination and (in bell hooks' terms) "the sexism perpetuated by institutions and social structures," it does not contribute to what we might call the "world-disclosing" aspect of a feminist theory.[49] It does not help us understand the ways in which the symbolic construction of gender has organized existing social practices and legitimized relations of domination.

Nevertheless, despite its inattention to issues related to sex and gender, *The Human Condition* has much to offer a feminist political theory. Accordingly, in the final section, I want to turn the tables and argue that Arendt's understanding of action and plurality as meaningful experiences of human freedom is something feminist theory should heed. In this respect, *The Human Condition* provides an orienting role for political self-understanding, and it encourages us to reconsider the way we think about the relationship between human practices and human identities.

Part of Arendt's critique of contemporary society involves her argument that politics as public life, as a space of appearances where citizens engage one another, deliberate, and debate, has nearly disappeared. As her emphasis on plurality indicates, Arendt means more by "participation in the space of appearances" than casting a ballot every four years or engaging in interest group activities. Indeed, the fact that we need to clarify the difference between voting and the active, public self-revelation of equals and peers as citizens is proof to Arendt that we have ceased to think of ourselves as, potentially, something more than just reproducers, producers, laborers, role-players, or fragile psyches. As the *vita activa* steadily becomes the province of *animal laborans*, so too, it seems, do our self-understandings. Our conceptualizations of who we are and what we are capable of doing are driven by the imperatives of "the last stage of laboring society"; hence we are less and less capable of imagining ourselves as mutually engaged citizens, or of thinking in terms of a political "we" rather than just an isolated "me." Our access to an understanding of politics as a public happiness has diminished; "mere" life overrules other considerations, the body supercedes the body politic, and the sheer survival of the individual as a "self" predominates over sensitivity to human plurality.

Athough it is not easy to say precisely what Arendt means by the notion that we have come to think what we are doing as *animal laborans*, she surely is getting at something more than just a cliché about the "me generation." Perhaps her argument is best summed up in terms of her own concepts: the modern age operates under the assumption that life, and not the world, is the highest good; the *immortality* of life – the possibility of achieving glory through speech and deed as public-spirited citizens – is a fading ideal. We are turned inward, and thrown back upon ourselves and our endlessly analyzed psyches. We are obsessed with society, wealth, and entertainment, but at a loss to comprehend the human condition as a being-in-the-presence-of-others in the *political* world. Remarking on the modern age, Arendt writes (in gendered language): "none of the higher capacities of man was any longer necessary to connect individual life with the life of the species; individual life became part of the life process, and to labor, to assure the continuity of one's own life and the life of the family, was all that was needed."[50]

Arendt intends for this indictment to cover philosophers of the modern age as well as ordinary agents. She numbers Marx, Kierkegaard, Nietzsche, and Bergson among those for whom political freedom and the worldliness of action have lost their meaning, or at least been radically transfigured. Hence the ultimate point of reference in their writings is not politics, action or plurality, but rather "life and life's fertility."[51] At least in the case of Kierkegaard and Nietzsche, the alternately agitated or aesthetic "I" replaces the politically engaged "we."

In the late twentieth century, a similar reluctance to theorize in political terms, by grounding the identity of human agents in the condition of plurality and in the capacity for speech and deed, seems to characterize certain forms of feminist theory. Nowhere perhaps is the temptation to theorize in the terms of *animal laborans* – with heightened attention to nature, reproduction, birth, the body, and the rhythmic processes of life itself – more prevalent than among those feminists who are concerned to argue that a privileged epistemological perspective emerges from specifically female practices and a generalizable women's condition. Consider, as examples, Mary O'Brien's emphasis on birth and reproduction as a starting point for a feminist theory of material relations, Nancy Hartsock's attention to the body's "desires, needs, and mortality" as a primary element in feminist epistemology, Adrienne Rich's concentration on "housework, childcare, and the repair of daily life" as the distinctive feature of women's community, Sara Ruddick's claim that daily nurturance and maternal work give women special insights into peace, and Julia Kristeva's case for the subversive potential of gestation, childbirth, and motherhood.[52] Although these theories are variously materialist, maternalist, and poststructuralist, they have in common an emancipatory vision that defends the moral (or subversive) possibilities of women's role as reproducer, nurturer, and preserver of vulnerable human life. O'Brien, for one, envisions a feminist theory "which celebrates once more the unity of cyclical time with historical time in the conscious and rational reproduction of the species. It will be a theory of the celebration of life in life rather than death in life."[53] Within this presumably celebratory vision an Arendtian might notice a tribute to *animal laborans*.

The temptation to theorize from the standpoint of women's bodies, and with an emphasis on reproduction, childbirth and mothering, bears a compelling logic. Women have been construed in terms of bodily processes and the so-called imperative of nature, and feminist theory, in its "world-disclosing" or critical aspects, confronts these putatively natural attributes and demystifies them. Feminist theory has revealed that, in O'Brien's words, "the private realm is where the new action is," insofar as the unmasking of structures of female subordination is concerend.[54] However, in the process of unmasking the manifold faces of power, many feminist theorists have, in effect, elevated the activities of *animal laborans* as the central features of women's identity and feminist politics. Guided by a reading of *The Human Condition* and Arendt's categories of the *vita activa*, we might consider why this feminist maneuver poses problems for a feminist theory of politics.

Unavoidably, when feminist theorists locate emancipatory or interventionist possibilities in "female reproductive consciousness" or within traditional female activities, they grant some warrant to the very patriarchal arrangements that have historically structured the *vita activa*. Of course, feminists appropriate these arrangements for purposes of emancipatory consciousness, but the subordination of women to *animal laborans* remains intact nonetheless. Accordingly, these feminist arguments – despite their transvaluation of women's work and bodily processes – legitimize a minimalist conception of women without considering a more expansive set of possibilities about what it means to be "in the presence of other human beings in the world." The celebration of *animal laborans* plays to a reduced, uniform conception of women's range of capabilities and their human identity within the *vita activa*. As Arendt's discussion of labor, work, and action invites us to see, however, being human involves more than just what Kristeva (appreciatively) calls "cycles, gestation, [and] the eternal recurrence of a biological rhythm which conforms to that of nature."[55] If female subjectivity has been traditionally linked to this latter form of temporality, then the goal of a feminist political theory should be to disengage female subjectivity from the straitjacket rather than to reinforce so restrictive a view of existential possibility and human potentiality.

Moreover, for an Arendtian, this disengagement from a theory of subjectivity rooted in *animal laborans* must be undertaken with a specifically political goal in mind. Whatever else we might wish to make of women as reproducers, mothers, or "celebrators of life in life," we should not confuse gender identification – or theories of subjectivity – with *political* emancipation. A feminist theory of political emancipation needs more than a focus on reproduction, birth, and childcare to sustain it. For, as much as we need to be reminded of the centrality of these experiences in the human condition, they do not and cannot serve as the focal point of a liberatory political theory. This is not only because, historically, reproduction, birth, and childcare have been practices as conducive to political oppression as to liberation. In addition, and perhaps more importantly, the language of birth and reproduction – constrained by its emphasis on a singular female physiology (or orientation) and the uniformity of women – simply does not provide feminism with the linguistic or conceptual context necessary for a theory of politics and political action. A theory of emancipatory politics must pay attention to diversity, solidarity, action-coordination, conflict, plurality, and the political equality (not the sameness) of women as citizens. None of these conceptual categories are forthcoming in theories grounded on singularity, physiology, necessity, uniformity, subjectivity, and the identity of women as reproducers.

Here, I think is where *The Human Condition* has the most to offer a feminist political theory. By articulating a conception of politics and political equality as collective action and the mutual engagement of peers in a public realm Arendt has us focus on what it means to be "speakers of words and doers of deeds" whose particular and distinctive identities deserve revelation in the public space of citizen politics. As a result, we shift our focus on human practices away from sheer biological, bodily processes on the one hand, and economic productivity on the other, and toward the constitution of public, political life. In this sense, Arendt forces theory to become expressly political, because she directs us toward the *public* aspect of human life and toward the human activity that determines all other human relations and arrangements in demonstrable ways. Moreover, she argues that the only polity that truly advances the freedom and plurality human beings are capable of experiencing, not to mention the conditions of existence they value and defend, is the polity that exhibits widespread participation in the public realm. To return to the notion of plurality, freedom is advanced when politics unfolds as the communicative interaction of diverse equals acting together as citizens.

Few feminist theorists have confronted the question of what constitutes a feminist politics in any systematic fashion, and fewer still have attempted to outline the contours of a feminist public realm.[56] In part, perhaps, this is because feminist theory has long had an ambivalence about matters public and political, and theoretical difficulties in distinguishing "politics" from "the patriarchal state." What has been historically constituted as the province of masculinity is often ceded to the male-stream, as feminists turn their attention toward the private domain of women's lives, thereby perpetuating the binary oppositions of "private woman, public man." As Arendt's existential analysis of the *vita activa* suggests, however, there is nothing intrinsically or essentially masculine about the public realm, just as there is nothing intrinsically or essentially feminine about laboring in the realm of necessity. The point is not to accept these gendered realms as fixed and immutable, but rather to undermine the gendering of public and private and move on to a more visionary and liberating conception of human practices, including those that constitute politics.

For feminists, Arendt's conception of plurality as politics may provide a promising place to begin. Plurality reinforces the notion of what Iris Young calls a "politics of difference," and emphasizes the heterogeneity of citizens. The unity Arendt imagines in the public realm is not mere uniformity, but rather a kind of solidarity engendered by the engagement of diversely constituted, unique individuals. Although Arendt did not pursue the concrete manifestations of plurality in any depth, she laid the groundwork for a political theory of action and difference, and a conception of civic "publics" as spaces where plurality can manifest itself. Without question, a feminist turn to plurality and politics would require the abandonment of some of the epistemological longings that underlie some current feminist theories – particularly the quest for univocality, certainty, and a fixed "standpoint" on reality. A feminist theory of politics as plurality needs to acknowledge multivocality, conflict, and the constantly shifting and ambiguous nature of politics itself. Given their appreciation of "otherness," however, and a growing attention to cultural diversity and heterogeneity, feminist theorists are also particularly well-situated for the task of developing our understanding of politics as plurality. Feminist theory also provides a powerful critique of the masculine virtue of "glory" that plays such an important role in Arendt's vision of action in the public realm. A feminist ethic of care, for example, might encourage us to imagine other dimensions of freedom, beyond glory, as vital to the public realm.

Equally significantly, Arendt's conception of politics places emphasis on a human capacity that has been central to much feminist theorizing – speech or "voice." Her case for political equality is informed by two basic insights concerning the human condition: that it is within the range of all human beings to insert themselves into the public realm through speech; and that the communicative interaction in which shared speakers engage as self-determining agents and representative thinkers is the essence of freedom. These insights raise other interesting questions for feminists that Arendt herself did not pursue, among them: what constitutes an ethic of communicative interaction among citizens? How can the diversity of speech and speakers be maintained and allowed to flourish? Do women bring a "different voice" or a "female consciousness" into the public realm? If so, how have these been manifested in practical, historical experience?[57] What should a feminist politics make of this voice and consciousness, if they indeed exist? All of these questions invite feminist attention, and encourage us to theorize both about who women are as citizens and about citizenship itself as a nongendered activity.

I have argued that Arendt's concepts of action and plurality provide an orienting role for a feminist theory of politics. Implicit in my argument is also an acceptance of the general distinctions she draws between labor, work, and action as general and permanent human capacities. In accepting the general framework of Arendt's theory, however, I do not mean to suggest that the distinctions she draws between these three modes of the *vita activa* are completely unproblematic. Nor are they exhaustive. Maternalist theorists, for instance, could rightly argue that mothering is as vital and perennial a human activity as labor, work, and action, and rightly insist that it does not fit easily under the parameters Arendt establishes for the *vita activa*. But neither are Arendt's analytical categories marked by the "artificiality" and "literal thoughtlessness" that O'Brien attributes to them. In some respects, of course, all analytical constructions are "artificial"; the issue is whether or not the theorist makes them a convincing and illuminating source for political reflection, as I think Arendt does.

In closing, then, I want briefly to reassert my case for *The Human Condition* as a source of political reflection, and with the hope of deflecting some possible responses to my appropriation of Arendt for a feminist theory of politics. Perhaps the most predictable response to this case for Arendt is that her theory not only privileges male "logocentric" reason but also continues in a tradition of disparaging the female body – or a "politics of the body" – and women's work. Rich comes close to the latter when she alludes to the "contempt and indifference" for the efforts of "women in labor" that typify theories like Arendt's.[58] But Rich misunderstands Arendt's characterization of labor. Nowhere does Arendt suggest that labor is a contemptible or insignificant activity. Her refusal to romanticize it should not be taken as offhand dismissal. To the contrary, Arendt writes that, "From the viewpoint of the life of the species, all activities indeed find their common denominator in laboring," and she says that the "blessing of life as a whole" is inherent in labor.[59] What Rich rightly wants to have philosophers acknowledge is not, however, in Arendt's view, the highest expression of human *freedom*. That comes only with collective action in the public realm. In fact, the glorification of *animal laborans* that Rich, like O'Brien, comes very close to exhibiting is precisely what Arendt thinks characterizes alienation and the loss of our capacity to think coherently about freedom in the contemporary world.

As for a "politics of the body," there is nothing in Arendt's discussion of plurality that posits "reason" over "passion" or condemns the literal body (or issues concerning life or the social control of the body) to the sphere of the private realm. In fact, Arendt's account of politics in the public realm brings courage, the spontaneity of passion, and "appearance" to the foreground, as crucial elements in the revelation of self that is part of collective speech and action. What she rejects, then, is not the presence of the body or a bodily politics but rather a political theory that locates the identity of persons only in a collective, singular, physiology – or in practices tied to the rhythmic cycles of nature. Arendt realizes human beings are ineliminably bound to nature, but we are also able to act in ways that at least temporarily defy the unremitting play of natural forces. Our bodies, in other words, are not merely the vessels of generative forces; they are also, along with our voices, integral to our appearance in the public world. This is one thing Arendt's discussion of plurality and individuals attempts to have us recognize. It is the *distinction* between the processes of repro- duction on the one hand, where the body is conceived in a singularly narrow way, and action on the other, the collective power of embodied persons made political, that Arendt wants to preserve. Thus, Nancy Hartsock's attempt to return Arendt's theory of power to the body at "the epistemological level of reproduction" misses a fundamental point. In Arendt's theory, a "bodily politics" exists and exhibits itself in the life of action within the public realm. To ground politics in reproduction, as Hartsock wants to do, and thereby make *animal laborans* the source of power, is apples and oranges – Arendt's theory simply cannot be trans- formed this way and remain coherent.[60]

Finally, the problem of "reason." Although Arendt obviously considers thinking and rational argumentation essential to the interaction of citizens in the public realm, she distinguishes between the communicative ration- ality indicative of plurality, and the instrumental rationality of *homo faber*, who thinks in terms of ends and means. In short, Arendt is rightly aware that there are many different forms of reason, some of which are appropriate to the realm of politics and not antithetical to the recognition of otherness, some of which are not. Representative thinking, the mentality that distin- guishes action in the public realm, is a good example of a form of reason that defies characterization in terms that would have us drive a wedge between reason and passion. It encompasses and incorporates both. Those who would dismiss her conception of public life as "too rational" or lacking in passion misapprehend the complexity of rationality in general and Arendt's "communications theory" of power more specifically.[61] We need only remember Tiananmen Square, a perfect example of the bound- less and unpredictable "space of appearances" as Arendt envisions it, to understand that her vision of public life admits of passion and spontaneity as well as rational discourse, and the drama of visual, bodily appearances as well as "*logos*" and reason.

My defense of *The Human Condition* as a possible starting place for a feminist theory of politics is not an endorsement of Arendt's theory *tout court*. As I hope I have shown, a feminist analysis reveals much about the inadequacies of Arendt's major work as a commentary on both the classical and the contemporary age. Still, feminism – at least in its academic guise – needs a calling back to politics. In this respect, *The Human Condition* gives feminist thought ground on which to stand and develop an action-co-ordinating theory of political emancipation. Because she articulates such a powerful defense of public, participatory citizenship and of empowerment as speech and action in plurality, Arendt provides feminist thinkers with a way to proceed toward politics. For a movement such as feminism, which has so vividly illuminated the inequalities and injustices of existing gender relations, but has not yet advanced a transformative vision of politics, *The Human Condition* offers a place to begin anew, as we try to imagine better political worlds.

Notes

1 Adrienne Rich, *On Lies, Secrets, and Silence: Selected Prose 1966–1978* (New York: W. W. Norton, 1979), p. 212; and Mary O'Brien, *The Politics of Reproduction* (London: Routledge and Kegan Paul, 1981), pp. 99–100.
2 O'Brien, *Politics of Reproduction*, p. 101.
3 Nancy Hartsock, *Money, Sex, and Power* (Boston: Northeastern University Press, 1985), p. 259.
4 Hanna Fenichel Pitkin, "Justice: On Relating Private and Public," *Political Theory*, 9, 1981, pp. 303–26.
5 Terry Winant, "The Feminist Standpoint: A Matter of Language," *Hypatia*, 2, 1987, p. 124.
6 Hanna Arendt, *The Human Condition* (Chicago: University of Chicago Press, 1958), p. 6.
7 Ibid., p. 7.
8 Ibid., p. 22.
9 Ibid., p. 5.
10 Arendt takes the phrase in quotes from Locke, and uses it to set off her discussion of labor and work as the human activities elevated in both liberal and Marxist thought.
11 Arendt, *Human Condition*, p. 96.
12 Ibid., p. 131. For a helpful clarification of the relationship between labor, work, and action and the mentalities Arendt associates with them, see Pitkin, "Justice."
13 Arendt, *Human Condition*, p. 144. Or, as she also puts it, *homo faber*, the creator of human artifice, is also a "destroyer of nature" (p. 139).
14 Ibid., pp. 136–7.
15 Ibid., p. 157.
16 Ibid., p. 305.
17 Ibid., p. 137.
18 Ibid., p. 190.
19 Ibid., p. 204.

20 Ibid., p. 7.

21 Ibid., p. 244.

22 Ibid., p. 175. The spontaneous political uprising of the Chinese people in Tiananmen Square was one of the most dramatic examples of what Arendt means by "action" and "plurality." What arose there was a community of equals, "where everybody has the same capacity to act . . . and the impossibility of remaining unique masters of what they do, of knowing its consequences and relying upon the future" (p. 244). Arendt calls this the "price paid for plurality" – for the joy of inhabiting together with others a world whose reality is guaranteed for each by the presence of all. Hence her emphasis on the "unpredictability" and the "boundlessness" of action, as well as its inherent glory and irreducible collectivity.

23 Ibid., p.8.

24 Ibid., pp. 52, 204.

25 Ibid., p. 205.

26 Ibid., p. 9.

27 Ibid., p. 204.

28 Arendt develops the dimensions of this mentality more fully in her essay, "The Crisis in Culture," in her *Between Past and Future* (New York: Viking Press, 1961), pp. 220–4. In contemporary terminology, the capacity to judge is communicative, not rational-instrumental.

29 Arendt is well aware that, throughout history, vast numbers of people have been prevented from realizing their existentially highest human activities. See *Human Condition*, p. 199.

30 Ibid., p. 72.

31 See O'Brien, *Politics of Reproduction*, pp. 103–7.

32 Arendt, *Human Condition*, pp. 118–19.

33 Ibid., p. 144.

34 Ibid., p. 28.

35 Ibid., p. 83.

36 Ibid., p. 72.

37 Ibid., p. 48.

38 Ibid., p. 71.

39 Arendt notes that the private "was like the other, the dark and hidden side of the public realm." Ibid., p. 64.

40 Ibid., pp. 8, 88, 111, 119.

41 Ibid., p. 106.

42 By putting this point in this way I do not mean to imply that the activity of labor has been everywhere the same for all women or that we can understand women's laboring in some universal, transhistorical fashion. For my purposes, what is significant is that Arendt leaves out of her discussion any acknowledgement that it is *women* who have in fact been assigned this activity she describes as the "lowest" in the human condition.

43 The phrase in quotes is from Rich, *On Lies, Secrets, and Silence*, p. 205. As far as I can tell, she was the first to make this prescient observation about Arendt's *animal laborans*.

44 I am not suggesting that women have never participated in political life, only

that, historically, they have not been accorded formal recognition as the equals and peers of men as citizens in the public realm. For a stimulating account of the ways in which women in the United States have found ways of participating in public life despite the denial of political equality, see Sara Evans, *Born for Liberty: A History of Women in America* (New York: Free Press, 1989).

45 Thanks to Ron Steiner.

46 See p. 195 above.

47 Hanna Fenichel Pitkin, "Food and Freedom in *The Founder*," *Political Theory*, 12, 1984, p. 481.

48 Arendt, *Human Condition*, p. 5.

49 bell hooks, *Feminist Theory from Margin to Center* (Boston: South End Press, 1984), p. 43. For a lucid discussion of the difference between "world-disclosing" and "action-coordinating" theories, see Stephen White, "Poststructuralism and Political Reflection," *Political Theory*, 16, 1988, pp. 186–208.

50 Arendt, *Human Condition*, p. 321.

51 Ibid., p. 313.

52 See O'Brien, *Politics of Reproduction*; Hartsock, *Money, Sex and Power*; Rich, *On Lies, Secrets, and Silence*; Sara Ruddick, *Maternal Thinking: Toward a Politics of Peace* (Boston: Beacon Press, 1989); and Ann Rosalind Jones, "Julia Kristeva on Femininity: The Limits of a Semiotic Politics," *Feminist Review*, 18, 1984, pp. 56–73.

53 O'Brien, *Politics of Reproduction*, p. 209.

54 Ibid., p. 208.

55 Julia Kristeva, "Women's Time," in *Feminist Theory: A Critique of Ideology*, ed. Nannerl O. Keohane, Michelle Z. Rosaldo, and Barbara C. Gelpi (Chicago: University of Chicago Press, 1981), pp. 31–54.

56 One exception is Iris Marion Young, whose work has expressly addressed the nature of a feminist politics and civic public. See "Impartiality and the Civic Public: Some Implications of Feminist Critiques of Moral and Political Theory," in *Feminism as Critique*, ed. Seyla Benhabib and Drucilla Cornell (Cambridge: Polity; Minneapolis: University of Minnesota Press, 1987), pp. 56–76; "The Ideal of Community and the Politics of Difference," *Social Theory and Practice*, 12, 1986, pp. 1–26; and "Polity and Group Difference: A Critique of the Ideal of Universal Citizenship," *Ethics*, 99, 1989, pp. 250–74. Also see Nancy Fraser, "Toward a Discourse Ethic of Solidarity," *Praxis International*, 5, 1986, pp. 425–9.

57 On the significance of a "female consciousness" in politics, see Temma Kaplan, "Female Consciousness and Collective Action: The Case of Barcelona, 1910–1915," in *Feminist Theory*, ed. Keohane et al., pp. 55–76.

58 Rich, *On Lies, Secrets and Silence*, p. 206.

59 Arendt, *Human Condition*, pp. 107–8.

60 Hartsock, *Money, Sex, and Power*, pp. 258–9.

61 For a cogent critique of how some feminists misapprehend rationality and reason, see Mary Hawkesworth, "Knowers, Knowing, and Known: Feminist Theory and Claims of Truth," *Signs: Journal of Women in Culture and Society*, 14, 1989, pp. 533–57.

14

What's Critical about Critical Theory? The Case of Habermas and Gender

Nancy Fraser

To my mind, no one has yet improved on Marx's 1843 definition of Critical Theory as "the self-clarification of the struggles and wishes of the age."[1] What is so appealing about this definition is its straightforwardly political character. A critical theory, it says, frames its research in the light of the contemporary social movements with which it has a partisan though not uncritical identification. For example, if struggles contesting the subordination of women figured among the most significant of a given age, then a critical social theory for that time would seek to shed light on the character and bases of such subordination. It would employ categories and explanatory models that revealed rather than occluded relations of male dominance and female subordination. And it would demystify as ideological rival approaches that obfuscated or rationalized those relations. In this situation, then, one of the standards for assessing a critical theory, once it had been subjected to all the usual tests of empirical adequacy, would be: how well does it theorize the situation and prospects of the feminist movement? To what extent does it serve the self-clarification of the struggles and wishes of contemporary women?

In what follows, I am going to presuppose the conception of critical theory that I have just outlined. In addition, I am going to take as the actual situation of our age the scenario I just sketched as hypothetical. On this basis, I shall examine the critical social theory of Jürgen Habermas as elaborated in *The Theory of Communicative Action* and related recent writings.[2] I shall ask: In what proportions does Habermas's theory clarify and/or mystify the bases of male dominance and female subordination in modern societies? In what respects does it challenge and/or replicate prevalent ideological rationalizations of such dominance and subordination? To what extent does it serve the self-clarification of the struggles and wishes of contemporary women's movements? In short, with respect to gender, what is critical and what is not in Habermas's social theory?

I shall proceed as follows. In the first section, I examine some elements of Habermas's social-theoretical framework in order to see how it casts childrearing and the male-headed, modern, restricted, nuclear family. In the second section, I look at his account of the relations between public and private spheres of life in classical capitalist societies and I reconstruct the unthematized gender subtext. Finally, in the third section, I consider Habermas's account of the dynamics, crisis tendencies, and conflict potentials specific to contemporary, Western, welfare state capitalism, so as to see in what light it casts contemporary feminist struggles.

The Social-theoretical Framework: A Feminist Interrogation

Let me begin by considering two distinctions that are central to Habermas's framework. The first is the distinction between the symbolic reproduction and the material reproduction of societies. On the one hand, claims Habermas, societies must reproduce themselves materially; they must successfully regulate the metabolic exchange of groups of biological in-dividuals with a nonhuman, physical environment and with other social systems. On the other hand, societies must reproduce themselves sym-bolically; they must maintain and transmit to new members the linguistic-ally elaborated norms and patterns of interpretation that are constitutive of social identities. Habermas claims that material reproduction transpires via "social labor." Symbolic reproduction, on the other hand, involves the socialization of the young, the cementing of group solidarity, and the transmission and extension of cultural traditions.[3] Finally, according to Habermas, in capitalist societies, the activities comprising the sphere of paid work count as material reproduction activities, since they are "social labor" and serve the function of material reproduction. In contrast, the childrearing practices performed without pay by women in the domestic sphere – let us call them "women's unpaid childrearing work" – count as symbolic reproduction activities, since, in his view, they serve socialization and the function of symbolic reproduction.[4]

It is worth noting, I think, that Habermas's distinction between symbolic and material reproduction is susceptible to two different interpretations. The first takes it to demarcate two objectively distinct "natural kinds," implying that childrearing, for example, simply *is* in itself a symbolic reproduction activity. The second interpretation, by contrast, treats the distinction pragmatically and contextually, implying only that it could be useful for certain purposes to consider childrearing practices from the standpoint of symbolic reproduction.

Now I want to argue that the natural kinds interpretation is conceptually inadequate and potentially ideological. I claim that it is not the case that childrearing practices serve symbolic as opposed to material reproduction. Granted, they comprise language-teaching and initiation into social mores, but also feeding, bathing, and protection from physical harm. Granted, they regulate children's interactions with other people, but also their interactions with physical nature. In short, not just the construction of children's social identities but also their biological survival is at stake. And so, therefore, is the biological survival of the societies they belong to. Thus, childrearing is not *per se* symbolic reproduction activity; it is equally and at the same time material reproduction activity. It is a "dual-aspect" activity.[5]

But the same is true of the activities institutionalized in modern capitalist paid work. Granted, the production of food and objects contributes to the biological survival of members of society. But it also and at the same time reproduces social identities. Not just nourishment and shelter *simpliciter* are produced, but culturally elaborated forms of nourishment and shelter. Moreover, such production occurs via symbolically mediated, norm-governed social practices. These serve to form, maintain, and modify the social identities of persons directly involved and indirectly affected. One need only think of an activity like computer programming for a wage in the US pharmaceutical industry to appreciate the thoroughly symbolic character of "social labor." Thus, such labor, like unpaid childrearing work, is a "dual-aspect" activity.

Thus, the distinction between women's unpaid childrearing work and other forms of work cannot be a distinction of natural kinds. Indeed, the classification of childrearing as symbolic reproduction and of other work as material reproduction is potentially ideological. It could be used, for example, to legitimate the institutional separation of childrearing from paid work, a separation that many feminists, including myself, consider a linchpin of modern forms of women's subordination. Whether Habermas uses the distinction in this way will be considered shortly.

The second component of Habermas's framework that I want to examine is his distinction between "socially integrated action contexts" and "system integrated action contexts." Socially integrated action contexts are those in which different agents coordinate their actions with one another by means of an explicit or implicit intersubjective consensus about norms, values, and ends. System-integrated action contexts, on the other hand, are those in which the actions of different agents are coordinated by the functional interlacing of unintended consequences, while each individual action is determined by self-interested, utility-maximizing calculations in the "media" of money and power.[6] Habermas considers the capitalist economic system to be the paradigm case of a system-integrated action context. By contrast, he takes the modern nuclear family to be a socially integrated action context.[7]

Once again, I think it useful to distinguish two possible interpretations of Habermas's position. The first takes the contrast between the two kinds of action contexts as registering an absolute difference. It implies that system-integrated contexts involve absolutely no consensuality or reference to moral norms and values, whereas socially integrated contexts involve absolutely no strategic calculations in the media of money and power. This "absolute differences" interpretation is at odds with a second possibility that takes the contrast, rather, to register a difference in degree.

Now I contend that the absolute differences interpretation is too extreme to be useful for social theory and that, in addition, it is potentially ideological. In few if any human action contexts are actions coordinated absolutely nonconsensually and nonnormatively. In the capitalist market-place, for example, strategic, utility-maximizing exchanges occur against a horizon of intersubjectively shared meanings and norms; agents normally subscribe to some commonly held notions of reciprocity and to some shared conceptions of the social meanings of objects, including what sorts of things are exchangeable. Similarly, in the capitalist workplace, managers and subordinates, as well as coworkers, normally coordinate their actions to some extent consensually and with some reference to normative assumptions, though the consensus be arrived at unfairly and the norms be incapable of withstanding critical scrutiny. Thus, the capitalist economic system has a moral-cultural dimension.

Similarly, few if any human action contexts are wholly devoid of strategic calculation. Gift rituals in noncapitalist societies, for example, once seen as veritable crucibles of solidarity, are now known to have a significant strategic, calculative dimension, one enacted in the medium of power, if not in that of money.[8] And, as I shall argue in more detail later, the modern nuclear family is not devoid of individual, self-interested, strategic calculations in either medium. These action contexts, then, while not officially counted as economic, have a strategic, economic dimension.

Thus, the absolute differences interpretation is not of much use in social theory. It fails to distinguish the capitalist economy – let us call it "the official economy" – from the modern nuclear family. For both of these institutions are mélanges of consensuality, normativity, and strategicality. But if this is so, then the classification of the official economy as a system-integrated action context and of the modern family as a socially integrated action context is potentially ideological. It could be used to exaggerate their differences and occlude their similarities, for example, by casting the family as the "negative," the complementary "other," of the (official) economic sphere, a "haven in a heartless world."

Now which of these possible interpretations of the two distinctions are the operative ones in Habermas's social theory? What use does he make of these distinctions? Habermas maps the distinction between action contexts onto the distinction between reproduction functions in order to model the institutional structure of modern societies. He holds that modern societies differ from premodern societies in that they split off some material reproduction functions from symbolic ones and hand over the former to two specialized institutions – the (official) economy and the state – which are system integrated. Modern societies also develop two "lifeworld" institutions, which specialize in symbolic reproduction and are socially integrated: the nuclear family, or "private sphere" and the space of political deliberation, or "public sphere." Thus, modern societies "uncouple," or separate, two distinct but previously undifferentiated aspects of society: "lifeworld" and "system."[9]

Now what are the critical insights and blindspots of this model? Consider, first, that Habermas's categorial divide between the "private sphere of the lifeworld" and the "private economic system" faithfully mirrors the institutional separation of family and official economy, household and paid workplace, in male-dominated, capitalist societies. It thus has some prima facie purchase on empirical social reality. But consider, too, that the characterization of the family as a socially integrated, symbolic reproduction domain and of the paid workplace, on the other hand, as a system-integrated material reproduction domain tends to exaggerate the differences and occlude the similarities between them. It directs attention away from the fact that the household, like the paid workplace, is a site of labor, albeit of unremunerated and often unrecognized labor. It obscures the fact that in the paid workplace, as in the household, women are assigned distinctively feminine, service-oriented and often sexualized occupations. And it fails to focalize the fact that in both spheres women are subordinated to men.

Moreover, this characterization casts the male-headed, nuclear family as having only an extrinsic and incidental relation to money and power. These "media" are taken as definitive of interactions in the official economy and the state but as only incidental to intrafamilial ones. But this assumption is counterfactual. Feminists have shown via analyses of contemporary familial decision-making, handling of finances, and wife-battering that families are thoroughly permeated with money and power. They are sites of egocentric, strategic, and instrumental calcuation as well as sites of usually exploitative exchanges of services, labor, cash, and sex, not to mention sites, frequently, of coercion and violence.[10] But Habermas's way of contrasting the modern family with the official capitalist economy occludes all this. It overstates the differences between these institutions and blocks the possibility of analyzing families as economic systems – as sites of labor, exchange, calculation, distribution, and exploitation.

Thus, Habermas's model has some empirical deficiencies. It is not easily able to capture some dimensions of male dominance in modern societies. Yet his framework does offer a conceptual resource suitable for understanding *other* aspects of modern male dominance. He subdivides the category of socially integrated action contexts into two subcategories. On the one hand, there are "normatively secured" forms of socially integrated action. These are actions coordinated on the basis of a conventional, prereflective, taken-for-granted consensus about values and ends, consensus rooted in the precritical internalization of cultural tradition. On the other hand, there are "communicatively achieved" forms of socially integrated action. These involve actions coordinated by explicit, reflectively achieved consensus, consensus reached by unconstrained discussion under conditions of freedom, equality, and fairness.[11]

This distinction constitutes a critical resource for analyzing the modern male-headed nuclear family. Such families can be understood as normatively secured rather than communicatively achieved action contexts, as contexts where actions are (sometimes) mediated by consensus and shared values, but where such consensus is suspect because prereflective or because achieved through dialogue vitiated by unfairness, coercion or inequality. This fits nicely with recent research on patterns of communication between husbands and wives. This research shows that men tend to control conversations, determining what topics are pursued, while women do more "interaction work" like asking questions and providing verbal support.[12]

Thus, Habermas's distinction enables us to capture something important about intrafamilial dynamics. What is insufficiently stressed, however, is that actions coordinated by normatively secured consensus are actions regulated by power. It is a grave mistake to restrict the use of the term "power" to bureaucratic contexts. Habermas would do better to distinguish different kinds of power, for example, domestic-patriarchal power, on the one hand, and bureaucratic-patriarchal power, on the other, not to mention other kinds as well.

Let me turn now to the normative political implications of Habermas's model. What sorts of social arrangements does it legitimate and what sorts of social transformations does it rule out? The view of modernization as the uncoupling of system and lifeworld tends to legitimate the modern institutional separation of family and official economy, childrearing and paid work. For Habermas claims that symbolic reproduction activities cannot be turned over to specialized systems set apart from the lifeworld; their inherently symbolic character requires that they be socially integrated.[13] It follows that women's unpaid childrearing work could not be incorporated into the (official) economic system without "pathological" results. Yet Habermas also holds that it is a mark of societal rationalization that systems be differentiated to handle material reproduction functions; the separation of a specialized (official) economic system enhances a society's capacity to deal with its natural and social environment. "System complexity," then, constitutes a "developmental advance." It follows that the (official) economic system of paid work could not be dedifferentiated with respect to childrearing without societal "regression." But if child-rearing could not be nonpathologically incorporated into the (official) economic system, and if the (official) economic system could not be nonregressively dedifferentiated, then the continued separation of child-rearing from paid work would be unavoidable.

This amounts to a defense of an arrangement that is widely held to be a linchpin of modern women's subordination, namely, the separation of the official economic sphere from the domestic sphere and the enclaving of childrearing from the rest of social labor. The fact that Habermas is a socialist does not alter the matter. For the (undeniably desirable) elimination of private ownership, profit orientation and hierarchical command in paid work would not of itself alter the official-economic/domestic separation.

Now I want to challenge several premises of the reasoning I have just reconstructed. First, this reasoning assumes the natural kinds interpretation of the symbolic reproduction versus material reproduction distinction. But since childrearing is a dual-aspect activity, and since it is not categorially different in this respect from other work, there is no warrant for assuming that the system-integrated organization of childrearing would be any more (or less) pathological than that of other work. Second, this reasoning assumes the absolute differences interpretation of the social integration versus system integration distinction. But since the modern male-headed nuclear family is a mélange of (normatively secured) con-sensuality, normativity and strategicality, and since it is in this respect not categorially different from the paid workplace, then privatized childrearing is already permeated by money and power. Third, the reasoning just sketched permits system complexity to trump proposed social transform-ations aimed at overcoming women's subordination. But this is at odds with Habermas's professions that system complexity is only one measure of "progress" among others. More importantly, it is at odds with any reasonable standard of justice.

What, then, should we conclude about the normative, political implica-tions of Habermas's model? If the conception of modernization as the uncoupling of system and lifeworld institutions does indeed have the implications I have just drawn from it, then it is in important respects androcentric and ideological.

Public and Private in Classical Capitalism:
Thematizing the Gender Subtext

The foregoing difficulties notwithstanding, Habermas offers an account of arenas of public and private life in classical capitalism that has some genuine critical potential. But in order to realize this potential fully, we need to reconstruct the unthematized gender subtext.

Consider Habermas's account of the ways in which the (official) economic and state systems are linked to the lifeworld. The "private sphere," or family, is linked to the (official) economy by means of a series of exchanges conducted in the medium of money; it supplies the (official) economy with appropriately socialized labor power in exchange for wages; and it provides monetarily measured demand for commodified goods and services. Exchanges between the family and the (official) economy, then, are channeled through the "roles" of worker and consumer. In contrast, the "public sphere," or space of political participation, is linked to the state-administrative system by exchanges in the "medium of power"; loyalty, obedience, and tax revenues are exchanged for "organizational results" and "political decisions." Exchanges between the public sphere and the state, then, are channeled through the "role" of citizen and, in late welfare state capitalism, that of client.[14]

This account has a number of important advantages. By modelling a relation among four terms – family, (official) economy, state, and "public sphere" – Habermas corrects standard dualistic approaches to the separation of public and private. His view suggests that in classical capitalism there are actually two distinct but interrelated public/private separations. There is one public/private separation at the level of "systems," namely, the separation of the state, or public system, from the (official) capitalist economy, or private system. There is another public/private separation at the level of the "lifeworld," namely, the separation of the family, or private sphere, from the space of political participation, or public sphere. Moreover, each of these public/private separations is coordinated with the other. One link runs between private system and private lifeworld sphere, that is, between (official) capitalist economy and nuclear family. Another runs between public system and public lifeworld sphere, or between state administration and arenas of political participation. In each case, the link consists in the institutionalization of specific roles: worker and consumer, citizen and (later) client.

Thus, Habermas provides a sophisticated account of the relations between public and private institutions in classical capitalist societies. Yet there are also some significant weaknesses. These are due to his failure to thematize the gender subtext of the material.

Take the role of the worker. In male-dominated, classical capitalist societies, this role is a masculine role. Masculinity here is in large part a matter of leaving home each day for a place of paid work and returning with a wage that provides for one's dependents. This internal relation between being a man and being a provider explains why in capitalist societies unemployment can be so psychologically as well as economically devastating for men. It also explains the centrality of the struggle for a "family wage" in the history of the workers' and trade union movements of the nineteenth and twentieth centuries. This was a struggle for a wage conceived not as a payment to a genderless individual for the use of labor power but, rather, as a payment to a man for the support of his economically dependent wife and children; and it rationalized the practice of paying women less for equal or comparable work.[15]

The masculine subtext of the worker role is confirmed by the vexed character of women's relation to paid work in male-dominated classical capitalism. As Carole Pateman puts it, it is not that women are absent from the paid workplace; it's rather that they are present differently[16] – for example, as feminized and sometimes sexualized "service" workers; as members of the "helping professions" utilizing mothering skills; as targets of sexual harassment; as low-waged, low-skilled, low-status workers in sex-segregated occupations; as part-time workers; as "working wives," "working mothers" and "supplemental earners." These differences in the quality of women's presence in the paid workplace testify to the conceptual dissonance between femininity and the worker role in classical capitalism and, so, to the masculine subtext of that role.

Conversely, the consumer, the other role linking the official economy and the family in Habermas's scheme, has a feminine subtext. For the sexual division of labor assigns to women the work – and it is indeed work, though unpaid and usually unrecognized work – of purchasing and preparing goods and services for domestic consumption. You can confirm this even today by visiting any supermarket or department store. Or by looking at the history of consumer goods advertising. Such advertising has nearly always addressed the consumer as feminine. It is only relatively recently, and with some difficulty, that advertisers have devised ways of interpellating a masculine subject of consumption. The difficulty and lateness of that development confirm the gendered character of the consumer role in classical capitalism. Men occupy it with conceptual strain and cognitive dissonance, much as women occupy the role of worker.

Moreover, Habermas's account of the roles linking family and (official) economy contains a significant omission. There is no mention in his schema of any childrearer role, although the material clearly requires one. For who else is performing the unpaid work of overseeing the production of the "appropriately socialized labor power" that the family exchanges for wages? Of course, the childrearer role in classical capitalism (as elsewhere) is patently a feminine role. Its omission here is a mark of androcentrism.

What, then, of the other set of roles and linkages identified by Habermas? What of the citizen role that connects the public system of the administrative state with the public lifeworld sphere of political participation? This role, too, is a gendered role in classical capitalism, indeed, a masculine role. And not simply in the sense that women did not win the vote in, for example, the US and Britain until the twentieth century. Rather, the lateness and difficulty of that victory are symptomatic of deeper strains. In Habermas's view, citizenship means participation in political debate and public opinion formation. It depends crucially on the capacities for consent and speech, the ability to participate on a par with others in dialogue. But these are capacities that are connected with masculinity in male-dominated, classical capitalism; they are often denied to women and deemed at odds with femininity. I have already cited studies about the effects of male dominance and female subordination on the dynamics of dialogue. Now consider that even today in most jurisdictions there is no such thing as marital rape. A wife is legally subject to her husband; she is not an individual who can give or withhold consent to his demands for sexual access. Consider also that even outside of marriage the legal test of rape is whether a "reasonable man" would have assumed that the woman had consented. Consider what that means when both popular and legal opinion widely holds that when a woman says "no" she means "yes." It means, says Carole Pateman, that "women find their speech . . . persistently and systematically invalidated in the crucial matter of consent, a matter that is fundamental to democracy. [But] if women's words about consent are consistently reinterpreted, how can they participate in the debate among citizens?"[17]

Thus, there is conceptual dissonance between femininity and the dialogical capacities central to Habermas's conception of citizenship. And there is another aspect of citizenship not discussed by him that is even more obviously bound up with masculinity. I mean the soldiering aspect of citizenship, the conception of the citizen as the defender of the polity and protector of those – women, children, the elderly – who allegedly cannot protect themselves. As Judith Stiehm has argued, this division between male protectors and female protected introduces further dissonance into women's relation to citizenship.[18] It confirms the gender subtext of the citizen role that links the state and the public sphere in male-dominated classical capitalism.

Thus, there are some major lacunae in Habermas's model. The gender-blindness of the model occludes important features of the arrangements he wants to understand. By omitting any mention of the childrearer role, and by failing to thematize the gender subtext underlying the roles of worker and consumer, Habermas fails to understand precisely how the capitalist workplace is linked to the modern male-headed, nuclear family. Similarly, by failing to thematize the masculine subtext of the citizen role, he misses the full meaning of the way the state is linked to the public sphere of political speech. Moreover, Habermas misses important cross-connections among the four elements of his model. He misses, for example, the way the masculine citizen-soldier-protector role links the state and public sphere not only to one another but also to the family and to the paid workplace, that is, the way the assumptions of man's capacity to protect and woman's need of man's protection run through all of them. He misses, too, the way the masculine citizen-speaker role links the state and public sphere not only to one another but also to the family and official economy, that is, the way the assumptions of man's capacity to speak and consent and woman's comparative incapacity run through all of them. He misses, also, the way the masculine worker-breadwinner role links the family and official economy not only to one another but also to the state and the political public sphere, that is, the way the assumptions of man's provider status and of woman's dependent status run through all of them. And he misses, finally, the way the feminine childrearer role links all four institutions to one another by overseeing the construction of the masculine and feminine gendered subjects needed to fill *every* role in classical capitalism.

Once the gender-blindness of Habermas's model is overcome, however, all these connections come into view. It then becomes clear that gender norms run like pink and blue threads through paid work, state adminis-tration, and citizenship as well as through familial and sexual relations. Moreover, a gender-sensitive reading of these connections has some im-portant theoretical and conceptual implications. It reveals that male dominance is intrinsic rather than accidental to classical capitalism, since the institutional structure of this social formation is actualized by means of gendered roles. It follows that the forms of male dominance at issue here are not properly understood as lingering forms of premodern status inequality. They are, rather, intrinsically modern in Habermas's sense, since they are premised on the separation of waged labor and the state from female childrearing and the household. It also follows that a critical social theory of capitalist societies needs gender-sensitive categories. The preceding analysis shows that, contrary to the usual androcentric under-standing, the relevant concepts of worker, consumer, and wage are not, in fact, strictly economic concepts. Rather, they have an implicit gender subtext and thus are "gender-economic" concepts. Likewise, the relevant concept of citizenship is not strictly a political concept; it has an implicit gender subtext and so, rather, is a "gender-political" concept. Thus, this analysis reveals the inadequacy of those critical theories that treat gender

as incidental to politics and political economy. It highlights the need for a
critical-theoretical categorial framework in which gender, politics, and
political economy are internally integrated.

In addition, a gender-sensitive reading of these arrangements reveals
the thoroughly multidirectional character of social motion in classical
capitalism. It gives the lie to the orthodox Marxist assumption that all or
most significant causal influence runs from the (official) economy to the
family and not vice versa. It shows that gender norms structure paid
work, state administration and political participation. Thus, it vindicates
Habermas's claim that in classical capitalism the (official) economy is not
all-powerful but is, rather, inscribed within and subject to the norms and
meanings of everyday life. Of course, Habermas assumed that in making
this claim he was saying something more or less positive. The norms and
meanings he had in mind were not the ones I have been discussing. Still,
the point is a valid one. It remains to be seen, though, whether it holds
also for late, welfare state capitalism, as I believe, or whether it ceases to
hold, as Habermas claims.

Finally, this reconstruction of the gender subtext of Habermas's model
has some normative political implications. It suggests that an emancipatory
transformation of male-dominated capitalist societies requires a transformation of these gendered roles and of the institutions they mediate. As
long as the worker and childrearer roles are fundamentally incompatible
with one another, it will not be possible to universalize either of them to
include both genders. Thus, some form of dedifferentiation of unpaid
childrearing and other work is required. Similarly, as long as the citizen
role is defined to encompass death-dealing soldiering but not life-fostering
childrearing, as long as it is tied to male-dominated modes of dialogue,
then it, too, will remain incapable of including women fully. Thus, changes
in the very concepts of citizenship, childrearing, and paid work are necessary, as are changes in the relationships among the domestic, official
economic, state, and political public spheres.

The Dynamics of Welfare State Capitalism: A Feminist Critique

Let me turn, then, to Habermas's account of late, welfare state capitalism.
Unlike his account of classical capitalism, its critical potential cannot be
released simply by reconstructing the gender subtext. Here, the problematical features of his framework inflect the analysis as a whole and diminish
its capacity to illuminate the struggles and wishes of contemporary women.
In order to show how this is the case, I shall present Habermas's view in
the form of six theses.

1 Welfare state capitalism emerges in response to instabilities inherent in classical capitalism. It realigns the relations between the (official) economy and state, rendering them more deeply intertwined with one another as the state actively engages in "crisis management." It tries to avert or manage economic crises by Keynesian "market replacing" strategies which create a "public sector." And it tries to avert or manage social and political crises by "market compensating" measures, including welfare concessions to trade unions and social movements. Thus welfare state capitalism partially overcomes the separation of public and private at the level of systems.[19]

2 The realignment of the (official) economy and the state brings changes in the roles linking those systems to the lifeworld. First, there is a major increase in the importance of the consumer role as dissatisfactions related to paid work are compensated by enhanced commodity consumption. Second, there is a major decline in the importance of the citizen role as journalism becomes mass media, political parties are bureaucratized, and participation is reduced to occasional voting. Finally, the relation to the state is increasingly channeled through a new role, the social welfare client.[20]

3 These developments are "ambivalent." On the one hand, there are gains in freedom with the institution of new social rights limiting the power of capital in the (paid) workplace and of the paterfamilias in the bourgeois family; and social insurance programs represent a clear advance over the paternalism of poor relief. On the other hand, the bureaucratic and monetary means employed to realize these new social rights tend perversely to endanger freedom. As these media structure the entitlements, benefits, and social services of the welfare system, they disempower clients, rendering them dependent on bureaucracies and therapeutocracies, and preempting their capacities to interpret their own needs, experiences and life problems.[21]

4 The most ambivalent welfare measures are those concerned with things like health care, care of the elderly, education, and family law, for when bureaucratic and monetary media structure these things, they intrude upon "core domains" of the lifeworld. They turn over symbolic reproduction functions like socialization and solidarity formation to modes of system integration. But given the inherently symbolic character of these functions, the results, *necessarily* are "pathological." Thus, these measures are more ambivalent than, say, reforms of the paid workplace. The latter bear on a domain that is already system integrated and that serves material as opposed to symbolic reproduction functions. So paid workplace reforms, unlike, say, family law reforms, do not necessarily generate "pathological" side-effects.[22]

5 Welfare state capitalism thus gives rise to an "inner colonization of

the lifeworld." Money and power cease to be mere media of exchange *between* system and lifeworld. Instead, they tend increasingly to penetrate the lifeworld's *internal* dynamics. The private and public spheres cease to subordinate (official) economic and administrative systems to the norms, values, and interpretations of everyday life. Rather, the latter are increasingly subordinated to the imperatives of the (official) economy and the administration. The roles of worker and citizen cease to channel the influence of the lifeworld to the systems. Instead, the newly inflated roles of consumer and client channel the influence of the system to the lifeworld. Moreover, the intrusion of system-integration mechanisms into domains inherently requiring social integration gives rise to "reification phenomena." The affected domains are detached not merely from traditional, normatively-secured consensus but from "value-orientations *per se*." The result is the "desiccation of communicative contexts" and the "depletion of the non-renewable cultural resources" needed to maintain personal and collective identity. Thus, symbolic reproduction is destabilized, identities are threatened, and social crisis tendencies develop.[23]

6 The colonization of the lifeworld sparks new forms of social conflict specific to welfare state capitalism. "New social movements" emerge in a "new conflict zone" at the "seam of system and lifeworld." They respond to system-induced identity threats by contesting the roles that transmit these. They contest the instrumentalization of professional labor transmitted via the worker role, the commodification of lifestyles transmitted via the inflated consumer role, the bureaucratization of life problems transmitted via the client role, and the rules and routines of interest politics transmitted via the impoverished citizen role. Thus, the conflicts at the cutting edge of developments in welfare state capitalism differ both from class struggles and from bourgeois liberation struggles. They respond to crisis tendencies in symbolic, as opposed to material, reproduction; and they contest reification and "the grammar of forms of life" as opposed to distribution or status inequality.[24]

The various new social movements can be classified with respect to their emancipatory potential. The criterion is the extent to which they advance the "decolonization of the lifeworld." Decolonization encompasses three things: first, the removal of system-integration mechanisms from symbolic reproduction spheres; second, the replacement of (some) normatively secured contexts by communicatively achieved ones; and third, the development of new, democratic institutions capable of asserting lifeworld control over state and (official) economic systems. Thus, those movements like religious fundamentalism which seek to defend traditional lifeworld norms against system intrusions are not genuinely emancipatory; they actively oppose the second element of decolonization and do not take up the third. Movements advocating peace and ecology are better; they aim both to resist system intrusions and also to instate new, reformed, communicatively achieved zones of interaction. But even these are "ambiguous" inasmuch as they tend to "retreat" into alternative communities and "particularistic" identities, thereby effectively renouncing the third element of decolonization and leaving the (official) economic and state systems unchecked. The feminist movement, on the other hand, represents something of an anomaly. It alone is "offensive," aiming to "conquer new territory," and it alone retains links to historic liberation movements. In principle, then, feminism remains rooted in "universalist morality." Yet it is linked to resistance movements by an element of "particularism." And it tends, at times, to "retreat" into identities and communities organized around the natural category of biological sex.[25]

Now what are the critical insights and blind spots of this account of the dynamics of welfare state capitalism? To what extent does it serve the self-clarification of the struggles and wishes of contemporary women? I shall take up the six theses one by one.

1 Habermas's first thesis is straightforward and unobjectionable. Clearly, the welfare state does engage in crisis management and does partially overcome the separation of public and private at the level of systems.

2 Habermas's second thesis contains some important insights. Clearly, welfare state capitalism does inflate the consumer role and deflate the citizen role, reducing the latter essentially to voting – and, we should add, also to soldiering. Moreover, the welfare state does increasingly position its subjects as clients. On the other hand, Habermas again fails to see the gender subtext of these developments. He overlooks that it is overwhelmingly women who are the clients of the welfare state: especially older women, poor women, single women with children. He overlooks, in addition, that many welfare systems are internally gendered. They include two basic kinds of programs: "masculine" ones tied to primary labor-force participation and designed to benefit principal breadwinners; and "feminine" ones oriented to "defective" households, that is, to families without a male breadwinner. Clients of feminine programs, virtually exclusively women and their children, are positioned in a distinctive, feminizing fashion as the "negatives of possessive individuals"; they are largely excluded from the market both as workers and as consumers and are often stigmatized, denied rights, subjected to surveillance and administrative harassment.[26] But this means that the rise of the client role in welfare state capitalism has a more complex meaning than Habermas allows. It is not only a change in the link between system and lifeworld institutions. It is also a change in the character of male dominance, a shift, in Carol Brown's phrase, "from private patriarchy to public patriarchy."[27]

3 This gives a rather different twist to the meaning of Habermas's

third thesis. It suggests that he is right about the "ambivalence" of welfare state capitalism, but not quite in the way he thought. Welfare measures do have a positive side insofar as they reduce women's dependence on an individual male breadwinner. But they also have a negative side insofar as they substitute dependence on a patriarchal and androcentric state bureaucracy. The benefits provided are, as Habermas says, "system-conforming" ones. But the system they conform to is not simply the system of the official, state-regulated capitalist economy. It is also the system of male dominance, which extends even to the lifeworld. The ambivalence, then, does not only stem, as Habermas implies, from the fact that the role of client carries effects of "reification." It stems also from the fact that this role perpetuates in a new "modernized" form women's subordination. Or so Habermas's third thesis might be rewritten in a feminist critical theory – without, of course, abandoning his insights into the ways in which welfare bureaucracies and therapeutocracies disempower clients by pre-empting their capacities to interpret their own needs, experiences, and life problems.

4 Habermas's fourth thesis, by contrast, is not so easily rewritten. This thesis states that welfare reforms of, for example, the domestic sphere are more ambivalent than reforms of the paid workplace. This is true empirically in the sense I have just described. But it is due to the patriarchal character of welfare systems, not to the inherently symbolic character of lifeworld institutions, as Habermas claims. His claim depends on two assumptions I have already challenged. First, it depends on the natural kinds interpretation of the distinction between symbolic reproduction activities and material reproduction activities, on the false assumption that childrearing is inherently more symbolic and less material than other work. Second, it depends on the absolute differences interpretation of the system-integrated versus socially integrated contexts distinction, on the false assumption that money and power are not already entrenched in the internal dynamics of the family. But once we repudiate these assumptions, then there is no categorial, as opposed to empirical, basis for differentially evaluating the two kinds of reforms. If it is basically progressive that paid workers acquire the means to confront their employers strategically and match power against power, right against right, then it must be just as progressive *in principle* that women acquire similar means to similar ends in the politics of familial and personal life. Likewise, if it is "pathological" that, in the course of achieving a better balance of power in familial and personal life, women become clients of state bureaucracies, then it must be just as "pathological" *in principle* that paid workers, too, become clients – which does not alter the fact that *in actuality* they become two different sorts of clients. But of course the real point is that the term "pathological"

is misused here insofar as it supposes that childrearing differs categorially from other work.

5 This sheds new light as well on Habermas's fifth thesis concerning the "inner colonization of the lifeworld." This thesis depends on three assumptions, two of which have just been rejected: the natural kinds interpretation of the distinction between symbolic and material reproduction activities, and the assumed virginity of the domestic sphere with respect to money and power. The third assumption is that the basic vector of motion in late capitalist society is from state-regulated economy to lifeworld and not vice versa. But the feminine gender subtext of the client role contradicts this assumption. It suggests that even in late capitalism gender norms continue to channel the influence of the lifeworld on to systems. These norms continue to structure the state-regulated economy, as the persistence, indeed exacerbation, of labor-force segmentation according to sex shows.[28] And they also structure state administration, as the gender segmentation of US and European social welfare systems shows.[29] Thus, it is not the case that in late capitalism "system intrusions" detach life contexts from "value-orientations *per se*." On the contrary, welfare capitalism simply uses other means to uphold the familiar "normatively secured consensus" concerning male dominance and female subordination. But Habermas's theory overlooks this and so it posits the evil of welfare state capitalism as the evil of a general and indiscriminate reification. It fails to account for the fact that it is disproportionately women who suffer the effects of bureaucratization and monetarization and for the fact that bureaucratization and monetarization are instruments of women's subordination.

6 This entails the revision, as well, of Habermas's sixth thesis concerning new social movements in late capitalist societies. He explains these movements as responses to colonization, that is, to the intrusion of system-integration mechanisms into symbolic reproduction spheres and to the consequent erosion and desiccation of contexts of interpretation and communication. But given the multidirectionality of causal influence in welfare state capitalism, the terms "colonization," "intrusion," "erosion," and "desiccation" are too negative and onesided to account for the identity shifts manifest in social movements. Let me attempt an alternative explanation, at least for women, by invoking the experience of millions of women, especially married women and women with children, who have in the postwar period become paid workers and/or social welfare clients. Granted, this has been an experience of new, acute forms of domination. But it has also been an experience in which many women could, often for the first time, taste the possibility of a measure of relative economic independence, an identity outside the domestic sphere, and expanded

political participation. Above all, it has been an experience of conflict and contradiction as women try to juggle the mutually incompatible roles of childrearer and worker, client and citizen. This experience of role conflict has been painful and identity-threatening, but not simply negative. Interpellated simultaneously in contradictory ways, women have become split subjects; and, as a result, the roles themselves, previously shielded in their separate spheres, have suddenly been opened to contestation. Should we, like Habermas, speak here of a "crisis in symbolic reproduction"? Surely not, if this means the desiccation of meaning and values wrought by the intrusion of money and organizational power into women's lives. Emphatically yes, if it means, rather, an opening on to new possibilities that cannot be realized within the established framework of gendered roles and institutions.

If colonization is not an adequate explanation of contemporary feminism, then decolonization cannot be an adequate conception of an emancipatory solution. The first element of decolonization, the removal of system-integration mechanisms from symbolic reproduction spheres, is conceptually and empirically askew of the real issues. If the real point is the moral superiority of cooperative and egalitarian interactions over strategic and hierarchical ones, then it mystifies matters to single out lifeworld institutions – the point should hold for paid work and political administration as well as for domestic life. Similarly, the third element of decolonization, namely, the reversal of the direction of influence and control from system to lifeworld, needs modification. Since the social meanings of gender still structure late-capitalist official economic and state systems, the question is not *whether* lifeworld norms will be decisive but, rather, *which* lifeworld norms will.

What, then, of the remaining element of decolonization, the replacement of normatively secured contexts of interaction by communicatively achieved ones? Something like this is occurring now as feminists criticize traditional gender norms embedded in legal, government, and corporate policy. It is also occurring as feminists and antifeminists clash over the social meanings of "femininity" and "masculinity," the interpretation of women's needs, and the social construction of women's bodies. In these cases, the political stake is hegemony over what I call the "means of interpretation and communication." Feminists are struggling to redistribute access to and control over these sociocultural discursive resources. We are, therefore, struggling for women's autonomy in the following special sense: a measure of collective control over the means of interpretation and communication sufficient to permit us to participate on a par with men in all types of social interaction, including political deliberation and decision-making.[30]

This suggests that a caution is in order concerning the use of the terms "particularism" and "universalism." Recall that Habermas emphasized feminism's links to historic liberation movements and its roots in universalist morality. Recall that he was critical of those tendencies within feminism, and in resistance movements in general, that retreat from political struggle into particularistic countercommunities defined, for example, by biological sex. Now I want to suggest that there are really three issues here and that they need to be disentangled from one another. One is the issue of political engagement versus apolitical countercultural activity. Insofar as Habermas's point is a criticism of separatist cultural feminism, it is well taken in principle, although it needs the following qualifications: cultural separatism, while inadequate as long-term political strategy, is in many cases a shorter-term necessity for women's physical, psychological, and moral survival; and separatist communities have been the source of many politically fruitful reinterpretations of women's experience. The second issue is the status of women's biology in the elaboration of new social identities. Insofar as Habermas's point is a criticism of reductive biologism, it is well taken. But this does not mean that one can ignore the fact that women's biology has nearly always been interpreted by men; and that women's struggle for autonomy necessarily and properly involves, among other things, the reinterpretation of the social meanings of our bodies. The third issue is the difficult and complex one of universalism versus particularism. Insofar as Habermas's endorsement of universalism pertains to the metalevel of access to and control over the means of interpretation and communication, it is well taken. At this level, women's struggle for autonomy can be understood in terms of a universalist conception of distributive justice. But it does not follow that the substantive content that is the fruit of this struggle, namely, the new social meanings we give our needs and our bodies, our new social identities and conceptions of femininity, can be dismissed as particularistic lapses from universalism. These, certainly, are no more particular than the sexist and androcentric meanings and norms they are meant to replace. More generally, at the level of substantive content, as opposed to dialogical form, the contrast between universalism and particularism is out of place. Substantive social meanings and norms are always necessarily culturally and historically specific; they always express distinctive shared but nonuniversal forms of life. Feminist meanings and norms will be no exception, but they will not, on that account, be particularistic in any pejorative sense. Let us simply say that they will be different.

Now what is the relation between feminist struggles over the means of interpretation and communication and institutional change? Such struggles, I claim, are implicitly and explicitly raising the following questions. Should the roles of worker, childrearer, citizen, and client be fully degendered? Can they be? Or do we, rather, require arrangements that permit women to be workers and citizens *as women*, just as men have always been workers and citizens *as men*? And what might that mean? In any case, how should the character and position of paid work, childrearing, and citizenship be defined *vis-à-vis* one another? Should democratic, socialist-feminist, self-managed paid work encompass childrearing? Or should childrearing, rather, replace soldiering as a component of trans- formed, democratic, socialist-feminist, participatory citizenship? What other possibilities are conceivable?

Let me conclude this discussion of the six theses by restating the most important critical points. First, Habermas's account fails to theorize the patriarchal, norm-mediated character of late-capitalist official-economic and administrative systems. Likewise, it fails to theorize the systemic, money- and power-mediated character of male dominance in the domestic sphere of the late-capitalist lifeworld. Consequently, his colonization thesis fails to grasp that the channels of influence between these institutions are multidirectional. And it tends to replicate, rather than to problematize, a major institutional support of women's subordination in late capitalism, namely, the gender-based separation of both the masculine public sphere and the state-regulated economy of sex-segmented paid work and social welfare from privatized female childrearing. Thus, while Habermas wants to be critical of male dominance, his diagnostic categories deflect attention elsewhere, to the allegedly overriding problem of gender-neutral reification. Finally, Habermas's categories tend to misrepresent the causes and under- estimate the scope of the feminist challenge to welfare state capitalism. In short, the struggles and wishes of contemporary women are not adequately clarified by a theory that draws the basic battle line between system and lifeworld institutions. From a feminist perspective, there is a more basic battle line between the forms of male dominance linking "system" to "lifeworld" *and us*.

Conclusion

In general, then, the principal blindspots of Habermas's theory with respect to gender are traceable to his categorial opposition between system and lifeworld institutions. And to the two more elementary oppositions from which it is compounded, the reproduction one and the action contexts one. Or, rather, the blindspots are traceable to the way in which these oppositions, ideologically and androcentrically interpreted, tend to over- ride and eclipse other, potentially more critical elements of Habermas's framework – elements like the distinction between normatively secured and communicatively achieved action contexts, and like the four-term model of public/private relations.

Habermas's blindspots are instructive, I think. They permit us to conclude something about what the categorial framework of a socialist-feminist critical theory of welfare state capitalism should look like. One crucial requirement is that this framework not be such as to put the male-headed nuclear family and the state-regulated official economy on two opposite sides of the major categorial divide. We require, rather, a framework sensitive to the similarities between them, since both appropriate our labor, short-circuit our participation in the interpretation of our needs, and shield normatively secured need interpretations from political contestation. A second crucial requirement is that this framework contain no a priori assumptions about the unidirectionality of social motion and causal influence, that it be sensitive to the ways in which allegedly disappearing institutions and norms persist in structuring social reality. A third crucial requirement, and the last I shall mention here, is that this framework not be such as to posit the evil of welfare state capitalism exclusively or primarily as the evil of reification. It must, rather, be capable of foregrounding the evil of dominance and subordination.[31]

Notes

I am grateful to John Brenkman, Thomas McCarthy, Carole Pateman and Martin Schwab for helpful comments and criticism; to Dee Marquez and Marina Rosiene for crackerjack word processing; and to the Stanford Humanities Center for financial support.

1 Karl Marx, "Letter to A. Ruge, September 1843" in *Karl Marx: Early Writings*, trans. Rodney Livingstone and Gregor Benton (New York: Vintage, 1975), p. 209.

2 Jürgen Habermas, *The Theory of Communicative Action*, vol. I, *Reason and the Rationalization of Society*, trans. Thomas McCarthy (Boston: Beacon Press, 1984). Hereafter, TCA I. Jürgen Habermas, *Theorie des kommunikativen Handelns*, vol. II, *Zur Kritik der funktionalistischen Vernunft* (Frankfurt am Main: Surhkamp Verlag, 1981). Hereafter TCA II. Both are also published in English by Polity Press.

3 TCA II, pp. 214, 217, 348–9; Habermas, *Legitimation Crisis*, trans. Thomas McCarthy (Boston: Beacon Press, 1975), pp. 8–9; Habermas, "A Reply to My Critics," in David Held and John B. Thompson, eds, *Habermas: Critical Debates* (Cambridge, Mass.: MIT Press, 1982), pp. 268, 278–9; Thomas McCarthy, "Translator's Introduction," TCA I, pp. xxv–xxvii; John B. Thompson, "Rationality and Social Rationalisation: An Assessment of Habermas's Theory of Communicative Action," *Sociology*, 17(2), 1983, pp. 278–94.

4 TCA II, p. 208; "A Reply to My Critics," pp. 223–5; McCarthy, "Translator's Introduction," pp. xxiv–xxv.

5 I am indebted to Martin Schwab for the expression "dual-aspect activity."

6 TCA I, pp. 85, 87–8, 101, 342, 357–60; TCA II, p. 179; *Legitimation Crisis*, pp. 4–5; "A Reply to My Critics," pp. 234, 237, 264–5; McCarthy, "Translator's Introduction", pp. ix, xxix–xxx.

7 TCA I, pp. 341, 357–9; TCA II, pp. 256, 266; McCarthy, "Translator's Introduction," p. xxx.

8 See Pierre Bourdieu, *Outline of a Theory of Practice*, trans. Richard Nice (New York: Cambridge University Press, 1977), and Arjun Appadurai, "Commodities and the Politics of Value," in *The Social Life of Things: Commodities in Cultural Perspective* ed. Arjun Appadurai (New York: Cambridge University Press, 1986).

9 TCA I, pp. 72, 341–2, 359–60; TCA II, p. 179; "A Reply to My Critics," pp. 268, 279–80; *Legitimation Crisis*, pp. 20–1; McCarthy, "Translator's Introduction," pp. xxviii–xxix; Thompson, "Rationality," pp. 285, 287. It should be noted that in TCA Habermas draws the contrast between system and lifeworld in two distinct senses. On the one hand, he contrasts them as two different methodological perspectives on the study of societies. The system perspective is objectivating and "externalist," while the lifeworld perspective is hermeneutical and "internalist." In principle, either can be applied to the study of any given set of societal phenomena. Habermas argues that neither alone is adequate. So he seeks to develop a methodology that combines both. On the other hand, Habermas also contrasts system and lifeworld in another way, namely, as two different kinds of institutions. It is this second system/lifeworld contrast that I am concerned with here. I do not explicitly treat the first one in this essay. I am sympathetic to Habermas's general methodological intention of combining or linking structural (in the sense of objectivating) and interpretive approaches to the study of societies. I do not, however, believe that this can be done by assigning structural properties to one set of institutions (the official economy and the state) and interpretive ones to another set (the family and the "public sphere"). I maintain, rather, that all of these institutions have both structural and interpretive dimensions and that all should be studied both structurally and hermeneutically. I have tried to develop an approch that meets these aims in "Women, Welfare and the Politics of Need Interpretation," and "Struggle over Needs: Outline of a Socialist-Feminist Critical Theory of Late Capitalist Political Culture," both in Nancy Fraser, *Unruly Practices: Power, Discourse and Gender in Contemporary Social Theory* (Minneapolis: University of Minnesota Press; Cambridge: Polity, 1989).

10 See, for example, the essays in Barrie Thorne and Marilyn Yalom, eds, *Rethinking the Family: Some Feminist Questions* (New York and London: Longman, 1982). Also, Michele Barrett and Mary McIntosh, *The Anti-Social Family* (London: Verso, 1982).

11 TCA I, pp. 85–6, 88–90, 101, 104–5; TCA II, p. 179; McCarthy, "Translator's Introduction," pp. ix, xxx.

12 Pamela Fishman, "Interaction: The Work Women Do," *Social Problems*, 25(4), 1978, pp. 397–406.

13 TCA II, pp. 523–4, 547; "A Reply to My Critics," p. 237; Thompson, "Rationality," pp. 288, 292.

14 TCA I, pp. 341–2, 359–60; TCA II, pp. 256, 473; "A Reply to My Critics,"

p. 280; McCarthy, "Translator's Introduction," p. xxxii; Thompson, "Rationality," pp. 286–8.

15 Carole Pateman, "The Personal and the Political: Can Citizenship be Democratic?", lecture 3 of her "Women and Democratic Citizenship," The Jefferson Memorial Lectures, delivered at the University of California, Berkeley, February 1985, unpublished typescript.

16 Ibid., p. 5.

17 Ibid., p. 8.

18 Judith Hicks Stiehm, "The Protected, the Protector, the Defender," in *Women and Men's Wars*, ed. Judith Hicks Stiehm (New York: Pergamon, 1983). This is not to say, however, that I accept Stiehm's conclusions about the desirability of integrating women fully into the US military as presently structured and deployed.

19 TCA II, pp. 505ff; *Legitimation Crisis*, pp. 33–6, 53–5; McCarthy, "Translator's Introduction," p. xxxiii.

20 TCA II, pp. 522–4; *Legitimation Crisis*, pp. 36–7, McCarthy, "Translator's Introduction," p. xxxiii.

21 TCA II, pp. 530–40; McCarthy, "Translator's Introduction," pp. xxxiii–xxxiv.

22 TCA II, pp. 540–7; McCarthy, "Translator's Introduction," p. xxxi.

23 TCA II, pp. 275–7, 452, 480, 522–4; "A Reply to My Critics," pp. 226, 280–1; Habermas, introduction to *Observations on "The Spiritual Situation of the Age"*: *Contemporary German Perspectives*, ed. Jürgen Habermas, trans. Andrew Buchwalter (Cambridge, Mass.: MIT Press, 1984), pp. 11–12, 16–20; McCarthy, "Translator's Introduction," pp. xxxi–xxxii; Thompson, "Rationality," pp. 286, 288.

24 TCA II, pp. 581–3; *Observations*, pp. 18–19, 27–8.

25 TCA II, pp. 581–3; *Observations*, pp. 16–17, 27–8.

26 For the US social welfare system, see the analysis of male versus female participation rates, and the account of the gendered character of the two subsystems in Fraser, "Women, Welfare and the Politics of Need Interpretation"; Barbara J. Nelson, "Women's Poverty and Women's Citizenship: Some Political Consequences of Economic Marginality," *Signs: Journal of Women in Culture and Society*, 10(2), 1985; Steven P. Erie, Martin Rein and Barbara Wiget, "Women and the Reagan Revolution: Thermidor for the Social Welfare Economy," in *Families, Politics and Public Policies: A Feminist Dialogue on Women and the State*, ed. Irene Diamond (New York: Longman, 1983); Diana Pearce, "Women, Work and Welfare: The Feminization of Poverty", in *Working Women and Families* ed. Karen Wolk Feinstein (Beverly Hills: Sage, 1979), and "Toil and Trouble: Women Workers and Unemployment Compensation," *Signs*, 10(3), 1985, pp. 439–59; Barbara Ehrenreich and Frances Fox Piven, "The Feminization of Poverty," *Dissent*, spring 1984, pp. 162–70. For an analysis of the gendered character of the British social welfare system, see Hilary Land, "Who Cares for the Family?" *Journal of Social Policy*, 7(3), 1978, pp. 257–84. For Norway, see the essays in Harriet Holter, ed., *Patriarchy in a Welfare Society* (Oslo: Universitetsforlaget, 1984). See also two comparative studies: Mary Ruggie, *The State and Working Women: A Comparative Study of Britain and Sweden* (Princeton, NJ: Princeton University Press, 1984); and Birte Siim "Women and the Welfare State:

Between Private and Public Dependence," unpublished typescript circulated at Stanford University, 1985.

27 Carol Brown, "Mothers, Fathers and Children: From Private to Public Patriarchy," in *Women and Revolution*, ed. Lydia Sargent (Boston: South End Press, 1981). Actually, I believe Brown's formulation is theoretically inadequate, since it presupposes a simple dualistic conception of public and private. Nonetheless, the phrase "from private to public patriarchy" evokes in a rough but suggestive way the phenomena a socialist-feminist critical theory of the welfare state would need to account for.

28 The most recent available data for the US indicate that sex segmentation in paid work is increasing, not decreasing. See Drew Christie, "Comparable Worth and Distributive Justice," paper read at meeting of the American Philosophical Association, Western Division, April 1985.

29 See note 26 above.

30 I develop this notion of the "sociocultural means of interpretation and communication" and the associated conception of autonomy in "Toward a Discourse Ethic of Solidarity," *Praxis International*, 5(4), January 1986, pp. 425–9, and in "Struggle over Needs." Both notions are extensions and modifications of Habermas's conception of "communicative ethics."

31 My own recent work attempts to construct a conceptual framework for a socialist-feminist critical theory of the welfare state which meets these requirements. See "Women, Welfare and the Politics of Need Interpretation," "Toward a Discourse Ethic of Solidarity" and "Struggle over Needs." Each of these essays draws on those aspects of Habermas's thought that I take to be unambiguously positive and useful, especially his conception of the irreducibly sociocultural, interpretive character of human needs, and his contrast between dialogical and monological processes of need interpretation. The present paper, on the other hand, focuses mainly on those aspects of Habermas's thought that I find problematical or unhelpful, and so does not convey the full range either of his work or of my views about it. Readers are warned, therefore, against drawing the conclusion that Habermas has little or nothing positive to contribute to a socialist-feminist critical theory of the welfare state. They are urged, rather, to consult the essays cited above for the other side of the story.

Index